STRATEGIC RISK TAKING

A FRAMEWORK FOR RISK MANAGEMENT

STRATEGIC

RISK TAKING

A FRAMEWORK
FOR
RISK MANAGEMENT

ASWATH DAMODARAN

Vice President, Publisher: Tim Moore
Wharton Editor: Yoram (Jerry) Wind
Executive Editor: Jim Boyd
Editorial Assistant: Pamela Boland
Development Editor: Russ Hall
Associate Editor-in-Chief and Director of Marketing: Amy Neidlinger
Publicist: Amy Fandrei
Marketing Coordinator: Megan Colvin
Cover Designer: Chuti Prasertsith
Managing Editor: Gina Kanouse
Project Editor: Jennifer Gallant
Copy Editor: Karen A. Gill
Proofreader: Water Crest Publishing
Senior Indexer: Cheryl Lenser
Compositor: Jake McFarland
Manufacturing Buyer: Dan Uhrig

Ш Wharton School Publishing
© 2008 by Pearson Education, Inc.
Publishing as Wharton School Publishing
Upper Saddle River, New Jersey 07458

Wharton School Publishing offers excellent discounts on this book when ordered in quantity for bulk purchases or special sales. For more information, please contact U.S. Corporate and Government Sales, 1-800-382-3419, corpsales@pearsontechgroup.com. For sales outside the U.S., please contact International Sales at international@pearsoned.com.

Company and product names mentioned herein are the trademarks or registered trademarks of their respective owners.

Printed in the United States of America
First Printing August 2007
ISBN-10: 0-13-199048-9
ISBN-13: 978-0-13-199048-7

Pearson Education LTD.
Pearson Education Australia PTY, Limited.
Pearson Education Singapore, Pte. Ltd.
Pearson Education North Asia, Ltd.
Pearson Education Canada, Ltd.
Pearson Educatión de Mexico, S.A. de C.V.
Pearson Education—Japan
Pearson Education Malaysia, Pte. Ltd.

Library of Congress Cataloging-in-Publication Data
Damodaran, Aswath.
  Strategic risk taking : a framework for risk management / Aswath Damodaran.
    p. cm.
  ISBN 978-0-13-199048-7 (pbk. : alk. paper) 1. Risk management. I. Title.
HD61.D23 2008
658.15'5--dc22
                        2007014971

To my wife, Michele, and my children, Ryan, Brendan, Kendra, and Kiran, who make it all worthwhile.

CONTENTS

CHAPTERS 5–8
Risk Assessment: Tools and Techniques 97

CHAPTER 5
Risk-Adjusted Value 99

CHAPTER 6
Probabilistic Approaches: Scenario Analysis, Decision Trees, and Simulations

CHAPTERS 9–12
Risk Management: The Big Picture 277

CHAPTER 9
Risk Management: The Big Picture 279

CHAPTER 10
Risk Management: Profiling and Hedging 309

ACKNOWLEDGMENTS

To risk takers everywhere.

ABOUT THE AUTHOR

Aswath Damodaran is a professor of finance and David Margolis teaching fellow at the Stern School of Business at New York University. He teaches the corporate finance and equity valuation courses in the MBA program. He received his MBA and PhD from the University of California at Los Angeles. His research interests lie in valuation, portfolio management, and applied corporate finance. He has been published in the *Journal of Financial and Quantitative Analysis*, the *Journal of Finance*, the *Journal of Financial Economics*, and the *Review of Financial Studies*. He has written three books on equity valuation (*Damodaran on Valuation*, *Investment Valuation*, and *The Dark Side of Valuation*) and two on corporate finance (*Corporate Finance: Theory and Practice*, *Applied Corporate Finance: A User's Manual*). He has coedited a book on investment management with Peter Bernstein (*Investment Management*) and has written a book on investment philosophies (*Investment Philosophies*). His newest book on portfolio management is titled *Investment Fables* and was published in 2004. He was a visiting lecturer at the University of California, Berkeley, from 1984 to 1986, where he received the Earl Cheit Outstanding Teaching Award in 1985. He has been at NYU since 1986 and received the Stern School of Business Excellence in Teaching Award (awarded by the graduating class) in 1988, 1991, 1992, 1999, 2001, and 2007, and was the youngest winner of the University-wide Distinguished Teaching Award (in 1990). He was profiled in *Business Week* as one of the top 12 business school professors in the United States in 1994.

A ROADMAP FOR
UNDERSTANDING RISK

This book is written for three very diverse and different audiences—people who have to manage and make the big decisions on risk (risk managers), analysts and others whose job it is to assess risk (risk assessors), and students of risk who are interested in getting a perspective on how the thinking on risk has evolved over time.

The study of risk has its deepest roots in economics and insurance. For centuries, researchers have attempted to grapple with the basic question of what risk is and how to measure risk aversion. Chapters 1 through 4 represent my attempt to give some historical perspective on how our thinking has evolved over the past few centuries, with a healthy dose of what psychologists have discovered in recent years about how human beings react to risk. In particular, these studies find that human beings are neither as rational nor as easy to categorize when it comes to behavior when confronted with risk as traditional economists had assumed them to be. Although much of this work would usually be categorized as behavioral economics or finance, understanding the findings is the first step to managing risk.

The next four chapters (Chapters 5–8) look at how risk assessment techniques have evolved over time. Chapter 5 has its roots in portfolio theory and examines ways in which we can adjust the value of risky assets for that risk. Chapter 6 borrows heavily from the decision sciences and statistics and discusses ways in which probabilistic approaches can be used to evaluate risk. Chapter 7 takes a closer look at value at risk (VaR), an extension of the probabilistic approach that has acquired a substantial following particularly in commercial and investment banks. Chapter 8 returns to financial theory and looks at how extensions of option pricing models can be used to incorporate the potential upside from risk exposure.

The last four chapters of this book represent an attempt to meld traditional finance and corporate strategy to arrive at a complete story for risk management, which goes beyond just risk hedging (which has been the finance focus) or competitive advantages (which has been the strategic imperative). These chapters represent the most innovative part of this book, because they attempt to bring together analyses and insights from different functional areas into a big picture of risk management.

The three groups—economists, risk assessors, and risk managers—have different skills and interests, and the tension shows in the book, with each part of the book reflecting these differences. Each group will find a portion of the book most attuned to their interests with the other parts representing more of a hike into unfamiliar but rewarding territory.

This book is modular and can be read in parts. In other words, there is little in the first eight chapters that I draw on in the last four chapters. Much as I would love to believe that you will buy this book and read it cover to cover, I am a realist. Given your time constraints and interests, you may skip through sections to get to the parts you want to read. In other words, if you are already familiar with risk assessment tools and are more interested in the big picture of risk management, skip forward to Chapter 9. If, on the other hand, you are more interested in risk assessment and how the different approaches fit together, you can browse through Chapters 5 through 8. Having said that, there is value added to looking at the parts not specifically aimed at you. In other words, risk assessors and analysts will be able to do their jobs better if they understand how what they do (from risk adjusting discount rates to simulations) fits into the big picture of risk management. At the same time, risk managers will be able to define what risk assessments they need if they can see the whole array of choices. Finally, economists studying risk aversion may gain from knowing the practical issues facing both risk assessors and risk managers. As I note, there is an extraordinary number of basic and critical questions that are unanswered in the theory.

There are excellent books and papers in each of the three areas right now, but they focus on one of the three, largely because different disciplines have been involved in each one: traditional economics and behavioral economics for the first part, corporate finance for the second, and corporate strategy for the third. I have tried to bridge the different functional areas across this book. It is entirely possible that people in any one of these functional areas will view what I say (in the section directed at them) as too simplistic or already well established, but I hope I have been able to bring insights into each of the three areas from being aware of the other two.

I do not claim that anything in this book, standing by itself, is new and revolutionary. In fact, I will concede that each chapter covers a topic that has been covered in more depth elsewhere, with entire books dedicated to some topics; there are several books on real options and quite a few on VaR, for instance. What I think is lacking in the areas of risk management is a spanning of work done in different areas with a link to practical risk management. Consequently, I used my own biased perspectives to try to create a narrative that would be useful to a decision maker involved in risk analysis and management. I hope you find it useful.

CHAPTERS 1–4

The Economists' View of Risk Aversion and the Behavioral Response

The study of risk has its roots in economics, with attempts to define risk and measure risk aversion going back several centuries. We begin Chapter 1, "What Is Risk," by defining risk and laying the groundwork for why understanding is so critical to every aspect of business and investing. Early in Chapter 2, "Why Do We Care About Risk?," we describe an experiment with a gamble by Bernoulli that laid the foundations of conventional economic theory on risk aversion, where individuals with well-behaved utility functions make reasoned judgments when confronted with risk. In Chapter 3, "What Do We Think about Risk?," we examine the evidence on risk aversion and conclude that individuals do not always behave in rational ways when faced with risk. In particular, we look at the implications of the findings in behavioral economics and finance for risk management. In Chapter 4, "How Do We Measure Risk?," we return to more traditional economics to look at how the models for measuring risk and estimating expected returns have evolved over time.

Just as a note of warning to the reader, these chapters say little directly about risk management. By their very nature, they use language that is familiar to economics—utility functions and risk aversion coefficients—but abstract to the rest of us. Risk management, though, has its beginnings here, with an understanding of risk and its consequences. There are insights on human behavior in these chapters that may prove useful in constructing risk management systems and in understanding why they sometimes break down.

Chapter	Questions for Risk Management
1	What is risk?
2	How do we measure risk aversion?
	Why do we care about risk aversion?

Chapter	Questions for Risk Management
3	How do human beings behave when confronted with risk?
	What do the known quirks in human behavior mean for risk management?
4	How do we measure risk?
	How have risk measures evolved over time?

1

WHAT IS RISK?

Risk is part of every human endeavor. From the moment we get up in the morning, drive or take public transportation to get to school or to work until we get back into our beds (and perhaps even afterwards), we are exposed to risks of different degrees. What makes the study of risk fascinating is that while some of this risk bearing may not be completely voluntary, we seek out some risks on our own (speeding on the highways or gambling, for instance) and enjoy them. Although some of these risks may seem trivial, others make a significant difference in the way we live our lives. On a loftier note, it can be argued that every major advance in human civilization, from the caveman's invention of tools to gene therapy, has been made possible because someone was willing to take a risk and challenge the status quo. In this chapter, we begin our exploration of risk by noting its presence through history and then look at how best to define what we mean by risk.

We close this chapter by restating the main theme of this book, which is that financial theorists and practitioners have chosen to take too narrow a view of risk, in general, and risk management, in particular. By equating risk management with risk hedging, they have underplayed the fact that the most successful firms in any industry get there not by avoiding risk but by actively seeking it out and exploiting it to their own advantage.

A Very Short History of Risk

For much of human history, risk and survival have gone hand in hand. Prehistoric humans lived short and brutal lives, as the search for food and shelter exposed them to physical danger from preying animals and poor weather.[1] Even as more established communities developed in Sumeria, Babylon, and Greece, other risks (such as war and disease) continued to ravage humanity. For much of early history, though, physical risk and material reward went hand in hand. The risk-taking caveman ended up with food, and the risk-averse one starved to death.

---

1   The average life span of prehistoric man was less than 30 years. Even the ancient Greeks and Romans were considered aged by the time they turned 40.

The advent of shipping created a new forum for risk taking for the adventurous. The Vikings embarked in superbly constructed ships from Scandinavia for Britain, Ireland, and even across the Atlantic to the Americas in search of new lands to plunder—the risk-return trade-off of their age. The development of the shipping trades created fresh equations for risk and return, with the risk of ships sinking and being waylaid by pirates offset by the rewards from ships that made it back with cargo. It also allowed for the separation of physical from economic risk as wealthy traders bet their money while the poor risked their lives on the ships.

The spice trade that flourished as early as 350 BC but expanded and became the basis for empires in the middle of the last millennium provides a good example. Merchants in India would load boats with pepper and cinnamon and send them to Persia, Arabia, and East Africa. From there, the cargo was transferred to camels and taken across the continent to Venice and Genoa, and then on to the rest of Europe. The Spanish and the Dutch, followed by the English, expanded the trade to the East Indies with an entirely seafaring route. Traders in London, Lisbon, and Amsterdam, with the backing of the crown, would invest in ships and supplies that would embark on the long journey. The hazards on the route were manifold, and it was common to lose half or more of the cargo (and those bearing the cargo) along the way, but the hefty prices that the spices commanded in their final destinations still made this a lucrative endeavor for both the owners of the ships and the sailors who survived.[2] The spice trade was not unique. Economic activities until the industrial age often exposed those involved in it to physical risk with economic rewards. Thus, Spanish explorers set off for the New World, recognizing that they ran a real risk of death and injury but also that they would be richly rewarded if they succeeded. Young men from England set off for distant outposts of the empire in India and China, hoping to make their fortunes while exposing themselves to risk of death from disease and war.

In the past couple of centuries, the advent of financial instruments and markets on the one hand and the growth of the leisure business on the other has allowed us to separate physical from economic risk. A person who buys options on technology stocks can be

---

2   A fascinating account of the spice trade is provided in *Nathaniel's Nutmeg*, a book by Giles Milton that follows Nathaniel Courthope, a British spice trader, through the wars between the Dutch East India Company and the British Crown for Run Island, a tiny Indonesian island where nutmeg grew freely. Milton provides details of the dangers that awaited the sailors on ships from foul weather, disease, malnutrition, and hostile natives as they made the long trip from Europe around the horn of Africa past southern Asia to the island. The huge markup on the price of nutmeg (about 3,200 percent between Run Island and London) offered sufficient incentive to fight for the island. An ironic postscript to the tale is that the British ultimately ceded Run Island to the Dutch in exchange for Manhattan. See Milton, G. *Nathaniel's Nutmeg*. New York: Farrar, Strous, and Giroux, 1999. For more on spices and their place in history, see Turner, J. *Spice: The History of a Temptation*. New York: Alfred A. Knopf, 2004.

exposed to significant economic risk without potential for physical risk, whereas a person who spends the weekend bungee jumping is exposed to significant physical risk with no economic payoff. Although there remain significant physical risks in the universe, this book is about economic risks and their consequences.

Defining Risk

Given the ubiquity of risk in almost every human activity, it is surprising how little consensus there is about how to define risk. The early discussion centered on the distinction between risk that could be quantified objectively and subjective risk. In 1921, Frank Knight summarized the difference between risk and uncertainty thus:[3]

> "…Uncertainty must be taken in a sense radically distinct from the familiar notion of Risk, from which it has never been properly separated… The essential fact is that "risk" means in some cases a quantity susceptible of measurement, while at other times it is something distinctly not of this character; and there are far-reaching and crucial differences in the bearings of the phenomena depending on which of the two is really present and operating… It will appear that a measurable uncertainty, or "risk" proper, as we shall use the term, is so far different from an un-measurable one that it is not in effect an uncertainty at all."

In short, Knight defined only quantifiable uncertainty to be risk and provided the example of two individuals drawing from an urn of red and black balls. The first individual is ignorant of the numbers of each color, whereas the second individual is aware that there are three red balls for each black ball. The second individual estimates (correctly) the probability of drawing a red ball to be 75 percent, but the first operates under the misperception that there is a 50 percent chance of drawing a red ball. Knight argues that the second individual is exposed to risk but that the first suffers from ignorance.

The emphasis on whether uncertainty is subjective or objective seems to us misplaced. It is true that risk that is measurable is easier to insure, but we *do* care about *all* uncertainty, whether measurable or not. In a paper on defining risk, Holton (2004) argues that two ingredients are needed for risk to exist.[4] The first is uncertainty about the potential outcomes from an experiment, and the other is that the outcomes have to matter in terms of providing utility. He notes, for instance, that a person jumping out of an airplane without a parachute faces no risk since he is certain to die (no uncertainty), and

---

3 Knight, F. H. *Risk, Uncertainty and Profit.* New York: Hart, Schaffner, and Marx, 1921.

4 Holton, Glyn A. "Defining Risk." *Financial Analysts Journal,* 60 (6), 19–25, 2004.

that drawing balls out of an urn does not expose one to risk because one's well being or wealth is unaffected by whether a red or a black ball is drawn. Of course, attaching different monetary values to red and black balls would convert this activity to a risky one.

Risk is incorporated into so many different disciplines from insurance to engineering to portfolio theory that it should come as no surprise that it is defined in different ways by each one. It is worth looking at some of the distinctions.

- **Risk versus probability**—Whereas some definitions of risk focus only on the probability of an event occurring, more comprehensive definitions incorporate both the probability of the event occurring and the consequences of the event. Thus, the probability of a severe earthquake may be small, but the consequences are so catastrophic that it would be categorized as a high-risk event.

- **Risk versus threat**—In some disciplines, a contrast is drawn between a risk and a threat. A *threat* is a low-probability event with large negative consequences, where analysts may be unable to assess the probability. A *risk*, on the other hand, is defined to be a higher probability event, where there is enough information to assess both the probability and the consequences.

- **All outcomes versus negative outcomes**—Some definitions of risk tend to focus only on the downside scenarios, whereas others are more expansive and consider all variability as risk. The engineering definition of risk is defined as the product of the probability of an event occurring, that is viewed as undesirable, and an assessment of the expected harm from the event occurring.

Risk = Probability of an accident * Consequence in lost money/deaths

In contrast, risk in finance is defined in terms of variability of actual returns on investment around an expected return, even when those returns represent positive outcomes.

Building on the last distinction, we should consider broader definitions of risk that capture both the positive and negative outcomes. The Chinese symbol for risk best captures this duality:

This Chinese symbol for risk is a combination of danger (crisis) and opportunity, representing the downside and the upside of risk. This is the definition of risk that we will

adhere to in this book because it captures perfectly both the essence of risk and the problems with focusing purely on risk reduction and hedging. Any approach that focuses on minimizing risk exposure (or danger) will also reduce the potential for opportunity.

Dealing with Risk

Although most of this book will be spent discussing why risk matters and how to incorporate it best into decisions, we will lay out two big themes that animate much of the discussion. The first is the link between risk and reward that has motivated much of risk taking throughout history. The other is the undermentioned link between risk and innovation, as new products and services have been developed to both hedge against and to exploit risk.

Risk and Reward

The "no free lunch" mantra has a logical extension. Those who desire large rewards have to be willing to expose themselves to considerable risk. The link between risk and return is most visible when making investment choices; stocks are riskier than bonds but generate higher returns over long periods. The presence of risk is less visible but just as important when making career choices; a job in sales and trading at an investment bank may be more lucrative than a corporate finance job at a corporation, but it does come with a greater likelihood that you will be laid off if you don't produce results.

Not surprisingly, therefore, the decisions on how much risk to take and what type of risks to take are critical to the success of a business. A business that decides to protect itself against all risk is unlikely to generate much upside for its owners; however, a business that exposes itself to the wrong types of risk may be even worse off, because it is more likely to be damaged than helped by the risk exposure. In short, the essence of good management is making the right choices when it comes to dealing with different risks.

Risk and Innovation

The other aspect of risk that needs examination is the role that risk taking plays in creating innovation. Over history, many of our most durable and valuable inventions have come from a desire to either remove risk or expose ourselves to it. Consider again the example of the spice trade. The risks at sea and from hostile forces created a need for more seaworthy crafts and powerful weapons, innovations designed to exploit risk.

The first full-fledged examples of insurance and risk pooling showed up at about the same time in history. While there were sporadic attempts at offering insurance in previous years, the first organized insurance business was founded in 1688 by merchants, ship owners, and underwriters in Lloyd's Coffee Shop in London in response to increased demands from ship owners for protection against risk.

Over the past few decades, innovations have come to financial markets at a dizzying pace, and we will consider the array of choices that individuals and businesses face, later in this book. Some of these innovations have been designed to help investors and businesses protect themselves against risk, but many have been offered as ways of exploiting risk for higher returns. In some cases, the same instruments (options and futures, for example) have played both risk-hedging and risk-exploiting roles, albeit to different audiences.

Risk Management

Risk clearly does matter, but what does managing risk involve? For too long, we have ceded the definition and terms of risk management to risk hedgers, who see the purpose of risk management as removing or reducing risk exposures. In this section, we will lay the foundation for a much broader agenda for risk managers, where increasing exposures to some risk is an integral part of success. In a later section in this book, we will consider the details, dangers, and potential payoffs to this expanded risk management.

The Conventional View and Its Limitations

There are risk management books, consultants, and services aplenty, but the definition of risk management used has tended to be cramped. In fact, many risk management offerings are really risk reduction or hedging products, with little or no attention paid to exploiting risk. In finance, especially, our definition of risk has been narrowed more and more over time to the point where we define risk statistically and think of it often as a negative when it comes to assessing value.

Several factors have contributed to the narrow definition of risk management. The first is that the bulk of risk management products are risk-hedging products, be they insurance, derivatives, or swaps. Because these products generate substantial revenues for those offering them, it should come as no surprise that they become the centerpieces for the risk management story. The second is that it is human nature to remember losses (the downside of risk) more than profits (the upside of risk); we are easy prey, especially after disasters, calamities, and market meltdowns for purveyors of risk-hedging products. The third is that the separation of management from ownership in most publicly traded firms creates a potential conflict of interest between what is good for the business (and its stockholders) and what is good for the mangers. Because it is the managers of firms and not the owners who decide how much and how to hedge risk, it is possible that the managers will hedge risks that the owners would never want hedged in the first place.

A More Expansive View of Risk Management

If the allure of risk is that it offers upside potential, risk management has to be more than risk hedging. Businesses that are in a constant defensive crouch when it comes to risk are in no position to survey the landscape and find risks that they are suited to take. In fact, all the most successful businesses of our time—from General Motors in the early part of the twentieth century to the Microsofts, Wal-Marts, and Googles of today—have risen to the top by finding particular risks that they are better at exploiting than their competitors.

This more complete view of risk management as encompassing both risk hedging at one end and strategic risk taking on the other is the central theme of this book. In the chapters to come, we will consider all aspects of risk management and examine ways in which businesses and individual investors can pick and choose through the myriad risks that they face, which risks they should ignore, which risks they should reduce or eliminate (by hedging), and which risks they should actively seek out and exploit. In the process, we will look at the tools that have been developed in finance to evaluate risk and examine ways in which we can draw on other disciplines—corporate strategy and statistics, in particular—to make these tools more effective.

Conclusion

Risk has been part of everyday life for as long as we have been on this planet. Although much of the risk that humans faced in prehistoric times was physical, the development of trade and financial markets has allowed for a separation of physical and economic risk. Investors can risk their money without putting their lives in danger.

The definitions of risk range the spectrum, with some focusing primarily on the likelihood of bad events occurring to those that weigh in the consequences of those events to those that look at both upside and downside potential. In this book, we will use that last definition of risk. Consequently, risk provides opportunities while exposing us to outcomes that we may not desire. It is the coupling of risk and reward that lies at the core of the risk definition. The innovations that have been generated in response make risk central to the study of not just finance but to all business.

In the final part of this chapter, we set up the themes for this book. We argue that risk has been treated far too narrowly in finance and in much of business, and that risk management has been equated for the most part with risk hedging. Successful businesses need a more complete vision of risk management, where they consider not only how to protect themselves against some risks but also which risks to exploit and how to exploit them.

2

WHY DO WE CARE ABOUT RISK?

D o human beings seek out risk or avoid it? How does risk affect behavior, and what are the consequences for business and investment decisions? The answers to these questions lie at the heart of any discussion about risk. Individuals may be averse to risk, but they are also attracted to it, and different people respond differently to the same risk stimuli.

In this chapter, we will begin by looking at the attraction that risk holds to human beings and how it affects behavior. We will then consider what we mean by risk aversion and why it matters for risk management. We will follow up and consider how best to measure risk aversion, looking at a range of techniques that have been developed in economics. In the final section, we will consider the consequences of risk aversion for corporate finance, investments, and valuation.

The Duality of Risk

In a world where people sky dive and bungee jump for pleasure and gambling is a multi-billion dollar business, it is clear that human beings collectively are sometimes attracted to risk and that some are more susceptible to its attraction than others. While psycho-analysts at the beginning of the twentieth century considered risk-taking behavior to be a disease, the fact that it is so widespread suggests that it is part of human nature to be attracted to risk, even when there is no rational payoff to being exposed to risk. The seeds, it could be argued, may have been planted in our hunter-gatherer days when survival mandated taking risks and there were no "play it safe" options.

At the same time, though, there is evidence that human beings try to avoid risk in both physical and financial pursuits. The same person who puts his life at risk, climb-ing mountains, may refuse to drive a car without his seat belt on or to invest in stocks, because he considers them to be too risky. As we will see in the next chapter, some people are risk takers on small bets but become more risk averse on bets with larger economic consequences. Also, risk-taking behavior can change as people age, become wealthier, and have families. In general, understanding what risk is and how we deal with it is the first step to effectively managing that risk.

I Am Rich, But Am I Happy? Utility and Wealth

While we can talk intuitively about risk and how human beings react to it, economists have used utility functions to capture how we react to at least economic risk. Individuals, they argue, make choices to maximize not wealth but expected utility. We can disagree with some of the assumptions underlying this view of risk, but it is as good a starting point as any for the analysis of risk. In this section, we will begin by presenting the origins of expected utility theory in a famous experiment and then consider possible special cases and issues that arise out of that theory.

The St. Petersburg Paradox and Expected Utility: The Bernoulli Contribution

Consider a simple experiment. I will flip a coin once and will pay you a dollar if the coin comes up tails on the first flip; the experiment will stop if it comes up heads. If you win the dollar on the first flip, though, you will be offered a second flip, where you can double your winnings if the coin comes up tails again but lose it all if it comes up heads. The game will thus continue, with the prize doubling at each stage, until you come up heads. How much would you be willing to pay to partake in this gamble?

This is the experiment that Nicholas Bernoulli proposed almost three hundred years ago, and he did so for a reason. This gamble, called the *St. Petersburg Paradox*, has an expected value of infinity, but most of us would pay only a few dollars to play this game. It was to resolve this paradox that his cousin, Daniel Bernoulli, proposed the following distinction between price and utility:[1]

---

1   Bernoulli, D. *Exposition of a New Theory on the Measurement of Risk*, 1738. Translated into English in *Econometrica*, January 1954. Daniel came from a family of distinguished mathematicians, and his uncle, Jakob, was one of the leading thinkers in early probability theory.

"…the value of an item must not be based upon its price, but rather on the utility it yields. The price of the item is dependent only on the thing itself and is equal for everyone; the utility, however, is dependent on the particular circumstances of the person making the estimate."

Bernoulli had two insights that continue to animate how we think about risk today. First, he noted that the value attached to this gamble would vary across individuals. Certain individuals would be willing to pay more than others, with people's difference a function of their risk aversion. His second insight was that the utility from gaining an additional dollar would decrease with wealth; he argued that "one thousand ducats is more significant to a pauper than to a rich man, although both gain the same amount." He was making an argument that the marginal utility of wealth decreases as wealth increases, a view that is at the core of most conventional economic theory today. Technically, diminishing marginal utility implies that utility increases as wealth increases, and at a declining rate.[2] Another way of presenting this notion is to graph total utility against wealth. Figure 2.1 presents the utility function for an investor who follows Bernoulli's dictums and contrasts it with utility functions for investors who do not.

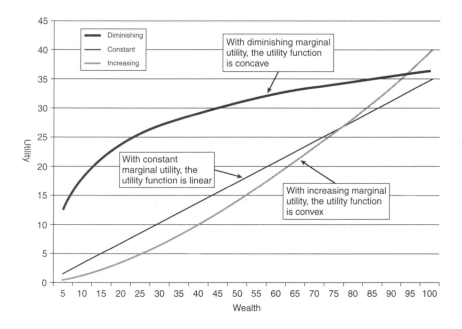

Figure 2.1: Utility and Wealth

---

2   In more technical terms, the first derivative of utility to wealth is positive, whereas the second derivative is negative.

If we accept the notion of diminishing marginal utility of wealth, it follows that a person's utility will decrease more with a loss of $1 in wealth than it would increase with a gain of $1. Thus, the foundations for risk aversion are laid because a rational human being with these characteristics will then reject a fair wager (a 50 percent chance of a gain of $100 and a 50 percent chance of a loss of $100) because she will be worse off in terms of utility. Bernoulli's conclusion, based upon his particular views on the relationship between utility and wealth, is that an individual would pay only about $2 to partake in the experiment proposed in the St. Petersburg paradox.[3]

While the argument for diminishing marginal utility seems eminently reasonable, it is possible that utility could increase in lock step with wealth (constant marginal utility) for some investors or even increase at an increasing rate (increasing marginal utility) for others. The classic risk lover, used to illustrate bromides about the evils of gambling and speculation, would fall into the latter category. The relationship between utility and wealth lies at the heart of whether we should manage risk, and if so, how. After all, in a world of risk-neutral individuals, there would be little demand for insurance, in particular, and risk hedging, in general. It is precisely because investors are risk averse that they care about risk, and the choices they make will reflect their risk aversion. Simplistic though it may seem in hindsight, Bernoulli's experiment was the opening salvo in the scientific analysis of risk.

Mathematics Meets Economics: Von Neumann and Morgenstern

In the bets presented by Bernoulli and others, success and failure were equally likely, although the outcomes varied. That's a reasonable assumption for a coin flip but not one that applies generally across all gambles. Whereas Bernoulli's insight was critical to linking utility to wealth, Von Neumann and Morgenstern shifted the discussion of utility from outcomes to probabilities.[4] Rather than think in terms of what it would take an individual to partake a specific gamble, they presented the individual with multiple gambles or lotteries with the intention of making him choose between them. They argued that the expected utility to individuals from a lottery can be specified in terms of both outcomes and the probabilities of those outcomes, and that individuals pick one gamble over another based on maximizing expected utility.

---

3   Bernoulli proposed the log utility function, where $U(W) = \ln(W)$. As we will see later in this chapter, this is but one of a number of utility functions that exhibit diminishing marginal utility.

4   Von Neumann, J., and O. Morgenstern. *Theory of Games and Economic Behavior*. 1953 edition. Princeton, NJ: Princeton University Press, 1944.

The Von Neumann-Morgenstern arguments for utility are based on what they called the basic *axioms of choice*. The first of these axioms, titled *comparability or completeness*, requires that the alternative gambles or choices be comparable and that individuals be able to specify their preferences for each one. The second, termed *transitivity*, requires that if an individual prefers gamble A to B and B to C, she has to prefer A to C. The third, referred to as the *independence axiom*, specifies that the outcomes in each lottery or gamble are independent of each other. This is perhaps the most important and the most controversial of the choice axioms. Essentially, we are assuming that the preference between two lotteries will be unaffected if they are combined in the same way with a third lottery. In other words, if we prefer lottery A to lottery B, we are assuming that combining both lotteries with a third lottery C will not alter our preferences. The fourth axiom, *measurability*, requires that the probability of different outcomes within each gamble be measurable with a probability. Finally, the *ranking axiom* presupposes that if an individual ranks outcomes B and C between A and D, the probabilities that would yield gambles on which he would be indifferent (between B and A&D and C and A&D) have to be consistent with the rankings. What these axioms allowed Von Neumann and Morgenstern to do was to derive expected utility functions for gambles that were linear functions of the probabilities of the expected utility of the individual outcomes. In short, the expected utility of a gamble with outcomes of $10 and $100 with equal probabilities can be written as follows:

$$E(U) = 0.5 \ U(10) + 0.5 \ U(100)$$

Extending this approach, we can estimate the expected utility of any gamble, as long as we can specify the potential outcomes and the probabilities of each one. As we will see later in this chapter, it is disagreements about the appropriateness of these axioms that have animated the discussion of risk aversion for the past few decades.

We cannot underestimate the importance of what Von Neumann and Morgenstern did in advancing our understanding and analysis of risk. By extending the discussion from whether an individual should accept a gamble or not to how he should choose between different gambles, they laid the foundations for modern portfolio theory and risk management. After all, investors have to choose between risky asset classes (stocks versus real estate) and assets within each risk class (Google versus Coca Cola) and the Von Neumann-Morgenstern approach allows for such choices. In the context of risk management, the expected utility proposition has allowed us not only to develop a theory of how individuals and businesses should deal with risk, but also to follow up by measuring the payoff to risk management. When we use betas to estimate expected returns for stocks or Value at Risk (VaR) to measure risk exposure, we are working with extensions of Von Neumann-Morgenstern's original propositions.

The Gambling Exception?

Gambling, whether on long shots on the horse tracks or card tables at the casinos, cannot be easily reconciled with a world of risk-averse individuals, such as those described by Bernoulli. Put another way, if the St. Petersburg Paradox can be explained by individuals being risk averse, those same individuals create another paradox when they go out and bet on horses at the track or play at the card table because they are giving up certain amounts of money for gambles with expected values that are lower in value. Economists have tried to explain away gambling behavior with a variety of stories.

The first argument is that it is a subset of strange human beings who gamble, and they cannot be considered rational. This small risk-loving group, it is argued, will only become smaller over time, as its members are parted from their money. Although this story allows us to separate ourselves from this unexplainable behavior, it clearly loses its resonance when the vast majority of individuals indulge in gambling, as the evidence suggests that they do, at least sometimes.

The second argument is that an individual may be risk averse over some segments of wealth, become risk loving over others, and revert to being risk averse again. Friedman and Savage, for instance, argued that individuals can be risk loving and risk averse at the same time, over different choices and for different segments of wealth. In effect, it is not irrational for an individual to buy insurance against certain types of risk on any given day and to go to the race track on the same day.[5] They were positing that we are all capable of behaving irrationally (at least relative to the risk-averse view of the world) when presented with risky choices under some scenarios. Why we would go through bouts of such pronounced risk-loving behavior over some segments of wealth, while being risk averse at others, is not addressed.

The third argument is that we cannot compare gambling to other wealth-seeking behavior because individuals enjoy gambling for its own sake, and they are willing to accept the loss in wealth for the excitement that comes from rolling the dice. Here again, we have to give pause. Why would individuals not feel the same excitement when buying stock in a risky company or bonds in a distressed firm? If they do, should the utility of a risky investment always be written as a function of both the wealth change it creates and the excitement quotient?

The final and most plausible argument is grounded in behavioral quirks that seem to be systematic. To provide one example, individuals seem to routinely overestimate their own

---

5   Friedman, M., and L. P. Savage. "The Utility Analysis of Choices Involving Risk." *Journal of Political Economy*, Vol. 56, 279–304, 1948. They developed a utility function that was concave (risk averse) for some segments of wealth and convex (risk loving) over others.

skills and the probabilities of success when playing risky games. As a consequence, gambles with negative expected values can be perceived (wrongly) to have positive expected value. Thus, gambling is less a manifestation of risk loving than it is of overconfidence. We will return to this topic in more detail later in this chapter and the next one.

Although much of the discussion about this topic has been restricted to individuals gambling at casinos and racetracks, it clearly has relevance to risk management. When a trader at a hedge fund puts the fund's money at risk in an investment where the potential payoffs clearly do not justify the price paid, he is gambling, as is a firm that invests money into an emerging market project with subpar cash flows. Rather than going through intellectual contortions trying to explain such phenomena in rational terms, we should accept the reality that such behavior is neither new nor unexpected in a world where some individuals, for whatever reason, are predisposed to risk seeking.

Small Versus Large Gambles

Assume that you are offered a choice between getting $10 with certainty or a gamble, where you will make $21 with 50 percent probability and nothing the rest of the time; the expected value of the gamble is $10.50. Which one would you pick? Now assume that you are offered the choice between getting $10,000 with certainty or a gamble, where you will make $21,000 with 50 percent probability and nothing the rest of the time; the expected value of the gamble is $10,500. With conventional expected utility theory, where investors are risk averse and the utility function is well behaved, the answer is clear. If you would reject the first gamble, you should reject the second one as well.

In a famous paper on the topic, Paul Samuelson offered one of his colleagues on the economics department at MIT a coin flip where he would win $200 if he guessed right and lose $100 if he did not.[6] The colleague refused but said he would be willing to accept the bet if he was allowed 100 flips with the same payoffs. Samuelson argued that rejecting the individual bet while accepting the aggregated bet was inconsistent with expected utility theory and that the error probably occurred because his colleague had mistakenly assumed that the variance of a repeated series of bets was lower than the variance of one bet.

In a series of papers, Rabin challenged this view of the world. He showed that an individual who showed even mild risk aversion on small bets would need to be offered huge amounts of money with larger bets, if one concave utility function (relating utility to wealth) covered all ranges of his wealth. For example, an individual who would reject

6   Samuelson, P. "Risk and Uncertainty: A Fallacy of Large Numbers." *Scientia.* 98, 108–113, 1963.

a 50:50 chance of making $11 or losing $10 would require a 50 percent chance of winning $20,242 to compensate for a 50 percent chance of losing $100 and would become infinitely risk averse with larger losses. The conclusion he drew was that individuals have to be close to risk neutral with small gambles for the risk aversion that we observe with larger gambles to be feasible, which would imply that there are different expected utility functions for different segments of wealth rather than one utility function for all wealth levels. Rabin's view is consistent with the behavioral view of utility in prospect theory, which we will touch upon later in this chapter and return to in the next one.

There are important implications for risk management. If individuals are less risk averse with small risks as opposed to large risks, whether they hedge risks or not and which tools they use to manage those risks should depend on the consequences. Large companies may choose not to hedge risks that smaller companies protect themselves against, and the same business may hedge against risks with large potential impact while letting smaller risks pass through to their investors. It may also follow that there can be no unified theory of risk management, because how we deal with risk will depend on how large we perceive the impact of the risk to be.

Measuring Risk Aversion

If we accept Bernoulli's proposition that it is utility that matters and not wealth per se, and we add the reality that no two human beings are alike, it follows that risk aversion can vary widely across individuals. Measuring risk aversion in specific terms becomes the first step in analyzing and dealing with risk in both portfolio and business contexts. In this section, we examine different ways of measuring risk aversion, starting with the widely used but still effective technique of offering gambles and observing what people choose to do and then moving on to more complex measures.

Certainty Equivalents

As we noted earlier, a risk-neutral individual would be willing to accept a fair bet. In other words, she would be willing to pay $20 for a 20 percent chance of winning $100 and an 80 percent chance of making nothing. The flip side of this statement is that if we can observe what someone is willing to pay for this bet (or any other where the expected value can be computed), we can draw inferences about this person's views on risk. A risk-averse individual, for instance, would pay less than $20 for this bet, and the amount paid would vary inversely with risk aversion.

In technical terms, the price that an individual is willing to pay for a bet where there is uncertainty and an expected value is called the *certainty equivalent value*. We can relate certainty equivalents back to utility functions. Assume that you as an individual are offered a choice between two risky outcomes, A and B, and that you can estimate the expected value across the two outcomes, based on the probabilities, p and (1–p), of each occurring:

$$V = p A + (1–p) B$$

Furthermore, assume that you know how much utility you would derive from each of these outcomes and label them U(A) and U(B). If you are risk neutral, you would in effect derive the same utility from obtaining V with certainty as you would if you were offered the risky outcomes with an expected value of V:

For a risk-neutral individual: $U(V) = p\, U(A) + (1–p)\, U(B)$

A risk-averse individual, though, would derive much greater utility from the guaranteed outcome than from the gamble:

For a risk-averse individual: $U(V) > p\, U(A) + (1–p)\, U(B)$

In fact, there would be some smaller guaranteed amount ($\bar{V}$), which would be labeled the certainty equivalent, that would provide the same utility as the uncertain gamble:

$$U(\bar{V}) = p\, U(A) + (1–p)\, U(B)$$

The difference between the expected value of the gamble and the certainty equivalent is termed the *risk premium*:

Risk Premium $= V – \bar{V}$

As the risk aversion of an individual increases, the risk premium demanded for any given risky gamble also increases. With risk-neutral individuals, the risk premium will be zero, because the utility they derive from the expected value of an uncertain gamble will be identical to the utility from receiving the same amount with certainty.

If this is too abstract, consider a simple example of an individual with a log utility function. Assume that you offer this individual a gamble where he can win $10 or $100, with 50 percent probability attached to each outcome. The expected value of this gamble can be written as follows:

Expected Value $= .50(\$10) + .50(\$100) = \$55$

The utility that this individual will gain from receiving the expected value with certainty is this:

U(Expected Value) = ln($55) = 4.0073 units

However, the utility from the gamble will be much lower, because the individual is risk averse:

U(Gamble) = 0.5 ln($10) + 0.5 ln ($100) = 0.5(2.3026) +0.5(4.6051) = 3.4538 units

The certainty equivalent will therefore be the guaranteed value that will deliver the same utility as the gamble:

U(Certainty Equivalent) = ln(X) = 3.4538 units

Solving for X, we get a certainty equivalent of $31.62.[7] The risk premium, in this specific case, is the difference between the expected value of the uncertain gamble and the certainty equivalent of the gamble:

Risk Premium = Expected Value – Certainty Equivalent = $55 – $31.62 = $23.38

Put another way, this individual should be indifferent between receiving $31.62 with certainty and a gamble where he will receive $ 10 or $100 with equal probability. Using different utility functions will deliver different values for the certainty equivalent.

Certainty equivalents not only provide us with an intuitive way of thinking about risk, but they are also effective devices for extracting information from individuals about their risk aversion. As we will see in the next chapter, many experiments in risk aversion have been based on making subjects choose between risky gambles and guaranteed outcomes and using the choices to measure their risk aversion. From a risk-management perspective, it can be argued that most risk-hedging products such as insurance and derivatives offer their users a certain cost (the insurance premium, the price of the derivative) in exchange for an uncertain cost (the expected cost of a natural disaster or movement in exchange rates). A significant subset of investors chooses the certain equivalent.

Risk Aversion Coefficients

Although observing certainty equivalents gives us a window into an individual's views on risk, economists want more precision in risk measures to develop models for dealing with risk. Risk aversion coefficients represent natural extensions of the utility functions

---

7   To estimate the certainty equivalent, we compute exp(3.4538) = 31.62.

introduced earlier in this chapter. If we can specify the relationship between utility and wealth in a function, the risk aversion coefficient measures how much utility we gain (or lose) as we add (or subtract) from our wealth. The first derivative of the utility function (dU/dW or U') should provide a measure of this, but it will be specific to an individual and cannot be easily compared across individuals with different utility functions. To get around this problem, Pratt and Arrow proposed that we look at the second derivative of the utility function, which measures how the change in utility (as wealth changes) itself changes as a function of wealth level, and divide it by the first derivative to arrive at a risk aversion coefficient.[8] This number will be positive for risk-averse investors and increase with the degree of risk aversion.

Arrow-Pratt Absolute Risk Aversion $= -U''(W)/U'(W)$

The advantage of this formulation is that we can compare it across different individuals with different utility functions to draw conclusions about differences in risk aversion across people.

We can also draw a distinction between how we react to absolute changes in wealth (an extra $100, for instance) and proportional changes in wealth (a 1 percent increase in wealth), with the former measuring absolute risk aversion and the latter measuring relative risk aversion. Decreasing absolute risk aversion implies that the amount of wealth that we are willing to put at risk increases as wealth increases, whereas decreasing relative risk aversion indicates that the proportion of wealth that we are willing to put at risk increases as wealth increases. With constant absolute risk aversion, the amount of wealth that we expose to risk remains constant as wealth increases, whereas the proportion of wealth remains unchanged with constant relative risk aversion. Finally, we stand willing to risk smaller and smaller amounts of wealth, as we get wealthier, with increasing absolute risk aversion, and decreasing proportions of wealth with increasing relative risk aversion. In terms of the Arrow-Pratt measure, the relative risk aversion measure can be written as follows:

Arrow-Pratt Relative Risk Aversion $= -W\,U''(W)/U'(W)$

where,

W = Level of wealth

8   Pratt, J. W. "Risk Aversion in the Small and in the Large." *Econometrica*, Vol. 32, 122–136, 1964.

Arrow, K. *Aspects of the Theory of Risk-Bearing*. Helsinki: Yrjö Hahnsson Foundation, 1965.

U'(W) = First derivative of utility to wealth, measuring how utility changes as wealth changes

U"(W) = Second derivative of utility to wealth, measuring how the change in utility itself changes as wealth changes

The concept can be illustrated using the log utility function.

$U = \ln(W)$

$U' = -1/W$

$U'' = -1/W^2$

Absolute Risk Aversion Coefficient $= U''/U' = 1/W$

Relative Risk Aversion Coefficient $= 1$

The log utility function therefore exhibits decreasing absolute risk aversion—individuals will invest larger dollar amounts in risky assets as they get wealthier—and constant relative risk aversion—individuals will invest the same percentage of their wealth in risky assets as they get wealthier. Most models of risk and return in practice are built on specific assumptions about absolute and relative risk aversion and whether they stay constant, increase, or decrease as wealth increases. Consequently, it behooves the users of these models to at least be aware of the underlying assumptions about risk aversion in individual utility functions. The appendix to this chapter provides a short introduction to the most commonly used utility functions in practice.

There is one final point that needs to be made in the context of estimating risk aversion coefficients. The Arrow-Pratt measures of risk aversion measure changes in utility for small changes in wealth and are thus local risk aversion measures rather than global risk aversion measures. Critics take issue with these risk aversion measures on two grounds.

- The risk aversion measures can vary widely, for the same individual, depending on how big the change in wealth is. As we noted in the discussion of small and large gambles in the "I Am Rich, But Am I Happy? Utility and Wealth" section, there are some economists who note that individuals behave very differently when presented with small gambles (where less of their wealth is at stake) than with large gambles.

- In a paper looking at conventional risk aversion measures, Ross argues that the Arrow-Pratt risk aversion axioms can yield counterintuitive results, especially when individuals have to pick between two risky choices, and provides two examples. In his first example, when two investors—one less risk averse (in the Arrow-Pratt sense) than the other—are presented with a choice between two risky assets, the less risk-averse investor may actually invest less (rather than more) in the more risky asset than the more risk-averse investor. In his second example, more risk-averse individuals (again in the Arrow-Pratt sense) may pay less for partial insurance against a given risk than less risk-averse individuals. The intuition he offers is simple: the Arrow-Pratt measures are too weak to be able to make comparisons across investors with different utility functions, when no risk-free option alternative exists. Ross argues for a stronger version of the risk aversion coefficient that takes into account global differences.[9]

There is little debate about the proposition that measuring risk aversion is important for how we think about and manage risk, but there remain two questions in putting the proposition into practice. The first is whether we can reliably estimate risk aversion coefficients when most individuals are unclear about the exact form and parameters of their utility functions, relative to wealth. The second is that whether the risk aversion coefficients, even if observable over some segment of wealth, can be generalized to cover all risky choices.

Other Views on Risk Aversion

All the assessments of risk aversion that we have referenced in this chapter have been built around the proposition that expected utility matters, and we can derive risk aversion measures by looking at utility functions. In the past few decades, there have been some attempts by researchers, who have been unconvinced by conventional utility theory or have been underwhelmed by the empirical support for it, to come up with alternative ways of explaining risk aversion.

The Allais Paradox

The trigger for much of the questioning of the von Neumann-Morgenstern expected utility theory was the paradox exposited by the French economist, Maurice Allais, in two pairs of lottery choices.[10] In the first pair, he presented individuals with two lotteries—P1 and P2—with the following outcomes:

9   Ross, S. A. "Some Stronger Measures of Risk Aversion in the Small and in the Large with Applications." *Econometrica*, Vol. 49 (3), 621–639, 1981.

10   Allais, M. "The So-Called Allais Paradox and Rational Decisions Under Uncertainty." *Allais and Hagen: Expected Utility Hypotheses and the Allais Paradox*. Dordrecht: D. Reidel, 1979.

P1: $100 with certainty

P2: $0 with 1 percent chance, $100 with 89 percent chance, $500 with 10 percent chance

Most individuals, given a choice, picked P1 over P2, which is consistent with risk aversion. In the second pair, Allais offered these same individuals two other lotteries—Q1 and Q2—with the following outcomes and probabilities:

Q1: $0 with 89 percent chance and $100 with 11 percent chance

Q2: $0 with 90 percent chance and $500 with 10 percent chance

Mathematically, it can be shown that an individual who picks P1 over P2 should pick Q1 over Q2 as well. In reality, Allais noted that most individuals switched, picking Q2 over Q1. To explain this paradox, he took issue with the von Neumann-Morgenstern computation of expected utility of a gamble as the probability weighted average of the utilities of the individual outcomes. His argument was that the expected utility on a gamble should reflect not just the utility of the outcomes and the probabilities of the outcomes occurring, but also the differences in utilities obtained from the outcomes. In the preceding example, Q2 is preferred simply because the variance across the utilities in the two outcomes is so high.

In a closely related second phenomenon, Allais also noted what he called the *common ratio effect*. Given a choice between a 25 percent probability of making $8,000 and a 20 percent probability of making $10,000, Allais noted that most individuals chose the latter, in direct contradiction of the dictums of expected utility theory.[11] Both of the propositions presented by Allais suggest that the independence axiom on which expected utility theory is built may be flawed.

By pointing out that individuals often behaved in ways that were not consistent with the predictions of conventional theory, Allais posed a challenge to those who continued to stay with the conventional models to try to explain the discordant behavior. The responses to his paradox have not only helped advance our understanding of risk considerably, but they have pointed out the limitations of conventional expected utility theory. If, as Allais noted, individuals collectively behave in ways that are not consistent with rationality, at least as defined by conventional expected utility theory, we should be cautious about using the risk measurement devices that come out of this theory and we should reconsider the risk management implications.

---

11   The two gambles have the same expected value of $2,000, but the second gamble is more risky than the first one. Any risk-averse individual who obeys the dictums of expected utility theory would pick the first gamble.

Expected Utility Responses

The first responses to the Allais paradox were within the confines of the expected utility paradigm. What these responses shared in common was that they worked with von Neuman-Morgenstern axioms of choice and attempted to modify one or more of them to explain the paradox. In one noted example, Machina proposed that the independence axiom be abandoned and that stochastic dominance be used to derive what he termed "local expected utility" functions.[12] In intuitive terms, he assumed that individuals became more risk averse as the prospects became better, which has consequences for how we choose between risky gambles.[13] A whole family of models are consistent with this reasoning and fall under the category of weighted utility functions, where different consequences are weighted differently (as opposed to the identical weighting given in standard expected utility models).

Loomes and Sugden relaxed the transitivity axiom in the conventional expected utility framework to develop what they called *regret theory*.[14] At its heart is the premise that individuals compare the outcomes they obtain within a given gamble and are disappointed when the outcome diverges unfavorably from what they might have had. Thus, large differences between what you get from a chosen action and what you could have received from an alternate action give rise to disproportionately large regrets. The net effect is that you can observe actions that are inconsistent with conventional expected utility theory.

Some other models are in the same vein, insofar as they largely stay within the confines of conventional expected utility theory and attempt to explain phenomena such as the Allais paradox with as little perturbation to the conventional axioms as possible. The problem, though, is that these models are not always internally consistent, and while they explain some of the existing paradoxes and anomalies, they create new paradoxes that they cannot explain.

---

12   Machina, Mark J. "'Expected Utility' Theory Without the Independence Axiom." *Econometrica*, 50, 277–323, 1982. Stochastic dominance implies that when you compare two gambles, you do at least as well or better under every possible scenario in one of the gambles as compared to the other.

13   At the risk of straying too far from the topic at hand, indifference curves in the von Neumann-Morgenstern world are upward sloping and parallel to each other and well behaved. In the Machina's modification, these curves fan out and create the observed Allais anomalies.

14   Loomes, Graham, and Robert Sugden. "Regret Theory: An Alternative Theory of Rational Choice Under Uncertainty," *Econ. J.* 92, 805–824, 1982.

Prospect Theory

Whereas many economists stayed within the conventional confines of rationality and attempted to tweak models to make them conform more closely to reality, Kahneman and Tversky posed a more frontal challenge to expected utility theory.[15] As psychologists, they brought a different sensibility to the argument and based their theory (which they called *prospect theory*) on some well-observed deviations from rationality, including the following:

- **Framing**—Decisions often seem to be affected by the way choices are framed, rather than the choices themselves. Thus, if we buy more of a product when it is sold at 20 percent off a list price of $2.50 than when it sold for a list price of $2.00, we are susceptible to framing. An individual may accept the same gamble he had rejected earlier if the gamble is framed differently.

- **Nonlinear preferences**—If an individual prefers A to B, B to C, and then C to A, she is violating one of the key axioms of standard preference theory (transitivity). In the real world, this type of behavior is common.

- **Risk aversion and risk seeking**—Individuals often simultaneously exhibit risk aversion in some of their actions while seeking out risk in others.

- **Source**—The mechanism through which information is delivered may matter, even if the product or service is identical. For instance, people will pay more for a good, based on how it is packaged, than for an identical good, even though they plan to discard the packaging instantly after the purchase.

- **Loss aversion**—Individuals seem to feel more pain from losses than from equivalent gains. Individuals will often be more willing to accept a gamble with uncertainty and an expected loss than a guaranteed loss of the same amount, in clear violation of basic risk-aversion tenets.

Kahneman and Tversky replaced the utility function, which defines utility as a function of wealth, with a value function, with value defined as deviations from a reference point that allows for different functions for gains and losses. In keeping with observed loss aversion, for instance, the value function for losses was much steeper (and convex) than the value function for gains (and concave).

The implication is that how individuals behave will depend on how a problem is framed, with the decision being different if the outcome is framed relative to a reference point to

---

15   Kahneman, D., and A. Tversky. "Prospect Theory: An Analysis of Decision Under Risk." *Econometrica*, Vol. 47, 263–292, 1979.

make it look like a gain as opposed to a different reference point to convert it into a loss. Stated in terms of risk aversion coefficients, Kahneman and Tversky assumed that risk aversion coefficients behave differently for upside than downside risk.

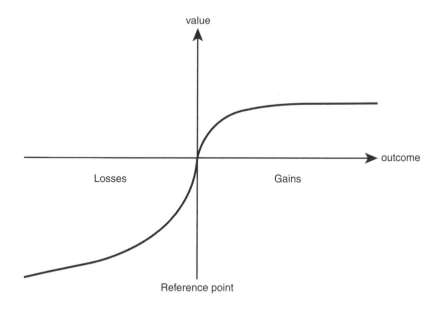

Figure 2.2: A Loss Aversion Function

Kahneman and Tversky also explained the Allais paradox in what they termed the *common consequence effect*. Their argument was that preferences could be affected by what they termed the *consolation price effect*, where the possibility of a large outcome can make individuals much more risk averse. This can be seen with the Allais paradox, where the expected utilities of the four lotteries can be written as follows:

$E(u; P1) = 0.1u(\$100) + 0.89u(\$100) + 0.01u(\$100)$

$E(u; P2) = 0.1u(\$500) + 0.89u(\$100) + 0.01u(\$0)$

$E(u; Q1) = 0.1u(\$100) + 0.01u(\$100) + 0.89u(\$0)$

$E(u; Q2) = 0.1u(\$500) + 0.01u(\$0) + 0.89u(\$0)$

Note that the common prize between the first pair of choices (P1 and P2) is 0.89 u($100), which is much larger than the common prize between the second pair of choices (Q1 and Q2), which is 0.89 u($0). With the higher common prize first pair, the individual is more risk averse than she is with the much lower common prize second pair.

If the earlier work by economists trying to explain observed anomalies (such as the Allais paradox) was evolutionary, Kahneman and Tversky's work was revolutionary because it suggested that the problem with expected utility theory was not with one axiom or another but with its view of human behavior. The influence of Kahneman and Tversky on the way we view investments, in general, and risk specifically has been profound. The entire field of behavioral finance that attempts to explain the so-called anomalies in investor behavior has its roots in their work. It is also entirely possible that the anomalies that we find in risk management, where some risks that we expect to see hedged are not hedged and other risks that should not be hedged are and may be attributable to quirks in human behavior.

Consequences of Views on Risk

Now that we have described how we think about risk and measuring risk aversion, we should turn our attention to why it is of such consequence. In this section, we will focus on how risk and our attitudes toward it affect everything that we do as human beings, but with particular emphasis on economic choices from where we invest our money to how we value assets and run businesses.

Investment Choices

Our views of risk have consequences for how and where we invest. In fact, the risk aversion of an investor affects every aspect of portfolio design, from allocating across different asset classes to selecting assets within each asset class to performance evaluation.

- **Asset allocation**—Asset allocation is the first and perhaps the most important step in portfolio management, where investors determine which asset classes to invest their wealth in. The allocation of assets across different asset classes will depend on how risk averse an investor is, with less risk-averse investors generally allocating a greater proportion of their portfolios to riskier assets. Using the most general categorization of stocks, bonds, and cash as asset classes, this would imply that less risk-averse investors will have more invested in stocks than more risk-averse investors, and the most risk-averse investors will not stray far from the safest asset class, which is cash.[16]

---

16   Cash includes savings accounts and money market accounts, where the interest rates are guaranteed and there is no or close to no risk of losing principal.

- **Asset selection**—Within each asset class, we have to choose specific assets to hold. Having decided to allocate specific proportions of a portfolio to stocks and bonds, the investor has to decide which stocks and bonds to hold. This decision is often made less complex by the existence of mutual funds of varying types, from sector funds to diversified index funds to bond funds. Investors who are less risk averse may allocate more of their equity investment to riskier stocks and funds, although they may pay a price in terms of less than complete diversification.

- **Performance evaluation**—Ultimately, our judgments on whether the investments we made in prior periods (in individual securities) delivered reasonable returns (and were therefore good investments) will depend on how we measure risk and what trade-off we demand in terms of higher returns.

The bottom line is that individuals are unique, and their risk preferences will largely govern the right investment choices for them.

Corporate Finance

Just as risk affects how we make portfolio decisions as investors, it also affects decisions that we make when running businesses. In fact, if we categorize corporate financial decisions into investment, financing and dividend decisions, the risk aversion of decision makers feeds into each of these decisions:

- **Investment decisions**—Few investments made by a business offer guaranteed returns. In fact, almost every investment comes with a full plate of risks, some of which are specific to the company and sector and some of which are macro risks. We have to decide whether to invest in these projects, given the risks and our expectations of the cash flows.

- **Financing decisions**—When determining how much debt and equity we should use in funding a business, we have to confront fundamental questions about risk and return again. Specifically, borrowing more to fund a business may increase the potential upside to equity investors but also increase the potential downside and put the firm at risk of default. The way we view this risk and its consequences will be central to how much we borrow.

- **Dividend decisions**—As the cash comes in from existing investments, we face the question of whether to return some or a lot of this cash to the owners of the business or hold on to it as a cash balance. Because one motive for holding onto cash is to meet contingencies in the future (an economic downturn, a need for new investment), how much we choose to hold as a cash balance will be determined by how we perceive the risk of these contingencies.

Although these are questions that every business, private and public, large and small, has to answer, an additional layer of complexity is added when the decision makers are not the owners of the business, which is all too often the case with publicly traded firms. In these firms, the managers who make investment, financing, and dividend decisions have different perspectives on risk and reward than the owners of the business. Later in this book, we will return to this conflict and argue that it may explain why so many risk-management products, which are peddled to the managers and not to the owners, are directed toward hedging risk and not exploiting it.

Valuation

In both portfolio management and corporate finance, the value of a business underlies decision making. With portfolio management, we try to find companies that trade at below their "fair" value, whereas in corporate finance, we try to make decisions that increase firm value. The value of any asset or collection of assets (which is what a business is) ultimately will be determined by the expected cash flows that we expect to generate and the discount rate we apply to these cash flows. In conventional valuation, risk matters primarily because it determines the discount rate, with riskier cash flows being discounted at higher rates.

Later in this book, we will argue that this is far too narrow a view of risk and that risk affects everything that a firm does, from cash flows to growth rates to discount rates. A rich valuation model will allow for this interplay between the way a firm deals with risk and its value, thus giving us a tool for evaluating the effects of all aspects of risk management. It is the first step in more comprehensive risk management.

Conclusion

As human beings, we have decidedly mixed feelings about risk and its consequences. On the one hand, we actively seek out risk in some of our pursuits, sometimes with no rewards, and on the other, we manifest a dislike for it when we are forced to make choices. It is this duality of risk that makes it so challenging.

In this chapter, we considered the basic tools that economists have devised for dealing with risk. We began with Bernoulli's distinction between price and utility and how the utility of a wager will be person specific. The same wager may be rejected by one person as unfair and embraced by another as a bargain because of their different utility functions. We then expanded on this concept by introducing the notion of certainty equivalents (where we looked at the guaranteed alternative to a risky outcome) and risk aversion coefficients (which can be compared across individuals). Whereas economists have long based their analysis of risk on the assumptions of rationality and diminishing marginal utility, we also presented the alternative theories based on the assumptions that individuals often behave in ways that are not consistent with the conventional definition of rationality.

In the final part of this chapter, we examined why measuring and understanding risk is so critical to us. Every decision that we are called on to make will be colored by our views on risk and how we perceive it. Understanding risk and how it affects decision makers is a prerequisite of success in portfolio management and corporate finance.

APPENDIX

Utility Functions and Risk Aversion Coefficients

In the chapter, we estimated the absolute and relative risk aversion coefficients for the log utility function, made famous by Bernoulli's use of it to explain the St. Petersburg paradox. In fact, the log utility function is not the only one that generates <u>decreasing absolute risk aversion</u> and <u>constant relative risk aversion</u>. A power utility function, which can be written as follows, also has the same characteristics:

$$U(W) = W^a$$

Figure 2A.1 graphs the log utility and power utility functions for an individual.

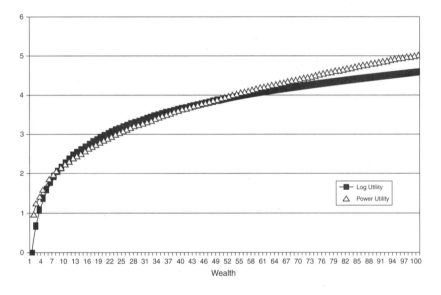

Figure 2A.1: Log Utility and Power Utility Functions

Other widely used functions generate combinations of absolute and relative risk aversion. Consider, for instance, the exponential utility function, which takes the following form:

$$U(W) = a - \exp^{-bW}$$

This function generates <u>constant absolute risk aversion</u> (where individuals invest the same dollar amount in risky assets as they get wealthier) and <u>increasing relative risk aversion</u> (where a smaller percentage of wealth is invested in risky assets as wealth increases). Figure 2A.2 graphs an exponential utility function.

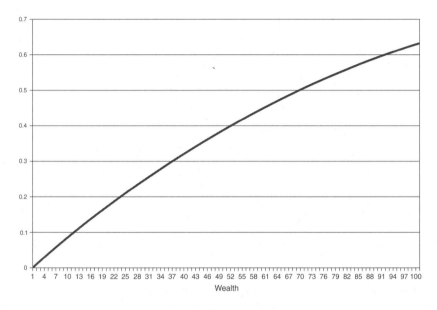

Figure 2A.2: Exponential Utility Function

The quadratic utility function has the attractive property of linking the utility of wealth to only two parameters: the expected level of wealth, and the standard deviation in that value.

$$U(W) = a + bW - c W^2$$

The function yields <u>increasing absolute risk aversion</u>, where investors invest less of their dollar wealth in risky assets as they get wealthier, which is a counterintuitive result. Figure 2A.3 graphs a quadratic utility function.

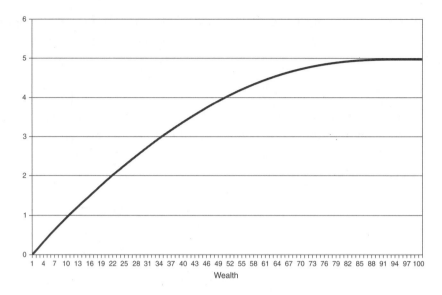

Figure 2A.3: Quadratic Utility Function

Now that you'd seen functions with constant and increasing relative risk aversion, consider a final example of a utility function that takes the following form:

$$U(W) = \frac{(W - \gamma)^{1-\alpha} - 1}{1 - \alpha} \text{ (with } \gamma > 0\text{)}$$

This function generates <u>decreasing relative risk aversion</u>, where the proportion of wealth invested in risky assets increases as wealth increases.

All the functions described in this appendix belong to a class of utility functions called *hyperbolic absolute risk aversion* (HARA). What these utility functions share in common is that the inverse of the risk aversion measure (also called *risk tolerance*) is a linear function of wealth.

Although utility functions have been mined by economists to derive elegant and powerful models, there are niggling details about them that should give us pause. The first is that no single utility function seems to fit aggregate human behavior very well. The second is that the utility functions that are easiest to work with, such as the quadratic utility functions, yield counterintuitive predictions about how humans will react to risk. The third is that there are such wide differences across individuals when it comes to risk aversion that finding a utility function to fit the representative investor or individual seems like an exercise in futility. Notwithstanding these limitations, a working knowledge of the basics of utility theory is a prerequisite for sensible risk management.

3

WHAT DO WE THINK ABOUT RISK?

In Chapter 2, "Why Do We Care About Risk?," we presented the ways in which economists go about measuring risk aversion and the consequences for investment and business decisions. In this chapter, we pull together the accumulated evidence of how individuals perceive risk. First, we look at experimental and survey studies that have focused on risk aversion in the population; then we turn our attention to what we can learn about risk aversion by looking at how risky assets are priced. Finally, we look at the explosion of game shows that require contestants to make choices between monetary prizes, thus providing fertile data for studies of risk aversion.

In the process of looking at the evidence on risk aversion, we examine some of the quirks that have been observed in how human beings react to risk, a topic we introduced in Chapter 2 in the context of prospect theory. Much of this work falls under the rubric of behavioral finance, but there are serious economic consequences, and they may be the basis for some well-known and hard-to-explain market anomalies.

General Principles

Before we look at the empirical evidence that has accumulated on how we react to risk, we should summarize what the theory posits about risk aversion in human beings. Most economic theory has been built on the proposition that individuals are risk averse and rational. The notion of diminishing marginal utility, introduced by Bernoulli, still lies at the heart of much of economic discussion. Although we may accept the arguments of these economists on faith, the reality is much more complex. As Kahneman and Tversky noted in their alternative view of the world, there are systematic anomalies in human behavior that are incompatible with rationality. We can act as if these aberrations are not widespread and will disappear, but the dangers of doing so are significant. We will both misprice and mismanage risk if we do not understand how humans really perceive it.

In this chapter, we will turn away from theoretical measures of risk aversion and arguments for rationality and look at the empirical evidence on risk aversion. In the process, we can determine for ourselves how much we can salvage of the conventional economic view of risk and whether the behavioral view of risk should replace it or supplement it in analysis.

Evidence on Risk Aversion

In the previous chapter, we presented the Arrow-Pratt measure of risk aversion, an elegant formulation that requires only two inputs: the first and the second derivatives of the utility function (relative to wealth) of an individual. The limitation in using it to measure risk aversion is that it requires specifying the utility function for wealth, which is a difficult exercise. Consequently, economists have struggled with how to give form to these unobservable utility functions. They have come up with three general approaches:

- Experimental studies, where they offer individuals simple gambles and observe how they react to changes in control variables

- Surveys of investors and consumers that seek to flesh out perspectives on risk

- Observations of market prices for risky assets, which offer a window into the price that investors charge for risk

Experimental Studies

Bernoulli's prospective gamble with coin flips, which we used to introduce utility theory in the previous chapter, can be considered the first published experimental study, although there were others that undoubtedly preceded it. However, experimental economics as an area is of relatively recent origin and has developed primarily in the past few decades. In experimental economics, we bring the laboratory tools of the physical sciences to economics. By designing simple experiments with subjects in controlled settings, we can vary one or more variables and record the effects on behavior, thus avoiding the common problems of full-fledged empirical studies, where we need to control for many other factors.

Experimental Design

In a treatise of experimental economics, Roth presents two ways in which an economic experiment can be designed and run. In the first, which he calls the method of *planned experimental design*, investigators run trials with a fixed set of conditions, and the design specifies which conditions will be varied under what settings. The results of the trials are used to fill in the cells of the experimental design, and then they're analyzed to test hypotheses. This is generally the standard when testing in physical science; it can be illustrated using a simple example of a test for a new drug to treat arthritis. The subjects are divided randomly into two groups, with one group being given the new drug and the other a placebo. The differences between the two groups are noted and attributed to the drug; breaking down into subgroups based on age may allow researchers to draw extended conclusions about whether the drug is more effective with older or younger patients. Once the experiment is designed, the experimenter is allowed little discretion on judgment, and the results from all trials usually are reported. In the second, which he calls the method of *independent trials*, each trial is viewed as a separate experiment, and the researcher reports the aggregate or average results across multiple trials.[1] Here, there is more potential for discretion and misuse because researchers determine which trials to report and in what form, a choice that may be affected by prior biases brought into the analyses. Most experiments in economics fall into this category and are thus susceptible to its weaknesses.

As experimental economics has developed as a discipline, more and more of conventional economic theory has been put to the test with experiments, and the experiments have become more complex and sophisticated. Although we have learned much about human behavior from these experiments, questions have also arisen about the proper design of and reporting on experiments. We can learn from the way the physical sciences, where experiments have a much longer tradition, have dealt with a number of issues relating to experiments.

- **Data mining and reporting**—The National Academy of Science's committee on the Conduct of Science explicitly categorizes as fraud the practice of "selecting only those data that support a hypothesis and concealing the rest." Consequently, researchers are encouraged to make the raw data that they use in their work available to others so that others can replicate their findings.

- **Researcher biases and preconceptions**—The biases that researchers bring into a study can play a key role in the way they read the data. It is for this reason that

---

1   Roth, A. E. "Let's Keep the Con Out of Experimental Econ: A Methodological Note," *Empirical Economics*, 19, 279...289, 1994.

experimental methods in the physical sciences try to shield the data from the subjective judgments of researchers (by using double-blind trials, for example).

- **Theory disproved or failed experiment**—A question that every experimental researcher faces when reporting on an experiment that fails to support an existing theory (especially when the theory is considered to be beyond questioning) is whether to view the contradictory information from the experiment as useful information and report it to other readers or to consider the experiment a failure. If it is the latter, the tendency will be to recalibrate the experiment until the theory is proven correct.

As we draw more and more on the findings in experimental economics, we should also bring a healthy dose of skepticism to the discussion. As with all empirical work, we have to make our own judgments on which researchers we trust more and how much we want to read into their findings.

Experimental Findings

Experimental studies on risk aversion have spanned the spectrum from testing whether human beings are risk averse, and if so, how much, to differences in risk aversion across different subgroups categorized by sex, age, and income. The findings from these studies can be categorized as follows.

Extent of Risk Aversion

Bernoulli's finding that most subjects would pay relatively small amounts to partake in a lottery with an infinite expected value gave rise to expected utility theory and laid the basis for how we measure risk aversion in economics. As a bookend, the experiments by Allais in the 1950s, also referenced in Chapter 2, provided evidence that conventional expected utility theory did not stand up to experimentation and that humans behaved in far more complicated ways than the theory would predict.

In the decades since, there have several studies of risk aversion using experiments. Some of these experiments used animals. One study used rats as subjects and made them choose between a safe alternative (a constant food source) and a risky one (a variable food source). It concluded that rats were risk averse in their choices and displayed mildly decreasing risk aversion as their consumption increased.[2] In a depressing afterthought

---

2   Battalio, Raymond C., John H. Kagel, and Don N. MacDonald. "Animals' Choices Over Uncertain Outcomes: Some Initial Experimental Results." *The American Economic Review*, Vol. 75, No. 4, 1985.

for risk-averse human beings, another study concluded that more risk-averse rats lived shorter, more stressful lives than their less risk-averse counterparts.[3]

Studies with human subjects have generally concluded that they are risk averse, although there are differences in risk aversion, depending on how much is at stake and how an experiment is structured. One study made its subjects, with varying levels of wealth, pick between guaranteed and risky investments. It found evidence of decreasing absolute risk aversion among the subjects—they were willing to risk more in dollar terms as they became wealthier—and no evidence of increasing relative risk aversion. The proportion of wealth that they were willing to put at risk did not decrease as wealth increased.[4]

The experimental research also finds interesting differences in risk aversion when subjects are presented with small gambles as opposed to large. Many of these studies offer their subjects choices between two lotteries with the same expected value but different spreads. For instance, 330 farmers in rural India were asked to pick between lottery A (which offers 50 percent probabilities of winning $50 or $100) and lottery B (with 50 percent probabilities of winning $25 or $125). That experiment concluded that there was mild risk aversion, with two-thirds of the subjects picking less risky lottery A over the more risky lottery B (with the rest of the respondents being risk lovers who picked the more risky lottery) when the payoffs were small. As the payoffs increased, risk aversion increased, and risk-loving behavior almost entirely disappeared.[5]

Holt and Laury expanded on this experiment by looking for the crossover point between the safer and the riskier lottery. In other words, using lottery A and B as examples again, they framed the question for subjects this way: What probability of success would you need on lottery B for it to be preferable to lottery A? Risk-averse subjects should require a probability greater than 50 percent, with higher probabilities reflecting higher risk aversion. They also found that risk aversion increased as the payoffs increased.[6]

Kachmeimeir and Shehata ran their experiments in China, eliciting certainty equivalent values from subjects for lotteries that they were presented with. Thus, subjects were asked how much they would accept as a guaranteed alternative to a lottery; the lower this certainty equivalent, relative to the expected value, the greater the risk aversion. They

---

3   Cavigelli, S.A., and McClintock, M.K. Fear of novelty in infant rats predicts adult corticosterone dynamics and an early death, Proceeds of the National Academy of the Sciences, 2003.

4   Levy, Hiam. "Absolute and Relative Risk Aversion: An Experimental Study." *Journal of Risk and Uncertainty*, 8:3 (May), 289...307, 1994.

5   Binswanger, Hans P. "Attitudes Towards Risk: Theoretical Implications of an Experiment in Rural India." *The Economic Journal*, Vol. 91, No. 364, 1981.

6   Holt, Charles A., and Susan K. Laury. "Risk Aversion and Incentive Effects." *The American Economic Review*, Vol. 92, No. 5, 2002.

also varied the probabilities on different lotteries, with some having 50 percent probabilities of success and others only 10 percent probabilities. Consistent with the other studies, they found that risk aversion increased with the magnitude of the payoffs, but they also found that risk aversion decreased with high-win probabilities. In other words, subjects were willing to accept a smaller certainty equivalent for a lottery with a 90 percent chance of making $10 and a 10 percent chance of making $110 (Expected value = .9(10) + .1 (110) = 20) than for a lottery with a 50 percent chance of making $10 and a 50 percent chance of making $30 (Expected value = .5(10) + .5 (30) =20).[7]

In summary, there seems to be clear evidence that human beings collectively are risk averse, and they become more so as the stakes become larger. There is also evidence of significant differences in risk aversion across individuals, with some showing no signs of risk aversion and some even seeking out risk.

Differences Across Different Gambles/Settings

Experimental studies of risk aversion indicate that the risk aversion of subjects varies depending on how an experiment is structured. For instance, risk-aversion coefficients that emerge from lottery choices seem to differ from those that come from experimental auctions, with the same subjects. Furthermore, subjects behave differently with differently structured auctions, and risk aversion varies with the information that is provided to them about assets and with whether they have won or lost in prior rounds. In this section, we consider some of the evidence of how experimental settings affect risk aversion and what their implications are.

- **Lotteries versus auctions**—Berg and Rietz found that subjects who were only slightly risk averse or even risk neutral in lottery choices became much more risk averse in bargaining games and in interactive auctions. They argued that interpersonal dynamics may play a role in determining risk aversion. If we carry this to its logical limit, we would expect investors buying stocks online (often sitting alone in front of their computer) to be less risk averse than investors who buy stocks through a broker or on a trading floor.[8]

7   Kachelmeier, Steven J., and Mohamed Shehata. "Examining Risk Preferences Under High Monetary Incentives: Experimental Evidence from the People's Republic of China." *The American Economic Review*, Vol. 82, No. 5, 1992.

8   Berg, Joyce E., and Thomas A. Rietz. "Do Unto Others: A Theory and Experimental Test of Interpersonal Factors in Decision Making Under Uncertainty." University of Iowa, Discussion Paper, 1997. This is backed up by Dorsey, R. E., and L. Razzolini. "Auctions versus Lotteries: Do Institutions Matter?" University of Mississippi, Discussion Paper, presented at the Summer 1998 ESA meeting.

- **Institutional setup**—Berg, Dickhaut, and McCabe compared the way the same set of subjects priced assets (and thus revealed their risk preferences) under an English clock auction and a first-price auction and found that subjects go from being risk loving in the English clock auction to risk averse in the first-price auction.[9] Isaac and James came to similar conclusions when comparing first-price auction markets to other auction mechanisms.[10] Because different markets are structured differently, this suggests that asset prices can vary depending on how markets are set up. To provide an illustration, Reynolds and Wooders compared auctions for the same items on Yahoo! and eBay and concluded that prices are higher on the former.[11]

- **Information effects**—Can risk aversion be affected by providing more information about possible outcomes in an experiment? There is some evidence that it can, especially in the context of *myopic loss aversion*—the tendency of human beings to be more sensitive to losses than equivalent gains and to become more so as they evaluate outcomes more frequently. Kahneman, Schwartz, Thaler, and Tversky found that subjects who got the most frequent feedback (and thus information about their gains and losses) were more risk averse than investors who got less information.[12] Camerer and Weigelt investigated the effects of revealing information to some traders and not to others in experiments and uncovered what they called *information mirages*, where traders who did not receive information attributed information to trades where such information did not exist. These mirages increase price volatility and result in prices drifting further from fair value.[13]

---

9   Berg, J, J. Dickhaut and K. McCabe. "Risk Preference Instability across Institutions: A Dilemma." *PNAS*, Vol. 102, 4209…4214, 2005. In an English clock auction, the price of an asset is set at the largest possible valuation, and potential sellers then exit the auction as the price is lowered. The last remaining seller sells the asset at the price at which the second-to-last seller exited the auction. In a first-price auction, potential buyers of an asset submit sealed bids simultaneously for an asset, and the highest bidder receives the asset at her bid-price.

10 Isaac, R. Mark, and Duncan James. "Just Who Are You Calling Risk Averse?" *Journal of Risk and Uncertainty*, Springer, Vol. 20(2), 177…187, 2000.

11 Reynolds, S. S., and J. Wooders. "Auctions with a Buy Price," Working Paper, University of Arizona, 2005. The key difference between the two auctions arises when the seller specifies a buy-now price; in the eBay auction, the buy-now option disappears as soon as a bid is placed, whereas it remains visible in the Yahoo! auction.

12 Kahneman, D., A. Schwartz, R. Thaler, and A. Tversky. "The Effect of Myopic Loss Aversion on Risk Taking: An Experimental Test." *Quarterly Journal of Economics*, Vol. 112, 647…661, 1997.

13 Camerer, C., and K. Weigelt. "Information Mirages in Experimental Asset Markets." *Journal of Business*, Vol. 64, 463…493, 1991.

In summary, the risk aversion of human beings depends not only on the choices they are offered but on the setting in which these choices are presented. The same investment may be viewed as riskier if offered in a different environment and at a different time to the same person.

Risk Aversion Differences Across Subgroups

Although most would concede that some individuals are more risk averse than others, are there significant differences across subgroups? In other words, are females more risk averse than males? How about older people versus younger people? What effect do experience and age have on risk aversion? In this section, we consider some of the experimental evidence in this regard.

- **Male versus female**—There seems to be some evidence that women, in general, are more risk averse than men, although the extent of the difference and the reasons for differences are still debated. In a survey of 19 other studies, Byrnes, Miller, and Schafer concluded that women are decidedly more risk averse than men.[14] In an investment experiment, Levy, Elron, and Cohen also found that women are less willing to take on investment risk and consequently earn lower amounts.[15] In contrary evidence, Holt and Laury found that increasing the stakes removed the sex differences in risk aversion.[16] In other words, while men may be less risk averse than women with small bets, they are as risk averse, if not more so, for larger, more consequential bets.

- **Naive versus experienced**—Does experience with an asset class make one more or less risk averse? A study by Dyer, Kagel and Levin compared the bids from naive student participants and experts from the construction industry for a common asset and concluded that although the winner's curse (where the winner overpays) was prevalent with both groups, the former (the students) were more risk averse than the experts.[17]

- **Young versus old**—Risk aversion increases as we age. In experiments, older people tend to be more risk averse than younger subjects, although the increase

14 Byrnes, James P., David C. Miller, and William D. Schafer. "Gender Differences in Risk Taking: A Meta-Analysis." *Psychological Bulletin*, 125: 367…383, 1999.

15 Levy, Haim, Efrat Elron, and Allon Cohen. "Gender Differences in Risk Taking and Investment Behavior: An Experimental Analysis." Unpublished manuscript, The Hebrew University, 1999.

16 Holt, Charles A., and Susan K. Laury. "Risk Aversion and Incentive Effects." *The American Economic Review*, Vol. 92, No. 5, 1644…1655, 2002.

17 Dyer, Douglas, John H. Kagel, and Dan Levin. "A Comparison of Naive and Experienced Bidders in Common Value Offer Auctions: A Laboratory Analysis." *Economic Journal*, 99:394 (March), 108…115, 1989.

in risk aversion is greater among women than men. Harrison, Lau, and Rustrom report that younger subjects (under 30 years) in their experiments, conducted in Denmark, had much lower relative risk aversion than older subjects (over 40 years). In a related finding, single individuals were less risk averse than married individuals, although having more children did not seem to increase risk aversion.[18]

- **Racial and cultural differences**—The experiments that we have reported on have spanned the globe from rural farmers in India to college students in the United States. The conclusion, though, is that human beings have a lot more in common when it comes to risk aversion than they have as differences. The Holt and Laury study from 2002, which we referenced earlier, found no race-based differences in risk aversion.

It should come as no surprise to any student of human behavior, but there are wide differences in risk aversion across individuals. The interesting question for risk management is whether policies on risk at businesses should be tailored to the owners of these businesses. In other words, should risk be perceived more negatively in a company where stockholders are predominantly older women than in a company held primarily by young males? If so, should there be more risk hedging at the former and strategic risk taking at the latter? Casual empiricism suggests that this proposition is not an unreasonable one and that the risk management practices at firms reflect the risk aversion of both the owners and the managers of these firms.

Other Risk Aversion Evidence

The most interesting evidence from experiments, though, is not in what they tell us about risk aversion in general but in what we learn about quirks in human behavior, even in the simplest of settings. In fact, Kahneman and Tversky's challenge to conventional economic utility theory was based on their awareness of the experimental research in psychology. In this section, we will cover some of the more important of these findings.

- **Framing**—Kahneman and Tversky noted that describing a decision problem differently, even when the underlying choices remain the same, can lead to different decisions and measures of risk aversion. In their classic example, they asked subjects to pick between two responses to a disease threat. The first response, they said, would save 200 people (out of a population of 600), but in the second, they noted that "there is a one-third probability that everyone will

---

18 Harrison, G. W., M. I. Lau, and E. E. Rutstrom. "Estimating Risk Attitudes in Denmark: A Field Experiment." Working Paper, University of Central Florida, 2004.

be saved and a two-thirds probability that no one will be saved." While the net effect of both responses is the same—400 will die and 200 will be saved—72 percent of the respondents pick the first option. They termed this phenomenon *framing* and argued that both utility models and experimenters have to deal with the consequences. In particular, the assumption of invariance that underlies the von Neumann-Morgenstern rational choice theory is violated by the existence of framing.[19]

- **Loss aversion**—*Loss aversion* refers to the tendency of individuals to prefer avoiding losses to making comparable gains. In an experiment, Kahneman and Tversky offered an example of loss aversion. The first offered subjects a choice between the following:

Option A: A guaranteed payout of $250

Option B: A 25 percent chance to gain $1,000 and a 75 percent chance of getting nothing

Of the respondents, 84 percent chose the sure option A over option B (with the same expected payout but much greater risk), which was not surprising, given risk aversion. They then reframed the question and offered the same subjects the following choices:

Option C: A sure loss of $750

Option D: A 75 percent chance of losing $ 1,000 and a 25 percent chance of losing nothing

Now, 73 percent of respondents preferred the gamble (with an expected loss of $750) over the certain loss. Kahneman and Tversky noted that stating the question in terms of a gain resulted in different choices from framing it in terms of a loss.[20] Loss aversion implies that individuals will prefer an uncertain gamble to a certain loss as long as the gamble has the possibility of no loss, even though the expected value of the uncertain loss may be higher than the certain loss.

Benartzi and Thaler combined loss aversion with the frequency with which individuals checked their accounts (what they called *mental accounting*) to create

19   Tversky, A. and D. Kahneman. "The Framing of Decisions and the Psychology of Choice." *Science* 211, 453…458, 1981.

20   Tversky, A. and D. Kahneman. "Loss Aversion in Riskless Choice: A Reference-Dependent Model." *Quarterly Journal of Economics*, 106, 1038…1061, 1991.

the composite concept of *myopic loss aversion*.[21] Haigh and List provided an experimental test that illustrates the proposition where they ran a sequence of nine lotteries with subjects but varied the way they provided information on the outcomes.[22] To one group, they provided feedback after each round, allowing them to thus react to success or failure on that round. To the other group, they withheld feedback until three rounds were completed and provided feedback on the combined outcome over the three rounds. They found that people were willing to bet far less in the frequent feedback group than in the pooled feedback group, suggesting that loss aversion becomes more acute if individuals have shorter time horizons and assess success or failure at the end of these horizons.

- **House money effect**—Generically, the *house money effect* refers to the phenomenon that individuals are more willing to take risks (and are thus less risk averse) with found money (that is, money obtained easily) than with earned money. Consider the experiment where 10 subjects were each given $30 at the start of the game and offered the choice of either doing nothing or flipping a coin to win or lose $9; seven chose the coin flip. Another set of 10 subjects were offered no initial funds but offered a choice of either taking $30 with certainty or flipping a coin and winning $39 if it came up heads or $21 if it came up tails. Only four in ten chose the coin flip, even though the final consequences (ending up with $21 or $39) were the same in both experiments. Thaler and Johnson illustrate the house money effect with an experiment where subjects were offered a sequence of lotteries. In the first lottery, subjects were given a chance to win $15 and were offered a subsequent lottery where they had a 50:50 chance of winning or losing $4.50. Although many of these same subjects would have rejected the second lottery, offered as an initial choice, 77 percent of those who won the first lottery (and made $15) took the second lottery.[23]

- **Break-even effect**—The *break-even effect* is the flip side of the house money effect and refers to the attempts of those who have lost money to make it back. In particular, subjects in experiments who have lost money seem willing to gamble on lotteries (that standing alone would be viewed as unattractive) that

21   Benartzi, Shlomo, and Richard Thaler. "Myopic Loss Aversion and the Equity Premium Puzzle." *Quarterly Journal of Economics*, 110, 73…92, 1995.

22   Haigh, M. S., and J. A. List. "Do Professional Traders Exhibit Myopic Loss Aversion? An Experimental Analysis." *Journal of Finance*, Vol. 45, 523…534, 2005.

23   Thaler, R. H., and E. J. Johnson. "Gambling with the House Money and Trying to Break Even: The Effects of Prior Outcomes on Risky Choice." *Management Science* 36, 643…660, 1990. They also document a house-loss effect, where those who lose in the initial lottery become more risk averse at the second stage, but the evidence from other experimental studies on this count is mixed.

offer them a chance to break even. The just-referenced study by Thaler and Johnson that uncovered the house money effect also found evidence in support of the break-even effect. In their sequenced lotteries, they found that subjects who lost money on the first lottery generally became more risk averse in the second lottery, except when the second lottery offered them a chance to make up their first-round losses and break even.[24]

In summary, the findings from experimental studies offer grist for the behavioral finance mill. Whether we buy into all the implications or not, there can be no arguing of the systematic quirks in human behavior.

As a side note, many of these experimental studies have been run using inexperienced subjects (usually undergraduate students) and professionals (traders in financial markets, experienced business people) to see if age and experience play a role in making people more rational. The findings are not promising for the "rational" human school, because the consensus view across these studies is that experience and age do not seem to confer rationality in subjects, and some of the anomalies noted in this section are exacerbated with experience. Professional traders exhibit more myopic loss aversion than undergraduate students, for instance. The behavioral patterns indicated in this section are also replicated in experiments using business settings (projects with revenues, profits, and losses) and experienced managers.[25]

Finally, we should resist the temptation to label these behaviors as irrational. Much of what we observe in human behavior seems to be hard wired into our systems and cannot be easily eliminated (if at all). In fact, a study in the journal *Psychological Science* in 2005 examined the decisions made by 15 people with normal IQs and reasoning skills but with damage to the portions of the brain that control emotions.[26] The researchers confronted this group and a control group of normal individuals with 20 rounds of a lottery, where they could win $2.50 or lose $1. They found that the inability to feel emotions such as fear and anxiety made the brain-damaged individuals more willing to take risks with high payoffs and less likely to react emotionally to previous wins and losses. Overall, the brain-impaired participants finished with about 13 percent higher winnings

24 Battalio, R. C., J. H. Kagel, and K. Jiranyakul. "Testing Between Alternative Models of Choice Under Uncertainty: Some Initial Results." *Journal of Risk and Uncertainty*, 3, 25–50, 1990.

25 Sullivan, K. "Corporate Managers' Risky Behavior: Risk Taking or Avoiding." *Journal of Financial and Strategic Decisions*, Vol. 10, 63…74, 1997.

26 Baba, S., G. Lowenstein, A. Bechara, H. Damasio, and A. Damasio. "Investment Behavior and the Negative Side of Emotion." *Psychological Science*, Vol. 16, 435…439, 2005. The damage to the individuals was created by strokes or disease and prevented them from feeling emotions.

than normal people who were offered the same gambles. Consequently, a computer or robot may be a much better risk manager than the most rational human being.

If we take these findings to heart, there are some interesting implications for risk management. First, it may be prudent to take at least some of the human element out of risk management systems because the survival skills that we human beings have accumulated from evolution undercut our abilities to be effective risk managers. Second, the notion that better and more timely information will lead to more effective risk management may be misplaced, because more frequent feedback seems to affect our risk aversion and skew our actions. Finally, the reason that risk management systems break down in a big way may be traced to one or more these behavioral quirks. Consider the example of Amaranth, a hedge fund that was forced to close down because a single trader exposed it to a loss of billions of dollars by doubling up his bets on natural gas prices, even as the market moved against him. This behavior is consistent with the break-even effect, as the trader attempted to make back what he had lost in prior trades with riskier new trades.

Survey Measures

In contrast to experiments, where relatively few subjects are observed in a controlled environment, survey approaches look at actual behavior—portfolio choices and insurance decisions, for instance—across large samples. Much of the evidence from surveys dovetails neatly into the findings from the experimental studies, although some differences emerge.

Survey Design

How can we survey individuals to assess their risk attitudes? Asking them whether they are risk averse and if so, by how much, is unlikely to yield any meaningful results because each individual's definition of both risk and risk aversion will be different. To get around this problem, we can survey for risk in three ways:

- **Investment choices**—By looking at the proportion of wealth invested in risky assets and relating this to other observable characteristics including level of wealth, researchers have attempted to back out the risk aversion of individuals. Friend and Blume estimated the Arrow-Pratt risk aversion measure using this approach and concluded that investors invested smaller proportions in risky assets as they got wealthier, thus exhibiting decreasing relative risk aversion. However, if wealth is defined to include houses, cars, and human capital, the proportion invested in risky assets stayed constant, consistent with constant relative risk aversion.[27] Other studies using the same approach also found evidence that wealthier people invested smaller proportions of their wealth in risky assets (declining relative risk aversion) than poorer people.

- **Questionnaires**—In this approach, participants in the survey are asked to answer a series of questions about the willingness to take risk. The answers are used to assess risk attitudes and measure risk aversion. In one example of this approach, 22000 German individuals were asked about their willingness to take risks on an 11-point scale. The results were double-checked (and found reasonable) against alternative risk assessment measures (including a conventional lottery choice).[28]

- **Insurance decisions**—Individuals buy insurance coverage because they are risk averse. A few studies have focused on insurance premiums and coverage purchased by individuals to get a sense of how risk averse they are. Szpiro looked at time series data on how much people paid for insurance and how much they purchased to conclude that they were risk averse.[29] Cichetti and Dubin confirmed Szpiro's finding by looking at a dataset of insurance for phone wiring bought by customers to a utility. They noted that the insurance cost was high ($0.45, a month) relative to the expected loss ($0.26) but still found that 57 percent of customers bought the insurance, which they attributed to risk aversion.[30]

Survey Findings

The evidence from surveys about risk aversion is for the most part consistent with the findings from experimental studies. Summarizing the findings:

- Individuals are risk averse, although the studies differed on what they found about relative risk aversion as wealth increases. Most found decreasing relative risk aversion, but there are exceptions that find constant relative risk aversion.

---

27 Friend, I. and M. E. Blume. "The Demand for Risky Assets." The American Economic Review, Vol. 65, No. 5, 900…922, 1975.

28 Dohmen, T., J. A. Falk, D. Huffman, J. Schuupp, U. Sunde, and G. G. Wagner. "Individual Risk Attitudes: New Evidence from a Large, Representative, Experimentally-Validated Survey." Working Paper, CEPR, 2006.

29 Szpiro, George G, "Measuring Risk Aversion: An Alternative Approach." *The Review of Economics and Statistics*, Vol. 68 (1), 156…159, 1986.

30 Cichetti, C. J., and J. A. Dubin. "A Microeconometric Analysis of Risk Aversion and the Decision to Self-Insure." *Journal of Political Economy*, Vol. 102, 169…186, 1994. An alternate story would be that the personnel selling this insurance are so persistent that most individuals are willing to pay $0.19 a month for the privilege of not having to listen to more sales pitches.

- Surveys have found that women are more risk averse than men, even after controlling for differences in age, income, and education. Jianakoplos and Bernasek used the Friend-Blume framework and data from the Federal Reserve's Survey of Consumers to estimate relative risk aversion by gender. They concluded that single women are relatively more risk averse than single men and married couples.[31] Riley and Chow also found that women are more risk averse than men. They concluded that never-married women are less risk averse than married women, who are, in turn, less risk averse than widowed and separated women.

- The life cycle risk aversion hypothesis posits that risk aversion should increase with age, but surveys cannot directly test this proposition because it would require testing the same person at different ages. In weak support of this hypothesis, Morin and Suarez found that older people are, in fact, more risk averse than younger people because they tend to invest less of their wealth in riskier assets.[32] In a rare study that looks at choices over time, Bakshi and Chen claim to find support for the lifecycle hypothesis by correlating the increase in equity risk premiums for the overall equity market to the aging of the population.[33]

- There is evidence linking risk aversion to both race/ethnicity and to education, but it is mixed. Although some studies claim to find a link between racial makeup and risk aversion, it is difficult to disentangle race from income and wealth, which do have much stronger effects on risk aversion. With respect to education, there have been contradictory findings, with some studies concluding that more educated people are more risk averse[34] and others that they are less.[35]

Critiquing Survey Evidence

Comparing experiments to surveys, surveys have the advantage of larger sample sizes but the disadvantage of not being able to control for other factors. Experiments allow researchers to analyze risk in tightly controlled environments, resulting in cleaner

31 Jianakoplos N. A., and A. Bernasek. "Are Women More Risk Averse?" *Economic Inquiry*, Vol. 36, No. 4, 1998.

32 Morin, R .A., and F. Suarez. "Risk Aversion Revisited." *Journal of Finance*, Vol. 38, No. 4, 1201...1216, 1983.

33 Bakshi, G., and Z. Chen. "Baby Boom, Population Aging, and Capital Markets." *Journal of Business*, Vol. 67, No. 2, 165...202, 1994.

34 Jianakoplos N. A., and A. Bernasek. "Are Women More Risk Averse?" *Economic Inquiry*, Vol. 36, No. 4, 1998.

35 Riley, W. B., and K.V. Chow. "Asset Allocation and Individual Risk Aversion." *Financial Analysts Journal*, Vol. 48, No. 6, 32...37, November/December 1992.

measures of risk aversion. However, as we noted earlier, the measures themselves are highly sensitive to the way the experiments are constructed and conducted.

The quality of the survey evidence is directly related to how carefully constructed a survey is. A good survey will draw a high proportion of the potential participants, have no sampling bias, and allow the researcher to draw clear distinctions between competing hypotheses. In practice, surveys tend to have low response rates, and there are serious problems with sampling bias. The people who respond to surveys might not be a representative sample. To give credit to the authors of the studies that we quote in this section, they are acutely aware of this possibility and try to minimize it through their survey design and subsequent statistical tests.

Pricing of Risky Assets

The financial markets represent experiments in progress, with millions of subjects expressing their risk preferences by the way they price risky assets. Although the environment is not tightly controlled, the size of the experiment and the reality that large amounts of money are at stake (rather than the small stakes that one sees in experiments) should mean that the market prices of risky assets provide more realistic measures of risk aversion than either simple experiments or surveys. In this section, we will consider how to use asset prices to back measures of risk aversion, and whether the evidence is consistent with the findings from other approaches.

Measuring the Equity Risk Premium

If we consider investing in stocks as a risky alternative to investing risklessly in treasury bonds, we can use a level of the stock market to back out how much investors are demanding for being exposed to equity risk. This is the idea behind an implied equity risk premium. Consider, for instance, a simple valuation model for stocks.

$$\text{Value} = \frac{\text{Expected Dividends Next Period}}{(\text{Required Return on Equity - Expected Growth Rate in Dividends})}$$

This is essentially the present value of dividends growing at a constant rate in perpetuity. We can obtain three of the four variables in this model externally: the current level of the market (that is, value), the expected dividends next period, and the expected growth rate in earnings and dividends in the long term. The only "unknown" is the required return on equity; when we solve for it, we get an implied expected return on stocks. Subtracting the risk-free rate will yield an implied equity risk premium. As investors become more risk averse, they will demand a larger premium for risk and pay less for the same set of cash flows (dividends).

To illustrate, assume that the current level of the S&P 500 Index is 900, the expected dividend yield on the index for the next period is 3 percent, and the expected growth rate in earnings and dividends in the long term is 6 percent. Solving for the required return on equity yields the following:

$$900 = \frac{900(0.03)}{r-0.06}$$

Solving for r,

$$r - 0.06 = 0.03$$

$$r = 0.09 = 9\%$$

If the current risk-free rate is 6 percent, this will yield an equity risk premium of 3 percent.

We can generalize this approach to allow for high growth for a period and extend it to cover cash flow-based, rather than dividend-based, models. To illustrate this, consider the S&P 500 Index on January 1, 2006. The index was at 1248.29, and the dividend yield on the index in 2005 was roughly 3.34 percent.[36] In addition, assume that the consensus estimate[37] of growth in earnings for companies in the index was approximately 8 percent for the next five years, and the 10-year treasury bond rate on that day was 4.39 percent. Because a growth rate of 8 percent cannot be sustained forever, we employ a two-stage valuation model, where we allow dividends and buybacks to grow at 8 percent for five years and then lower the growth rate to the treasury bond rate of 4.39 percent after the five-year period.[38] Table 3.1 summarizes the expected cash flows for the next five years of high growth and the first year of stable growth thereafter.

---

36   Stock buybacks during the year were added to the dividends to obtain a consolidated yield.

37   We used the average of the analyst estimates for individual firms (bottom-up). Alternatively, we could have used the top-down estimate for the S&P 500 earnings.

38   The treasury bond rate is the sum of expected inflation and the expected real rate. If we assume that real growth is equal to the real rate, the long-term stable growth rate should be equal to the treasury bond rate.

Table 3.1 Expected Cash Flows on S&P 500

Year	Cash Flow on Index
1	44.96
2	48.56
3	52.44
4	56.64
5	61.17
6	61.17 (1.0439)

Cash flow in the first year = 3.34 percent of 1248.29 (1.08)

If we assume that these are reasonable estimates of the cash flows and that the index is correctly priced, then

$$\text{Index level} = 1248.29 = \frac{44.96}{(1+r)} + \frac{48.56}{(1+r)^2} + \frac{52.44}{(1+r)^3} + \frac{56.64}{(1+r)^4} + \frac{61.17}{(1+r)^5} + \frac{61.17(1.0439)}{(r-.0439)(1+r)^5}$$

Note that the last term of the equation is the terminal value of the index, based on the stable growth rate of 4.39 percent, discounted back to the present. Solving for r in this equation yields us the required return on equity of 8.47 percent. Subtracting the treasury bond rate of 4.39 percent yields an implied equity premium of 4.08 percent.

The advantage of this approach is that it is market driven and current, and it does not require historical data. Thus, it can be used to estimate implied equity premiums in any market. It is, however, bound by whether the model used for the valuation is the right one and the availability and reliability of the inputs to that model.

Equity Risk Premium over Time

The implied equity premiums change over time much more than historical risk premiums. In fact, the contrast between these premiums and the historical premiums is best illustrated by graphing the implied premiums in the S&P 500 going back to 1960 in Figure 3.1.

In terms of mechanics, we use historical growth rates in earnings as our projected growth rates for the next five years, set growth equal to the risk-free rate beyond that point in time, and value stocks using a two-stage dividend discount model (with stock buybacks added back to dividends). We can draw at least two conclusions from this table:

- **Investors are risk averse**—The fact that the implied equity risk premium is positive indicates that investors require a reward (in the form of higher expected returns) for taking on risk.

- **Risk aversion changes over time**—If we consider the risk premium as a measure of risk aversion for investors collectively, there seems to be clear evidence that investors becomes more risk averse over some periods and less risk averse in others. In Figure 3.1, for instance, this collective measure of risk aversion increased during the inflationary 1970s and then went through a two-decade period where it declined to reach historic lows at the end of 1999 (coinciding with the peak of the bull market of the 1990s). It bounced back again in the short and sharp market correction that followed and has remained fairly stable since 2001.

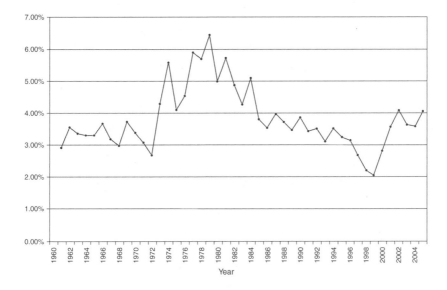

Figure 3.1: Implied Premium for US Equity Market

The implied equity risk premium also brings home an important point. Risk premiums and stock prices generally move in opposite directions. Stock prices are highest when investors demand low-risk premiums and should decrease as investors become more risk averse, pushing up risk premiums.

The Equity Risk Premium Puzzle

Although the previous section provided a forward-looking estimate of equity risk premiums, we can also obtain a historical equity risk premium by looking at how much investors have earned investing in stocks, as opposed to investing in government securities in the past. For instance, an investment in stocks in the United States would have earned 4.80 percent more annually, on a compounded basis between 1928 and 2005, than an investment in 10-year treasury bonds over the same period.[39] Although the premium does change depending on the period examined, stocks have consistently earned 3 to 5 percent more, on an annual basis, than government bonds for much of the past century.

In a widely cited paper, Mehra and Prescott argued that the observed historical risk premiums (which they estimated at about 6 percent at the time of their analysis) were too high and that investors would need implausibly high risk aversion coefficients to demand these premiums.[40] In the years since, there have been many attempts to provide explanations for this puzzle.

- **Statistical artifact**—The historical risk premium obtained by looking at U.S. data is biased upward because of a survivor bias, induced by picking one of the most successful equity markets of the twentieth century. The true premium, it is argued, is much lower because equity markets in other parts of the world did not do as well as the U.S. market during this period. Consequently, a wealthy investor in 1928 looking to invest in stocks would have been just as likely to invest in the Austrian stock market as the U.S. stock market and would have had far less success with his investment over the rest of the century. This view is backed up by a study of 17 equity markets over the twentieth century, which concluded that the historical risk premium is closer to 4 percent than the 6 percent cited by Mehra and Prescott.[41] However, even the lower risk premium would have been too high, if we assumed reasonable risk aversion coefficients.

- **Disaster insurance**—A variation on the statistical artifact theme, albeit with a theoretical twist, is that the observed risk in an equity market does not fully capture the potential risk, which includes rare but disastrous events that reduce consumption and wealth substantially. Thus, the fact that there has not been a catastrophic drop in U.S. equity markets in the past 50 years cannot be taken

---

39 On a simple average basis, the premium is even larger and exceeds 6 percent.

40 Mehra, Rajnish, and Edward C. Prescott. "The Equity Premium: A Puzzle." *Journal Monetary Economics*, Vol. 15, 145...161, 1985. Using a constant relative risk-aversion utility function and plausible risk-aversion coefficients, they demonstrate that the equity risk premiums should be much lower (less than 1 percent).

41 Dimson, E., P. March, and M. Staunton. *Triumph of the Optimists*. Princeton University Press, 2002.

to imply that the probability of such an occurrence is zero.[42] In effect, forward-looking risk premiums incorporate the likelihood of these low-probability, high-impact events, whereas the historical risk premium does not.

- **Taxes**—One possible explanation for the high equity returns in the period after the Second World War is that taxes on equity income declined during that period. McGrattan and Prescott, for instance, provide a hypothetical illustration where a drop in the tax rate on dividends from 50 percent to 0 percent over 40 years would cause equity prices to rise about 1.8 percent more than the growth rate in GDP; adding the dividend yield to this expected price appreciation generates returns similar to the observed returns.[43] In reality, though, the drop in marginal tax rates was much smaller and cannot explain the surge in equity risk premiums.

- **Preference for stable wealth and consumption**—Some argue that the equity risk premium puzzle stems from its dependence on conventional expected utility theory to derive premiums. In particular, the constant relative risk aversion function used by Mehra and Prescott in their paper implies that if an investor is risk averse to variation in consumption across different states of nature at a point in time, he will also be equally risk averse to consumption variation across time. The counter argument is that individuals will choose a lower and more stable level of wealth and consumption that they can sustain over the long term over a higher level of wealth that varies widely from period to period.[44] One reason may be that individuals become used to maintaining past consumption levels, and even small changes in consumption can cause big changes in marginal utility.[45] Investing in stocks works against this preference by creating more instability in wealth over periods, adding to wealth in good periods and taking away from it in bad periods. In more intuitive terms, your investment in stocks will tend to do well when the economy in doing well and do poorly

---

42   To those who argue that this will never happen in a mature equity market, we offer the example of the Nikkei, which dropped from 40,000 in the late 1980s to less than 10,000 a decade later. Investors who bought stocks at the peak will probably not live to see capital gains on their investments.

43   McGrattan, E. R., and E. C. Prescott. "Taxes, Regulations, and Asset Prices." Working Paper No. 610, Federal Reserve Bank of Minneapolis, 2001.

44   Epstein, L. G., and S. E. Zin. "Substitution, Risk Aversion, and the Temporal Behavior of Consumption and Asset Returns: An Empirical Analysis." *Journal of Political Economy*, Vol. 99, No. 2, 263…286, 1991.

45   Constantinides, G. M. "Habit Formation: A Resolution of the Equity Premium Puzzle." *Journal of Political Economy*, Vol. 98, No. 3, 519…543, 1990.

during recessions, when you may very well find yourself out of a job. To compensate, you will demand a larger premium for investing in equities.

- **Myopic loss aversion**—Earlier in this chapter, we introduced the notion of myopic loss aversion, where the loss aversion already embedded in individuals becomes more pronounced as the frequency of their monitoring increases. If investors bring myopic risk aversion into investing, the equity risk premiums they will demand will be much higher than those obtained from conventional expected utility theory. The paper that we cited earlier by Benartzi and Thaler yields estimates of the risk premium very close to historical levels using a one-year time horizon for investors with plausible loss aversion characteristics.

The bottom line is that observed equity risk premiums cannot be explained using conventional expected utility theory. Here again, the behavioral quirks that we observed in both experiments and surveys may help in explaining how people price risky assets and why the prices change over time.

Beyond Equities

The approach that we used to estimate the equity risk premium and, by extension, get a measure of risk aversion can be generalized to look at any asset class or even individual assets. By looking at how investors price risky assets, we can get a sense of how investors assess risk and how much they charge for bearing it.

For instance, we could look at how investors price bonds with default risk, relative to risk-free bonds, to gauge their attitudes toward risk. If investors are risk neutral, the prices and interest rates on bonds should reflect the likelihood of default and the expected cost to the bondholder of such default; risk-averse investors will attach a bigger discount to the bond price for the same default risk. Studies of default spreads on corporate bonds yield results that are consistent not only with the proposition that bond investors are risk averse, but also with changing risk aversion over time.[46]

We could also look at the pricing of options to measure investor risk aversion. For instance, we can back out the risk-neutral probabilities of future stock prices changes from option prices today.[47] Comparing these probabilities with the actual returns can tell us about the risk aversion of option investors. A study that estimated risk aversion

---

46   Wu, C. and C. Yu. "Risk Aversion and the Yield of Corporate Debt." *Journal of Banking and Finance*, Vol. 20, 267...281, 1996.

47   The risk-neutral probability can be written as a function of the subjective (and conventional) probability estimate and a risk aversion coefficient.

Risk neutral probability = Subjective probability * Risk aversion coefficient.

coefficients using options on the S&P 500 Index, in conjunction with actual returns on the index, concluded that they were well behaved prior to the 1987 stock market crash—risk-aversion coefficients were positive and decreased with wealth—but that they changed dramatically after the crash, becoming negative in some cases and increasing with wealth.[48] An examination of options on the FTSE 100 and S&P 500 options from 1992 to 2001 concluded that risk-aversion coefficients were consistent across utility functions and markets but that they tended to decline with forecast horizon and increase during periods of low market volatility.[49]

In summary, studies of other risky asset markets confirm the findings in equity markets that investors are risk averse, in the aggregate, and that this risk aversion changes over time.

The Limitations of Market Prices

Although markets are large, ongoing experiments, they are also complicated, and isolating risk aversion can be difficult. Unlike a controlled experiment, where all subjects are faced with the same risky choices, investors in markets tend to have different information about and views on the assets they are pricing. Thus, we have to make simplifying assumptions to back out measures of the risk premium. With the equity risk premium, for instance, we used a two-stage dividend discount model and analyst estimates of growth to compute the equity risk premium. Any errors we make in model specification and inputs will spill over into our risk premium estimates.

Notwithstanding these limitations, market prices offer valuable clues about changes in risk aversion over time. In summary, they indicate that expected utility models fall short in explaining how individuals price risky assets, and there are significant shifts in the risk aversion of populations over time.

Evidence from Racetracks, Gambling, and Game Shows

Some of the most anomalous evidence on risk aversion comes from studies of how individuals behave when at the racetracks and in casinos, and in recent years, on game shows. In many ways, explaining why humans gamble has been a challenge to economists, because the expected returns (at least based on probabilities) are negative and the

---

48   Jackwerth, J. C. "Recovering Risk Aversion from Option Prices and Realized Returns." *The Review of Financial Studies*, Vol. 13, 433...451, 2000.

49   Bliss, R. R., and N. Panigirtzoglou. "Recovering Risk Aversion from Options." Working Paper, Federal Reserve Bank of Chicago, 2001.

risk is often substantial. Risk-averse investors with well-behaved utility functions would not be gamblers, but this section presents evidence that risk seeking is common.

Racetracks and Gambling

Gambling is big business. At racetracks, casinos, and sporting events, individuals bet huge amounts of money each year. While some may contest the notion, there can be no denying that gambling is a market like any other, where individuals make their preferences clear by what they do. Over the past few decades, the data from gambling events has been examined closely by economists, trying to understand how individuals behave when confronted with risky choices.

In a survey article, Hausch, Ziemba, and Rubinstein examined the evidence from studies of racetrack betting and found that there were strong and stable biases in their findings. First, they found that people paid too little for favorites and too much for long shots.[50] In particular, one study that they quote computed rates of returns from betting on horses in different categories. First, they concluded that bettors could expect to make positive returns by betting on favorites (9.2 percent) but very negative returns (...23.7 percent) by betting on long odds.[51] Second, they noted that bettors tended to bet more on longer-odds horses as they lost money, often in a desperate attempt to recover from past losses.

This long-shot bias is now clearly established in the literature, and there have been many attempts to explain it. One argument challenges the conventional view (and the evidence from experimental studies and surveys) that human beings are risk averse. Instead, it posits that gamblers are risk lovers and are therefore drawn to the higher risk in long-shot bets.[52] The other arguments are consistent with risk aversion but require assumptions about behavioral quirks or preferences and include the following.

- The long-shot bias can be explained if individuals underestimate large probabilities and overestimate small probabilities, behavior that is inconsistent with rational, value-maximizing individuals but entirely feasible if we accept psychological studies of human behavior.[53]

---

50   Hausch, D. B., W. T. Ziemba, and M. Rubinstein. "Efficiency of the Market for Racetrack Betting." *Management Science*, 1981.

51   Snyder, W. W., "Horse Racing: Testing the Efficient Markets Model." *Journal of Finance*, 33, 1109...1118, 1978.

52   Quandt, R. "Betting and Equilibrium." *Quarterly Journal of Economics*, 101, 201...207, 1986.

53   Griffith, R. "Odds Adjustment by American Horses Race Bettors." *American Journal of Psychology*, 62, 290...294, 1949.

- Another argument is that betting on long shots is more exciting and that excitement itself generates utility for individuals.[54]

- Some argue that the preference for long shots comes not from risk-loving behavior on the part of bettors but from a preference for large positive payoffs; that is, individuals attach additional utility to large payoffs, even when the probabilities of receiving them are small.[55]

Researchers have also used data from racetrack betting to fit utility functions to bettors. Wietzman looked at betting in 12,000 races between 1954 and 1963 and generated utility functions that are consistent with risk-loving rather than risk-averse individuals.[56] Although a few other researchers back up this conclusion, Jullien and Salane argue that gamblers are risk averse and that their seeming risk-seeking behavior can be attributed to incorrect assessments of the probabilities of success and failure.[57] Extending the analysis from racetracks to other gambling venues—casino gambling and lotteries, for instance—studies find similar results. Gamblers willingly enter into gambles where the expected returns from playing are negative and exhibit a bias toward gambles with low probabilities of winning but big payoffs (the long-shot bias).

Game Shows

The final set of studies that we will reference are relatively recent and mine data obtained from the way contestants behave on game shows, especially when there is no skill involved and substantial amounts of money at stake.

- A study examined the way contestants behave in *Card Sharks*, a game show where contestants are asked to bet in a bonus round on whether the next card in the deck is higher or lower than the card that they had open in front of them. The study found evidence that contestants behave in risk-averse ways, but a subset of decisions deviate from what you would expect with a rational,

54   Thaler, R., and W. Ziemba. "Anomalies—Parimutuel Betting Markets: Racetracks and Lotteries." *Journal of Economic Perspectives*, 2, 161…174, 1988.

55   Golec, J., and M. Tamarkin. "Bettors Love Skewness, Not Risk, at the Horse Track." *Journal of Political Economy*, 106, 205…225, 1998. A study of lottery game players by Garrett and Sobel backs up this view; Garrett, T. A, and R. S. Sobel, "Gamblers Favor Skewness, Not Risk: Further Evidence from United States' Lottery Games." Working Paper, 2004.

56   Weitzman, M. "Utility Analysis and Group Behavior: An Empirical Study." *Journal of Political Economy*, 73, 18…26, 1965.

57   Jullien, B., and B. Salanie. "Empirical Evidence on the Preferences of Racetrack Bettors." *Efficiency of Sports and Lottery Markets*, Ed. D. Hausch and W. Ziemba, 2005.

utility-maximizing individual.[58] In contrast, another study found that contestants reveal more risk neutrality than aversion when they wager their winnings in Final Jeopardy, and they make more "rational" decisions when their problems are simpler.[59]

- In a study of the popular game show *Deal or No Deal*, Post, Baltussen, and Van den Assem examined the way contestants behave when asked to make choices in 53 episodes from Australia and the Netherlands. In the show, 26 models each hold a briefcase that contains a sum of money (varying from one cent to $1 million in the U.S. game). The contestant picks one briefcase as her own and then begins to open the other 25, each time, by process of elimination, revealing a little more about what her own case might hold. At the end, the contestant can also trade her briefcase for the last unopened one. Thus, contestants are offered numerous opportunities where they can either take a fixed sum (the suitcase that was open) or an uncertain gamble (the unopened suitcase). Because both the fixed sum and the gamble change with each attempt, we are observing certainty equivalents in action. The researchers found evidence of overall risk aversion, but they also noted big differences across contestants, with some even exhibiting risk-seeking behavior. Finally, they backed up some of the behavioral quirks we noted earlier when talking about experimental studies, with evidence that contestant risk aversion depends on prior outcomes (with failure making contestants more risk averse) and for the break-even effect (where risk aversion decreases following earlier losses and a chance to recoup these losses).[60]

- Tenorio and Cason examined the spin or no spin segment of *The Price Is Right*, a long-running game show.[61] In this segment, three contestants spin a wheel with 20 uniform partitions numbered from 5 to 100 (in fives). They are allowed up to two spins, and the sum of the scores of the two spins is computed. The contestant who scores closest to 100 points, without going over, wins and moves on to the next round and a chance to win big prizes. Scoring exactly 100 points earns a bonus for the contestant. The key component examined in this paper was whether the contestant would choose to use the second spin, because spinning

58 Gertner, R. "Game Shows and Economic Behavior: Risk-Taking on 'Card Sharks.'" *Quarterly Journal of Economics*, Vol. 108, No. 2, 507…521, 1993.

59 Metrick, A. "A Natural Experiment in 'Jeopardy!' *American Economic Review*, Vol. 58, 240…253, 1995. In Final Jeopardy, the three contestants on the show decide how much of the money winnings that they have accumulated over the show they want to bet on the final question, with the recognition that only the top money winner will win.

60 Post, T., G. Baltussent, and M. Van den Assem, "Deal or No Deal." Working Paper, Erasmus University, 2006.

61 Tenorio R., and T.N. Cason. To spin or not to spin? Natural and laboratory experiments from The Price is Right, *Economic Journal*, v112, 170–195, 2002.

again increases the point total but also increases the chance of going over 100. This study found that contestants are more likely to make "irrational" decisions when faced with complicated scenarios than with simple ones, suggesting that risk aversion is tied to computational ability and decision biases.

- *Lingo* is a word guessing game on Dutch TV, where two couples play each other, and the one that guesses the most words moves on to the finals, which is composed of five rounds. At the end of each round, each couple is offered a chance to take home what they have won so far or go on to the next round; if they survive, they double their winnings, but they risk losing it all if they lose. The odds of winning decrease with each round. A study of this game show found that although contestants are risk averse, they tend to overestimate the probability of winning by as much as 15 percent.[62] A study of contestants on *Who Wants to Be a Millionaire?* in the UK backed up this finding. In fact, the researchers contended that contestant behavior on this show is consistent with logarithmic utility functions, a throwback to Daniel Bernoulli's solution to the St. Petersburg Paradox.[63]

In summary, game shows offer us a chance to observe how individuals behave when the stakes are large (relative to the small amounts offered in experimental studies) and decisions have to be made quickly. The consensus finding from these studies is that contestants on game shows are risk averse but not always rational, overestimating their probabilities of success in some cases and behaving in unpredictable (and not always sensible) ways in complicated scenarios.

Propositions about Risk Aversion

The evidence about risk aversion comes from a variety of sources, and there are both common findings and differences across the different approaches. We can look at all the evidence and summarize what we see as the emerging consensus on risk aversion:

- Individuals are generally risk averse and are more so when the stakes are large than when they are small. Although there are some differences across the studies, the evidence does support the view that individuals are willing to invest larger amounts in risky assets (decreasing absolute risk aversion) as they get wealthier.

---

62 Beetsma, R. and P. Schotman. "Measuring Risk Attitudes in a Natural Experiment: Data from the Television Game Show Lingo." *Economic Journal*, October 2001.

63 Hartley, R., G. Lanot, and I. Walker. "Who Really Wants to be a Millionaire: Estimates of Risk Aversion from Game Show Data." Working Paper, University of Warwick, 2005.

However, the evidence is mixed on relative risk aversion, with support for increasing, constant, and decreasing relative risk aversion in different settings.

- There are big differences in risk aversion across the population and noticeable differences across subgroups. Women tend to be more risk averse than men, and older people are more risk averse than younger people. More importantly, there are significant differences in risk aversion within homogeneous groups, with some individuals exhibiting risk aversion and a sizable minority seeking out risk. This may help explain why studies that have focused on gambling find that a large percentage (albeit not a majority) of gamblers exhibit risk-loving behavior. It seems reasonable to believe that risk seekers are more likely to be drawn to gambling.

- Although the evidence of risk aversion in individuals may make believers in expected utility theory happy, the other evidence that has accumulated about systematic quirks in individual risk taking will not. In particular, the evidence indicates the following:

  - Individuals are far more affected by losses than equivalent gains (loss aversion), and this behavior is made worse by frequent monitoring (myopia).

  - The choices that people make (and the risk aversion they manifest) when presented with risky choices or gambles can depend on how the choice is presented (framing).

  - Individuals tend to be much more willing to take risks with what they consider "found money" than with money that they have earned (house money effect).

  - There are two scenarios where risk aversion seems to decrease and even be replaced by risk seeking. One is when individuals are offered the chance of making an extremely large sum with a small probability of success (long-shot bias). The other is when individuals who have lost money are presented with choices that allow them to make their money back (break-even effect).

  - When faced with risky choices, whether in experiments or game shows, individuals often make mistakes in assessing the probabilities of outcomes, overestimating the likelihood of success. This problem gets worse as the choices become more complex.

In summary, the notion of a representative individual, whose utility function and risk aversion coefficient can stand in for the entire population, is difficult to hold on to, given both the diversity in risk aversion across individuals and the anomalies (at least from the perspective of the perfectly rational utility seeker) that remain so difficult to explain.

Conclusion

Investors hate risk and love it. They show clear evidence of both risk aversion and risk seeking. In this chapter, we examined the basis for these contradictory statements by looking at the evidence on risk aversion in the population, acquired through a number of approaches, including experiments, surveys, financial market prices, and observations of gamblers. Summing up the evidence, investors are generally risk averse, but some are much more so than others. In fact, a few are risk neutral or even risk loving. Some of the differences in risk aversion can be attributed to systematic factors such as age, sex, and income, but a significant portion is random.

The interesting twist in the findings is that there are clear patterns in risk taking that are not consistent with the rational utility maximizer in classical economics. The ways we act when faced with risky choices seem to be affected by whether we face gains or losses and how the choices are framed. Although it is tempting to label this behavior as anomalous, it occurs far too often and in such a wide cross section of the population that it should be considered the norm rather than the exception. Consequently, the way we measure and manage risk has to take into account these behavioral quirks.

4

HOW DO WE MEASURE RISK?

If you accept the argument that risk matters and that it affects how managers and investors make decisions, it follows logically that measuring risk is a critical first step toward managing it. In this chapter, we look at how risk measures have evolved over time, from a fatalistic acceptance of bad outcomes to probabilistic measures that allow us to begin getting a handle on risk, and the logical extension of these measures into insurance. We then consider how the advent and growth of markets for financial assets has influenced the development of risk measures. Finally, we build on modern portfolio theory to derive unique measures of risk and explain why they might not be in accordance with probabilistic risk measures.

Fate and Divine Providence

Risk and uncertainty have been part and parcel of human activity since its beginnings, but they have not always been labeled as such. For much of recorded time, events with negative consequences were attributed to divine providence or to the supernatural. The responses to risk under these circumstances were prayer, sacrifice (often of innocents), and an acceptance of whatever fate meted out. If the gods intervened on our behalf, we got positive outcomes, and if they did not, we suffered; sacrifice, on the other hand, appeased the spirits that caused bad outcomes. No measure of risk was therefore considered necessary because everything that happened was predestined and driven by forces outside our control.

This is not to suggest that the ancient civilizations, be they Greek, Roman, or Chinese, were completely unaware of probabilities and the quantification of risk. Games of chance were common in those times, and the players of those games must have recognized that there was an order to the uncertainty.[1] As Peter Bernstein notes in his splen-

---

1   Chances are.... Kaplan, M. and E. Kaplan. *Adventures in Probability*. New York: Viking Books, 2006. The authors note that dice litter ancient Roman campsites and that the citizens of the day played a variant of craps using either dice or knucklebones of sheep.

did book on the history of risk, it is a mystery why the Greeks, with their considerable skills at geometry and numbers, never seriously attempted to measure the likelihood of uncertain events, be they storms or droughts, occurring, turning instead to priests and fortune-tellers.[2]

Notwithstanding the advances over the past few centuries and our shift to more modern, sophisticated ways of analyzing uncertainty, the belief that powerful forces beyond our reach shape our destinies is never far below the surface. The same traders who use sophisticated computer models to measure risk consult their astrological charts and rediscover religion when confronted with the possibility of large losses.

Estimating Probabilities: The First Step to Quantifying Risk

Given the focus on fate and divine providence that characterized the way we thought about risk until the Middle Ages, it is ironic then that it was an Italian monk who initiated the discussion of risk measures by posing a puzzle in 1494 that befuddled people for almost two centuries. The solution to his puzzle and subsequent developments laid the foundations for modern risk measures.

Luca Pacioli, a monk in the Franciscan order, was a man of many talents. He is credited with inventing double-entry bookkeeping and teaching Leonardo DaVinci mathematics. He also wrote a book on mathematics, *Summa de Arithmetica*, that summarized all the knowledge in mathematics at that point in time. In the book, he also presented a puzzle that challenged mathematicians of the time. Assume, he said, that two gamblers are playing a best-of-five dice game and are interrupted after three games, with one gambler leading two to one. What is the fairest way to split the pot between the two gamblers, assuming that the game cannot be resumed but taking into account the state of the game when it was interrupted?

With the hindsight of several centuries, the answer may seem simple, but we have to remember that the notion of making predictions or estimating probabilities had not developed yet. The first steps toward solving the Pacioli Puzzle came in the early part of the sixteenth century when an Italian doctor and gambler, Girolamo Cardano, estimated the likelihood of different outcomes of rolling a dice. His observations were contained in a book titled *Books on the Game of Chance*, where he estimated not only the likelihood of rolling a specific number on a dice (1/6), but also the likelihood of obtaining values

---

2   Much of the history recounted in this chapter is stated much more lucidly and in greater detail by Peter Bernstein in his books *Against the Gods: The Remarkable Story of Risk* (1996) and *Capital Ideas: The Improbable Origins of Modern Wall Street* (1992). The former explains the evolution of our thinking on risk through the ages, whereas the latter examines the development of modern portfolio theory.

on two consecutive rolls; he, for instance, estimated the probability of rolling two 1s in a row to be 1/36. Galileo, taking a break from discovering the galaxies, came to the same conclusions for his patron, the Grand Duke of Tuscany, but he did not go much further than explaining the roll of the dice.

It was not until 1654 that the Pacioli puzzle was fully solved when Blaise Pascal and Pierre de Fermat exchanged a series of five letters on the puzzle. In these letters, Pascal and Fermat considered all the possible outcomes to the Pacioli puzzle and noted that with a fair dice, the gambler who was ahead two games to one in a best-of-five dice game would prevail three times out of four, if the game were completed, and was thus entitled to three quarters of the pot. In the process, they established the foundations of probabilities and their usefulness not just in explaining the past but also in predicting the future. It was in response to Pacioli's challenge that Pascal developed his triangle of numbers for equal-odds games, shown in Figure 4.1:[3]

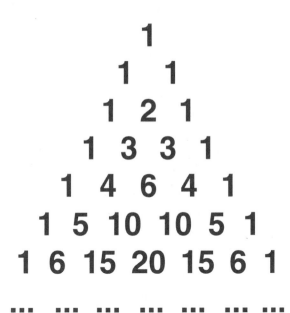

Figure 4.1: Pascal's Triangle

Pascal's triangle can be used to compute the likelihood of any event with even odds occurring. Consider, for instance, the odds that a couple expecting their first child will

3   It should be noted that Chinese mathematicians constructed the same triangle 500 years before Pascal and are seldom credited for the discovery.

have a boy; the answer, with even odds, is one-half and is in the second line of Pascal's triangle. If they have two children, what are the odds of them having two boys, or a boy and a girl, or two girls? The answer is in the second line, with the odds being 1/4 on the first and the third combinations and 1/2 on the second. In general, Pascal's triangle provides the number of possible combinations if an even-odds event is repeated a fixed number of times; if repeated N times, adding the numbers in the N+1 row and dividing each number by this total should yield the probabilities. Thus, the couple who has six children can compute the probabilities of the various outcomes by going to the seventh row and adding up the numbers (which yields 64) and dividing each number by the total. There is only a 1/64 chance that this couple will have six boys (or six girls), a 6/64 chance of having five boys and a girl (or five girls and a boy), and so on.

Sampling, The Normal Distributions, and Updating

Pascal and Fermat fired the opening volley in the discussion of probabilities with their solution to the Pacioli puzzle, but the muscle power for using probabilities was provided by Jacob Bernoulli, with his discovery of the *law of large numbers*. Bernoulli proved that a random sampling of items from a population has the same characteristics, on average, as the population.[4] He used coin flips to illustrate his point by noting that the proportion of heads (and tails) approached 50 percent as the number of coin tosses increased. In the process, he laid the foundation for generalizing population properties from samples, a practice that now permeates both the social and economic sciences.

In 1738, an English mathematician of French extraction, Abraham de Moivre, introduced the normal distribution as an approximation for binomial distributions as sample sizes became larger. This provided researchers with a critical tool for linking sample statistics with probability statements.[5] Figure 4.2 provides a picture of the normal distribution.

The bell curve, which characterizes the normal distribution, was refined by other mathematicians, including Laplace and Gauss, and the distribution is still referred to as the Gaussian distribution. One of the advantages of the normal distribution is that it can be described with just two parameters—the *mean* and the *standard deviation*—and allows us to make probabilistic statements about sampling averages. In the normal distribution,

---

4 Since Bernoulli's exposition of the law of large numbers, two variants of it have developed in statistical literature. The weak law of large numbers states that the average of a sequence of uncorrelated random numbers drawn from a distribution with the same mean and standard deviation will converge on the population average. The strong law of large numbers extends this formulation to a set of random variables that are independent and identically distributed.

5 De Moivre, A. *Doctrine of Chances*. New York: Chelsea Publishing, 1738.

approximately 68 percent of the distribution is within one standard deviation of the mean, 95 percent is within two standard deviations, and 98 percent is within three standard deviations. In fact, the distribution of a sum of independent variables approaches a normal distribution, which is the basis for the central limit theorem and allows us to use the normal distribution as an approximation for other distributions (such as the binomial).

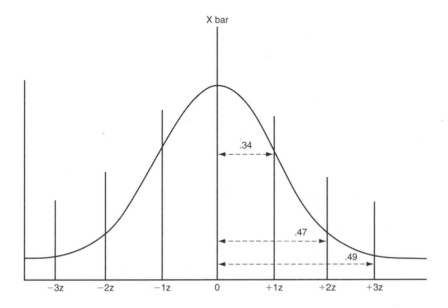

Figure 4.2: Normal Distribution

In 1763, Reverend Thomas Bayes published a simple way of updating existing beliefs in the light of new evidence. In Bayesian statistics, the existing beliefs are called prior probabilities, and the revised values after considering the new evidence are called posterior or conditional probabilities.[6] Bayes provided a powerful tool for researchers who wanted to use probabilities to assess the likelihood of negative outcomes and to update these probabilities as events unfolded. In addition, Bayes' rule allows us to start with subjective judgments about the likelihood of events occurring and to modify these judgments as new data or information is made available about these events.

In summary, these developments allowed researchers to see that they could extend the practice of estimating probabilities from simple equal-odds events such as rolling a dice

---

6   Bayes, Rev. T. *An Essay Toward Solving a Problem in the Doctrine of Chances*. Philos. Trans. R. Soc. London 53, 370–418, 1763. Reprinted in *Biometrika*, 45, 293–315, 1958.

to any events that had uncertainty associated with it. The law of large numbers showed that sampling means could be used to approximate population averages, with the precision increasing with sample size. The normal distribution allows us to make probability statements about the sample mean. Finally, Bayes' rule allows us to estimate probabilities and revise them based on new sampling data.

The Use of Data: Life Tables and Estimates

The work done on probability, sampling theory, and the normal distribution provided a logical foundation for the analysis of raw data. In 1662, John Graunt created one of the first mortality tables by counting for every 100 children born in London, each year from 1603 to 1661, how many were still living. In the course of constructing the table, Graunt not only refined the use of statistical tools and measures with large samples, but he also considered ways of dealing with data errors. He estimated that although 64 out of every 100 made it to age to 6 alive, only 1 in 100 survived to be 76. In an interesting aside, Graunt estimated the population of London in 1663 to be only 384,000, well below the then-prevailing estimate of 6 to 7 million. He was eventually proven right; London's population did not exceed 6 million until three centuries later. In 1693, Edmund Halley, the British mathematician, constructed the first life table from observations and devised a method for valuing life annuities. He pointed out that the government, which was selling life annuities to citizens at that time, was pricing them too low and was not setting the price independently of the age of the annuitant.

Actuarial risk measures have become more sophisticated over time and draw heavily on advances in statistics and data analysis, but the foundations still lie in the work done by Graunt and Halley. Using historical data, actuaries estimate the likelihood of events occurring—from hurricanes in Florida to deaths from cancer—and the consequent losses.

The Insurance View of Risk

As long as risk has existed, people have been trying to protect themselves against its consequences. As early as 1000 BC, the Babylonians developed a system where merchants who borrowed money to fund shipments could pay an extra amount to cancel the loan if the shipment was stolen. The Greeks and the Romans initiated life insurance with "benevolent societies," which cared for families of society members if they died. However, the development of the insurance business was stymied by the absence of ways of measuring risk exposure. The advances in assessing probabilities and the subsequent development of statistical measures of risk laid the basis for the modern insurance business. In the aftermath of the great fire of London in 1666, Nicholas Barbon opened The Fire Office, the first fire insurance company to insure brick homes. Lloyd's of London became the first large company to offer insurance to ship owners.

Insurance is offered when the timing or occurrence of a loss to an individual is unpredictable but the likelihood and magnitude of the loss are relatively predictable. It is in the latter pursuit that probabilities and statistics contribute mightily. Consider, for instance, how a company can insure your house against fire. Historical data on fires can be used to assess the likelihood that your house will catch fire and the extent of the losses, if a fire occurs. Thus, the insurance company can get a sense of the expected loss from the fire and charge an insurance premium that exceeds that cost, thus earning a profit. By insuring a large number of houses against fire, insurance companies are drawing on Bernoulli's law of large numbers to ensure that their profits exceed the expected losses over time.

Even large, well-funded insurance companies have to worry, though, about catastrophes so large that they will be unable to meet their obligations. Katrina, one of the most destructive hurricanes in memory, destroyed much of New Orleans in 2005 and left two states, Louisiana and Mississippi, in complete devastation; the total cost of damages was in excess of $50 billion. Insurance companies paid out billions of dollars in claims, and some of them were put in financial jeopardy by the magnitude of the losses.

Because insurers are concerned primarily about losses (and covering those losses), insurance measures of risk are almost always focused on the downside. Thus, a company that insures merchant ships will measure risk in terms of the likelihood of ships and cargo being damaged and the loss that accrues from the damage. The potential for upside that exists has little or no relevance to the insurer because he does not share in it.

Financial Assets and the Advent of Statistical Risk Measures

As stock and bond markets developed around the world in the nineteenth century, investors started looking for richer measures of risk. In particular, because investors in financial assets share in both upside and downside, the notion of risk primarily as a loss function (the insurance view) was replaced by a sense that risk could be a source of profit.

There was little access to information and few ways of processing even that limited information in the eighteenth and nineteenth centuries. Not surprisingly, the risk measures used were qualitative and broad. Investors in the financial markets during that period defined risk in terms of stability of income from their investments in the long-term and capital preservation. Thus, perpetual British government bonds called Consols, which offered fixed coupons forever, were considered close to risk free, and a fixed-rate long-term bond was considered preferable to a shorter-term bond with a higher rate. In the risk hierarchy of that period, long-term government bonds ranked as safest, followed by corporate bonds and stocks paying dividends. At the bottom were nondividend-paying stocks, a ranking that has not changed much since.

Given that there were few quantitative measures of risk for financial assets, how did investors measure and manage risk? One way was to treat entire groups of investments as sharing the same risk level; thus, stocks were categorized as risky and inappropriate investments for risk-averse investors, no matter what their dividend yield. The other way was to categorize investments based on how much information was available about the entity issuing it. Thus, equity issued by a well-established company with a solid reputation was considered safer than equity issued by a more recently formed entity about which less was known. In response, companies started providing more data on operations and making them available to potential investors.

By the early part of the twentieth century, services were already starting to collect return and price data on individual securities and computing basic statistics such as the expected return and standard deviation in returns. For instance, in 1909, the *Financial Review of Reviews*, a British publication, examined portfolios of 10 securities, including bonds, preferred stock, and ordinary stock, and they measured the volatility of each security using prices over the prior 10 years. In fact, they made an argument for diversification by estimating the impact of correlation on their hypothetical portfolios. (Appendix 1 includes the table from the publication.) Nine years previously, Louis Bachelier, a postgraduate student of mathematics at the Sorbonne, examined the behavior of stock and option prices over time in a remarkable thesis. He noted that there was little correlation between the price change in one period and the price change in the next, thus laying the foundation for the random walk and efficient market hypothesis, although they were not fleshed out until almost 60 years later.[7]

At about the same time, the access to and the reliability of financial reports from corporations were improving, and analysts were constructing risk measures that were based on accounting numbers. Ratios of profitability (such as margin and return on capital) and financial leverage (debt to capital) were used to measure risk. By 1915, services including the Standard Statistics Bureau (the precursor to Standard and Poor's), Fitch, and

---

7   Bachelier, L. "Theorie de la speculation." *Annales Scientifiques de l'E´cole Normale Supe´rieure*, 21–86, 1900. For an analysis of this paper's contribution to mathematical finance, see Courtault, J. M., Y. Kabanov, B. Bru, and P. Crepel. "Louis Bachelier: On the Centenary of the Theorie de la speculation." Mathematical Finance, Vol. 10, 341–350, 2000.

Moody's were processing accounting information to provide bond ratings as measures of credit risk in companies. Similar measures were slower to evolve for equities, but stock rating services were beginning to make their presence felt well before the Second World War. Although these services did not exhibit a consensus on the right way to measure risk, the risk measures drew on both price volatility and accounting information.

In his first edition of Security Analysis in 1934, Ben Graham argued against measures of risk based on past prices (such as volatility), noting that price declines can be temporary and not reflective of a company's true value. He argued that risk comes from paying too high a price for a security relative to its value and that investors should maintain a "margin of safety" by buying securities for less than their true worth.[8] This is an argument that value investors from the Graham school, including Warren Buffett, continue to make to this day.

By 1950, investors in financial markets were using measures of risk based on past prices and accounting information, in conjunction with broad risk categories, based on security type and issuer reputation, to make judgments about risk. There was, however, no consensus on how best to measure risk and what the exact relationship is between risk and expected return.

The Markowitz Revolution

The belief that diversification was beneficial to investors was already well in place before Harry Markowitz turned his attention to it in 1952. In fact, our earlier excerpt from the *Financial Review of Reviews* from 1909 used correlations between securities to make the argument that investors should spread their bets and that a diversified portfolio would be less risky than investing in an individual security, while generating similar returns. However, Markowitz changed the way we think about risk by linking the risk of a portfolio to the co-movement between individual assets in that portfolio.

Efficient Portfolios

As a young graduate student at the University of Chicago in the 1940s, Harry Markowitz was influenced by the work done by von Neumann, Friedman, and Savage on uncer-

---

8   Graham, B. *The Intelligent Investor*. New York: McGraw Hill, 1949. Originally in Graham, B., and D. Dodd. *Security Analysis*. New York: McGraw Hill, 1934. In *The Intelligent Investor*, Graham proposed to measure the margin of safety by looking at the difference between the earnings yield on a stock (earnings per share/ market price) and the treasury bond rate; the larger the difference (with the former exceeding the latter), the greater the margin for safety.

tainty. In describing how he came up with the idea that gave rise to modern portfolio theory, Markowitz explains that he was reading John Burr Williams's *Theory of Investment Value*, the book that first put forth the idea that the value of a stock is the present value of its expected dividends.[9] He noted that if the value of a stock were the present value of its expected dividends and an investor were intent on only maximizing returns, he would invest in the one stock that had the highest expected dividends. That practice was clearly at odds with both practice and theory at that time, which recommended investing in diversified portfolios. Investors, Markowitz reasoned, must diversify because they care about risk, and the risk of a diversified portfolio must therefore be lower than the risk of the individual securities that went into it. His key insight was that the variance of a portfolio could be written as a function not only of how much was invested in each security and the variances of the individual securities but also of the correlation between the securities. By explicitly relating the variance of a portfolio to the covariances between individual securities, Markowitz didn't just put into concrete form what had been conventional wisdom for decades. He also formulated a process by which investors could generate optimally diversified portfolios—that is, portfolios that would maximize returns for any given level of risk (or minimize risk for any given level of return). In his thesis, Markowitz derived the set of optimal portfolios for different levels of risk and called it the *efficient frontier*.[10] He refined the process in a subsequent book that he wrote while he worked at the RAND Corporation.[11]

The Mean-Variance Framework

The Markowitz approach, while powerful and simple, boils investor choices down to two dimensions. The "good" dimension is captured in the expected return on an investment, and the "bad" dimension is the variance or volatility in that return. In effect, the approach assumes that all risk is captured in the variance of returns on an investment and that all other risk measures, including the accounting ratios and the Graham margin of safety, are redundant. You can justify the mean-variance focus in two ways: assuming that returns are normally distributed, or by assuming that investors' utility functions push them to focus on just expected return and variance.

---

9   See the Markowitz autobiography for the Nobel committee. You can access it online at http://nobelprize.org/economics/laureates/1990/markowitz-autobio.html.

10   Markowitz, H. M. "Portfolio Selection." The *Journal of Finance*, 7(1): 77–91, 1952.

11   Markowitz, H. M. *Portfolio Selection: Efficient Diversification of Investments*. New York: Wiley, 1959. (Yale University Press, 1970; Basil Blackwell, 1991.)

Consider first the normal distribution assumption. As we noted earlier in this chapter, the normal distribution is not only symmetric but also can be characterized by just the mean and the variance.[12] If returns were normally distributed, it follows then that the only two choice variables for investors would be the expected returns and standard deviations, thus providing the basis for the mean variance framework. The problem with this assumption is that returns on most investments cannot be normally distributed. The worst outcome you can have when investing in a stock is to lose your entire investment, translating into a return of -100 percent (and not $-\infty$ as required in a normal distribution).

As for the utility distribution argument, consider the quadratic utility function, where utility is written as follows.

$$U(W) = a + bW - cW^2$$

The quadratic utility function is graphed in Figure 4.3.

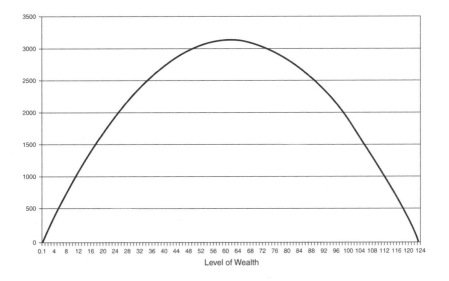

Figure 4.3: Quadratic Utility Function

Investors with quadratic utility functions care about only the level of their wealth and the variance in that level; thus, they have a mean-variance focus when picking investments. Although assuming a quadratic utility function may be convenient, it is not a

---

12 Portfolios of assets that each exhibit normally distributed returns will also be normally distributed. Lognormally distributed returns can also be parameterized with the mean and the variance, but portfolios of assets exhibiting lognormal returns may not exhibit lognormality.

plausible measure of investor utility for three reasons. The first reason is that it assumes that investors are equally averse to deviations of wealth below the mean (bad outcomes) as they are to deviations above the mean (good outcomes). The second is that individuals with quadratic utility functions exhibit decreasing absolute risk aversion—that is, individuals invest less of their wealth (in absolute terms) in risky assets as they become wealthier. Finally, there are ranges of wealth where investors actually prefer less wealth to more wealth; the marginal utility of wealth becomes negative.

Because both the normal distribution and quadratic utility assumptions can only be justified with contorted reasoning, how then how do you defend the mean-variance approach? The many supporters of the approach argue that the decisions based on decisions based on the mean and the variance come reasonably close to the optimum with utility functions other than the quadratic. They also rationalize the use of the normal distribution by pointing out that returns may be log-normally distributed (in which case the log of the returns should be normally distributed) and that the returns on portfolios (rather than individual stocks), especially over shorter periods, are more symmetric and thus closer to normality. Ultimately, their main argument is that what is lost in precision is gained in simplicity when we use the mean-variance as opposed to more realistic but complex frameworks.[13]

Implications for Risk Assessment

If we accept the mean-variance framework, the implications for risk measurement are significant.

- The argument for diversification becomes irrefutable. A portfolio of assets will almost always generate a higher return for a given level of variance than any single asset. Investors should diversify even if they have special access to information and there are transactions costs, although the extent of diversification may be limited.[14]

- In general, the risk of an asset can be measured by the risk it adds to the portfolio that it becomes part of and, in particular, by how much it increases the vari-

---

13 Markowitz, defending the quadratic utility assumptions, notes that focusing on just the mean and the variance makes sense for changes in wealth.

14 The only exception is if the information is perfect—that is, investors have complete certainty about what will happen to a stock or investment. In that case, they can invest their wealth in that individual asset and it will be risk free. In the real world, inside information gives you an edge over other investors but does not bestow its possessor with guaranteed profits. Investors with such information would be better served spreading their wealth over multiple stocks on which they have privileged information rather than just one source.

ance of the portfolio to which it is added. Thus, the key component determining asset risk will not be its volatility per se, but how the asset price co-moves with the portfolio. An asset that is extremely volatile but moves independently of the rest of the assets in a portfolio will add little or even no risk to the portfolio. Mathematically, the covariance between the asset and the other assets in the portfolio becomes the dominant risk measure, rather than its variance.

- The other parameters of an investment, such as the potential for large payoffs and the likelihood of price jumps, become irrelevant after they have been factored into the variance computation.

Whether one accepts the premise of the mean-variance framework or not, its introduction changed the way we think about risk from one where the risk of individual assets was assessed independently to one where asset risk is assessed relative to a portfolio of which the asset is a part.

Introducing the Riskless Asset—The Capital Asset Pricing Model (CAPM) Arrives

The revolution initiated by Harry Markowitz was carried to its logical conclusion by John Lintner, Jack Treynor, and Bill Sharpe, with their development of the capital asset pricing model (CAPM).[15] Sharpe and Linter added a riskless asset to the mix and concluded that there existed a superior alternative to investors at every risk level, created by combining the riskless asset with one supremely diversified portfolio on the efficient frontier. Combinations of the riskless asset and the one super-efficient portfolio generate higher expected returns for every given level of risk than holding just a portfolio of risky assets. (Appendix 2 contains a more complete proof of this conclusion.) For those investors who desire less risk than that embedded in the market portfolio, this translates into investing a portion of their wealth in the super-efficient portfolio and the rest in the riskless assets. Investors who want to take more risk are assumed to borrow at the riskless rate and invest that money in the super-efficient portfolio. If all investors follow this dictum, they should hold the one super-efficient portfolio, which should be supremely

15 Sharpe, William F. "Capital Asset Prices: A Theory of Market Equilibrium under Conditions of Risk. *Journal of Finance*, 19 (3), 425–442, 1961. Lintner, J. 1965. The valuation of risk assests and the selection of risky investments in stock portfolios and capital budgets. *Review of Economics and Staticstics* 47: 13–37.

Treynor, Jack. "The Valuation of Risk Assets and the Selection of Risky Investments in Stock Portfolios and Capital Budgets" *The Review of Economics and Statistics*, 47: 13–37, 1961.

diversified. (It should include every traded asset in the market, held in proportion to its market value.) Thus, it is termed the *market portfolio*.

To reach this result, the original version of the model did assume that there were no transactions costs or taxes and that investors had identical information about assets (and thus shared the same estimates for the expected returns, standard deviations, and correlation across assets). In addition, the model assumed that all investors shared a single period time horizon and that they could borrow and invest at the risk-free rate. Intuitively, the model eliminates any rationale for holding back on diversification. After all, without transactions costs and differential information, why settle for any portfolio that is less than fully diversified? Consequently, any investor who holds a portfolio other than the market portfolio is not fully diversified and bears the related cost with no offsetting benefit.

If we accept the assumptions (unrealistic though they may seem) of the capital asset pricing model, the risk of an individual asset becomes the risk added on to the market portfolio and can be measured statistically as follows.

$$\text{Risk of an asset} = \frac{\text{Covariance of asset with the market portfolio}}{\text{Variance of the market portfolio}} = \text{Asset Beta}$$

Thus, the CAPM extends the Markowitz insight that investors should diversify to its logical limit where investors hold a market portfolio of all traded assets. Thus, the risk of any asset is a function of how it covaries with the market portfolio. Dividing the covariance of every asset by the market portfolio to the market variance allows for the scaling of betas around 1; an average risk investment has a beta around 1, whereas investments with above-average risk and below-average risk have betas greater than and less than 1, respectively.

In closing, though, accepting the CAPM requires us to accept the assumptions that the model makes about transactions costs and information in addition to the underlying assumptions of the mean-variance framework. Notwithstanding its many critics, whose views we will examine in the next two sections, the widespread acceptance of the model and its survival as the default model for risk to this day is testimony to its intuitive appeal and simplicity.

Mean Variance Challenged

From its beginnings, the mean variance framework has been controversial. Although there have been many who have challenged its applicability, we will consider these challenges in three groups. The first group argues that stock prices, in particular, and investment returns, in general, exhibit too many large values to be drawn from a normal distribution. They argue that the "fat tails" on stock price distributions lend themselves better to a class of distributions, called *power-law distributions*, which exhibit infinite variance and long periods of price dependence. The second group takes issue with the symmetry of the normal distribution and argues for measures that incorporate the asymmetry observed in actual return distributions into risk measures. The third group posits that distributions that allow for price jumps are more realistic, and risk measures should consider the likelihood and magnitude of price jumps.

Fat Tails and Power-Law distributions

Benoit Mandelbrot, a mathematician who also did pioneering work on the behavior of stock prices, was one of those who took issue with the use of normal and lognormal distributions.[16] He argued, based on his observation of stock and real asset prices, that a power-law distribution characterized them better.[17] In a power-law distribution, the relationship between two variables, Y and X, can be written as follows:

$$Y = \alpha^k$$

In this equation, α is a constant (constant of proportionality), and k is the power-law exponent. Mandelbrot's key point was that the normal and log normal distributions were best suited for series that exhibited mild and well-behaved randomness, whereas power-law distributions were more suited for series that exhibited large movements and what he termed *wild randomness*. Wild randomness occurs when a single observation can affect the population in a disproportionate way. Stock and commodity prices, with their long periods of relatively small movements, punctuated by wild swings in both directions, seem to fit better into the wild randomness group.

What are the consequences for risk measures? If asset prices follow power-law distributions, the standard deviation or volatility ceases to be a good risk measure and a good basis for computing probabilities. Assume, for instance, that the standard deviation in

---

16   Mandelbrot, B. "The Variation of Certain Speculative Prices." *Journal of Business*, Vol. 34, 394–419, 1961.

17   H. E. Hurst, a British civil servant, is credited with bringing the power-law distribution into popular usage. Faced with the task of protecting Egypt against floods on the Nile river, he did an exhaustive analysis of the frequency of high and low water marks at dozens of other rivers around the world. He found that the range widened far more than would be predicted by the normal distribution. In fact, he devised a measure, called the *Hurst exponent*, to capture the widening of the range. The Hurst exponent, which has a value of 0.5 for the normal distribution, had a value of 0.73 for the rivers that he studied. In intuitive terms, Hurst's findings suggested that there were extended periods of rainfall that were better than expected and worse than expected that caused the widening of the ranges. Mandelbrot's awareness of this research allowed him to bring the same thinking into his analysis of cotton prices on the Commodity Exchange.

annual stock returns is 15 percent, and the average return is 10 percent. Using the normal distribution as the base for probability predictions, this implies that the stock returns will exceed 40 percent (average plus two standard deviations) only once every 44 years and 55 percent only (average plus three standard deviations) once every 740 years. In fact, stock returns will be greater than 85 percent (average plus five standard deviations) only once every 3.5 million years. In reality, stock returns exceed these values far more frequently, a finding consistent with power-law distributions, where the probability of larger values declines linearly as a function of the power-law exponent. As the value is doubled, the probability of its occurrence drops by the square of the exponent. Thus, if the exponent in the distribution is 2, the likelihood of returns of 25 percent, 50 percent, and 100 percent can be computed as follows:

Returns will exceed 25 percent: Once every 6 years

Returns will exceed 50 percent: Once every 24 years

Returns will exceed 100 percent: Once every 96 years

Note that as the returns are doubled, the likelihood increases fourfold (the square of the exponent). As the exponent decreases, the likelihood of larger values increases; an exponent between 0 and 2 will yield extreme values more often than a normal distribution. An exponent between 1 and 2 yields power-law distributions called stable Paretian distributions, which have infinite variance. In an early study, Fama[18] estimated the exponent for stocks to be between 1.7 and 1.9, but subsequent studies have found that the exponent is higher in both equity and currency markets.[19]

In practical terms, the power law proponents argue that using measures such as volatility (and its derivatives such as beta) underestimate the risk of large movements. The power law exponents for assets, in their view, provide investors with more realistic risk measures for these assets. Assets with higher exponents are less risky (because extreme values become less common) than assets with lower exponents.

Mandelbrot's challenge to the normal distribution was more than a procedural one. Mandelbrot's world, in contrast to the Gaussian mean-variance one, is one where prices move jaggedly over time and look like they have no pattern at a distance, but where patterns repeat themselves, when observed closely. In the 1970s, Mandelbrot created

---

18   Fama, E. F. "The Behavior of Stock Market Prices." *Journal of Business*, Vol. 38, 34–105, 1965.

19   In a paper in *Nature*, researchers looked at stock prices on 500 stocks between 1929 and 1987 and concluded that the exponent for stock returns is roughly 3. Gabaix, X., P. Gopikrishnan, V. Plerou, and H. E Stanley. "A Theory of Power-Law Distributions in Financial Market Fluctuations." *Nature*, 423, 267–270, 2003.

a branch of mathematics called *fractal geometry* where processes are not described by conventional statistical or mathematical measures but by fractals; a *fractal* is a geometric shape that when broken down into smaller parts replicates that shape. To illustrate the concept, he uses the example of the coastline that, from a distance, looks irregular but up close looks roughly the same—fractal patterns repeat themselves. In fractal geometry, higher fractal dimensions translate into more jagged shapes; the rugged Cornish Coastline has a fractal dimension of 1.25, whereas the much smoother South African coastline has a fractal dimension of 1.02. Using the same reasoning, stock prices that look random when observed at longer intervals start revealing self-repeating patterns when observed over shorter periods. More volatile stocks score higher on measures of fractal dimension, thus making it a measure of risk. With fractal geometry, Mandelbrot was able to explain not only the higher frequency of price jumps (relative to the normal distribution) but also long periods where prices move in the same direction and the resulting price bubbles.[20]

Asymmetric Distributions

Intuitively, it should be downside risk that concerns us and not upside risk. In other words, it is not investments going up significantly that create heartburn and unease but investments going down significantly. However, the mean-variance framework, by weighting both upside volatility and downside movements equally, does not distinguish between the two. With a normal or any other symmetric distribution, the distinction between upside and downside risk is irrelevant because the risks are equivalent. With asymmetric distributions, though, there can be a difference between upside and downside risk. As we noted in Chapter 3, "What Do We Think about Risk," studies of risk aversion in humans conclude the following:

- They are loss averse—that is, they weigh the pain of a loss more than the joy of an equivalent gain.

- They value very large positive payoffs—long shots—far more than they should given the likelihood of these payoffs.

In practice, return distributions for stocks and most other assets are not symmetric. Instead, as shown in Figure 4.4, asset returns exhibit fat tails and are more likely to have extreme positive values than extreme negative values (simply because returns are constrained to be no less than −100 percent).

---

20 Mandelbrot has expanded on his thesis in a book on the topic: Mandelbrot, B. and R. L. Hudson. *The (Mis)behavior of Markets: A Fractal View of Risk, Ruin, and Reward*. New York: Basic Books, 2004.

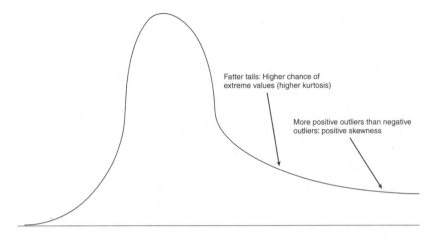

Fatter tails: Higher chance of
extreme values (higher kurtosis)

More positive outliers than negative
outliers: positive skewness

Figure 4.4 : Return distributions on Stocks

Note that the distribution of stock returns has a higher incidence of extreme returns (fat tails or *kurtosis*) and a tilt toward very large positive returns (positive skewness). Critics of the mean variance approach argue that it takes too narrow a view of both rewards and risk. In their view, a fuller return measure should consider not just the magnitude of expected returns but also the likelihood of very large positive returns or skewness,[21] and more complete risk measure should incorporate both variance and the possibility of big jumps (co-kurtosis).[22] Note that even as these approaches deviate from the mean-variance approach in terms of the way they define risk, they stay true to the portfolio measure of risk. In other words, it is not the possibility of large positive payoffs (skewness) or big jumps (kurtosis) that they argue should be considered, but only that portion of the skewness (co-skewness) and kurtosis (co-kurtosis) that is market related and not diversifiable.

---

21   The earliest paper on this topic was by Kraus, Alan, and Robert H. Litzenberger. "Skewness Preference and the Valuation of Risk Assets." *Journal of Finance*, 31, 1085–1100, 1976. They generated a three-moment CAPM, with a measure of co-skewness (of the asset with the market) added to capture preferences for skewness, arguing that it helped better explain differences across stock returns.

In a more recent paper, Harvey and Siddique use co-skewness to explain why small companies and low price-to-book companies earn higher returns. See Harvey, C. and A. Siddique. "Conditional Skewness in Asset Pricing Tests." *Journal of Finance*, 55, 1263–1295, 2000.

22   Fang, H., and Lai T-Y. "Co-Kurtosis and Capital Asset Pricing." *The Financial Review*, 32, 293–307, 1997. In this paper, the authors introduce a measure of co-kurtosis (stock price jumps that are correlated with market jumps) and argue that it adds to the risk of a stock.

Jump Process Models

The normal, power-law, and asymmetric distributions that form the basis for the models we have discussed in this section are continuous distributions. Observing the reality that stock prices do jump, some have argued for the use of jump process distributions to derive risk measures.

Press, in one of the earliest papers that attempted to model stock price jumps, argued that stock prices follow a combination of a continuous price distribution and a Poisson distribution, where prices jump at irregular intervals. The key parameters of the Poisson distribution are the expected size of the price jump (μ), the variance in this value (δ^2), and the likelihood of a price jump in any specified period (λ). Press estimated these values for ten stocks. In subsequent papers, Beckers and Ball and Torous suggest ways of refining these estimates.[23] In an attempt to bridge the gap between the CAPM and jump process models, Jarrow and Rosenfeld derive a version of the capital asset pricing model that includes a jump component that captures the likelihood of market jumps and an individual asset's correlation with these jumps.[24]

Although jump process models have gained some traction in option pricing, they have had limited success in equity markets, largely because the parameters of jump process models are difficult to estimate with any degree of precision. Thus, while everyone agrees that stock prices jump, there is little consensus on the best way to measure how often this happens, whether these jumps are diversifiable, and how best to incorporate their effect into risk measures.

Data Power: Arbitrage Pricing and Multifactor Models

Two developments in the past three decades have changed the way we think about risk measurement. The first was access to richer data on stock and commodity market information; researchers could not only get information on weekly, daily, or even intraday prices but also on trading volume and bid-ask spreads. The other was the increase in both personal and mainframe computing power, allowing researchers to bring powerful

---

23   Beckers, S. "A Note on Estimating the Parameters of the Diffusion-Jump Process Model of Stock Returns." *Journal of Financial and Quantitative Analysis*, Vol. 16, 127–140, 1981.

Ball, C. A., and W. N. Torous. "A Simplified Jump Process for Common Stock Returns." *Journal of Financial and Quantitative Analysis*, Vol. 18, 53–65, 1983.

24   Jarrow, R. A., and E. R. Rosenfeld. "Jump Risks and the Intertemporal Capital Asset Pricing Model." *Journal of Business*, Vol. 57, 337–351, 1984.

statistical tools to bear on the data. As a consequence of these two trends, we have seen the advent of risk measures that are based almost entirely on observed market prices and financial data.

Arbitrage Pricing Model

The first direct challenge to the capital asset pricing model came in the mid-seventies, when Steve Ross developed the arbitrage pricing model using the fundamental proposition that two assets with the same exposure to risk had to be priced the same by the market to prevent investors from generating risk-free or arbitrage profits.[25] In a market where arbitrage opportunities did not exist, he argued that you can back out measures of risk from observed market returns. Appendix 2 provides a short summary of the derivation of the arbitrage pricing model.

The statistical technique that Ross used to extract these risk measures was factor analysis. He examined (or rather got a computer to analyze) returns on individual stocks over a long period and asked a fundamental question: are there common factors that seem to cause large numbers of stock to move together in particular periods? The factor analysis suggested that there were multiple factors affecting overall stock prices; these factors were termed *market risk factors* because they affected many stocks at the same time. As a bonus, the factor analysis measured each stock's exposure to each of the multiple factors; these measures were titled *factor betas*.

In the parlance of the capital asset pricing model, the arbitrage pricing model replaces the single market risk factor in the CAPM (captured by the market portfolio) with multiple market risk factors. It replaces the single market beta in the CAPM (which measures risk added by an individual asset to the market portfolio) with multiple factor betas (measuring an asset's exposure to each of the market risk factors). More importantly, the arbitrage pricing model does not make restrictive assumptions about investor utility functions or the return distributions of assets. The trade-off, though, is that the arbitrage pricing model depends heavily on historical price data for its estimates of both the number of factors and factor betas and is at its core more of a statistical than an economic model.

---

25   Ross, Stephen A. "The Arbitrage Theory of Capital Asset Pricing." *Journal of Economic Theory.* Vol. 13(3), 341–360, 1976.

Multifactor and Proxy Models

Although arbitrage pricing models restrict themselves to historical price data, multifactor models expand the data used to include macroeconomic data in some versions and firm-specific data (such as market capitalization and pricing ratios) in others. Fundamentally, multifactor models begin with the assumption that market prices usually go up or down for good reason, and stocks that earn high returns over long periods must be riskier than stocks that earn low returns over the same periods. With that assumption in place, these models then look for external data that can explain the differences in returns across stocks.

One class of multifactor models restricts the external data that it uses to macroeconomic data, arguing that the risk that is priced into stocks should be market risk and not firm-specific risk. For instance, Chen, Roll, and Ross suggest that the following macroeconomic variables are highly correlated with the factors that come out of factor analysis: the level of industrial production, changes in the default spread (between corporate and treasury bonds), shifts in the yield curve (captured by the difference between long- and short-term rates), unanticipated inflation, and changes in the real rate of return.[26] These variables can then be correlated with returns to come up with a model of expected returns, with firm-specific betas calculated relative to each variable. In summary, Chen, Roll, and Ross found that stock returns were more negative in periods when industrial production fell, and the default spread, unanticipated inflation, and the real rate of return increased. Stocks did much better in periods when the yield curve was more upward sloping—long-term rates were higher than short-term rates—and worse in periods when the yield curve was flat or downward sloping. With this approach, the measure of risk for a stock or asset becomes its exposure to each of these macroeconomic factors (captured by the beta relative to each factor).

Although multifactor models may stretch the notion of market risk, they remain true to its essence by restricting the search to only macroeconomic variables. A second class of models weakens this restriction by widening the search for variables that explain differences in stock returns to include firm-specific factors. The most widely cited study using this approach was by Fama and French, where they presented strong evidence that differences in returns across stocks between 1962 and 1990 were best explained not by CAPM betas but by two firm-specific measures: the market capitalization of a company and its book-to-price ratio.[27] Smaller market cap companies and companies with higher

---

26 Chen, N., R. Roll, and S. A. Ross. "Economic Forces and the Stock Market." *Journal of Business*, Vol. 59, 383–404, 1986.

27 Fama, E. F., and K. R. French. "The Cross-Section of Expected Returns." *Journal of Finance*, Vol. 47, 427–466, 1992. There were numerous other studies prior to this one that had the same conclusions as this one, but their focus was different. These earlier studies used their findings that low PE, low PBV, and small companies earned higher returns than expected (based on the CAPM) to conclude that either markets were not efficient or that the CAPM did not work.

book-to-price ratios generated higher annual returns over this period than larger market cap companies with lower book-to-price ratios. If markets are reasonably efficient in the long term, they argued that this must indicate that market capitalization and book-to-price ratios were good stand-ins or proxies for risk measures. In the years since, other factors have added to the list of risk proxies—price momentum, price level per share, and liquidity are a few that come to mind.[28]

Multifactor and proxy models will do better than conventional asset pricing models in explaining differences in returns because the variables chosen in these models are those that have the highest correlation with returns. Put another way, researchers can search through hundreds of potential proxies and pick the ones that work best. It is therefore unfair to argue for these models based purely on their better explanatory power.

The Evolution of Risk Measures

The way in which we measure risk has evolved over time, reflecting the developments in statistics and economics on the one hand and the availability of data on the other. In Figure 4.5, we summarize the key developments in the measurement of risk and the evolution of risk measures over time.

It is worth noting that as new risk measures have evolved, the old ones have not been entirely abandoned. Thus, although much of academic research may have jumped on the portfolio theory bandwagon and its subsequent refinements, there are still many investors who are more comfortable with subjective judgments about risk or overall risk categories. (Stocks are risky and bonds are not.)

Conclusion

To manage risk, we first have to measure it. In this chapter, we look at the evolution of risk measures over time. For much of recorded time, human beings attributed negative events to fate or divine providence; therefore, they made little effort to measure it quantitatively. After all, if the gods decided to punish you, no risk measurement device or risk management product could protect you from retribution.

---

28 Stocks that have gone up strongly in the recent past (his momentum), trade at low prices per share, and are less liquid earn higher returns than stocks without these characteristics.

Key Event		Risk Measure Used
Risk was considered to be either fated and thus impossible to change or divine providence, in which case it could be altered only through prayer or sacrifice.	Pre-1494	None or gut feeling
Luca Pacioli posits his puzzle with two gamblers in a coin tossing game.	1494	
Pascal and Fermal solve the Pacioli puzzle and lay foundations for probability estimation and theory.	1654	Computed probabilities
Graunt generates life table using data on births and deaths in London.	1662	
Bernoulli states the "law of large numbers," providing the basis for sampling from large populations.	1711	Sample-based probabilities
de Moivre derives the normal distribution as an approximation to the binomial and Gauss & Laplace refine it.	1738	
Bayes published his treatise on how to update prior beliefs as new information is acquired.	1763	
Insurance business develops and with it come actuarial measures of risk, based upon historical data.	1800s	Expected loss
Bachelier examines stock and option prices on Paris exchanges and defends his thesis that prices follow a random walk.	1900	Price variance
Standard Statistics Bureau, Moody's, and Fitch start rating corporate bonds using accounting information.	1909–1915	Bond & stock ratings
Markowitz lays statistical basis for diversification and generates efficient portfolios for different risk levels.	1952	Variance added to portfolio
Sharpe and Lintner introduce a riskless assest and show that combinations of it and a market portfolio (including all traded assets) are optimal for all investors. The CAPM is born.	1964	Market beta
Risk and return models based upon alternatives to normal distribution - Power law, asymmetric, and jump process distributions.	1960–	
Using the "no arbitrage" argument, Ross derives the arbitrage pricing model; multiple market risk factors are derived from the historical data.	1976	Factor betas
Macroeconomic variables examined as potential market risk factors, leading the multi-factor model.	1986	Macro economic betas
Fama and French, examining the link between stock returns and firm-specific factors, conclude that market cap and book to price at better proxies for risk than beta or betas.	1992	Proxies

Figure 4.5: Key Developments in Risk Analysis and Evolution of Risk Measures

The first break in this karmic view of risk occurred in the Middle Ages when mathematicians, more in the interests of success at the card tables than in risk measurement, came up with the first measures of probability. Subsequent advances in statistics—sampling distributions, the law of large numbers, and Bayes' rule, to provide three examples—extended the reach of probability into the uncertainties that individuals and businesses faced day to day. Consequently, the insurance business was born, where companies offered to protect individuals and businesses from expected losses by charging premiums. The key, though, was that risk was still perceived almost entirely in terms of potential downside and losses.

The growth of markets for financial assets created a need for risk measures that captured both the downside risk inherent in these investments as well as the potential for upside or profits. The growth of services that provided estimates of these risk measures parallels the growth in access to pricing and financial data on investments. The bond rating agencies in the early part of the twentieth century provided risk measures for corporate bonds. Measures of equity risk appeared at about the same time but were primarily centered on price volatility and financial ratios.

Although the virtues of diversifying across investments had been well publicized at the time of his arrival, Markowitz laid the foundation for modern portfolio theory by making explicit the benefits of diversification. In the aftermath of his derivation of efficient portfolios—that is, portfolios that maximized expected returns for given variances—three classes of models that allowed for more detailed risk measures developed. One class included models like the CAPM that stayed true to the mean variance framework and measured risk for any asset as the variance added on to a diversified portfolio. The second set of models relaxed the normal distribution assumption inherent in the CAPM and allowed for more general distributions (like the power-law and asymmetric distributions) and the risk measures emanating from these distributions. The third set of models trusted the market to get it right, at least on average, and derived risk measures by looking at history. Implicitly, these models assumed that investments that earned high returns in the past must have done so because they were riskier and looked for factors that best explained these returns. These factors remained unnamed and were statistical in the arbitrage pricing model. They were macroeconomic variables in multifactor models and firm-specific measures (like market cap and price-to-book ratios) in proxy models.

APPENDIX 1

Mean-Variance Framework and the CAPM

Consider a portfolio of two assets. Asset A has an expected return of μ_A and a variance in returns of σ^2_A, whereas asset B has an expected return of μ_B and a variance in returns of σ^2_B. The correlation in returns between the two assets, which measures how the assets move together, is ρ_{AB}. The expected returns and variance of a two-asset portfolio can be written as a function of these inputs and the proportion of the portfolio going to each asset.

$$\mu_{portfolio} = w_A\,\mu_A + (1 - w_A)\,\mu_B$$

$$\sigma^2_{portfolio} = w_A^2\,\sigma^2_A + (1 - w_A)^2\,\sigma^2_B + 2\,w_A\,w_B\rho_{AB}\,\sigma_A\,\sigma_B$$

where

w_A = Proportion of the portfolio in asset A

The last term in the variance formulation is sometimes written in terms of the covariance in returns between the two assets, which is:

$$\sigma_{AB} = \rho_{AB}\,\sigma_A\,\sigma_B$$

The savings that accrue from diversification are a function of the correlation coefficient. Other things remaining equal, the higher the correlation in returns between the two assets, the smaller the potential benefits from diversification. The following example illustrates the savings from diversification.

If there is a diversification benefit of going from one asset to two, as the preceding discussion illustrates, there must be a benefit in going from two assets to three, and from three assets to more. The variance of a portfolio of three assets can be written as a function of the variances of each of the three assets, the portfolio weights on each, and the correlations between pairs of the assets. It can be written as follows:

$$\sigma_p^{2} = w_A^2\,\sigma^2_A + w_B^2\,\sigma^2_B + w_C^2\,\sigma^2_C + 2\,w_A\,w_B\rho_{AB}\,\sigma_A\,\sigma_B + 2\,w_A\,w_C\rho_{AC}\,\sigma_A\,\sigma_C + 2\,w_B\,w_C\rho_{BC}\,\sigma_B\,\sigma_C$$

where

w_A, w_B, w_C = Portfolio weights on assets

$\sigma^2_A, \sigma^2_B, \sigma^2_C$ = Variances of assets A, B, and C

$\rho_{AB}, \rho_{AC}, \rho_{BC}$ = Correlation in returns between pairs of assets (A&B, A&C, B&C)

Note that the number of covariance terms in the variance formulation has increased from one to three. This formulation can be extended to the more general case of a portfolio of n assets.

$$\sigma^2_p = \sum_{i=1}^{i=n} \sum_{j=1}^{j=n} w_i \, w_j \, \rho_{ij} \, \sigma_i \, \sigma_j$$

The number of terms in this formulation increases exponentially with the number of assets in the portfolio, largely because of the number of covariance terms that have to be considered. In general, the number of covariance terms can be written as a function of the number of assets.

Number of covariance terms = n (n–1) /2

where n is the number of assets in the portfolio. Table 4A.1 lists the number of covariance terms we would need to estimate the variances of portfolios of different sizes.

We can use this formulation to estimate the variance of a portfolio and the effects of diversification on that variance. For purposes of simplicity, assume that the average asset has a standard deviation in returns of σ, and the average covariance in returns between any pair of assets is σ_{ij}. Furthermore, assume that the portfolio is always equally weighted across the assets in that portfolio. The variance of a portfolio of n assets can then be written as follows:

$$\sigma^2_p = n \left(\frac{1}{n} \right)^2 \overline{\sigma}^2 + \frac{(n-1)}{n} \overline{\sigma}_{ij}$$

Table 4A.1   Number of Covariance Terms

Number of Assets	Number of Covariance Terms
2	1
10	45
100	4,950
1,000	499,500
10,000	49,995,000

The fact that variances can be estimated for portfolios made up of a large number of assets suggests an approach to optimizing portfolio construction, in which investors trade off expected return and variance. If an investor can specify the maximum amount of risk he is willing to take on (in terms of variance), the task of portfolio optimization becomes the maximization of expected returns subject to this level of risk. Alternatively, if an investor specifies her desired level of return, the optimum portfolio is the one that minimizes the variance subject to this level of return. These optimization algorithms can be written as follows:

Return maximization   Risk minimization

Maximize expected return   Minimize return variance

$$E(R_p) = \sum_{i=1}^{i=n} w_i \, E(R_i) \qquad \sigma_p^2 = \sum_{i=1}^{i=n} \sum_{j=1}^{j=n} w_i w_j \sigma_{ij}$$

subject to

$$\sigma_p^2 = \sum_{i=1}^{i=n} \sum_{j=1}^{j=n} w_i w_j \sigma_{ij} \leq \hat{\sigma}^2 \qquad E(R_p) = \sum_{i=1}^{i=n} w_i \, E(R_i) = E(\hat{R})$$

where

$\hat{\sigma}$ = Investor's desired level of variance

$E(\hat{R})$ = Investor's desired expected returns

The portfolios that emerge from this process are called *Markowitz portfolios*. They are considered efficient because they maximize expected returns given the standard deviation, and the entire set of portfolios is referred to as the *Efficient Frontier*. Graphically, these portfolios are shown on the expected return/standard deviation dimensions in Figure 4A.1.

The Markowitz approach to portfolio optimization, while intuitively appealing, suffers from two major problems. The first is that it requires a large number of inputs because the covariances between pairs of assets are required to estimate the variances of portfolios. Although this may be manageable for small numbers of assets, it becomes less so when the entire universe of stocks or all investments are considered. The second problem is that the Markowitz approach ignores a very important asset choice that most investors have—riskless default-free government securities—in coming up with optimum portfolios.

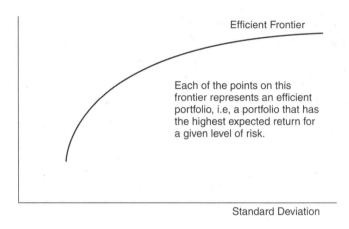

Efficient Frontier

Each of the points on this frontier represents an efficient portfolio, i.e, a portfolio that has the highest expected return for a given level of risk.

Standard Deviation

Figure 4A.1: Markowitz Portfolios

To get from Markowitz portfolios to the capital asset pricing model, let us consider adding a riskless asset to the mix of risky assets. By itself, the addition of one asset to the investment universe may seem trivial, but the riskless asset has some special characteristics that affect optimal portfolio choice for all investors.

- The riskless asset, by definition, has an expected return that will always be equal to the actual return. The expected return is known when the investment is made, and the actual return should be equal to this expected return; the standard deviation in returns on this investment is zero.

- While risky assets' returns vary, the absence of variance in the riskless asset's returns make it uncorrelated with returns on any of these risky assets. To examine what happens to the variance of a portfolio that combines a riskless asset with a risky portfolio, assume that the variance of the risky portfolio is σ_r^2 and that w_r is the proportion of the overall portfolio invested to these risky assets. The balance is invested in a riskless asset, which has no variance, and is uncorrelated with the risky asset. The variance of the overall portfolio can be written as follows:

$$\sigma^2\text{portfolio} = w_r^2\, \sigma^2_r$$

$$\sigma\text{portfolio} = w_r\, \sigma_r$$

Note that the other two terms in the two-asset variance equation drop out, and the standard deviation of the overall portfolio is a linear function of the portfolio invested in the risky portfolio.

The significance of this result can be illustrated by returning to Figure 4A.1 and adding the riskless asset to the choices available to the investor. The effect of this addition is explored in Figure 4A.2.

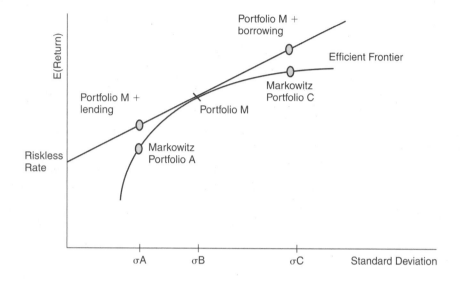

Figure 4A.2: Introducing a Riskless Asset

Consider investor A, whose desired risk level is σ_A. This investor, instead of choosing portfolio A, the Markowitz portfolio containing only risky assets, will choose to invest in a combination of the riskless asset and a much riskier portfolio, because he will be able to make a much higher return for the same level of risk. The expected return increases as the slope of the line drawn from the riskless rate increases, and the slope is maximized when the line is tangential to the efficient frontier; the risky portfolio at the point of tangency is labeled as risky portfolio M. Thus, investor A's expected return is maximized by holding a combination of the riskless asset and risky portfolio M. Investor B, whose desired risk level is σ_B, which happens to be equal to the standard deviation of the risky portfolio M, will choose to invest her entire portfolio in that portfolio. Investor C, whose desired risk level is σ_C, which exceeds the standard deviation of the risky portfolio M, will borrow money at the riskless rate and invest in the portfolio M.

In a world in which investors hold a combination of only two assets—the riskless asset and the market portfolio—the risk of any individual asset will be measured relative to the market portfolio. In particular, the risk of any asset will be the risk it adds onto the market portfolio. To arrive at the appropriate measure of this added risk, assume that

σ^2_m is the variance of the market portfolio prior to the addition of the new asset, and the variance of the individual asset being added to this portfolio is σ^2_i. The market value portfolio weight on this asset is w_i, and the covariance in returns between the individual asset and the market portfolio is σ_{im}. The variance of the market portfolio prior to and after the addition of the individual asset can then be written like this:

Variance prior to asset i being added $= \sigma^2_m$

Variance after asset i is added $= \sigma^2_{m'} = w_i^2\, \sigma^2_i + (1 - w_i)^2\, \sigma^2_m + 2\, w_i\, (1-w_i)\, \sigma_{im}$

The market value weight on any individual asset in the market portfolio should be small because the market portfolio includes all traded assets in the economy. Consequently, the first term in the equation should approach zero, and the second term should approach σ^2_m, leaving the third term (σ_{im}, the covariance) as the measure of the risk added by asset i. Dividing this term by the variance of the market portfolio yields the beta of an asset.

$$\text{Beta of asset} = \frac{\sigma_{im}}{\sigma^2_m}$$

APPENDIX 2

Derivation of the Arbitrage Pricing Model

Like the capital asset pricing model, the arbitrage pricing model begins by breaking down risk into firm-specific and market risk components. As in the capital asset pricing model, firm-specific risk covers information that affects primarily the firm, whereas market risk affects many or all firms. Incorporating both types of risk into a return model, we get the following.

$$R \quad = \quad E(R) \quad + \quad m \quad + \quad \varepsilon$$

where R is the actual return, $E(R)$ is the expected return, m is the market-wide component of unanticipated risk, and ε is the firm-specific component. Thus, the actual return can be different from the expected return, either because of market risk or firm-specific actions. In general, the market component of unanticipated returns can be decomposed into economic factors.

$$R \quad = \quad R \quad + \quad m \quad + \quad \varepsilon$$

$$= \quad R \quad + (\beta_1 \, F_1 + \beta_2 \, F_2 + \,.... + \beta_n \, F_n) \quad + \quad \varepsilon$$

where

β_j = Sensitivity of investment to unanticipated changes in factor j

F_j = Unanticipated changes in factor j

Note that the measure of an investment's sensitivity to any macroeconomic factor takes the form of a beta, called a *factor beta*. In fact, this beta has many of the same properties as the market beta in the CAPM.

The arbitrage pricing model assumes that firm-specific risk component (ε) can be diversified away and concludes that the return on a portfolio will not have a firm-specific component of unanticipated returns. The return on a portfolio can be written as the sum of two weighted averages: that of the anticipated returns in the portfolio and that of the market factors.

$$R_p = (w_1R_1+w_2R_2+...+w_nR_n)+ (w_1\beta_{1,1}+w_2\beta_{1,2}+...+w_n\beta_{1,n}) \, F_1 + (w_1\beta_{2,1}+w_2\beta_{2,2}+...+w_n\beta_{2,n}) \, F_2 \, ...$$

where

w_j = Portfolio weight on asset j

R_j = Expected return on asset j

$\beta_{i,j}$ = Beta on factor i for asset j

The final step in this process is estimating an expected return as a function of the betas specified earlier. To do this, we should first note that the beta of a portfolio is the weighted average of the betas of the assets in the portfolio. This property, in conjunction with the absence of arbitrage, leads to the conclusion that expected returns should be linearly related to betas. To see why, assume that there is only one factor and three portfolios. Portfolio A has a beta of 2.0 and an expected return of 20 percent; portfolio B has a beta of 1.0 and an expected return of 12 percent; and portfolio C has a beta of 1.5 and an expected return of 14 percent. Note that the investor can put half of his wealth in portfolio A and half in portfolio B and end up with a portfolio with a beta of 1.5 and an expected return of 16 percent. Consequently, no investor will choose to hold portfolio C until the prices of assets in that portfolio drop and the expected return increases to 16 percent. By the same rationale, the expected returns on every portfolio should be a linear function of the beta. If they were not, we could combine two other portfolios—one with a higher beta and one with a lower beta—to earn a higher return than the portfolio in question, creating an opportunity for arbitrage. This argument can be extended to multiple factors with the same results. Therefore, the expected return on an asset can be written as follows.

$$E(R) = R_f + \beta_1 \, [E(R_1) - R_f] + \beta_2 \, [E(R_2) - R_f] \, ...+ \beta_n \, [E(R_n) - R_f]$$

where

R_f = Expected return on a zero-beta portfolio

$E(R_j)$ = Expected return on a portfolio with a factor beta of 1 for factor j, and zero for all other factors

The terms in the brackets can be considered to be risk premiums for each of the factors in the model.

CHAPTERS 5–8

Risk Assessment: Tools and Techniques

R isk management begins with the assessment of risk. In the past 50 years, the confluence of developments in economic and financial theory with computing and data advancements has allowed us to develop new tools for assessing risk and improve existing ones. On the one hand, portfolio theory and risk and return models (such as the capital asset and arbitrage pricing models) have allowed us to become more sophisticated in adjusting the expected value of risky assets for that risk. Chapter 5, "Risk-Adjusted Value," provides a broad overview of the choices when it comes to risk-adjusting the value. The decision sciences and statistics have contributed their own tools to risk assessment. Chapter 6, "Probabilistic Approaches: Scenario Analysis, Decision Trees, and Simulations," examines these tools and why you may choose one over the other and how probabilistic approaches relate to the risk-adjusted values in Chapter 5. Chapters 7, "Value at Risk (VaR)," and 8, "Real Options," cover two relatively new tools in risk assessment, value at risk (VaR), focused primarily on downside risk and with a particular focus on financial service firms, and real options, more oriented toward upside risk and its payoff, with roots in the mining and technology businesses.

To the extent that risk assessment has to grapple with numbers and put a value on risk, these chapters are the most quantitative in the book. Although many risk managers do not do risk assessments themselves, they use risk assessments done by others. These chapters should provide some insight into how the risk assessment tools differ in what they do and what types of follow-up questions you should have with each one.

Chapter	Questions for Risk Management
5	What are the different ways of adjusting the value of a risky asset for risk? Which approach should you use and why?
6	How do probabilistic approaches help us get a handle on risk? How do these approaches differ from each other?

Chapter	Questions for Risk Management
7	What is VaR, and how does it relate to other assessment approaches?
	When does it make sense to use VaR?
8	How do real options differ from other risk assessment tools?
	When is it appropriate to use real options?

5

RISK-ADJUSTED VALUE

R isk-averse investors will assign lower values to assets that have more risk associated with them than to otherwise similar assets that are less risky. The most common way of adjusting for risk is to compute a value that is risk adjusted. In this chapter, we will consider four ways in which we can make this risk adjustment. The first two approaches are based on discounted cash flow valuation, where we value an asset by discounting the expected cash flows on it at a discount rate. The risk adjustment here can take the form of a higher discount rate or a reduction in expected cash flows for risky assets, with the adjustment based on some measure of asset risk. The third approach is to do a post-valuation adjustment to the value obtained for an asset, with no consideration given for risk, with the adjustment taking the form of a discount for potential downside risk or a premium for upside risk. In the final approach, we adjust for risk by observing how much the market discounts the value of assets of similar risk.

Although we will present these approaches as separate and potentially self-standing, we will also argue that analysts often employ combinations of approaches. For instance, it is common for an analyst to estimate value using a risk-adjusted discount rate and then attach an additional discount for liquidity to that value. In the process, they often double-count or miscount risk.

Discounted Cash Flow Approaches

In discounted cash flow valuation, the value of any asset can be written as the present value of the expected cash flows on that asset. Thus, the value of a default free government bond is the present value of the coupons on the bond, discounted at a riskless rate. As we introduce risk into the cash flows, we face a choice of how best to reflect this risk. We can continue to use the same expected cash flows that a risk-neutral investor would have used and add a risk premium to the risk-free rate to arrive at a risk-adjusted discount rate to use in discounting the cash flows. Alternatively, we can continue to use the risk-free rate as the discount rate and adjust the expected cash flows for risk; in effect, we replace the uncertain expected cash flows with certainty-equivalent cash flows.

The DCF Value of an Asset

We buy most assets because we expect them to generate cash flows for us in the future. In discounted cash flow valuation, we begin with a simple proposition. The value of an asset is not what someone perceives it to be worth but is a function of the expected cash flows on that asset. Put simply, assets with predictable cash flows should have higher values than assets with volatile cash flows. We can value assets with risk in two ways.

- We can estimate the value of a risky asset by discounting the expected cash flows on the asset over its life at a risk-adjusted discount rate.

$$\text{Value of asset} = \frac{E(CF_1)}{(1+r)} + \frac{E(CF_2)}{(1+r)^2} + \frac{E(CF_3)}{(1+r)^3} \ldots + \frac{E(CF_n)}{(1+r)^n}$$

  where the asset has an n-year life, $E(CF_t)$ is the expected cash flow in period t, and r is a discount rate that reflects the risk of the cash flows.

- Alternatively, we can replace the expected cash flows with the guaranteed cash flows we would have accepted as an alternative (certainty equivalents) and discount these certain cash flows at the risk-free rate.

$$\text{Value of asset} = \frac{CE(CF_1)}{(1+r_f)} + \frac{CE(CF_2)}{(1+r_f)^2} + \frac{CE(CF_3)}{(1+r_f)^3} \ldots + \frac{CE(CF_n)}{(1+r_f)^n}$$

  where $CE(CF_t)$ is the certainty equivalent of $E(CF_t)$ and r_f is the risk-free rate.

The cash flows will vary from asset to asset—dividends for stocks, coupons (interest), and the face value for bonds and after-tax cash flows for an investment that a business makes. The principles of valuation will not vary.

Using discounted cash flow models is in some sense an act of faith. We believe that every asset has an intrinsic value, and we try to estimate that intrinsic value by looking at an asset's fundamentals. What is intrinsic value? Consider it the value that would be attached to an asset by an analyst with access to all information available right now and a perfect valuation model. No such analyst exists, of course, but we all aspire to be as close as we can to this perfect analyst. The problem lies in the fact that none of us ever gets to see what the true intrinsic value of an asset is, so we have no way of knowing whether our discounted cash flow valuations are close to the mark.

Risk-Adjusted Discount Rates

Of the two approaches for adjusting for risk in discounted cash flow valuation, the more common one is the risk-adjusted discount rate approach, where we use higher discount rates to discount expected cash flows when valuing riskier assets, and we use lower discount rates when valuing safer assets.

Risk-and-Return Models

In Chapter 4, "How Do We Measure Risk," we examined the development of risk-and-return models in economics and finance. From the capital asset pricing model (CAPM) in 1964 to the multifactor models of today, a key output from these models is the expected rate of return for an investment, given its risk. This expected rate of return is the risk-adjusted discount rate for the asset's cash flows. In this section, we will revisit the CAPM, the arbitrage pricing model, and the multifactor model and examine the inputs we need to compute the required rate of return with each one.

In the CAPM, the expected return on an asset is a function of its beta, relative to the market portfolio.

Expected return = risk-free rate + market beta * equity risk premium

There are two inputs that all assets have in common in risk-and-return models. The first is the *risk-free rate*, which is the rate of return that you can expect to make with certainty on an investment. This is usually measured as the current market interest rate on a default-free (usually Government) security; the U.S. Treasury bond rate or bill rate is used as the long term or short-term risk-free rate in U.S. dollars. It is worth noting that the risk-free rate will vary across currencies, because the expected inflation rate is different with each currency. The second is the *equity risk premium*, which can be estimated in one of two ways. The first way is a historical risk premium, obtained by looking at returns you would have earned on stocks, relative to a riskless investment. The other way is to compute a forward-looking or implied premium by looking at the pricing of stocks, relative to the cash flows you expect to get from investing in them. In Chapter 3, "What Do We Think About Risk," we estimated both for the U.S. market and came up with 4.80 percent for the former and 4.09 percent for the latter in early 2006, relative to the Treasury bond rate. The only risk parameter that is investment specific is the beta, which measures the covariance of the investment with the market portfolio. In practice, it is estimated by either regressing returns on the investment (if it is publicly traded) against returns on a market index, or by looking at the betas of other publicly traded firms in the same business. The latter is called a *bottom-up beta* and generally yields more reliable estimates than a *historical regression beta*, which, in addition to being backward looking, also yields betas with large error terms.

Consider a simple example. In January 2006, the 10-year Treasury bond rate in the United States was 4.25 percent. At that time, the regression beta for Google was 1.83, with a standard error of 0.35, and the bottom-up beta for Google, looking at other Internet firms, was 2.25. If we accept the latter as the best estimate of the beta, the expected return on Google stock, using the implied risk premium of 4.09 percent, would have been as follows.

Expected return on Google = 4.25 percent + 2.25 (4.09 percent) = 13.45 percent

If you were valuing Google's equity cash flows, this would have been the risk-adjusted discount rate that you would have used.[1]

The arbitrage pricing and multifactor models are natural extensions of the CAPM. The risk-free rate remains unchanged, but risk premiums now have to be estimated for each factor; the premiums are for the unspecified market risk factors in the arbitrage pricing model and for the specified macroeconomic risk factors in the multifactor models. For individual investments, the betas have to be estimated, relative to each factor, and as with the CAPM betas, they can come from examining historical returns data on each investment or by looking at betas that are typical for the business that the investment is in.

As we noted in Chapter 4, the risk-and-return models in use share the common assumption of a marginal investor who is well diversified and measure risk as the risk added on to a diversified portfolio. They also share a common weakness insofar as they make simplifying assumptions about investor behavior—that investors have quadratic utility functions, for instance, or return distributions—that returns are log-normally distributed. They do represent a convenient way of adjusting for risk, and it is no surprise that they are in the toolboxes of most analysts who deal with risky investments.

Proxy Models

In Chapter 4, we examined some of the variables that have historically characterized stocks that have earned high returns; small market capitalization and low price-to-book ratios are two variables that come to mind. We also highlighted the findings of Fama and French, who regressed returns on stocks against these variables, using data from 1963 to 1990, to arrive at the following result for monthly returns.

---

1   When firms are funded with a mix of equity and debt, we can compute a consolidated cost of capital that is a weighted average of the cost of equity (computed using a risk-and-return model) and a cost of debt (based on the default risk of the firm). To value the entire business (rather than just the equity), we would discount the collective cash flows generated by the business for its equity investors and lenders at the cost of capital.

$$\text{Return}_j = 1.77\% - 0.11 \ln\left(MV_j\right) + 0.35 \ln\left(\frac{BV_j}{MV_j}\right)$$

where

Return_j = Monthly return on company j

$\ln(MV_j)$ = Natural log of the market value of equity of company j

$\ln(BV/MV)$ = Natural log of ratio of book value tom value of equity

Plugging a company's market value and book-to-price ratio into this equation will generate an expected return for that investment, which, in turn, is an estimate of the risk-adjusted discount rate that you could use to value it. Thus, the expected monthly return for a company with a market value of equity of $500 million and a book value of equity of $300 million can be written as follows:

Expected monthly return = 1.77 percent – 0.11 ln(500) + 0.35 ln (300/500) = 0.9076 percent

Annualized, this would translate into an expected annual return of 11.45 percent.

Expected annual return = $(1.009076)^{12} - 1 = .1145$ or 11.45 percent

This would be the risk-adjusted discount rate that you would use to value the company's cash flows (to equity investors).

In recent years, other variables have been added to proxy models. Adding price momentum, price level, and trading volume have been shown to improve the predictive power of the regression; strong stock price performance in the past six months, low stock price levels, and low trading volume are leading indicators of high returns in the future.

Proxy models have developed a following among analysts, especially those whose primary focus is valuing companies. Many of these analysts use an amalgam of risk-and-return models and proxy models to generate risk-adjusted discount rates to use in valuing stocks. For instance, the CAPM will be used to estimate an expected return for a small company, and a small-stock premium (usually based on historical return premium earned by small stocks relative to the market index) will be added on to arrive at the "right" discount rate for a small company. The approach has been less useful for those who are called upon to analyze either real or nontraded investments, because the inputs to the model (market capitalization and price-to-book ratio) require a market price.

Implied Discount Rates

For assets that are traded in the market, we can use a third approach to estimate discount rates. If we are willing to make estimates of the expected cash flows on the asset, we can back out the risk-adjusted discount rate from the market price. Thus, if an asset has a market value of $1,000, expected cash flow next year of $100, and a predicted growth rate of 3 percent in perpetuity, the risk-adjusted discount rate implied in the price can be computed as follows:

> Market value = Expected cash flow next year / (Risk-adjusted discount rate – Expected growth)

> $1,000 = $100/(r – .03)

Solving for r, we obtain a risk-adjusted discount rate of 13 percent.

Although the implied discount rate removes the requirements of making assumptions about risk-and-return models, it has two critical flaws that have prevented its general usage.

- It requires that the investment be traded and have a market price. Thus, it cannot be used without substantial modification for a nontraded asset.

- Even if the asset has a market price, this approach assumes that the market price is correct. Therefore, it becomes useless to an analyst who is called upon to make a judgment on whether the market price is correct; put another way, using the implied discount rate to value any risky asset will yield the not-surprising conclusion that everything is always fairly priced.

Practitioners have gotten around these problems in a couple of interesting ways. One way is to compute implied risk-adjusted discount rates for every asset in a class of risky assets—all cement companies, for example—and to average the rate across the assets. Implicitly, we are assuming that all the assets have equivalent risk and that they should all share the same average risk-adjusted rate of return. The other way is to compute risk-adjusted discount rates for the same asset for each year for a long period and to average the rate obtained over the period. Here, the assumption is that the risk-adjusted discount rate does not change over time and that the average across time is the best estimate of the risk-adjusted rate today.

General Issues

Although the use of risk-adjusted discount rates in computing value is widespread in both business valuation and capital budgeting, there are a surprising number of unresolved or overlooked issues in their usage.

- **Single-period models and multiperiod projects**—The risk-and-return models that we usually draw on for estimating discount rates such as the CAPM or the APM are single-period models, insofar as they help us forecast expected returns for the next period. Most assets have cash flows over multiple periods, and we discount these cash flows at the single-period discount rate, compounded over time. In other words, when we estimate the risk-adjusted return at Google to be 13.45 percent, it is an expected return for the next year. When valuing Google, we discount cash flows in years 2, 3, and beyond using the same discount rate. Myers and Turnbull (1977) note that this is appropriate only if we assume that the systematic risk of the project (its beta in the CAPM) and the market risk premium do not change over time.[2] They also go on to argue that this assumption will be violated when a business or asset has growth potential, because the systematic risk (beta) of growth is likely to be higher than the systematic risk of investments already made, and this will cause the systematic risk of an asset to change over time. One approximation worth considering in this scenario is to change the risk-adjusted discount rate each period to reflect changes in the systematic risk.

- **Composite discount rate versus item-specific discount rate**—In most discounted cash flow valuations, we estimate the expected cash flows of the asset by netting all outflows against inflows and then discount these cash flows using one risk-adjusted cost of capital. Implicitly, we are assuming that all cash flow items have equivalent exposure to systematic risk, but what if this assumption is not true? We can use different risk-adjusted discount rates for each set of cash flows; for instance, revenues and variable operating expenses can be discounted at the cost of capital, whereas fixed operating expenses, where the firm may have precommitted to making the payments, can be discounted back at a lower rate (such as the cost of debt). The question, though, is whether the risk variations are large enough to make a difference. At the minimum, the one or two cash flow items that diverge most from the average risk assumption (underlying the risk-adjusted cost of capital) can be separately valued.

- **Negative versus positive cash flows**—Generally, we penalize riskier assets by increasing the discount rate that we use to discount the cash flows. This presupposes that the cash flows are positive. When cash flows are negative, using a higher discount rate will have the perverse impact of reducing their present value and perhaps increasing the aggregate value of the asset. Although some analysts get around this by discounting negative cash flows at the risk-free rate

---

2   Myers, S. C., and S. M. Turnbull. "Capital Budgeting and the Capital Asset Pricing Model: Good News and Bad News." *Journal of Finance*, Vol. 32, 321–333, 1977.

(or a low rate variant) and positive cash flows at the risk-adjusted discount rate, they are being internally inconsistent in the way they deal with risk. In our view, any value benefits that accrue from discounting negative cash flows at the risk-adjusted rate will be more than lost when the eventual positive cash flows are discounted back at the same risk adjusted rate, compounded over time. Consider, for instance, a growth business with negative cash flows of $10 million each year for the first three years and a terminal value of $100 million at the end of the third year. Assume that the risk-free rate is 4 percent and the risk-adjusted discount rate is 10 percent. The value of the firm using the risk-free rate for the first three years and the risk-adjusted rate only on the terminal value is as follows:

$$\text{Value of firm} = \frac{-10}{(1.04)^1} + \frac{-10}{(1.04)^2} + \frac{-10}{(1.04)^3} + \frac{100}{(1.04)^3} = 61.15$$

Note that the terminal value is being discounted back at the risk-free rate for three years.[3] In contrast, the value of the same firm using the risk-adjusted discount rate on all the cash flows is as follows:

$$\text{Value of firm} = \frac{-10}{(1.10)^1} + \frac{-10}{(1.10)^2} + \frac{-10}{(1.10)^3} + \frac{100}{(1.10)^3} = 50.26$$

Put another way, it is reasonable to discount back negative cash flows at a lower rate if they are more predictable and stable, but not just because they are negative.

Certainty-Equivalent Cash Flows

Although most analysts adjust the discount rate for risk in DCF valuation, some prefer to adjust the expected cash flows for risk. In the process, they are replacing the uncertain expected cash flows with the certainty-equivalent cash flows, using a risk-adjustment process akin to the one used to adjust discount rates.

Misunderstanding Risk Adjustment

At the outset of this section, it should be emphasized that many analysts misunderstand what risk-adjusting the cash flows requires them to do. Some analysts consider the cash

---

3   Some use the risk-adjusted rate only on the terminal value, but that is patently unfair because you are using two different discount rates for the same periods. The only exception is if the negative cash flows are guaranteed and the terminal value is uncertain.

flows of an asset under a variety of scenarios, ranging from best case to catastrophic, assign probabilities to each one, take an expected value of the cash flows, and consider it risk adjusted. Although it is true that bad outcomes have been weighted in to arrive at this cash flow, it is still an expected cash flow and is not risk adjusted. To see why, assume that you were given a choice between two alternatives. In the first one, you are offered $95 with certainty, and in the second, you will receive $100 with probability 90 percent and only $50 the rest of the time. The expected value of both alternatives is $95, but risk-averse investors would pick the first investment with guaranteed cash flows over the second one.

If this argument sounds familiar, it is because it is a throwback to the beginnings of utility theory and the St. Petersburg Paradox that we examined in Chapter 2, "Why Do We Care About Risk?" In that chapter, we unveiled the notion of a certainty equivalent, a guaranteed cash flow that we would accept instead of an uncertain cash flow, and argued that more risk-averse investors would settle for lower-certainty equivalents for a given set of uncertain cash flows than less risk-averse investors. In the example given in the previous paragraph, a risk-averse investor would have settled for a guaranteed cash flow of well below $95 for the second alternative with an expected cash flow of $95.

The practical question that we will address in this section is how best to convert uncertain expected cash flows into guaranteed-certainty equivalents. Although we do agree with the notion that it should be a function of risk aversion, the estimation challenges remain daunting.

Utility Models: Bernoulli Revisited

In Chapter 2, we introduced the first (and oldest) approach to computing certainty equivalents, rooted in the utility functions for individuals. If we can specify the utility function of wealth for an individual, we are well set to convert risky cash flows to certainty equivalents for that individual. For instance, an individual with a log utility function would have demanded a certainty equivalent of $93.30 for the risky gamble presented in the previous section (90 percent chance of $100 and 10 percent chance of $50):

Utility from gamble = $.90 \ln(100) + .10 \ln(50) = 4.5359$

Certainty equivalent = $\exp^{4.5359} = \$93.30$

The certainty equivalent of $93.30 delivers the same utility as the uncertain gamble with an expected value of $95. We can repeat this process for more complicated assets and convert each expected cash flow into a certainty equivalent.[4]

One quirk of using utility models to estimate certainty equivalents is that the certainty equivalent of a positive expected cash flow can be negative. Consider, for instance, an investment where you can make $2,000 with probability 50 percent and lose $1,500 with probability 50 percent. The expected value of this investment is $250, but the certainty equivalent may very well be negative, with the effect depending on the utility function assumed.

In practice, this approach has two problems. The first is that specifying a utility function for an individual or analyst is difficult, if not impossible, to do with any degree of precision. In fact, as we noted in Chapter 3, most utility functions that are well behaved (mathematically) do not seem to explain actual behavior very well. The second is that, even if we were able to specify a utility function, this approach would require us to lay out all the scenarios that can unfold for an asset (with corresponding probabilities) for every period. Not surprisingly, certainty equivalents from utility functions have been largely restricted to analyzing simple gambles.

Risk-and-Return Models

A more practical approach to converting uncertain cash flows into certainty equivalents is offered by risk-and-return models. In fact, we would use the same approach to estimating risk premiums that we employed while computing risk-adjusted discount rates but we would use the premiums to estimate certainty equivalents instead.

Certainty equivalent cash flow = Expected cash flow / (1 + Risk premium in risk – adjusted discount rate)

Consider the risk-adjusted discount rate of 13.45 percent that we estimated for Google in early 2006.

Expected return on Google = 4.25 percent + 2.25 (4.09 percent) = 13.45 percent

4   Gregory, D. D. "Multiplicative Risk Premiums." *Journal of Financial and Quantitative Analysis*, Vol. 13, 947–963, 1978. This paper derives certainty equivalent functions for quadratic, exponential, and gamma-distributed utility functions and examines their behavior.

Instead of discounting the expected cash flows on the stock at 13.45 percent, we would decompose the expected return into a risk-free rate of 4.25 percent and a compounded risk premium of 8.825 percent.[5]

$$\text{Compounded risk premium} = \frac{(1+\text{Risk} - \text{adjusted Discount Rate})}{(1+\text{Risk} - \text{free Rate})} - 1 = \frac{(1.1345)}{(1.0425)} - 1 = .08825$$

If the expected cash flow in years 1 and 2 is $100 million and $120 million respectively, we can compute the certainty-equivalent cash flows in those years.

Certainty-equivalent cash flow in year 1 = $100 million / 1.08825 = $ 91.89 million

Certainty-equivalent cash flow in year 2 = $120 million / 1.08825^2 = $ 101.33 million

This process would be repeated for all the expected cash flows. The adjustment process for certainty equivalents can be written more formally as follows (where the risk-adjusted return is r and the risk-free rate is r_f:[6])

$$CE\ (CF_t) = \alpha_t\ E(CF_t) = \frac{(1+r_f)^t}{(1+r)^t} E(CF_t)$$

This adjustment has two effects. The first is that expected cash flows with higher uncertainty associated with them have lower certainty equivalents than more predictable cash flows at the same point in time. The second is that the effect of uncertainty compounds over time, making the certainty equivalents of uncertain cash flows further into the future lower than uncertain cash flows that will occur sooner.

Cash Flow Haircuts

A far more common approach to adjusting cash flows for uncertainty is to *haircut* the uncertain cash flows subjectively. Thus, an analyst, faced with uncertainty, will replace uncertain cash flows with conservative or lowball estimates. This is a weapon commonly employed by analysts, who are forced to use the same discount rate for projects of different risk levels and want to even the playing field. They will haircut the cash flows of

---

5   A more common approximation used by many analysts is the difference between the risk-adjusted discount rate and the risk-free rate. In this case, that would have yielded a risk premium of 9.2 percent (13.45 percent – 4.25 percent = 9.20 percent).

6   This equation was first derived in a paper in 1966: Robichek, A. A. and S. C. Myers. "Conceptual Problems in the Use of Risk Adjusted Discount Rates." *Journal of Finance*, Vol. 21, 727–730,1966.

riskier projects to make them lower, thus hoping to compensate for the failure to adjust the discount rate for the additional risk.

In a variant of this approach, some investors consider only those asset cash flows that are predictable and ignore risky or speculative cash flows when valuing the asset. Warren Buffet expresses his disdain for the CAPM and other risk-and-return models and claims to use the risk-free rate as the discount rate. We suspect that he can get away with doing so because of a combination of the types of companies he chooses to invest in and his inherent conservatism when it comes to estimating the cash flows.

Although cash flow haircuts retain their intuitive appeal, we should be wary of their usage. After all, gut feelings about risk can vary widely across analysts looking at the same asset; more risk-averse analysts will tend to haircut the cash flows on the same asset more than less risk-averse analysts. Furthermore, the distinction between diversifiable and market risk that we drew in the previous chapter can be completely lost when analysts are making intuitive adjustments for risk. In other words, the cash flows may be adjusted downward for risk that will be eliminated in a portfolio. The absence of transparency about the risk adjustment can also lead to the double counting of risk, especially when there are multiple layers of analysis. As a means of illustration, after the first analyst looking at a risky investment decides to use conservative estimates of the cash flows, the analysis may pass to a second stage, where his superior may decide to make an additional risk adjustment to the cash flows.

Risk-Adjusted Discount Rate or Certainty-Equivalent Cash Flow

Adjusting the discount rate for risk or replacing uncertain expected cash flows with certainty equivalents are alternative approaches to adjusting for risk, but do they yield different values, and if so, which one is more precise? The answer lies in how we compute certainty equivalents. If we use the risk premiums from risk-and-return models to compute certainty equivalents, the values obtained from the two approaches will be the same. After all, adjusting the cash flow, using the certainty equivalent, and then discounting the cash flow at the risk-free rate is equivalent to discounting the cash flow at a risk-adjusted discount rate. To see this, consider an asset with a single cash flow in one year and assume that r is the risk-adjusted cash flow, r_f is the risk-free rate, and RP is the compounded risk premium computed as described earlier in this section.

$$\text{Certainty-equivalent value} = \frac{\text{CE}}{(1+r_f)} = \frac{\text{E(CF)}}{(1+\text{RP})(1+r_f)} = \frac{\text{E(CF)}}{\frac{(1+r)}{(1+r_f)}(1+r_f)} = \frac{\text{E(CF)}}{(1+r)}$$

This analysis can be extended to multiple periods and will still hold.[7] Note, though, that if the approximation for the risk premium, computed as the difference between the risk-adjusted return and the risk-free rate, had been used, this equivalence would no longer hold. In that case, the certainty equivalent approach would give lower values for any risky asset, and the difference would increase with the size of the risk premium.

Are there other scenarios where the two approaches will yield different values for the same risky asset? The first is when the risk-free rates and risk premiums change from period to period; the risk-adjusted discount rate will also then change from period to period. Robichek and Myers, in the paper we referenced earlier, argue that the certainty-equivalent approach yields more precise estimates of value in this case. The other is when the certainty equivalents are computed from utility functions or subjectively, whereas the risk-adjusted discount rate comes from a risk-and-return model. The two approaches can yield different estimates of value for a risky asset. Finally, the two approaches deal with negative cash flows differently. The risk-adjusted discount rate discounts negative cash flows at a higher rate, and the present value becomes less negative as the risk increases. If certainty equivalents are computed from utility functions, they can yield certainty equivalents that are negative and become more negative as you increase risk, a finding that is more consistent with intuition.[8]

Hybrid Models

Risk-adjusted discount rates and certainty equivalents come with pluses and minuses. For some market-wide risks, such as exposure to interest rates, economic growth, and inflation, it is often easier to estimate the parameters for a risk-and-return model and the risk-adjusted discount rate. For other risks, especially those occurring infrequently but that can have a large impact on value, it may be easier to adjust the expected cash flows. Consider, for instance, the risk that a company is exposed to from an investment in India, China, or any other large emerging market. In most periods, the investment will be like an investment in a developed market; however, in some periods, there is the potential for major political and economic disruptions and consequent changes in value. Although we can attempt to incorporate this risk into the discount rate,[9] it may be easier to adjust the cash flows for this risk, especially if the possibility of insuring against this

---

7   The proposition that risk-adjusted discount rates and certainty equivalents yield identical net present values is shown in the following paper: Stapleton, R. C. "Portfolio Analysis, Stock Valuation, and Capital Budgeting Decision Rules for Risky Projects." *Journal of Finance.* Vol. 26, 95–117, 1971.

8   Beedles, W. L. "Evaluating Negative Benefits." *Journal of Financial and Quantitative Analysis*, Vol. 13, 173–17,1978.

9   Damodaran, A. *Investment Valuation.* New York: John Wiley and Sons, 2002. Several approaches for adjusting discount rates for country risk are presented in this book.

risk exists. If so, the cost of buying insurance can be incorporated into the expenses, and the resulting cash flow can be adjusted for the insured risk (but not against other risks). An alternate approach to adjusting cash flows can be used if a risk is triggered by a specific contingency. For instance, a gold mining company that will default on its debt if the gold price drops below $250 an ounce can either obtain or estimate the cost of a put option on gold, with a strike price of $250, and include the cost when computing cash flows.

The biggest dangers arise when analysts use an amalgam of approaches, where the cash flows are adjusted partially for risk, usually subjectively, and the discount rate is also adjusted for risk. It is easy to double-count risk in these cases. The risk adjustment to value often becomes difficult to decipher. To prevent this from happening, it is best to categorize the risks that a project faces and then to be explicit about how the risk will be adjusted in the analysis. In the most general terms, risks can then be categorized as follows in Table 5.1.

Table 5.1   Risks: Types and Adjustment

Type of Risk	Examples	Risk Adjustment in Valuation
Continuous market risk where buying protection against consequences is difficult or impossible to do.	Interest rate risk, inflation risk, exposure to economic cyclicality.	Adjust the discount rate for risk.
Discontinuous market risk, with small likelihood of occurrence but large economic consequences.	Political risk, risk of expropriation, terrorism risk.	If insurance markets exist, include the cost of insurance as an operating expense and adjust cash flows. If not, adjust the discount rate.
Market risk that is contingent on a specific occurrence.	Commodity price risk.	Estimate the cost of an option required to hedge against risk, include it as an operating expense, and adjust cash flows.
Firm-specific risks.	Estimation risk, competitive risk, technology risk.	If investors in the firm are diversified, no risk adjustment is needed. If investors are not diversified, follow the same rules used for market risk.

We will use a simple example to illustrate the risk-adjusted discount rate, the certainty equivalent, and the hybrid approaches. Assume that Disney is considering investing in a new theme park in Thailand and that Table 5.2 contains the estimates of the cash flows that they believe they can generate over the next 10 years on this investment.

Table 5.2   Expected Cash Flows for Bangkok Disney (in U.S. Dollars)

Year	Annual Cash Flow (in millions)	Terminal Value (in millions)
0	−$2,000	
1	−$1,000	
2	−$880	
3	−$289	
4	$324	
5	$443	
6	$486	
7	$517	
8	$571	
9	$631	
10	$663	$7,810

Note that the cash flows are estimated in dollars, purely for convenience, and that the entire analysis could have been done in the local currency. The negative cash flows in the first three years represent the initial investment, and the terminal value is an estimate of the value of the theme park investments at the end of the tenth year.

We will first estimate a risk-adjusted discount rate for this investment, based on both the riskiness of the theme park business and the fact that the theme parks will be located in Thailand, thus exposing Disney to some additional political and economic risk.

Cost of capital = Risk-free rate + Business risk premium + Country risk premium

= 4 percent + 3.90 percent + 2.76 percent = 10.66 percent

The business risk premium is reflective of the nondiversifiable or market risk of being in the theme park business,[10] whereas the country risk premium reflects the risk involved in the location.[11] Appendix 5.1 includes a fuller description of these adjustments. The risk-adjusted value of the project can be estimated by discounting the expected cash flows at the risk-adjusted cost of capital (in Table 5.3).

Table 5.3   Risk-Adjusted Value: Risk-Adjusted Discount Rate Approach

Year	Annual Cash Flow	Salvage Value	Present Value @10.66 percent
0	−$2,000		−$2,000
1	−$1,000		−$904
2	−$880		−$719
3	−$289		−$213
4	$324		$216
5	$443		$267
6	$486		$265
7	$517		$254
8	$571		$254
9	$631		$254
10	$663	$7,810	$3,077
Risk-Adjusted Value =			$751

As an alternative, let's try the certainty-equivalent approach. For purposes of simplicity, we will strip the total risk premium in the cost of capital and use this number to convert the expected cash flows into certainty equivalents in Table 5.4.

$$\text{Risk premium in cost of capital} = \frac{1+\text{Risk}-\text{adjusted Cost of Capital}}{1+\text{Risk}-\text{free Rate}} - 1$$

$$= 1.1066 / 1.04 - 1 = 6.4038 \text{ percent}$$

---

10   For a more detailed discussion of the computation, check Damodaran, A. *Applied Corporate Finance*, Second Edition. New York: John Wiley and Sons, 2005.

11   The additional risk premium was based on Thailand's country rating and default spread as a country, augmented for the additional risk of equity. The details of this calculation are also in Damodaran, A. *Applied Corporate Finance*, Second Edition. New York: John Wiley and Sons, 2005.

Table 5.4 Certainty-Equivalent Cash Flows and Risk-Adjusted Value

Year	Annual Cash Flow (in millions)	Terminal Value (in millions)	Certainty Equivalent	Present Value @ 4 Percent
0	−$2,000		−$2,000	−$2,000
1	−$1,000		−$940	−$904
2	−$880		−$777	−$719
3	−$289		−$240	−$213
4	$324		$252	$216
5	$443		$324	$267
6	$486		$335	$265
7	$517		$335	$254
8	$571		$348	$254
9	$631		$361	$254
10	$663	$7,810	$4,555	$3,077
Risk-Adjusted Value =				$751

Note that the certainty-equivalent cash flows are discounted back at the risk-free rate to yield the same risk-adjusted value as in the first approach. Not surprisingly, the risk-adjusted value is identical to this approach.[12]

Finally, let us assume that we could insure at least against country risk and that the after-tax cost of buying this insurance will be $150 million a year, each year for the next 10 years. Reducing the expected cash flows by the after-tax cost of insurance yields the after-tax cash flows in Table 5.5.

These cash flows are discounted back at a risk-adjusted discount rate of 7.90 percent (that is, without the country risk adjustment) to arrive at the present value in the last column. The risk-adjusted value in this approach of $670 million is different from the estimates in the first two approaches because the insurance market's perceptions of risk are different from those that gave rise to the country risk premium of 2.76 percent in the first two analyses.

---

12 Using the approximate risk premium of 6.66 percent (risk-adjusted cost of capital minus the risk-free rate) would have yielded a value of $661 million.

Table 5.5   Expected Cash Flows After Insurance Payments

Year	Annual Cash Flow (in millions)	Terminal Value (in millions)	Insurance Payment (in millions)	Adjusted Cash Flow	PV @ 7.90 Percent
0	−$2,000		$150	−$2,150	−$2,150
1	−$1,000		$150	−$1,150	−$1,066
2	−$880		$150	−$1,030	−$885
3	−$289		$150	−$439	−$350
4	$324		$150	$174	$128
5	$443		$150	$293	$200
6	$486		$150	$336	$213
7	$517		$150	$367	$216
8	$571		$150	$421	$229
9	$631		$150	$481	$243
10	$663	$7,810	$150	$8,324	$3,891
					$670

DCF Risk Adjustment: Pluses and Minuses

There are good reasons why risk adjustment is most often done in a discounted cash flow framework. When the risk adjustment is made through a risk-and-return model, whether it is the CAPM, the arbitrage pricing model, or a multifactor model, the effect is transparent and clearly visible to others looking at the valuation. If they disagree with the computation, they can change it. In addition, the models are explicit about the risks that are adjusted for and the risks that do not affect the discount rate. In the CAPM, for instance, it is only the risks that cannot be diversified away by a well-diversified investor that are reflected in the beta.

There are, however, costs associated with letting risk-and-return models carry the burden of capturing the consequences of risk. Analysts take the easy way out when it comes to assessing risk, using the beta or betas of assets to measure risk and them moving on to estimate cash flows and value, secure in the comfort that they have already considered the effects of risk and its consequences for value. In reality, risk-and-return models make assumptions about how both markets and investors behave that are at odds with actual behavior. Given the complicated relationship between investors and risk, we may not be able to capture the effects of risk fully into a discount rate or a cash flow adjustment.

Post-Valuation Risk Adjustment

A second approach to assessing risk is to value a risky investment or asset as if it had no risk and then to adjust the value for risk after the valuation. These post-valuation adjustments usually take the form of discounts to assessed value, but there are cases where the potential for upside from risk is reflected in premiums.

It is possible to adjust for all risk in the post-valuation phase—by discounting expected cash flows at a risk-free rate and then applying a discount to that value—but the tools that are necessary for making this adjustment are the same ones we use to compute risk-adjusted discount rates and certainty equivalents. Consequently, it is uncommon, and most analysts who want to adjust for risk prefer to use the conventional approach of adjusting the discount rates or cash flows. The more common practice with post-valuation adjustments is for analysts to capture some of the risks that they perceive in a risk-adjusted discount rate and deal with other risks in the post-valuation phase as discounts or premiums. Thus, an analyst valuing a private company will first value it using a high discount rate to reflect its business risk but then apply an illiquidity discount to the computed value to arrive at the final value estimate.

In this section, we will begin by looking at why analysts are drawn to the practice of post-valuation discounts and premiums and follow up by taking a closer look at some of the common risk adjustments. We will end the section by noting the dangers of what we call value garnishing.

Rationale for Post-Valuation Adjustments

Post-valuation risk discounts reflect the belief on the part of analysts that conventional risk-and-return models shortchange or even ignore what they see as significant risks. Consider again the illiquidity discount. The CAPM and multifactor models do not explicitly adjust expected returns for illiquidity. In fact, the expected return on two stocks with the same beta will be equal, even though one might be widely traded and liquid and the other not. Analysts valuing illiquid assets or businesses therefore feel that they are overvaluing these investments, using conventional risk-and-return models; the illiquidity discount is their way of bringing the estimated value down to a more "reasonable" number.

The rationale for applying post-valuation premiums is different. Premiums are usually motivated by the concern that the expected cash flows do not fully capture the potential for large payoffs in some investments. An analyst who believes that there is synergy in a merger and does not feel that the cash flows reflect this synergy will add a premium for it to the estimated value.

Downside Risks

It is common to see valuations where the initial assessments of value of a risky asset are discounted by 30 percent or 40 percent for one potential downside risk or another. In this section, we will examine perhaps the most common of these discounts—for illiquidity or lack of marketability—in detail and the dangers associated with the practice.

Illiquidity Discount

When you invest in an asset, you generally would like to preserve the option to liquidate that investment if you need to. The need for liquidity arises not only because your views on the asset value change over time—you may perceive it as a bargain today, but it may become overpriced in the future—but also because you may need the cash from the liquidation to meet other contingencies. Some assets can be liquidated with almost no cost—Treasury bills are a good example—whereas others involve larger costs—such as stock in a lightly traded over-the-counter stock or real estate. With investments in a private business, liquidation cost as a percent of firm value can be substantial. Consequently, the value of equity in a private business may need to be discounted for this potential illiquidity. In this section, we will consider measures of illiquidity, how much investors value illiquidity, and how analysts try to incorporate illiquidity into value.

Measuring Illiquidity

You can sell any asset, no matter how illiquid it is perceived to be, if you are willing to accept a lower price for it. Consequently, we should not categorize assets into liquid and illiquid assets but allow for a continuum on liquidity, where all assets are illiquid but the degree of illiquidity varies across them. One way of capturing the cost of illiquidity is through transactions costs, with less liquid assets bearing higher transactions costs (as a percent of asset value) than more liquid assets.

With publicly traded stock, some investors undoubtedly operate under the misconception that the only cost of trading is the brokerage commission that they pay when they buy or sell assets. Although this might be the only cost that they pay explicitly, they will incur other costs in the course of trading that generally dwarf the commission cost. When we trade any asset, there are three other ingredients that go into the trading costs.

- The first cost is the *spread* between the price at which you can buy an asset (the dealer's ask price) and the price at which you can sell the same asset at the same point in time (the dealer's bid price). For heavily traded stocks on the New York Stock Exchange, this cost will be small (10 cents on a $50 stock, for instance), but the costs will increase as we move to smaller, less-traded companies. A lightly traded stock may have an ask price of $2.50 and a bid price of $2.00, and the resulting bid-ask spread of 50 cents will be 20 percent of the ask price.

■ The second cost is the *price impact* that an investor can create by trading on an asset, pushing the price up when buying the asset and pushing it down while selling. As with the bid-ask spread, this cost will be highest for the least liquid stocks, where even relatively small orders can cause the price to move. It will also vary across investors, with the costs being higher for large institutional investors like Fidelity who have to buy and sell large blocks of shares, and lower for individual investors.

■ The third cost, which was first proposed by Jack Treynor in his article[13] on transactions costs, is the *opportunity cost* associated with waiting to trade. Although being a patient trader may reduce the first two components of trading cost, the waiting can cost profits both on trades that are made and in terms of trades that would have been profitable if made instantaneously but which became unprofitable as a result of the waiting.

It is the sum of these costs, in conjunction with the commission costs, that makes up the trading cost of an asset.

If the cost of trading stocks can be substantial, it should be even larger for assets that are not traded regularly, such as real assets or equity positions in private companies.

■ Real assets can range from gold to real estate to fine art, and the transactions costs associated with trading these assets can vary substantially. The smallest transactions costs are associated with commodities—gold, silver, or oil—because they tend to come in standardized units and are widely traded. With residential real estate, the commission that you have to pay a real estate broker or salesperson can be 5–6 percent of the value of the asset. With commercial real estate, commissions may be smaller for larger transactions, but they will be well in excess of commissions on financial assets. With fine art or collectibles, the commissions become even higher. If you sell a Picasso through one of the auction houses, you may have to pay 15–20 percent of the value of the painting as a commission. Why are the costs so high? The first reason is that there are far fewer intermediaries in real asset businesses than there are in the stock or bond

---

13 This was proposed in his article titled "What does it take to win the trading game?" *Financial Analysts Journal*, January–February 1981.

markets. The second is that real estate and fine art are not standardized products. In other words, one Picasso can be very different from another, and you often need the help of experts to judge value. This adds to the cost in the process.

- The trading costs associated with buying and selling a private business can range from substantial to prohibitive, depending on the size of the business, the composition of its assets, and its profitability. There are relatively few potential buyers, and the search costs (associated with finding these buyers) will be high. Later in this chapter, we will put the conventional practice of applying 20–30 percent illiquidity discounts to the values of private businesses under the microscope.

- The difficulties associated with selling private businesses can spill over into smaller equity stakes in these businesses. Thus, private equity investors and venture capitalists have to consider the potential illiquidity of their private company investments when considering how much they should pay for them (and what stake they should demand in private businesses in return).

In summary, the costs of trading assets that are usually not traded are likely to be substantial.

Theoretical Backing for an Illiquidity Discount

Assume that you are an investor trying to determine how much you should pay for an asset. In making this determination, you have to consider the cash flows that the asset will generate for you and how risky these cash flows are to arrive at an estimate of intrinsic value. You will also have to consider how much it will cost you to sell this asset when you decide to divest it in the future. In fact, if the investor buying the asset from you builds in a similar estimate of transactions cost she will face when she sells it, the value of the asset today should reflect the expected value of all future transactions cost to all future holders of the asset. This is the argument that Amihud and Mendelson used in 1986, when they suggested that the price of an asset would embed the present value of the costs associated with expected transactions costs in the future.[14] In their model, the bid-ask spread is used as the measure of transactions costs, and even small spreads can translate into big illiquidity discounts on value, if trading is frequent. The magnitude of the discount will be a function of investor holding periods and turnover ratios, with shorter holding periods and higher turnover associated with bigger discounts. In more intuitive terms, if you face a 1 percent bid-ask spread and you expect to trade once a year, the value of the asset today should be reduced by the present value of the costs you will pay in perpetuity. With an 8 percent discount rate, this will work out to roughly an illiquidity discount of 12.5 percent (.01/.08).

---

14 Amihud, Y., and H. Mendelson. "Asset Pricing and the Bid-Ask Spread." *Journal of Financial Economics,* Vol. 17, 223–250,1986.

What is the value of liquidity? Put differently, when does an investor feel the loss of liquidity most strongly when holding an asset? Some would argue that the value of liquidity lies in being able to sell an asset, when it is most overpriced; the cost of illiquidity is not being able to do this. In the special case where the owner of an asset has the information to know when this overpricing occurs, the value of illiquidity can be considered an option. Longstaff presents an upper bound for the option by considering an investor with perfect market timing abilities who owns an asset on which she is not allowed to trade for a period (t). In the absence of trading restrictions, this investor would sell at the maximum price that an asset reached during the period. The value of the look-back option estimated using this maximum price should be the outer bound for the value of illiquidity.[15] Using this approach, Longstaff estimates how much marketability would be worth as a percent of the value of an asset for different illiquidity periods and asset volatilities. The results are graphed in Figure 5.1.

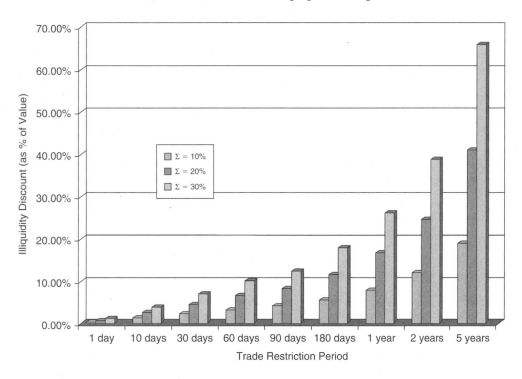

Figure 5.1: Upper bounds on Marketability Discount - Option Pricing Model

---

15   Longstaff, F. A. "How much can marketability affect security values?" *Journal of Finance*, Vol. 50, 1767–1774, 1995.

It is worth emphasizing that these are upper bounds on the value of illiquidity because it is based on the assumption of a perfect market timer. To the extent that investors are unsure about when an asset has reached its maximum price, the value of illiquidity will be lower than these estimates. The more general lessons will still apply. The cost of illiquidity, stated as a percent of firm value, will be greater for more volatile assets and will increase with the length of the period for which trading is restricted.

Empirical Evidence that Illiquidity Matters

If we accept the proposition that illiquidity has a cost, the next question becomes an empirical one. How big is this cost, and what causes it to vary across time and across assets? The evidence on the prevalence and the cost of illiquidity is spread over a number of asset classes.

- **Bond market**—There are wide differences in liquidity across bonds issued by different entities, and even across bonds issued by the same entity. These differences in liquidity offer us an opportunity to examine whether investors price liquidity and if so, how much, by comparing the yields of liquid bonds with otherwise similar illiquid bonds.

  Amihud and Mendelson compared the yields on treasury bonds with less than six months left to maturity with Treasury bills that had the same maturity.[16] They concluded that the yield on the less liquid Treasury bond was 0.43 percent higher on an annualized basis than the yield on the more liquid Treasury bill, a difference that they attributed to illiquidity. A study of more than 4,000 corporate bonds in both investment-grade and speculative categories concluded that illiquid bonds had much higher yield spreads than liquid bonds. Comparing yields on these corporate bonds, the study concluded that the yield increases 0.21 percent for every 1 percent increase in transactions costs for investment-grade bonds, whereas the yield increases 0.82 percent for every 1 percent increase in transactions costs for speculative bonds.[17] Looking across the studies, the consensus finding is that liquidity matters for all bonds, but it matters more with risky bonds than with safer bonds.

- **Publicly traded stocks**—It can be reasonably argued that the costs associated with trading equities are larger than the costs associated with trading Treasury bonds or bills. It follows, therefore, that some of the equity risk premium, which we discussed in Chapter 4, has to reflect these additional transactions costs.

---

16   Amihud, Y., and H. Mendelson. "Liquidity, Maturity and the Yield on U.S. Treasury Securities." *Journal of Finance*, 46, 1411–1425, 1991.

17   Chen, L., D. A. Lesmond, and J. Wei. "Corporate Yield Spreads and Bond Liquidity." Working Paper, SSRN, 2005.

Jones, for instance, examined bid-ask spreads and transactions costs for the Dow Jones stocks from 1900 to 2000 and concluded that the transactions costs are about 1 percent lower today than they were in the early 1900s, and this may account for the lower equity risk premium in recent years.[18] Within the stock market, some stocks are more liquid than others, and studies have looked at the consequences of these differences in liquidity for returns. The consensus conclusion is that investors demand higher returns when investing in more illiquid stocks. Put another way, investors are willing to pay higher prices for more liquid investments relative to less liquid investments.

- **Restricted stocks**—Much of the evidence on illiquidity discounts comes from examining "restricted stock" issued by publicly traded firms. Restricted securities are securities issued by a publicly traded company, not registered with the SEC, and sold through private placements to investors under SEC Rule 144. They cannot be resold in the open market for a one-year holding period,[19] and limited numbers can be sold after that. When this stock is issued, the issue price is set much lower than the prevailing market price, which is observable, and the difference can be viewed as a discount for illiquidity. The results of two of the earliest and most quoted studies that have looked at the magnitude of this discount are summarized here.

  - Maher examined restricted stock purchases made by four mutual funds in the period 1969 to 1973 and concluded that they traded an average discount of 35.43 percent on publicly traded stock in the same companies.[20]

  - Silber examined restricted stock issues from 1981 to 1988 and found that the median discount for restricted stock is 33.75 percent.[21] He also noted that the discount was larger for smaller and less healthy firms and for bigger blocks of shares.

  Other studies confirm these findings of a substantial discount, with discounts ranging from 30–35 percent, although one recent study by Johnson did find a

---

18   This becomes clear when we look at forward-looking or implied equity risk premiums rather than historical risk premiums. The premiums during the 1990s averaged about 3 percent, whereas there were more than 5 percent prior to 1960. Jones, C. M. "A Century of Stock Market Liquidity and Trading Costs." Working Paper, Columbia University, 2002.

19   The holding period was two years prior to 1997 and has been reduced to one year since.

20   Maher, J. M. "Discounts for Lack of Marketability for Closely Held Business Interests." *Taxes*, 54, 562–571, 1976.

21   Silber, W. L. "Discounts on Restricted Stock: The Impact of Illiquidity on Stock Prices." *Financial Analysts Journal*, Vol. 47, 60–64, 1991.

smaller discount of 20 percent.[22] These studies have been used by practitioners to justify large marketability discounts, but there are reasons to be skeptical. First, these studies are based on small sample sizes, spread out over long periods, and the standard errors in the estimates are substantial. Second, most firms do not make restricted stock issues, and the firms that do make these issues tend to be smaller, riskier, and less healthy than the typical firm. This selection bias may be skewing the observed discount. Third, the investors with whom equity is privately placed may be providing other services to the firm, for which the discount is compensation.

- **Private equity**—Private equity and venture capital investors often provide capital to private businesses in exchange for a share of the ownership in these businesses. Implicit in these transactions must be the recognition that these investments are not liquid. If private equity investors value liquidity, they will discount the value of the private business for this illiquidity and demand a larger share of the ownership of illiquid businesses for the same investment. Looking at the returns earned by private equity investors, relative to the returns earned by those investing in publicly traded companies, should provide a measure of how much value they attach to illiquidity. Ljungquist and Richardson estimate that private equity investors earn excess returns of 5 to 8 percent, relative to the public equity market, and this generates about 24 percent in risk-adjusted additional value to a private equity investor over 10 years. They interpret it to represent compensation for holding an illiquid investment for 10 years.[23] Das, Jagannathan, and Sarin take a more direct approach to estimating private company discounts by looking at how venture capitalists value businesses (and the returns they earn) at different stages of the life cycle. They conclude that the discount is only 11 percent for late-stage investments but can be as high as 80 percent for early-stage businesses.[24]

Illiquidity Discounts in Practice

The standard practice in many private company valuations is to either use a fixed illiquidity discount for all firms or, at best, to have a range for the discount, with the analyst's subjective judgment determining where in the range a particular company's

---

22   B. A. Johnson. "Quantitative Support for Discounts for Lack of Marketability." *Business Valuation Review*, Vol. 16, 152–155, 1999.

23   Ljungquist, A., and M. Richardson. "The Cashflow, Return and Risk Characteristics of Private Equity." Working Paper, Stern School of Business, 2003.

24   Das, S., M. Jagannathan, and A. Sarin. "The Private Equity Discount: An Empirical Examination of the Exit of Venture Capital Companies." Working Paper, SSRN, 2002.

discount should fall. The evidence for this practice can be seen in both the handbooks most widely used in private company valuation and in the court cases where these valuations are often cited. The genesis for these fixed discounts seems to be in the early studies of restricted stock that we noted in the previous section. These studies found that restricted (and therefore illiquid) stocks traded at discounts of 25–35 percent, relative to their unrestricted counterparts, and private company appraisers have used discounts of the same magnitude in their valuations.[25] Because many of these valuations are for tax court, we can see the trail of "restricted stock"-based discounts littering the footnotes of dozens of cases in the past three decades.[26]

In recent years, analysts have become more creative in their measurement of the illiquidity discount. They have used option pricing models and studies of transactions just prior to initial public offerings to motivate their estimates and been more willing to estimate firm-specific illiquidity discounts.[27] Appendix 5.2 describes some of the approaches used to compute liquidity discounts.

Other Discounts

Although illiquidity discounts are the most common example of post-valuation discounts, other risks also show up as post-valuation adjustments. For instance, analysts valuing companies that are subject to regulation will sometimes discount the value for uncertainty about future regulatory changes and companies that have exposure to lawsuits for adverse judgments on these cases. In each of these cases, analysts have concluded that the risk was significant but difficult to incorporate into a discount rate. In practice, the discounts tend to be subjective and reflect the analysts' overall risk aversion and perception of the magnitude of the risk.

---

25 In recent years, some appraisers have shifted to using the discounts on stocks in IPOs in the years prior to the offering. The discount is similar in magnitude to the restricted stock discount.

26 As an example, in one widely cited tax court case (McCord versus Commissioner, 2003), the expert for the taxpayer used a discount of 35 percent that he backed up with four restricted stock studies.

27 One common device used to compute illiquidity discounts is to value an at-the-money put option with the illiquidity period used as the life of the option and the variance in publicly traded stocks in the same business as the option volatility. The IPO studies compare prices at which individuals sell their shares in companies just prior to an IPO to the IPO price; the discounts range from 40–60 percent and are attributed to illiquidity.

Upside Risks

Just as analysts try to capture downside risk that is missed by the discount rates in a post-valuation discount, they try to bring in upside potential that is not fully incorporated into the cash flows into valuations as premiums. In this section, we will examine two examples of such premiums—control and synergy premiums—that show up widely in acquisition valuations.

Control Premium

It is common in private company and acquisition valuations to see premiums of 20 percent to 30 percent attached to estimated value to reflect the "value of control." But what exactly is this premium for? The value of controlling a firm derives from the fact that you believe that you or someone else would operate the firm differently from the way it is operated currently. When we value a business, we make implicit or explicit assumptions about both who will run that business and how they will run it. In other words, the value of a business will be much lower if we assume that it is run by incompetent managers rather than by competent ones. When valuing an existing company, private or public, where there is already a management in place, we are faced with a choice. We can value the company run by the incumbent managers and derive what we can call a *status quo value*. Or we can revalue the company with a hypothetical "optimal" management team and estimate an *optimal value*. The difference between the optimal and the status quo values can be considered the value of controlling the business.

If we apply this logic, the value of control should be much greater at badly managed and run firms and much smaller at well-managed firms. In addition, the expected value of control will reflect the difficulty you will face in replacing incumbent management. Consequently, the expected value of control should be smaller in markets where corporate governance is weak and larger in markets where hostile acquisitions and management changes are common.

Analysts who apply control premiums to value are therefore rejecting the path of explicitly valuing control by estimating an optimal value and computing a probability of management change in favor of a simpler but less precise approximation. To prevent double counting, they have to ensure that they are applying the premium to a status quo value and not to an optimal value. Implicitly, they are also assuming that the firm is badly run and that its value can be increased by a new management team.

Synergy Premium

Synergy is the additional value that is generated by combining two firms, creating opportunities that would not have been available to these firms operating independently. Operating synergies affect the operations of the combined firm and include economies of scale, increased pricing power, and higher growth potential. They generally show up as higher expected cash flows. Financial synergies, on the other hand, are more focused and include tax benefits, diversification, a higher debt capacity, and uses for excess cash. They sometimes show up as higher cash flows and sometimes take the form of lower discount rates.

Because we can quantify the impact of synergy on cash flows and discount rates, we can explicitly value it. Many analysts, though, are either unwilling or unable to go through this exercise, arguing that synergy is too subjective and qualitative for the estimates to be reliable. Instead, they add significant premiums to estimated value to reflect potential synergies.

The Dangers of Post-Valuation Adjustments

Although the temptation is strong to adjust value for overlooked downside and upside risk, there are clearly significant dangers. The first is that these risks can be easily double-counted, if analysts bring their concerns about the risk into the estimation of discount rates and cash flows. In other words, an analyst valuing an illiquid asset may decide to use a higher discount rate for that asset because of its lack of marketability, thus pushing down value, and then proceed to apply a discount to that value. Similarly, an analyst evaluating an acquisition may increase the growth rate in cash flows to reflect the control and synergy benefits from the acquisition and thus increase value; attaching control and synergy premiums to this value will risk double-counting the benefits.

The second problem is that the magnitude of the discounts and premiums is, if not arbitrary, based on questionable evidence. For instance, the 20 percent control premium used so often in practice comes from looking at the premiums (over the market price) paid in acquisitions, but these premiums reflect not just control and synergy but also any overpayment on acquisitions. When these premiums become accepted in practice, they are seldom questioned or analyzed.

The third problem is that adjusting an estimated value with premiums and discounts opens the door for analysts to bring their biases into the number. Thus, an analyst who arrives at an estimate of $100 million for the value of a company and feels it is too low can always add a 20 percent control premium to get to $120 million, even though it may not be merited in this case.

Relative Valuation Approaches

The risk adjustment approaches we have talked about in this chapter have been built around the premise that assets are valued using discounted cash flow models. Thus, we can increase the discount rate, replace uncertain cash flows with certainty-equivalent numbers, or apply discounts to estimated value to bring risk into the value. Most valuations, in practice, are based on relative valuation—that is, the values of most assets are estimated by looking at how the market prices similar or comparable assets. In this section, we will examine the way analysts adjust for risk when doing relative valuation.

Basis for Approach

In relative valuation, the value of an asset is derived from the pricing of comparable assets, standardized using a common variable. Included in this description are two key components of relative valuation. The first is the notion of *comparable or similar* assets. From a valuation standpoint, this would imply assets with similar cash flows, risk, and growth potential. In practice, it is usually taken to mean other companies that are in the same business as the company being valued. The other is a *standardized price*. After all, the price per share of a company is in some sense arbitrary because it is a function of the number of shares outstanding; a two-for-one stock split would halve the price. Dividing the price or market value by some measure that is related to that value will yield a standardized price. When valuing stocks, this essentially translates into using multiples where we divide the market value by earnings, book value, or revenues to arrive at an estimate of standardized value. We can then compare these numbers across companies.

The simplest and most direct applications of relative valuations are with real assets where it is easy to find similar assets or even identical ones. The asking price for a Mickey Mantle rookie baseball card or a 1965 Ford Mustang is relatively easy to estimate given that there are other Mickey Mantle cards and 1965 Ford Mustangs out there and that the prices at which they have been bought and sold can be obtained. With equity valuation, relative valuation becomes more complicated by two realities. The first is the absence of similar assets, requiring us to stretch the definition of comparable to include companies that are different from the one that we are valuing. After all, what company in the world is similar to Microsoft or GE? The other is that different ways of standardizing prices (different multiples) can yield different values for the same company.

Risk Adjustment

The adjustments for risk in relative valuations are surprisingly rudimentary and require strong assumptions to be justified. To make matters worse, the adjustments are often implicit, rather than explicit, and completely subjective.

- **Sector comparisons**—In practice, analysts who are called upon to value a software company will compare it to other software companies and make no risk adjustments. Implicit is the assumption that all software firms are of equivalent risk and that their price earnings ratios can therefore be compared safely. As the risk characteristics of firms within sectors diverge, this approach will lead to misleading estimates of value for firms that have more or less risk than the average firm in the sector; the former will be overvalued and the latter will be undervalued.

- **Market capitalization or size**—In some cases, especially in sectors with lots of firms, analysts will compare a firm only to firms of roughly the same size (in terms of revenues or market capitalization). The implicit assumption is that smaller firms are riskier than larger firms and should trade at lower multiples of earnings, revenues, and book value.

- **Ratio-based comparisons**—An approach that adds a veneer or sophistication to relative valuation is to compute a ratio of value or returns to a measure of risk. For instance, portfolio managers will often compute the ratio of the expected return on an investment to its standard deviation; the resulting Sharpe ratio can be considered a measure of the returns you can expect to earn for a given unit of risk. Assets that have higher Sharpe ratios are considered better investments.

- **Statistical controls**—We can control for risk in a relative valuation statistically. Reverting to the software sector example, we can regress the PE ratios of software companies against their expected growth rates and some measure of risk (standard deviation in stock price or earnings, market capitalization, or beta) to see if riskier firms are priced differently from safer firms. The resulting output can be used to estimate predicted PE ratios for individual companies that control for the growth potential and risk of these companies.

DCF Versus Relative Valuation

It should come as no surprise that the risk adjustments in relative valuation do not match up to the risk adjustments in discounted cash flow valuation. The fact that risk is usually considered explicitly in discounted cash flow models gives them an advantage over relative valuations, with its ad-hoc treatment of risk. This advantage can be quickly dissipated, though, if we are sloppy about the way we risk-adjust the cash flows or discount rates or if we use arbitrary premiums and discounts on estimated value.

The nature of the risk adjustment in discounted cash flow valuation makes it more time and information intensive; we need more data, and it takes longer to adjust discount rates than to compare a software company's PE to the average for the software sector. If time or data is scarce, it should come as no surprise that individuals choose the less precise risk adjustment procedure embedded in relative valuation.

There is one final difference. In relative valuation, we are far more dependent on markets being right, at least on average, for the risk adjustment to work. In other words, even if we are correct in our assessment that all software companies have similar risk exposures, the market still has to price software companies correctly for the average price earnings ratio to be a good measure of an individual company's equity value. We may be dependent upon markets for some inputs in a DCF model—betas and risk premiums, for instance—but the assumption of market efficiency is less consequential.

The Practice of Risk Adjustment

In this chapter, we have described four ways of adjusting for risk: use a higher discount rate for risky assets, reduce uncertain expected cash flows, apply a discount to estimated value, and look at how the market is pricing assets of similar risk. Although each of these approaches can be viewed as self-standing and sufficient, analysts often use more than one approach to adjust for risk in the same valuation. In many discounted cash flow valuations, the discount rate is risk adjusted (using the CAPM or multifactor model), the cash flow projections are conservative (reflecting a cash flow risk adjustment), the terminal value is estimated using a multiple obtained by looking at comparable companies (relative valuation risk adjustment), and there is a post-valuation discount for illiquidity.

At the risk of repeating what we said in an earlier section, using multiple risk adjustment procedures in the same valuation not only makes it difficult to decipher the effect of the risk adjustment but also creates the risk of double-counting or even triple-counting the same risk in value.

Conclusion

With risk-adjusted values, we try to incorporate the effect of risk into our estimates of asset value. In this chapter, we began by looking at ways in which we can do this in a valuation. First, we can estimate a risk-adjusted discount rate, relying if need be on a risk-and-return model, which measures risk and converts it into a risk premium. Second, we can discount uncertain expected cash flows to reflect the uncertainty; if the risk premium computed in a risk-and-return model is used to accomplish this, the value obtained in this approach will be identical to the one estimated with risk-adjusted discount rates. Third, we can discount the estimated value of an asset for those risks that we believe have not been incorporated into the discount rate or the cash flows. Finally, we can use the market pricing of assets of similar risk to estimate the value for a risky asset. The difficulty of finding assets that have similar risk exposure leads to approximate solutions such as using other companies in the same business as the company being valued.

APPENDIX 5.1

Adjusting Discount Rates for Country Risk

In many emerging markets, there is little historical data, and the data that exists is too volatile to yield a meaningful estimate of the risk premium. To estimate the risk premium in these countries, let us start with the basic proposition that the risk premium in any equity market can be written as follows:

Equity risk premium = Base premium for mature equity market + Country premium

The country premium could reflect the extra risk in a specific market. This boils down our estimation to answering two questions:

- What should the base premium for a mature equity market be?

- How do we estimate the additional risk premium for individual countries?

To answer the first question, we will make the argument that the U.S. equity market is a mature market, and there is sufficient historical data in the United States to make a reasonable estimate of the risk premium. In fact, reverting to our discussion of historical premiums in the U.S. market, we will use the geometric average premium earned by stocks over Treasury bonds of 4.82 percent between 1928 and 2003. We chose the long period to reduce standard error, the Treasury bond to be consistent with our choice of a risk-free rate, and geometric averages to reflect our desire for a risk premium that we can use for longer-term expected returns. We can use three approaches to estimate the country risk premium.

- **Country bond default spreads**—Although there are several measures of country risk, one of the simplest and most easily accessible is the rating assigned to a country's debt by a ratings agency (S&P, Moody's, and IBCA all rate countries). These ratings measure default risk (rather than equity risk), but they are affected by many of the factors that drive equity risk—the stability of a country's currency, its budget and trade balances, and its political stability, for instance.[28]

---

28 The process by which country ratings are obtained is explained on the S&P Web site at http://www.ratings.standard-poor.com/criteria/index.htm.

The other advantage of ratings is that they come with default spreads over the U.S. Treasury bond. For instance, Brazil was rated B2 in early 2004 by Moody's, and the 10-year Brazilian C-bond, which is a dollar-denominated bond, was priced to yield 10.01 percent, or 6.01 percent more than the interest rate (4 percent) on a 10-year Treasury bond at the same time.[29] Analysts who use default spreads as measures of country risk typically add them on to both the cost of equity and debt of every company traded in that country. For instance, the cost of equity for a Brazilian company, estimated in U.S. dollars, will be 6.01 percent higher than the cost of equity of an otherwise similar U.S. company. If we assume that the risk premium for the United States and other mature equity markets is 4.82 percent, the cost of equity for a Brazilian company can be estimated as follows (with a U.S. Treasury bond rate of 4 percent and a beta of 1.2):

Cost of equity = Risk-free rate + Beta *(U.S. risk premium) + Country bond default spread

= 4 percent + 1.2 (4.82 percent) + 6.01 percent = 15.79 percent

In some cases, analysts add the default spread to the U.S. risk premium and multiply it by the beta. This increases the cost of equity for high beta companies and lowers them for low beta firms.

- **Relative standard deviation**—Some analysts believe that the equity risk premiums of markets should reflect the differences in equity risk, as measured by the volatilities of these markets. A conventional measure of equity risk is the standard deviation in stock prices; higher standard deviations are generally associated with more risk. If you scale the standard deviation of one market against another, you obtain a measure of relative risk.

$$\text{Relative Standard Deviation}_{\text{Country X}} = \frac{\text{Standard Deviation}_{\text{Country X}}}{\text{Standard Deviation}_{\text{US}}}$$

This relative standard deviation when multiplied by the premium used for U.S. stocks should yield a measure of the total risk premium for any market.

$$\text{Equity Risk Premium}_{\text{Country X}} = \text{Risk Premum}_{\text{US}} *\text{Relative Standard Deviation}_{\text{Country X}}$$

---

29 These yields were as of January 1, 2004. Although this is a market rate and reflects current expectations, country bond spreads are extremely volatile and can shift significantly from day to day. To counter this volatility, the default spread can be normalized by averaging the spread over time or by using the average default spread for all countries with the same rating as Brazil in early 2004.

Assume, for the moment, that you are using a mature market premium for the United States of 4.82 percent and that the annual standard deviation of U.S. stocks is 20 percent. The annualized standard deviation[30] in the Brazilian equity index was 36 percent, yielding a total risk premium for Brazil.

$$\text{Equity Risk Premium}_{\text{Brazil}} = 4.82\% * \frac{36\%}{20\%} = 8.67\%$$

The country risk premium can be isolated as follows.

$$\text{Country Risk Premium}_{\text{Brazil}} = 8.67\% - 4.82\% = 3.85\%$$

Although this approach has intuitive appeal, there are problems with using standard deviations computed in markets with widely different market structures and liquidity. There are risky emerging markets that have low standard deviations for their equity markets because the markets are illiquid. This approach will understate the equity risk premiums in those markets.

- **Default spreads + relative standard deviations**—The country default spreads that come with country ratings provide an important first step but still only measure the premium for default risk. Intuitively, we would expect the country equity risk premium to be higher than the country default risk spread. To address the issue of how much higher, we look at the volatility of the equity market in a country relative to the volatility of the bond market used to estimate the spread. This yields the following estimate for the country equity risk premium.

$$\text{Country Risk Premium} = \text{Country Default Spread} * \left(\frac{\sigma_{\text{Equity}}}{\sigma_{\text{Country Bond}}} \right)$$

To illustrate, consider the case of Brazil. As noted earlier, the dollar-denominated bonds issued by the Brazilian government trade with a default spread of 6.01 percent over the U.S. Treasury bond rate. The annualized standard deviation in the Brazilian equity index over the previous year was 36 percent, whereas the annualized standard deviation in the Brazilian dollar-denominated C-bond was

---

30 Both the U.S. and Brazilian standard deviations were computed using weekly returns for two years from the beginning of 2002 to the end of 2003. Although you could use daily standard deviations to make the same judgments, they tend to have much more noise in them.

27 percent.[31] The resulting additional country equity risk premium for Brazil is as follows.

$$\text{Brazil's Country Risk Premium} = 6.01\% \left(\frac{36\%}{27\%} \right) = 7.67\%$$

Note that this country risk premium will increase if the country rating drops or if the relative volatility of the equity market increases. It is also in addition to the equity risk premium for a mature market. Thus, the total equity risk premium for a Brazilian company using the approach and a 4.82 percent premium for the United States would be 12.49 percent.

Why should equity risk premiums have any relationship to country bond spreads? A simple explanation is that an investor who can make 11 percent on a dollar-denominated Brazilian government bond would not settle for an expected return of 10.5 percent (in dollar terms) on Brazilian equity. Both this approach and the previous one use the standard deviation in equity of a market to make a judgment about country risk premium, but they measure it relative to different bases. This approach uses the country bond as a base, whereas the previous one uses the standard deviation in the U.S. market. This approach assumes that investors are more likely to choose between Brazilian government bonds and Brazilian equity, whereas the previous approach assumes that the choice is across equity markets.

The three approaches to estimating country risk premiums will generally give you different estimates, with the bond default spread and relative equity standard deviation approaches yielding lower country risk premiums than the melded approach that uses both the country bond default spread and the equity and bond standard deviations. In the case of Brazil, for instance, the country risk premiums range from 3.85 percent using the relative equity standard deviation approach to 7.67 percent for the melded approach. We believe that the larger country risk premiums that emerge from the last approach are the most realistic for the immediate future, but that country risk premiums may decline over time. Just as companies mature and become less risky over time, countries also can mature and become less risky.

---

31 The standard deviation in C-bond returns also was computed using weekly returns over two years. Because their returns are in dollars and the returns on the Brazilian equity are in real, there is an inconsistency here. We did estimate the standard deviation on the Brazilian equity in dollars, but it made little difference to the overall calculation because the dollar standard deviation was close to 36 percent.

APPENDIX 5.2

Estimating the Illiquidity Discount

In conventional valuation, there is little scope for showing the effect of illiquidity. The cash flows are expected, the discount rate is usually reflective of the risk in the cash flows, and the present value we obtain is the value for a liquid business. With publicly traded firms, we then use this value, making the implicit assumption that illiquidity is not a large enough problem to factor into valuation. In private company valuations, analysts have been less willing (with good reason) to make this assumption. The standard practice in many private company valuations is to apply an illiquidity discount to this value. But how large should this discount be, and how can we best estimate it? This is a difficult question to answer empirically because the discount in private company valuations cannot be observed. Even if we were able to obtain the terms of all private firm transactions, note that what is reported is the *price* at which private firms are bought and sold. The *value* of these firms is not reported, and the illiquidity discount is the difference between the value and the price. In this section, we will consider four approaches that are in use—a fixed discount (with marginal and subjective adjustments for individual firm differences), a firm-specific discount based on a firm's characteristics, a discount obtained by estimating a synthetic bid-ask spread for an asset, and an option-based illiquidity discount.

Fixed Discount

The standard practice in many private company valuations is either to use a fixed illiquidity discount for all firms or, at best, to have a range for the discount, with the analyst's subjective judgment determining where in the range a particular company's discount should fall. The evidence for this practice can be seen in both the handbooks most widely used in private company valuation and in the court cases where these valuations are often cited. The genesis for these fixed discounts seems to be in the early studies of restricted stock that we noted in the chapter. These studies found that restricted (and therefore illiquid) stocks traded at discounts of 25–35 percent, relative to their unrestricted counterparts, and private company appraisers have used discounts of the same magnitude in their valuations.[32] Because many of these valuations are for tax court, we can see the trail of references to "restricted stock" in the footnotes of dozens of cases in the past three decades.[33]

As we noted in the chapter, some researchers have argued that these discounts are too large because of the sampling bias inherent in using restricted stock and that they should be replaced with smaller discounts. In recent years, the courts have begun to look favorably at these arguments. In a 2003 case,[34] the Internal Revenue Service, often at the short end of the illiquidity discount argument, was able to convince the judge that the conventional restricted stock discount was too large and to accept a smaller discount.

Firm-Specific Discount

Much of the theoretical and empirical discussion supports the view that illiquidity discounts should vary across assets and business. In particular, with a private company, you would expect the illiquidity discount to be a function of the size and the type of assets that the company owns. In this section, we will consider the determinants of the illiquidity discount and practical ways of estimating it.

Determinants of Illiquidity Discounts

With any asset, the illiquidity discount should be a function of the number of potential buyers for the asset and the ease with which that asset can be sold. Thus, the illiquidity discount should be relatively small for an asset with a large number of potential buyers (such as real estate) compared to an asset with a relatively small number of buyers (an expensive collectible). With private businesses, the illiquidity discount is likely to vary across both firms and buyers, which renders rules of thumb useless. Let us consider first some of the factors that may cause the discount to vary across firms.

---

32 In recent years, some appraisers have shifted to using the discounts on stocks in IPOs in the years prior to the offering. The discount is similar in magnitude to the restricted stock discount.

33 As an example, in one widely cited tax court case (McCord versus Commissioner, 2003), the expert for the taxpayer used a discount of 35 percent that he backed up with four restricted stock studies.

34 The court case was McCord versus Commissioner. In that case, the taxpayer's expert argued for a discount of 35 percent based on the restricted stock studies. The IRS argued for a discount of 7 percent, on the basis that a big portion of the observed discount in restricted stock, and IPO studies reflect factors other than liquidity. The court ultimately decided on an illiquidity discount of 20 percent.

- **Liquidity of assets owned by the firm**—The fact that a private firm is difficult to sell may be rendered moot if its assets are liquid and can be sold with no significant loss in value. A private firm with significant holdings of cash and marketable securities should have a lower illiquidity discount than one with factories or other assets for which there are relatively few buyers.

- **Financial health and cash flows of the firm**—A private firm that is financially healthy should be easier to sell than one that is not healthy. In particular, a firm with strong earnings and positive cash flows should be subject to a smaller illiquidity discount than one with losses and negative cash flows.

- **Possibility of going public in the future**—The greater the likelihood that a private firm can go public in the future, the lower the illiquidity discount that should be attached to its value. In effect, the probability of going public is built into the valuation of the private firm. To illustrate, the owner of a private e-commerce firm in 1998 or 1999 would not have had to apply much of a illiquidity discount to his firm's value, if any, because of the ease with which it could have been taken public in those years.

- **Size of the firm**—If we state the illiquidity discount as a percent of the value of the firm, it should become smaller as the size of the firm increases. In other words, the illiquidity discount should be smaller as a percent of firm value for private firms like Cargill and Koch Industries, which are worth billions of dollars, than it should be for a small firm worth $5 million.

- **Control component**—Investing in a private firm is decidedly more attractive when you acquire a controlling stake with your investment. A reasonable argument can be made that a 51 percent stake in a private business should be more liquid than a 49 percent stake in the same business.[35]

The illiquidity discount is also likely to vary across potential buyers because the desire for liquidity varies among investors. It is likely that those buyers who have deep pockets, longer time horizons, and see little or no need to cash out their equity positions will attach much lower illiquidity discounts to value, for similar firms, than buyers who do not possess these characteristics. The illiquidity discount is also likely to vary across time, as the market-wide desire for liquidity ebbs and flows. In other words, the illiquidity discount attached to the same business will change over time even for the same buyer.

---

35 See the companion paper on the value of control (http://www.damodaran.com: Look under Research & Papers).

Estimating Firm-Specific Illiquidity Discount

Although it is easy to convince skeptics that the illiquidity discount should vary across companies, it is much more difficult to get consensus on how to estimate the illiquidity discount for an individual company. In this section, we revert to the basis for the fixed discount studies and look for clues on why discounts vary across companies and how to incorporate these differences into illiquidity discounts.

Restricted Stock Studies

Earlier in this chapter, we looked at studies of the discount in restricted stock. One of the papers that we referenced by Silber (1991) examined factors that explained differences in discounts across various restricted stock by relating the size of the discount to observable firm characteristics including revenues and the size of the restricted stock offering. Silber reported the following regression.

$$LN(RPRS) = 4.33 + 0.036 \ln(REV) - 0.142\ LN(RBRT) + 0.174\ DERN + 0.332\ DCUST$$

where

RPRS = Restricted stock price / unrestricted stock price = 1 – illiquidity discount

REV = Revenues of the private firm (in millions of dollars)

RBRT = Restricted block relative to total common stock (in percent)

DERN = 1 if earnings are positive; 0 if earnings are negative

DCUST = 1 if there is a customer relationship with the investor; 0 otherwise

The illiquidity discount tends to be smaller for firms with higher revenues, decreases as the block offering decreases, and is lower when earnings are positive and when the investor has a customer relationship with the firm. These findings are consistent with some of the determinants that we identified in the previous section for the illiquidity premium. In particular, the discounts tend to be smaller for larger firms (at least as measured by revenues) and for healthy firms (with positive earnings being the measure of financial health). This would suggest that the conventional practice of using constant discounts across private firms is wrong and that we should be adjusting for differences across firms.

Consider again the regression that Silber presents on restricted stock. Not only does it yield a result specific to restricted stock, but it also provides a measure of how much lower the discount should be as a function of revenues. A firm with revenue of $20 million should have an illiquidity discount that is 1.19 percent lower than a firm with revenues of $10 million. Thus, we could establish a benchmark discount for a profitable firm with specified revenues (say $10 million) and adjust this benchmark discount for individual firms that have revenues much higher or lower than this number. The regression can also be used to differentiate between profitable and unprofitable firms. Figure 5A.1 presents the difference in illiquidity discounts across both profitable and unprofitable firms with different revenues, using a benchmark discount of 25 percent for a firm with positive earnings and $10 million revenues.

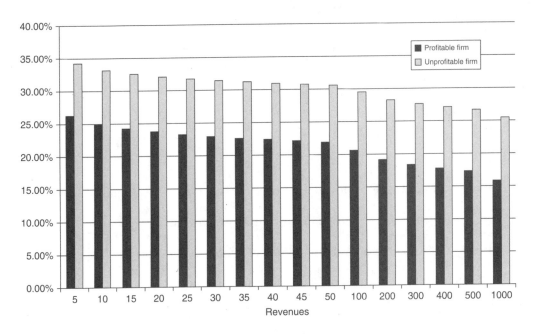

Figure 5A.1: Illiquidity Discounts: Base Discount of 25% for profitable firm with $10 million in revenue

There are clearly dangers associated with extending a regression run on a small number of restricted stocks to estimating discounts for private firms, but it does provide at least a road map for adjusting discount factors.

Private Placements

Just as Silber considered fundamental factors that cause restricted stock discounts to vary across firms, Bajaj et al. considered various fundamental factors that may cause illiquidity discounts to vary across firms in private placements.[36] Their regression, run across 88 private placements between 1990 and 1995, is summarized here.

$$DISC = 4.91\% + 0.40\ SHISS - 0.08\ Z - 7.23\ DREG + 3.13\ SDEV$$
$$(0.89)\quad(1.99)\qquad(2.51)\quad(2.21)\qquad(3.92)$$

where

DISC = Discount on the market price

SHISS = Private placement as percent of outstanding shares

Z = Altman Z-score (for distress)

DREG = 1 if registered; 0 if unregistered (restricted stock)

SDEV = Standard deviation of returns

Other things remaining equal, the discount is larger for larger private placements (as a percent of outstanding stocks) by risky and distressed firms and smaller for safer firms. The discount is larger for restricted stock than for registered stock, indicative of the sampling bias in the former. Hertzel and Smith ran a similar regression with 106 private placements between 1980 and 1987 and found larger private placement discounts at more distressed, riskier, and smaller firms.[37]

These regressions are a little more difficult to adapt for use with private company valuations because they are composite regressions that include registered private placements (where there is no illiquidity). However, the results reinforce the Silber regression findings that troubled or distressed firms should have larger illiquidity discounts than healthy firms.

Legitimate criticisms can be mounted against the regression approach. The first is that the R squared of these regressions is moderate (30–40 percent) and that the estimates will have large standard errors associated with them. The second is that the regression coefficients are unstable and likely to change over time. Although both criticisms are valid, they really can be mounted against any cross-sectional regression and cannot be used to justify a constant discount for all firms. After all, these regressions clearly reject the hypothesis that the discount is the same across all firms.

---

36 Bajaj, M., D.J. Dennis, S.P. Ferris, and A.Sarin, 2001, "Firm Value and Marketability Discounts," *Journal of Corporate Law*, v27.

37 Hertzel, M. and R.L. Smith, 1993, "Market Discounts and Shareholder Gains from Placing Equity Privately," *Journal of Finance*, v48, 459-486.

Synthetic Bid-Ask Spread

The biggest limitation of using studies based on restricted stock or private placements is that the samples are small. We would be able to make estimates that are far more precise if we could obtain a large sample of firms with illiquidity discounts. We would argue that such a sample exists, if we consider the fact that an asset that is publicly traded is not completely liquid. In fact, liquidity varies widely across publicly traded stock. A small company listed over-the-counter is much less liquid than a company listed on the New York Stock Exchange, which in turn is much less liquid than a large capitalization company that is widely held. If, as we argued earlier, the bid-ask spread is a measure of the illiquidity of a stock, we can compute the spread as a percent of the market price and relate it to a company's fundamentals. Although the bid-ask spread might only be a quarter or half a dollar, it looms as a much larger cost when it is stated as a percent of the price per unit. For a stock that is trading at $2, with a bid-ask spread of 1/4, this cost is 12.5 percent. For higher price and very liquid stocks, the illiquidity discount may be less than 0.5 percent of the price, but it is not zero. What relevance does this have for illiquidity discounts on private companies? Think of equity in a private company as a stock that never trades. On the continuum described earlier, you would expect the bid-ask spread to be high for such a stock, and this would essentially measure the illiquidity discount.

To make estimates of the illiquidity discounts using the bid-ask spread as the measure, you would need to relate the bid-ask spreads of publicly traded stocks to variables that can be measured for a private business. For instance, you could regress the bid-ask spread against the revenues of the firm and a dummy variable, reflecting whether the firm is profitable or not, and extend the regression done on restricted stocks to a much larger sample. You could even consider the trading volume for publicly traded stocks as an independent variable and set it to zero for a private firm. Using data from the end of 2000, for instance, we regressed the bid-ask spread against annual revenues, a dummy variable for positive earnings (DERN: 0 if negative and 1 if positive), cash as a percent of firm value, and trading volume.

$$\text{Spread} = 0.145 - 0.0022 \ln (\text{annual revenues}) - 0.015 \, (\text{DERN}) - 0.016$$
$$(\text{cash/firm value}) - 0.11 \, (\$ \text{ monthly trading volume / firm value})$$

Plugging in the corresponding values—with a trading volume of zero—for a private firm should yield an estimate of the synthetic bid-ask spread for the firm. This synthetic spread can be used as a measure of the illiquidity discount on the firm.

Option-Based Discount

In the chapter, we examined an option-pricing based approach, which allowed you to estimate an upper bound for the illiquidity discount, by assuming an investor with perfect market timing skills. There have been attempts to extend option pricing models to valuing illiquidity, with mixed results. In one widely used variation, liquidity is modeled as a put option for the period when an investor is restricted from trading. Thus, the illiquidity discount on value for an asset where the owner is restricted from trading for two years will be modeled as a two-year at-the-money put option.[38] This approach has several flaws, both intuitive and conceptual. The first is that liquidity does not give you the right to sell a stock at today's market price anytime over the next two years. What it does give you is the right to sell at the prevailing market price anytime over the next two years.[39] The second (and smaller) problem is that option-pricing models are based on continuous price movements and arbitrage, and it is difficult to see how these assumptions will hold up for an illiquid asset.

The value of liquidity ultimately has to derive from the investor being able to sell at some predetermined price during the nontrading period rather than being forced to hold until the end of the period. The look-back option approach that assumes a perfect market timer, explained earlier in this chapter, assumes that the sale would have occurred at the high price and allows us to estimate an upper bound on the value. Can we use option pricing models to value illiquidity without assuming perfect market timing? Consider one alternative. Assume that you have a disciplined investor who always sells investments, when the price rises 25 percent above the original buying price. Not being able to trade on this investment for a period (say, two years) undercuts this discipline, and it can be argued that the value of illiquidity is the product of the value of the put option (estimated using a strike price set 25 percent above the purchase price and a two-year life) and the probability that the stock price will rise 25 percent or more over the next two years.

If you decide to apply option pricing models to value illiquidity in private businesses, the value of the underlying asset (which is the private business) and the standard deviation in that value will be required inputs. Although estimating them for a private busi-

---

38   In a 1993 study, David Chaffe used this approach to estimate illiquidity discounts ranging from 28–49 percent for an asset, using the Black Scholes option pricing model and volatilities ranging from 60–90 percent for the underlying asset.

39   There is a simple way to illustrate that this put option has nothing to do with liquidity. Assume that you own stock in a liquid, publicly traded company and that the current stock price is $50. A two-year put option on this stock with a strike price of $50 will have substantial value, even though the underlying stock is completely liquid. The value has nothing to do with liquidity but is a price you are willing to pay for insurance.

ness is more difficult to do than for a publicly traded firm, we can always use industry averages.

6

PROBABILISTIC APPROACHES: SCENARIO ANALYSIS, DECISION TREES, AND SIMULATIONS

In the previous chapter, we examined ways in which we can adjust the value of a risky asset for its risk. Notwithstanding their popularity, all these approaches share a common theme. The riskiness of an asset is encapsulated in one number—a higher discount rate, lower cash flows, or a discount to the value—and the computation almost always requires us to make assumptions (often stringent) about the nature of risk.

In this chapter, we consider a different and potentially more informative way of assessing and presenting the risk in an investment. Rather than compute an expected value for an asset that tries to reflect the different possible outcomes, we can provide information on what the value of the asset will be under each outcome or at least a subset of outcomes. We will begin this section by looking at the simplest version, which is an analysis of an asset's value under three scenarios—a best case, most likely case, and worst case—and then extend the discussion to look at scenario analysis more generally. We will move on to examine the use of decision trees, which is a more complete approach to dealing with discrete risk. We will close the chapter by evaluating Monte Carlo simulations, the most complete approach of assessing risk across the spectrum.

Scenario Analysis

We can estimate the expected cash flows that we use to value risky assets in one or two ways. They can represent a probability-weighted average of cash flows under all possible scenarios, or they can be the cash flows under the most likely scenario. Although the former is the more precise measure, it is seldom used simply because it requires far more information to compile. In both cases, there are other scenarios where the cash flows will be different from expectations—higher than expected in some and lower than expected in others. In scenario analysis, we estimate expected cash flows and asset value under various scenarios, with the intent of getting a better sense of the effect of risk on value. In this section, we first look at an extreme version of scenario analysis where we consider the value in the best-case and the worst-case scenarios, and then we look at a more generalized version of scenario analysis.

Best Case/Worst Case

With risky assets, the actual cash flows can be very different from expectations. At the minimum, we can estimate the cash flows if everything works to perfection—a best-case scenario—and if nothing does—a worst-case scenario. In practice, we can structure this analysis in two ways. In the first, each input into asset value is set to its best (or worst) possible outcome and the cash flows estimated with those values. Thus, when valuing a firm, we can set the revenue growth rate and operating margin at the highest possible level while setting the discount rate at its lowest level, and compute the value as the best-case scenario. The problem with this approach is that it may not be feasible; after all, to get the high revenue growth, the firm may have to lower prices and accept lower margins. In the second, the best possible scenario is defined in terms of what is feasible while allowing for the relationship between the inputs. Thus, instead of assuming that both revenue growth and margins will be maximized, we will choose that combination of growth and margin that is feasible and yields the best outcome. Although this approach is more realistic, it does require more work to put into practice.

How useful is a best-case/worse-case analysis? There are two ways in which decision makers can utilize the results from this analysis. First, they can use the difference between the best-case and worst-case value as a measure of risk on an asset; the range in value (scaled to size) should be higher for riskier investments. Second, firms that are concerned about the potential spillover effects on their operations of an investment going bad may be able to gauge the effects by looking at the worst-case outcome. Thus, a firm that has significant debt obligations may use the worst-case outcome to make a judgment as to whether an investment has the potential to push the company into default.

In general, though, best-case/worse-case analyses are not very informative. After all, there should be no surprise in knowing that an asset will be worth a lot in the best case and not very much in the worst case. Thus, an equity research analyst who uses this approach to value a stock, priced at $50, may arrive at values of $80 for the best case and $10 for the worst case. With a range that large, it would be difficult to judge whether the stock was a good investment at its current price of $50.

Multiple Scenario Analysis

Scenario analysis does not have to be restricted to the best and worst cases. In its most general form, the value of a risky asset can be computed under a number of different scenarios, varying the assumptions about both macroeconomic and asset-specific variables.

Steps in Scenario Analysis

Although the concept of sensitivity analysis is a simple one, it has four critical components:

1. The first is the determination of which factors the scenarios will be built around. These factors can range from the state of the economy for an automobile firm considering a new plant, to the response of competitors for a consumer product firm introducing a new product, to the behavior of regulatory authorities for a phone company considering a new phone service. In general, analysts should focus on the two or three most critical factors that will determine the value of the asset and build scenarios around these factors.

2. The second component is determining the number of scenarios to analyze for each factor. Although more scenarios may be more realistic than fewer, it becomes more difficult to collect information and differentiate between the scenarios in terms of asset cash flows. Thus, estimating cash flows under each scenario will be easier if the firm lays out 5 scenarios, for instance, than if it lays out 15. The question of how many scenarios to consider will depend then on how different the scenarios are and how well the analyst can forecast cash flows under each one.

3. The third component is the estimation of asset cash flows under each scenario. It is to ease the estimation at this step that we focus on only two or three critical factors and build relatively few scenarios for each factor.

4. The final component is the assignment of probabilities to each scenario. For some scenarios, involving macroeconomic factors such as exchange rates, interest rates, and overall economic growth, we can draw on the expertise of services that forecast these variables. For other scenarios, involving either the sector or competitors, we have to draw on our knowledge about the industry. Note, though, that this makes sense only if the scenarios cover the full spectrum of possibilities. If the scenarios represent only a subset of the possible outcomes on an investment, the probabilities will not add up to one.

We can present the output from a scenario analysis as values under each scenario and as an expected value across scenarios (if we can estimate the probabilities in the fourth step).

This quantitative view of scenario analysis may be challenged by strategists, who have traditionally viewed scenario analysis as a qualitative exercise whose primary benefit is to broaden the thinking of decision makers. As one strategist put it, scenario analysis is about devising "plausible future narratives" rather than probable outcomes; in other words, there are benefits to considering scenarios that have a very low probability of occurring.[1] The benefit of the exercise is that it forces decision makers to consider views of what may unfold that differ from the "official view."

Examples of Scenario Analysis

To illustrate scenario analysis, consider a simple example. The Boeing 747, introduced in 1974, is the largest capacity airplane[2] that Boeing manufactures for the commercial aerospace market. Assume that Boeing is considering the introduction of a new large-capacity airplane, capable of carrying 650 passengers, called the *Super Jumbo*, to replace the Boeing 747. Arguably, as the largest and longest-serving firm in the commercial aircraft market, Boeing knows the market better than any other firm in the world. Surveys and market testing of Boeing's primary customers, the airline companies, are unlikely to be useful tools in this case, for the following reasons.

- Even if the demand exists now, it will be several years before Boeing will actually be able to produce and deliver the aircraft; the demand can change by then.

- Technologically, it is not feasible to produce a few Super Jumbo Jets for test marketing, because the cost of retooling plant and equipment will be huge.

- There are relatively few customers (the airlines) in the market, and Boeing is in constant contact with them. Thus, Boeing should already have a reasonable idea of what the customers current preferences are, in terms of the types of commercial aircraft.

---

1   Randall, D., and C. Ertel. "Moving beyond the official future." *Financial Times Special Reports/Mastering Risk*. London: Financial Times, September 15, 2005.

2   The Boeing 747 has the capacity to carry 416 passengers.

At the same time, there is considerable uncertainty as to whether airlines will be interested in a Super Jumbo jet. The demand for this jet will be greatest on long-haul,[3] international flights, because smaller airplanes are much more profitable for short-haul, domestic flights. In addition, the demand is unlikely to support two large-capacity airplanes, produced by different companies. Thus, Boeing's expected revenues will depend on two fundamental factors.

- The growth in the long-haul, international market, relative to the domestic market. Arguably, a strong Asian economy will play a significant role in fueling this growth, because a large proportion[4] of growth will have to come from an increase in flights from Europe and North America to Asia.

- The likelihood that Airbus, Boeing's primary competitor, will come out with a larger version of its largest capacity airplane, the A-300, over the period of the analysis.

We will consider three scenarios for the first factor.

- A high growth scenario, where real growth in the Asian economies exceeds 7 percent a year

- An average growth scenario, where real growth in Asia falls between 4 and 7 percent a year

- A low growth scenario, where real growth in Asia falls below 4 percent a year

For the Airbus response, we will also consider three scenarios.

- Airbus produces an airplane that has the same capacity as the Super Jumbo jet, capable of carrying 650+ passengers.

- Airbus produces an improved version of its existing A-300 jet that is capable of carrying 300+ passengers.

- Airbus decides to concentrate on producing smaller airplanes and abandons the large-capacity airplane market.

In Table 6.1, we estimate the number of Super Jumbo jets that Boeing expects to sell under each of these scenarios.

---

3   Because these planes cost a great deal more to operate, they tend to be most economical for flights over long distances.

4   Flights from Europe to North America are clearly the largest segment of the market currently. It is also the segment least likely to grow because both markets are mature.

Table 6.1   Planes Sold by Boeing Under Scenarios

	Airbus Large Jet	Airbus A-300	Airbus Abandons Large-Capacity Airplane
High growth in Asia	120	150	200
Average growth in Asia	100	135	160
Low growth in Asia	75	110	120

These estimates are based on both Boeing's knowledge of this market and responses from potential customers (willingness to place large advance orders). The cash flows can be estimated under each of the nine scenarios, and the value of the project can be computed under each scenario.

Although many scenario analyses do not take this last step, we next estimate the probabilities of each of these scenarios occurring and report them in Table 6.2.

Table 6.2   Probabilities of Scenarios

	Airbus Large Jet	Airbus A-300	Airbus Abandons Large-Capacity Airplane	Sum
High growth in Asia	0.125	0.125	0.00	0.25
Average growth in Asia	0.15	0.25	0.10	0.50
Low growth in Asia	0.05	0.10	0.10	0.25
Sum	0.325	0.475	0.20	1.00

These probabilities represent joint probabilities; the probability of Airbus going ahead with a large jet that will directly compete with the Boeing Super Jumbo in a high-growth Asian economy is 12.5 percent. Note also that the probabilities sum to 1; that summing up the probabilities, by column, yields the overall probabilities of different actions by Airbus; and that summing up the probabilities by row yields probabilities of different growth scenarios in Asia. Multiplying the probabilities by the value of the project under each scenario should yield an expected value for the project. Multiplying the probabilities of each scenario by the number of planes that will be sold under that scenario yields the expected number of planes sold:

$$\text{Expected sales} = 120(.125)+100(.15)+75(.05)+150(.125)+135(.25)+110(.10)$$
$$+200(0)+160(.10)+120(.10) = 125$$

If the assessments across scenarios is correct, Boeing can expect to sell 125 planes. If we were estimating the expected cash flow for a risk-adjusted value, we would use this number to derive expected revenues and cash flows. In a scenario analysis, the cash flows will be estimated under each scenario separately and can breakeven points (for profits and value added) can be computed across scenarios.

Use in Decision Making

How useful is scenario analysis in value assessment and decision making? The answer, as with all tools, depends on how it is used. The most useful information from a scenario analysis is the range of values across different scenarios, which provides a snapshot of the riskiness of the asset; riskier assets will have values that vary more across scenarios, and safer assets will manifest more value stability. In addition, scenario analysis can be useful in determining the inputs into an analysis that have the most effect on value. In the Boeing Super Jumbo jet example, the inputs that have the biggest effect on the project's value are the health and growth prospects of the Asian economy and the decision of Airbus about building a competing aircraft. Given the sensitivity of the decision to these variables, Boeing may devote more resources to estimating them better. With Asian growth, in particular, it may pay to have a more thorough analysis and forecast of Asian growth prospects before Boeing commits to this large investment.

Scenario analysis has one final advantage. Assuming Boeing decides that investing in the Super Jumbo makes economic sense, it can take proactive steps to minimize the damage that the worst-case scenarios create to value. To reduce the potential downside from Asian growth, Boeing may try to diversify its revenue base and sell more aircraft in Latin America and Eastern Europe. It could even try to alter the probability of Airbus developing a competitive aircraft by using a more aggressive low-price strategy, where it gives up some margin in return for a lower likelihood of competition in the future.

If nothing else, the process of thinking through scenarios is a useful exercise in examining how the competition will react under different macroeconomic environments and what can be done to minimize the effect of downside risk and maximize the effect of potential upside on the value of a risky asset. An article in the *Financial Times* illustrates how scenario analysis can be used by firms, considering investing large amounts in China, to gauge potential risks.[5] They consider four scenarios, built around how China will evolve over time.

---

5   Clemons, E. K., S. Barnett, and J. Lanier. "Fortune favors the forward-thinking." *Financial Times Special Reports /Mastering Risk*. London: Financial Times, September 22, 2005.

- **Global economic partner**—In this scenario (which they label the official future because so many firms seem to subscribe to it now), China grows both as an exporter of goods and as a domestic market for consumer goods, while strengthening legal protections for ownership rights.

- **Global economic predator**—China remains a low-cost producer, with a tightly controlled labor force and an intentionally undervalued currency. The domestic market for consumer goods is constrained, and the protection of ownership right does not advance significantly.

- **Slow-growing global participant**—China continues to grow, but at a much slower pace, as the challenges of entering a global marketplace prove to be more difficult than anticipated. However, the government stays in control of the environment, and there is little overt trouble.

- **Frustrated and unstable outsider**—China's growth stalls, and political and economic troubles grow, potentially spilling over into the rest of Asia. The government becomes destabilized, and strife spreads.

Forward-looking firms, they argue, may go into China expecting the first scenario (global economic partner), but they need to be prepared if the other scenarios unfold.

Issues

Multiple scenario analysis provides more information than a best-case/worst-case analysis by providing asset values under each of the specified scenarios. It does, however, have its own set of problems.

- **Garbage in, garbage out**—It goes without saying that the key to doing scenario analysis well is the setting up of the scenarios and the estimation of cash flows under each one. Not only do the outlined scenarios have to be realistic, but they also have to try to cover the spectrum of possibilities. After the scenarios have been laid out, the cash flows have to be estimated under each one; this trade-off has to be considered when determining how many scenarios will be run.

- **Continuous risk**—Scenario analysis is best suited for dealing with risk that takes the form of discrete outcomes. In the Boeing example, whether Airbus develops a Super Jumbo or not is a discrete risk, and the modeling of the scenarios is straightforward. When the outcomes can take on any of a large number of potential values or the risk is continuous, it becomes more difficult to set up scenarios. In the Boeing example, we have categorized the "growth in Asia" variable into three groups—high, average, and low—but the reality is that the cutoff points that we used of 4 percent and 7 percent are subjective. Thus, a growth rate of 7.1 percent will put us in the high growth scenario, but a growth rate of 6.9 percent will yield an average growth scenario.

- **Double counting of risk**—As with the best-case/worst-case analysis, there is the danger that decision makers will double-count risk when they do scenario analysis. Thus, an analyst looking at the Boeing Super Jumbo jet analysis may decide to reject the investment even though the value of the investment (estimated using the risk-adjusted discount rate) exceeds the cost at the expected production and sale of 125 planes. Why? Because there is a significant probability (30 percent) that the sales will fall below the breakeven of 115 planes. Because the expected value is already risk adjusted, this would represent a double counting of potentially the same risk or risk that should not be a factor in the decision in the first place (because it is diversifiable).

Decision Trees

In some projects and assets, risk is not only discrete but also sequential. In other words, for the asset to have value, it has to pass through a series of tests, with failure at any point potentially translating into a complete loss of value. This is the case, for instance, with a pharmaceutical drug that is just being tested on human beings. The three-stage FDA approval process lays out the hurdles that have to be passed for this drug to be commercially sold, and failure at any of the three stages dooms the drug's chances. Decision trees allow us not only to consider the risk in stages but also to devise the right response to outcomes at each stage.

Steps in Decision Tree Analysis

The first step in understanding decision trees is to distinguish among root nodes, decision nodes, event nodes, and end nodes.

- The root node represents the start of the decision tree, where a decision maker can be faced with a decision choice or an uncertain outcome. The objective of the exercise is to evaluate what a risky investment is worth at this node.

- Event nodes represent the possible outcomes on a risky gamble; whether a drug passes the first stage of the FDA approval process or not is a good example. We have to figure out the possible outcomes and the probabilities of the outcomes occurring, based on the information we have available today.

- Decision nodes represent choices that the decision maker can make—to expand from a test market to a national market after a test market's outcome is known.

- End nodes usually represent the outcomes of earlier risky outcomes and decisions made in response.

Consider a simple example. We are offered a choice where we can take a certain amount of $20 or partake in a gamble, where we can win $50 with probability 50 percent and $10 with probability 50 percent. The decision tree for this offered gamble is shown in Figure 6.1.

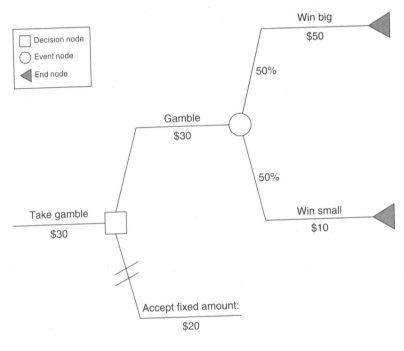

Figure 6.1: Simple Decision Tree

Note the key elements in the decision tree. First, only the event nodes represent uncertain outcomes and have probabilities attached to them. Second, the decision node represents a choice. On a pure expected-value basis, the gamble is better (with an expected value of $30) than the guaranteed amount of $20; the double slash on the latter branch indicates that it would not be selected. Although this example may be simplistic, the elements of building a decision tree are in it.

In general, developing a decision tree requires us to go through the following steps, although the details and the sequencing can vary from case to case.

1. **Divide analysis into risk phases**—The key to developing a decision tree is outlining the phases of risk that we will be exposed to in the future. In some cases, such as the FDA approval process, this will be easy to do because there are only two outcomes—the drug gets approved to move on to the next phase, or it does not. In other cases, it will be more difficult. For instance, a test market of a new consumer product can yield hundreds of potential outcomes; here, we will have to create discrete categories for what would qualify as success in the test market.

2. **Estimate the probabilities of the outcomes in each phase**—Once the phases of the analysis have been put down and the outcomes at each phase are defined, we have to compute the probabilities of the outcomes. In addition to the obvious requirement that the probabilities across outcomes have to sum up to one, the analyst also has to consider whether the probabilities of outcomes in one phase can be affected by outcomes in earlier phases. For example, how does the probability of a successful national product introduction change when the test market outcome is only average?

3. **Define decision points**—Embedded in the decision tree are decision points where we will get to determine, based on observing the outcomes at earlier stages and expectations of what will occur in the future, what our best course of action will be. With the test market example, for instance, we will get to determine, at the end of the test market, whether we want to conduct a second test market, abandon the product, or move directly to a national product introduction.

4. **Compute cash flows/value at end nodes**—The next step in the decision tree process is estimating what the final cash flow and value outcomes will be at each end node. In some cases, such as abandonment of a test market product, this will be easy to do and will represent the money spent on the test marketing of the product. In other cases, such as a national launch of the same product, this will be more difficult to do because we will have to estimate expected cash flows over the life of the product and discount these cash flows to arrive at value.

5. **Fold back the tree**—The last step in a decision tree analysis is termed *folding back* the tree, where we compute the expected values, working backward through the tree. If the node is a chance node, we compute the expected value as the probability weighted average of all the possible outcomes. If it is a decision node, we compute the expected value for each branch, and we choose the highest value (as

the optimal decision). The process culminates in an expected value for the asset or investment today.[6]

Two key pieces of output emerge from a decision tree. The first is the expected value today of going through the entire decision tree. This expected value incorporates the potential upside and downside from risk and the actions that we will take along the way in response to this risk. In effect, this is analogous to the risk-adjusted value that we talked about in the previous chapter. The second is the range of values at the end nodes, which should encapsulate the potential risk in the investment.

An Example of a Decision Tree

To illustrate the steps involved in developing a decision tree, let us consider the analysis of a pharmaceutical drug for treating Type 1 diabetes that has gone through preclinical testing and is about to enter phase 1 of the FDA approval process.[7] Assume that we are provided with the additional information on each of the three phases:

1. Phase 1 is expected to cost $50 million and will involve 100 volunteers to determine safety and dosage; it is expected to last one year. There is a 70 percent chance that the drug will successfully complete the first phase.

2. In phase 2, the drug will be tested on 250 volunteers for effectiveness in treating diabetes over a two-year period. This phase will cost $100 million, and the drug will have to show a statistically significant impact on the disease to move on to the next phase. There is only a 30 percent chance that the drug will prove successful in treating type 1 diabetes, but there is a 10 percent chance that it will be successful in treating both type 1 and type 2 diabetes and a 10 percent chance that it will succeed only in treating type 2 diabetes.

3. In phase 3, the testing will expand to 4,000 volunteers to determine the long-term consequences of taking the drug. If the drug is tested on only type 1 or type 2 diabetes patients, this phase will last four years and cost $250 million; there is an 80

---

6   There is a significant body of literature examining the assumptions that have to hold for this folding-back process to yield consistent values. In particular, if a decision tree is used to portray concurrent risks, the risks should be independent of each other. See Sarin, R., and P. Wakker. "Folding Back in Decision Tree Analysis." *Management Science*, Vol. 40, 625–628, 1994.

7   In type 1 diabetes, the pancreas does not produce insulin. The patients are often young children, and the disease is unrelated to diet and activity; they have to receive insulin to survive. In type 2 diabetes, the pancreas produces insufficient insulin. The disease manifests itself in older people and can sometimes be controlled by changing lifestyle and diet.

percent chance of success. If it is tested on both types, the phase will last four years and cost $300 million; there is a 75 percent chance of success.

The following table shows the costs of developing the drug and the annual cash flows if the drug passes through all three phases.

Disease Treatment	Cost of Development	Annual Cash Flow
Type 1 diabetes only	$500 million	$300 million for 15 years
Type 2 diabetes only	$500 million	$125 million for 15 years
Type 1 and 2 diabetes	$600 million	$400 million for 15 years

Assume that the cost of capital for the firm is 10 percent.

We now have the information to draw the decision tree for this drug. We will first draw the tree in Figure 6.2, specifying the phases, the cash flows at each phase, and the probabilities.

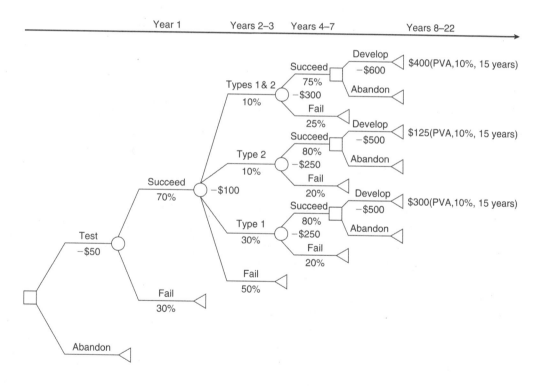

Figure 6.2: Decision Tree for Drug Development

The decision tree shows the probabilities of success at each phase and the additional cash flow or marginal cash flow associated with each step. Because it takes time to go through the phases, there is a time value effect that has to be built into the expected cash flows for each path. We introduce the time value effect and compute the cumulative present value (today) of cash flows from each path, using the 10 percent cost of capital as the discount rate, in Figure 6.3.

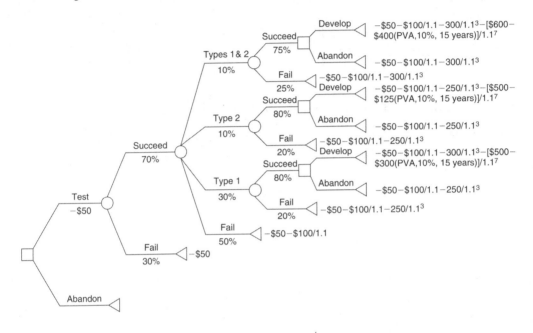

Figure 6.3: Present Value of Cash Flows at End Nodes: Drug Development Tree

Note that the present value of the cash flows from development after the third phase gets discounted back an additional seven years (to reflect the time it takes to get through three phases). In the last step in the process, we compute the expected values by working backward through the tree and estimating the optimal action in each decision phase in Figure 6.4.

The expected value of the drug today, given the uncertainty over its success, is $50.36 million. This value reflects all the possibilities that can unfold over time and shows the choices at each decision branch that are suboptimal and thus should be rejected. For example, after the drug passes phase 3, developing the drug beats abandoning it in all three cases—as a treatment for type 1, type 2, or both types. The decision tree also provides a range of outcomes, with the worst-case outcome being failure in phase 3 of the drug as a treatment for both phase 1 and 2 diabetes (−$366.30 million in today's dollars) to the best-case outcome of approval and development of the drug as treatment for both types of diabetes ($887.05 million in today's dollars).

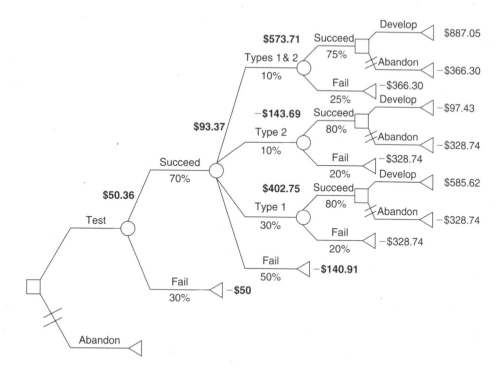

Figure 6.4: Drug Decision Tree Folded Back

One element in the last set of branches may seem puzzling. Note that the present value of developing the drug as a treatment for just type 2 diabetes is negative (–$97.43 million). Why would the company still develop the drug? Because the alternative of abandoning the drug at the late stage in the process has an even more negative net present value (–$328.74 million). Another way to see this is to look at the marginal effect of developing the drug just for type 2 diabetes. Once the firm has expended the resources to take the firm through all three phases of testing, the testing becomes a sunk cost and is not a factor in the decision.[8] The marginal cash flows from developing the drug after phase 3 yield a positive net present value of $451 million (in year 7 cash flows).

---

8   It would be more accurate to consider only the costs of the first two phases as sunk, because by the end of phase 2, the firm knows that the drug is effective only against type 2 diabetes. Even if we consider only the costs of the first 2 phases as sunk, it still makes sense on an expected value basis to continue to phase 3.

Present value of developing drug to treat type 2 diabetes in year $7 = -500 + 125$
(PV of annuity, 10 percent, 15 years) = \$451 million

At each stage in the decision tree, we make our judgments based on the marginal cash flows at that juncture. Rolling back the decision tree allows us to see what the value of the drug is at each phase in the process.

Use in Decision Making

Several benefits accrue from using decision trees, and it is surprising that they are not used more often in analysis.

- **Dynamic response to risk**—By linking actions and choices to outcomes of uncertain events, decision trees encourage firms to consider how they should act under different circumstances. As a consequence, firms will be prepared for whatever outcome may arise rather than be surprised. In the example in the previous section, for instance, the firm will be ready with a plan of action, no matter what the outcome of phase 3 happens to be.

- **Value of information**—Decision trees provide a useful perspective on the value of information in decision making. Although it is not as obvious in the drug development example, it can be seen clearly when a firm considers whether to test-market a product before commercially developing it. By test-marketing a product, we acquire more information on the chances of eventual success. We can measure the expected value of this improved information in a decision tree and compare it to the test marketing cost.

- **Risk management**—Because decision trees provide a picture of how cash flows unfold over time, they are useful in deciding what risks should be protected against and the benefits of doing so. Consider a decision tree on the value of an asset, where the worst-case scenario unfolds if the dollar is weak against the Euro. Because we can hedge against this risk, we can compare the cost of hedging the risk to the loss in cash flows in the worst-case scenario.

In summary, decision trees provide a flexible and powerful approach for dealing with risk that occurs in phases, with decisions in each phase depending on outcomes in the previous one. In addition to providing us with measures of risk exposure, they force us to think through how we will react to both adverse and positive outcomes that may occur at each phase.

Issues

Decision trees are capable of handling some types of risk and not others. In particular, decision trees are best suited for risk that is sequential; the FDA process where approval occurs in phases is a good example. Risks that affect an asset concurrently cannot be easily modeled in a decision tree.[9] Looking back at the Boeing Super Jumbo jet example in the scenario analysis, for instance, the key risks that Boeing faces relate to Airbus developing its own version of a super-sized jet and growth in Asia. If we had wanted to use a decision tree to model this investment, we would have had to assume that one of these risks leads the other. For instance, we could assume that Airbus will base its decision on whether to develop a large plane on growth in Asia; if growth is high, Airbus is more likely to do it. If, however, this assumption in unreasonable and the Airbus decision will be made while Boeing faces growth risk in Asia, a decision tree may not be feasible.

As with scenario analysis, decision trees generally look at risk in terms of discrete outcomes. Again, this is not a problem with the FDA approval process where there are only two outcomes—success or failure. However, there is a much wider range of outcomes with most other risks, and we have to create discrete categories for the outcomes to stay within the decision tree framework. For instance, when looking at a market test, we may conclude that selling more than 100,000 units in a test market qualifies as a success, selling between 60,000 and 100,000 units qualifies as an average outcome, and selling below 60,000 qualifies as a failure.

Assuming risk is sequential and can be categorized into discrete boxes, we are faced with estimation questions to which there may be no easy answers. In particular, we have to estimate the cash flow under each outcome and the associated probability. With the drug development example, we had to estimate the cost and the probability of success of each phase. The advantage that we have when it comes to these estimates is that we can draw on empirical data about how frequently drugs that enter each phase make it to the next one and historical costs associated with drug testing. To the extent that there may be wide differences across different phase 1 drugs in terms of success—some may be longer shots than others—there can still be errors that creep into decision trees.

The expected value of a decision tree depends heavily on the assumption that we will stay disciplined at the decision points in the tree. In other words, if the optimal decision is to abandon if a test market fails and the expected value is computed, based on this assumption, the integrity of the process and the expected value will quickly fall apart if managers decide to overlook the market testing failure and go with a full launch of the product anyway.

---

9   If we choose to model such risks in a decision tree, the risks have to be independent of each other. In other words, the sequencing should not matter.

Risk-Adjusted Value and Decision Trees

Are decision trees an alternative or an addendum to discounted cash flow valuation? The question is an interesting one because some analysts believe that decision trees, when factoring in the possibility of good and bad outcomes, are already risk adjusted. In fact, they go on to make the claim that the right discount rate to use estimating present value in decision trees is the risk-free rate; using a risk-adjusted discount rate, they argue, would be double-counting the risk. Barring a few exceptional circumstances, they are incorrect in their reasoning.

- **Expected values are not risk adjusted**—Consider decision trees, where we estimate expected cash flows by looking at the possible outcomes and their probabilities of occurrence. The probability-weighted expected value that we obtain is not risk adjusted. The only rationale that can be offered for using a risk-free rate is that the risk embedded in the uncertain outcomes is asset-specific and will be diversified away, in which case the risk adjusted discount rate would be the risk-free rate. In the FDA drug development example, for instance, this may be offered as the rationale for why we would use the risk-free rate to discount cash flows for the first seven years, when the only the risk we face is drug approval risk. After year 7, though, the risk is likely to contain a market element, and the risk-adjusted rate will be higher than the risk-free rate.

- **Double-counting of risk**—We do have to be careful about making sure that we don't double-count for risk in decision trees by using risk-adjusted discount rates that are set high to reflect the possibility of failure at the earlier phases. One common example of this phenomenon is in venture capital valuation. A conventional approach that venture capitalists have used to value young start-up companies is to estimate an exit value, based on projected earnings and a multiple of those earnings in the future, and then to discount the exit value at a target rate. Using this approach, for instance, the value today for a firm that is losing money currently but is expected to make profits of $10 million in 5 years (when the earnings multiple at which it will be taken public is estimated to be 40) can be computed as follows (if the target rate is 35 percent):

Value of the firm in 5 years = Earnings in year 5 * PE = 10 * 40 = $400 million

Value of the firm today = $400 / 1.35^5 = $89.20 million

Note, however, that the target rate is set at a high level (35 percent) because of the probability that this young firm will not make it to a public offering. In fact, we could frame this as a simple decision tree in Figure 6.5.

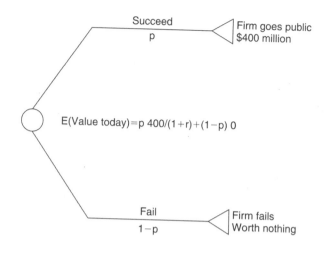

Figure 6.5: Decision Tree for start-up firm

Assume that r is the correct discount rate, based on the nondiversifiable risk that the venture capitalist faces on this venture. Going back to the numeric example, assume that this discount rate would have been 15 percent for this venture. We can solve for the implied probability of failure, embedded in the venture capitalist's estimate of value of $89.20 million.

$$\text{Estimated value} = \$89.20 = \frac{\$400}{1.15^5}(p)$$

Solving for p, we estimate the probability of success at 44.85 percent. With this estimate of probability in the decision tree, we would have arrived at the same value as the venture capitalist, assuming that we use the right discount rate. Using the target rate of 35 percent as the discount rate in a decision tree would have led to a drastically lower value, because risk would have been counted twice. Using the same reasoning, we can see why using a high discount rate in assessing the value of a biotechnology drug in a decision tree will undervalue the drug, especially if the discount rate already reflects the probability that the drug will not make it to commercial production. If the risk of the approval process is specific to that drug, and thus diversifiable, this would suggest that discount rates should be set at reasonable levels in decision tree analysis, even for drugs with high likelihoods of not making it through the approval process.

■ **The right discount rate**—If the right discount rate to use in a decision tree should reflect the nondiversifiable risk looking forward, it is not only possible but also likely that discount rates we use will be different at various points in the tree. For instance, extraordinary success at the test market stage may yield more predictable cash flows than an average test market outcome; this would lead us to use a lower discount rate to value the former and a higher discount rate to value the latter. In the drug development example, it is possible that the expected cash flows, if the drug works for both types of diabetes, will be more stable than if is a treatment for only one type. It would follow that a discount rate of 8 percent may be the right one for the first set of cash flows, whereas a 12 percent discount rate may be more appropriate for the second.

Reviewing the discussion, decision trees are not alternatives to risk-adjusted valuation. Instead, they can be viewed as a different way of adjusting for discrete risk that may be difficult to bring into expected cash flows or into risk-adjusted discount rates.

Simulations

If scenario analysis and decision trees are techniques that help us to assess the effects of discrete risk, simulations provide a way of examining the consequences of continuous risk. To the extent that most risks that we face in the real world can generate hundreds of possible outcomes, a simulation will give us a fuller picture of the risk in an asset or investment.

Steps in Simulation

Unlike scenario analysis, where we look at the values under discrete scenarios, simulations allow for more flexibility in the way we deal with uncertainty. In its classic form, distributions of values are estimated for each parameter in the analysis (growth, market share, operating margin, beta, and so on). In each simulation, we draw one outcome from each distribution to generate a unique set of cash flows and value. Across a large number of simulations, we can derive a distribution for the value of an investment or an asset that will reflect the underlying uncertainty we face in estimating the inputs to the valuation. The steps associated with running a simulation are as follows.

1. **Determine "probabilistic" variables**—Any analysis has potentially dozens of inputs, some of which are predictable and some of which are not. Unlike scenario analysis and decision trees, where the number of variables that are changed and the potential outcomes have to be few in number, there is no constraint on how many variables can be allowed to vary in a simulation. At least in theory, we can define probability distributions for each input in a valuation. The reality, though, is that this will be time consuming and may not provide much of a

payoff, especially for inputs that have only marginal impact on value. Consequently, it makes sense to focus attention on a few variables that have a significant impact on value.

2. **Define probability distributions for these variables**—This is a key and the most difficult step in the analysis. Generically, there are three ways in which we can go about defining probability distributions.

   a. **Historical data**—For variables that have a long history and reliable data over that history, it is possible to use the historical data to develop distributions. Assume, for instance, that we are trying to develop a distribution of expected changes in the long-term Treasury bond rate (to use as an input in investment analysis). We could use the histogram in Figure 6.6, based on the annual changes in Treasury bond rates every year from 1928 to 2005, as the distribution for future changes.

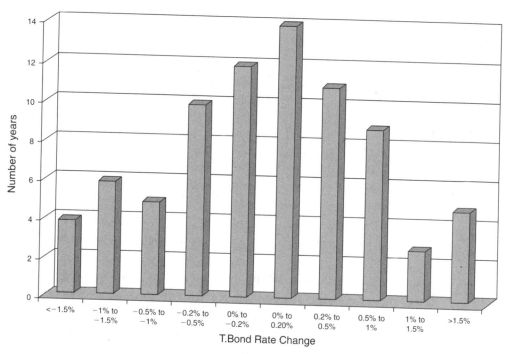

Figure 6.6: Change in T.Bond Rate - 1928 – 2005

Implicit in this approach is the assumption that there have been no structural shifts in the market that will render the historical data unreliable.

b. Cross-sectional data—In some cases, we may be able to substitute data on differences in a specific variable across existing investments that are similar to the investment being analyzed. Consider two examples. Assume that we are valuing a software firm and are concerned about the uncertainty in operating margins. Figure 6.7 provides a distribution of pretax operating margins across software companies in 2006.

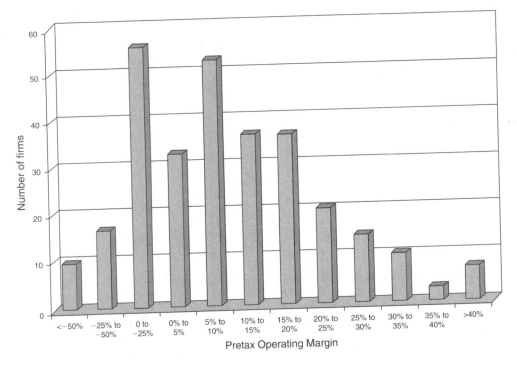

Figure 6.7: Pre-tax Operating Margin across Software Companies (US) - January 2006

If we use this distribution, we are in effect assuming that the cross-sectional variation in the margin is a good indicator of the uncertainty we face in estimating it for the software firm in question. In a second example, assume that we work for Target, the retailer, and that we are trying to estimate the sales per square foot for a new store investment. Target could use the distribution on this variable across existing stores as the basis for its simulation of sales at the new store.

c. Statistical distribution and parameters—For most variables that we are trying to forecast, the historical and cross-sectional data will be insufficient or unreliable. In these cases, we have to pick a statistical distribution that best captures the variability in the input and estimate the parameters for that distribution. Thus, we may conclude that operating margins will be distributed uniformly, with a minimum of 4 percent and a maximum of 8 percent, and that revenue growth is normally distributed with an expected value of 8 percent and a standard deviation of 6 percent. Many simulation packages available for personal computers now provide a rich array of distributions to choose from, but picking the right distribution and the parameters for the distribution remains difficult for two reasons. The first reason is that few inputs that we see in practice meet the stringent requirements that statistical distributions demand; revenue growth, for instance, cannot be normally distributed because the lowest value it can take on is –100 percent. Consequently, we have to settle for statistical distributions that are close enough to the real distribution that the resulting errors will not wreak havoc on our conclusion. The second is that the parameters still need to be estimated after the distribution is picked. For this, we can draw on historical or cross-sectional data; for the revenue growth input, we can look at revenue growth in prior years or revenue growth rate differences across peer group companies. The caveats about structural shifts that make historical data unreliable and peer group companies incomparable continue to apply.

The probability distributions can be discrete for some inputs and continuous for others, be based upon historical data for some and statistical distributions for others. Appendix 6.1 provides an overview of the statistical distributions that are most commonly used in simulations and their characteristics.

3. **Check for correlation across variables**—Although it is tempting to jump to running simulations right after the distributions have been specified, it is important that we check for correlations across variables. Assume, for instance, that we are developing probability distributions for both interest rates and inflation. Although both inputs may be critical in determining value, they are likely to be correlated with each other; high inflation is usually accompanied by high interest rates. When there is strong correlation, positive or negative, across inputs, we have two choices. One is to pick only one of the two inputs to vary; it makes sense to focus on the input that has the bigger impact on value. The other is to build the correlation explicitly into the simulation; this does require more sophisticated simulation packages and adds more detail to the estimation process. As with the parameters of the distributions, we can estimate the correlations by looking at the past.

4. **Run the simulation**—For the first simulation, we draw one outcome from each distribution and compute the value based on those outcomes. We can repeat this process as many times as desired, although the marginal contribution of each

simulation drops off as the number of simulations increases. The number of simulations we run will be determined by the following:

a. **Number of probabilistic inputs**—The larger the number of inputs that have probability distributions attached to them, the greater the required number of simulations.

b. **Characteristics of probability distributions**—The greater the diversity of distributions in an analysis, the larger the number of required simulations. Thus, the number of required simulations will be smaller in a simulation where all the inputs have normal distributions than in one where some have normal distributions, some are based on historical data distributions, and some are discrete.

c. **Range of outcomes**—The greater the potential range of outcomes on each input, the greater the number of simulations.

Most simulation packages allow users to run thousands of simulations, with little or no cost attached to increasing that number. Given that reality, it is better to err on the side of too many simulations than too few.

There have generally been two impediments to good simulations. The first is informational; estimating distributions of values for each input into a valuation is difficult to do. In other words, it is far easier to estimate an expected growth rate of 8 percent in revenues for the next 5 years than it is to specify the distribution of expected growth rates—the type of distribution, parameters of that distribution—for revenues. The second is computational; until the advent of personal computers, simulations tended to be too time and resource intensive for the typical analysis. Both these constraints have eased in recent years, and simulations have become more feasible.

An Example of a Simulation

Running a simulation is simplest for firms that consider the same kind of projects repeatedly. These firms can use their experience from similar projects that are already in operation to estimate expected values for new projects. The Home Depot, for instance, analyzes dozens of new home improvement stores every year. It also has hundreds of stores in operation,[10] at different stages in their life cycles; some of these stores have been in operation for more than 10 years, and others have been around only for a couple of years. Thus, when forecasting revenues for a new store, the Home Depot can draw on this rich database to make its estimates more precise. The firm has a reasonable idea of

---

10   At the end of 2005, the Home Depot had 743 stores in operation, 707 of which were in the United States.

how long it takes a new store to become established and how store revenues change as the store ages and new stores open close by.

There are other cases where experience can prove useful for estimating revenues and expenses on a new investment. An oil company, in assessing whether to put up an oil rig, comes into the decision with a clear sense of what the costs are of putting up a rig and how long it will take for the rig to be productive. Similarly, a pharmaceutical firm, when introducing a new drug, can bring to its analysis its experience with other drugs in the past, how quickly such drugs are accepted and prescribed by doctors, and how responsive revenues are to pricing policy. We are not suggesting that the experience these firms have had in analyzing similar projects in the past removes uncertainty about the project from the analysis. The Home Depot is still exposed to considerable risk on each new store that it analyzes today, but the experience does make the estimation process easier and the estimation error smaller than it would be for a firm that is assessing a unique project.

Assume that the Home Depot is analyzing a new home improvement store that will follow its traditional format.[11] The Home Depot needs to make several estimates when analyzing a new store. Perhaps the most important is the likely revenues at the store. Given that the Home Depot's store sizes are similar across locations, the firm can get an idea of the expected revenues by looking at revenues at their existing stores. Figure 6.8 summarizes the distribution[12] of annual revenues at existing stores in 2005.

This distribution not only yields an expected revenue per store of about $44 million, but it also provides a measure of the uncertainty associated with the estimate, in the form of a standard deviation in revenues per store.

The second key input is the operating margin that the Home Depot expects to generate at this store. Although the margins are fairly similar across all its existing stores, there are significant differences in margins across different building supply retailers, reflecting their competitive strengths or weaknesses. Figure 6.9 summarizes differences in pretax operating margins across building supply retailers.

Note that this distribution, unlike the revenue distribution, does not have a noticeable peak. In fact, with one outlier in either direction, it is distributed evenly between 6 percent and 12 percent.

---

11 A typical Home Depot store has store space of about 100,000 square feet and carries a wide range of home improvement products, from hardware to flooring.

12 This distribution is a hypothetical one, because the Home Depot does not provide this information to outsiders. It does have the information internally.

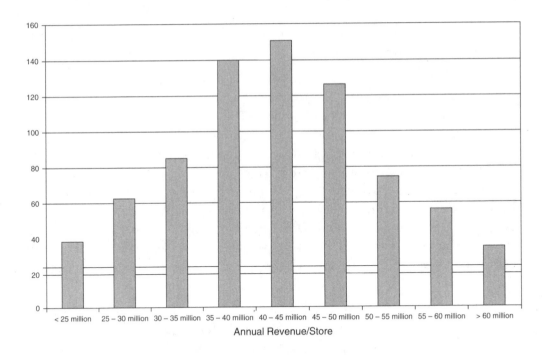

Figure 6.8: Revenues/Store: Home Depot US Stores in 2005

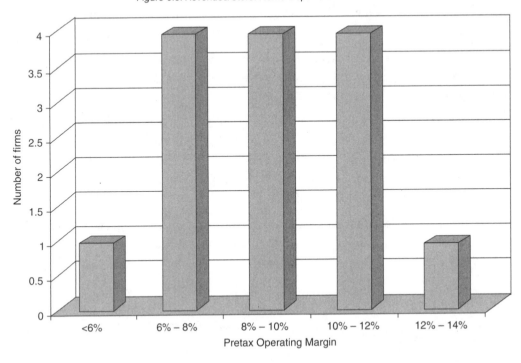

Figure 6.9: Pre-tax Operating Margin at Building Retailers (US) - January 2006

Finally, the store's future revenues will be tied to an estimate of expected growth, which we will assume will be strongly influenced by overall economic growth in the United States. To get a measure of this growth, we looked at the distribution of real GDP growth from 1925 to 2005 in Figure 6.10.

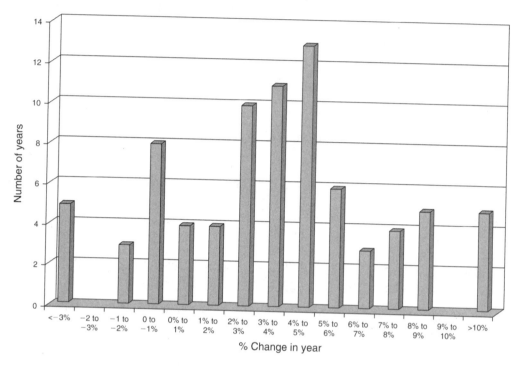

Figure 6.10: Annual % Change in Real GDP for US - 1925 to 2005

To run a simulation of the Home Depot's store's cash flows and value, we will make the following assumptions.

- **Base revenues**—We will base our estimate of the base year's revenues on Figure 6.8. For computational ease, we will assume that revenues will be normally distributed with an expected value of $44 million and a standard deviation of $10 million.

- **Pretax operating margin**—Based on Figure 6.9, the pretax operating margin is assumed to be uniformly distributed, with a minimum value of 6 percent, a maximum value of 12 percent, and an expected value of 9 percent. Nonoperating expenses are anticipated to be $ 1.5 million per year.

- **Revenue growth**—We used a slightly modified version of the actual distribution of historical real GDP changes as the distribution of future changes in real GDP.[13] The average real GDP growth over the period was 3 percent, but there is substantial variation with the worst year delivering a drop in real GDP of more than 8 percent and the best an increase of more than 8 percent. The expected annual growth rate in revenues is the sum of the expected inflation rate and the growth rate in real GDP. We will assume that the expected inflation rate is 2 percent.

- The store is expected to generate cash flows for 10 years, and there is no expected salvage value from the store closure.

- The cost of capital for the Home Depot is 10 percent, and the tax rate is 40 percent.

We can compute the value of this store to the Home Depot, based entirely on the expected values of each variable:

Expected base-year revenue = $44 million

Expected base-year after-tax cash flow = (revenue * pretax margin – nonoperating expenses) (1 – tax rate) = (44*.09 – 1.5) (1 – .4) = $1.476 million

Expected growth rate = GDP growth rate + expected inflation = 3 percent + 2 percent = 5 percent

$$\text{Value}[14] \text{ of store} = CF\,(1+g)\frac{(1-\frac{(1+g)^n}{(1+r)^n})}{(r-g)} = 1.476\,(1.05)\,\frac{(1-\frac{1.05^{10}}{1.10^{10}})}{(.10-.05)} = \$11.53 \text{ million}$$

The risk-adjusted value for this store is $11.53 million.

We then did a simulation with 10,000 runs, based on the probability distributions for each of the inputs.[15] The resulting values are graphed in Figure 6.11.

The key statistics on the values obtained across the 10,000 runs are summarized next.

- The average value across the simulations was $11.67 million, a trifle higher than the risk-adjusted value of $11.53 million; the median value was $10.90 million.

---

13   In the modified version, we smoothed out the distribution to fill in the missing intervals and moved the peak of the distribution slightly to the left (to 3–4 percent from 4–5 percent), reflecting the larger size of the economy today.

14   The equation presented here is the equation for the present value of a growing annuity.

15   We used Crystal Ball as the computational program. Crystal Ball is a simulation program produced by Decisioneering Inc.

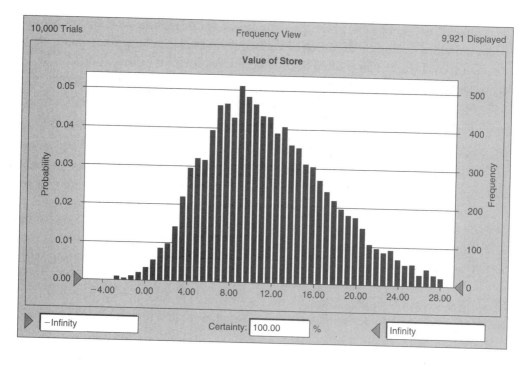

Figure 6.11: Distribution of Estimated Values for HD Store from Simulation

- There was substantial variation in values, with the lowest value across all runs −$5.05 million and the highest value of $39.42 million; the standard deviation in values was $5.96 million.

Use in Decision Making

A well-done simulation provides us with more than just an expected value for an asset or investment.

- **It offers better input estimation**—In an ideal simulation, analysts will examine both the historical and cross-sectional data on each input variable before making a judgment on the distribution to use and the parameters of the distribution. In the process, they may be able to avoid the sloppiness that is associated with the use of "single best" estimates; many discounted cash flow valuations are based on expected growth rates that are obtained from services such as Zack's or IBES, which report analysts' consensus estimates.

- **It yields a distribution for expected value rather than a point estimate**— Consider the valuation example that we completed in the previous section.

In addition to reporting an expected value of $11.67 million for the store, we estimated a standard deviation of $5.96 million in that value and a breakdown of the values, by percentile. The distribution reinforces the obvious but important point that valuation models yield estimates of value for risky assets that are imprecise and explains why different analysts valuing the same asset may arrive at different estimates of value.

Note that there are two claims about simulations that we are unwilling to make. The first is that simulations yield better estimates of expected value than conventional risk-adjusted value models. In fact, the expected values from simulations should be fairly close to the expected value that we would obtain using the expected values for each of the inputs (rather than the entire distribution). The second is that simulations, by providing estimates of the expected value and the distribution in that value, lead to better decisions. This may not always be the case because the benefits that decision makers receive by getting a fuller picture of the uncertainty in value in a risky asset may be more than offset by misuse of that risk measure. As we will argue later in this chapter, it is all too common for risk to be double-counted in simulations and for decisions to be based on the wrong type of risk.

Simulations with Constraints

To use simulations as a tool in risk analysis, we have to introduce a constraint, which, if violated, creates very large costs for the firm and perhaps even causes its demise. We can then evaluate the effectiveness of risk-hedging tools by examining the likelihood that the constraint will be violated with each one and weighing that against the cost of the tool. In this section, we will consider some common constraints that are introduced into simulations.

Book Value Constraints

The book value of equity is an accounting construct and, by itself, means little. Firms like Microsoft and Google trade at market values that are several times their book values. At the other extreme are firms that trade at half their book value or less. In fact, there are several hundred firms in the United States, some with significant market values that have negative book values for equity. There are two types of restrictions on book value of equity that may call for risk hedging.

- **Regulatory capital restrictions**—Financial service firms such as banks and insurance companies are required to maintain book equity as a fraction of loans or other assets at or above a floor ratio specified by the authorities. Firms that violate these capital constraints can be taken over by the regulatory authorities, with the equity investors losing everything if that occurs. Not surprisingly, financial service firms not only keep a close eye on their book value of equity (and the related ratios), but they also are conscious of the possibility that the risk in their investments or positions can manifest itself as a drop in book equity. In fact, value at risk (VaR), which we will examine in the next chapter, represents the efforts by financial service firms to understand the potential risks in their investments and to be ready for the possibility of a catastrophic outcome, although the probability of its occurring might be small. By simulating the values of their investments under a variety of scenarios, financial service firms can identify not only the possibility of falling below the regulatory ratios but also look for ways of hedging against this event occurring. The payoff to risk hedging then manifests itself as a decline in or even an elimination of the probability that the firm will violate a regulatory constraint.

- **Negative book value for equity**—As noted, there are hundreds of firms in the United States with negative book values of equity that survive its occurrence and have high market values for equity. In some countries, a negative book value of equity can create substantial costs for the firm and its investors. For instance, companies with negative book values of equity in parts of Europe are required to raise fresh equity capital to bring their book values above zero. In some countries in Asia, companies that have negative book values of equity are barred from paying dividends. Even in the United States, lenders to firms can have loan covenants that allow them to gain at least partial control of a firm if its book value of equity turns negative. As with regulatory capital restrictions, we can use simulations to assess the probability of a negative book value for equity and to protect against it.

Earnings and Cash Flow Constraints

Earnings and cash flow constraints can be internally or externally imposed. In some firms, managers may decide that the consequences of reporting a loss or not meeting analysis estimates of earnings are so dire, including perhaps the loss of their jobs, that they are willing to expend the resources on risk-hedging products to prevent this from happening. The payoff from hedging risk then has nothing to do with firm value maximization and much to do with managerial compensation and incentives. In other firms, the constraints on earnings and cash flows can be externally imposed. For instance, loan covenants can be related to earnings outcomes. Not only can the interest rate on the loan be tied to whether a company makes money or not, but the control of the firm can itself shift to lenders in some cases if the firm loses money. In either case, we can use simulations to both assess the likelihood that these constraints will be violated and to examine the effect of risk-hedging products on this likelihood.

Market Value Constraints

In discounted cash flow valuation, the value of the firm is computed as a going concern, by discounting expected cash flows at a risk-adjusted discount rate. Deducting debt from this estimate yields equity value. The possibility and potential costs of not being able to meet debt payments are considered only peripherally in the discount rate. In reality, the costs of not meeting contractual obligations can be substantial. In fact, these costs are generally categorized as indirect bankruptcy costs and could include the loss of customers, tighter supplier credit, and higher employee turnover. The perception that a firm is in trouble can lead to further trouble. By allowing us to compare the value of a business to its outstanding claims in all possible scenarios (rather than just the most likely one), simulations allow us to not only quantify the likelihood of distress but also build the cost of indirect bankruptcy costs into valuation. In effect, we can explicitly model the effect of distress on expected cash flows and discount rates.

Issues

The use of simulations in investment analysis was first suggested in an article by David Hertz in the Harvard Business Review.[16] He argued that using probability distributions for input variables, rather than single best estimates, would yield more informative output. In the example that he provided in the paper, he used simulations to compare the distributions of returns of two investments; the investment with the higher expected return also had a higher chance of losing money (which was viewed as an indicator of its riskiness). In the aftermath, there were several analysts who jumped on the simulation bandwagon, with mixed results. In recent years, there has been a resurgence in interest in simulations as a tool for risk assessment, especially in the context of using and valuing derivatives. There are several key issues, though, that we have to deal with in the context of using simulations in risk assessment:

- **Garbage in, garbage out**—For simulations to have value, the distributions chosen for the inputs should be based on analysis and data, rather than guesswork. It is worth noting that simulations yield great-looking output, even when the inputs are random. Unsuspecting decision makers may therefore be getting

---

16   Hertz, D. "Risk Analysis in Capital Investment." *Harvard Business Review*, v16, 95-102, 1964.

meaningless pictures of the risk in an investment. It is also worth noting that simulations require more than a passing knowledge of statistical distributions and their characteristics; analysts who cannot assess the difference between normal and lognormal distributions should not be doing simulations.

- **Real data may not fit distributions**—The problem with the real world is that the data seldom fits the stringent requirements of statistical distributions. Using a probability distribution that bear little resemblance to the true distribution underlying an input variable will yield misleading results.

- **Nonstationary distributions**—Even when the data fits a statistical distribution or where historical data distributions are available, shifts in the market structure can lead to shifts in the distributions. In some cases, this can change the form of the distribution, and in other cases, it can change the parameters of the distribution. Thus, the mean and variance estimated from historical data for an input that is normally distributed may change for the next period. What we would really like to use in simulations, but seldom can assess, are forward looking probability distributions.

- **Changing correlation across inputs**—Earlier in this chapter, we noted that correlation across input variables can be modeled into simulations. However, this works only if the correlations remain stable and predictable. To the extent that correlations between input variables change over time, it becomes far more difficult to model them.

Risk-Adjusted Value and Simulations

In our discussion of decision trees, we referred to the common misconception that decision trees are risk adjusted because they consider the likelihood of adverse events. The same misconception is prevalent in simulations, where the argument is that the cash flows from simulations are somehow risk adjusted because of the use of probability distributions and that the risk-free rate should be used in discounting these cash flows. With one exception, this argument does not make sense. Looking across simulations, the cash flows that we obtain are expected cash flows and are not risk adjusted. Consequently, we should be discounting these cash flows at a risk-adjusted rate.

The exception occurs when we use the standard deviation in values from a simulation as a measure of investment or asset risk and make decisions based on that measure. In this case, using a risk-adjusted discount rate will result in a double counting of risk. Consider a simple example. Assume that we are trying to choose between two assets, both of which we have valued using simulations and risk-adjusted discount rates. Table 6.3 summarizes our findings.

Table 6.3   Results of Simulation

Asset	Risk-Adjusted Discount Rate	Simulation Expected Value	Simulation Standard Deviation
A	12%	$100	15%
B	15%	$100	21%

Note that we view asset B to be riskier and have used a higher discount-rate-to-compute value. If we now proceed to reject asset B because the standard deviation is higher across the simulated values, we would be penalizing it twice. We can redo the simulations using the risk-free rate as the discount rate for both assets, but a note of caution needs to be introduced. If we then base our choice between these assets on the standard deviation in simulated values, we are assuming that all risk matters in investment choice, rather than only the risk that cannot be diversified away. Put another way, we may end up rejecting an asset because it has a high standard deviation in simulated values, even though adding that asset to a portfolio may result in little additional risk (because much of its risk can be diversified away).

This is not to suggest that simulations are not useful to us in understanding risk. Looking at the variance of the simulated values around the expected value provides a visual reminder that we are estimating value in an uncertain environment. It is also conceivable that we can use it as a decision tool in portfolio management in choosing between two stocks that are equally undervalued but have different value distributions. The stock with the less volatile value distribution may be considered a better investment than another stock with a more volatile value distribution.

An Overall Assessment of Probabilistic Risk Assessment Approaches

Now that we have looked at scenario analysis, decision trees, and simulations, we can consider not only when each one is appropriate but also how these approaches complement or replace risk-adjusted value approaches.

Comparing the Approaches

Assuming that we decide to use a probabilistic approach to assess risk and could choose between scenario analysis, decision trees, and simulations, which one should we pick? The answer will depend upon how we plan to use the output and what types of risk we are facing:

- **Selective versus full risk analysis**—In the best-case/worst-case scenario analysis, we look at only three scenarios (the best case, the most likely case, and the worst case) and ignore all other scenarios. Even when we consider multiple scenarios, we will not have a complete assessment of all possible outcomes from risky investments or assets. With decision trees and simulations, we attempt to consider all possible outcomes. In decision trees, we try to accomplish this by converting continuous risk into a manageable set of possible outcomes. With simulations, we use probability distributions to capture all possible outcomes. Put in terms of probability, the sum of the probabilities of the scenarios we examine in scenario analysis can be less than one, whereas the sum of the probabilities of outcomes in decision trees and simulations has to equal one. Consequently, we can compute expected values across outcomes in the latter, using the probabilities as weights. These expected values are comparable to the single estimate risk-adjusted values that we talked about in the previous chapter.

- **Type of risk**—As noted earlier, scenario analysis and decision trees are generally built around discrete outcomes in risky events, whereas simulations are better suited for continuous risks. Focusing on just scenario analysis and decision trees, the latter are better suited for sequential risks, because risk is considered in phases, whereas the former is easier to use when risks occur concurrently.

- **Correlation across risks**—If the various risks that an investment is exposed to are correlated, simulations allow for explicitly modeling these correlations (assuming that we can estimate and forecast them). In scenario analysis, we can deal with correlations subjectively by creating scenarios that allow for them; the high (low) interest rate scenario will also include slower (higher) economic growth. Correlated risks are difficult to model in decision trees.

Table 6.4 summarizes the relationship between risk type and the probabilistic approach used.

Table 6.4 Risk Type and Probabilistic Approaches

Discrete/Continuous	Correlated/ Independent	Sequential/ Concurrent	Risk Approach
Discrete	Independent	Sequential	Decision Tree
Discrete	Correlated	Concurrent	Scenario Analysis
Continuous	Either	Either	Simulations

Finally, the quality of the information will be a factor in our choice of approach. Because simulations heavily depend on being able to assess probability distributions and parameters, they work best in cases with substantial historical and cross-sectional data available that can be used to make these assessments. With decision trees, we need estimates of the probabilities of the outcomes at each chance node, making them best suited for risks that can be assessed either using past data or population characteristics. Thus, it should come as no surprise that when confronted with new and unpredictable risks, analysts continue to fall back on scenario analysis, notwithstanding its slapdash and subjective ways of dealing with risk.

Complement or Replacement for Risk Adjusted Value

As we noted in our discussion of both decision trees and simulations, we can use these approaches as either complements to or substitutes for risk-adjusted value. Scenario analysis, on the other hand, will always be a complement to risk-adjusted value, because it does not look at the full spectrum of possible outcomes.

When any of these approaches is used as a complement to risk-adjusted value, the caveats that we offered earlier in the chapter continue to apply and bear repeating. All of these approaches use expected rather than risk-adjusted cash flows, and the discount rate that is used should be a risk-adjusted one; we cannot use the risk-free rate to discount expected cash flows. In all three approaches, though, we still preserve the flexibility to change the risk-adjusted discount rate for different outcomes. Because all these approaches will also provide a range for estimated value and a measure of variability (in terms of value at the end nodes in a decision tree or as a standard deviation in value in a simulation), it is important that we do not double-count for risk. In other words, it is patently unfair to risky investments to discount their cash flows back at a risk-adjusted rate (in simulations and decision trees) and then to reject them because the variability in value is high.

We can use both simulations and decision trees as alternatives to risk-adjusted valuation, but there are constraints on the process. The first is that the cash flows will be discounted back at a risk-free rate to arrive at value. The second is that we now use the measure of variability in values that we obtain in both these approaches as a measure of risk in the investment. Comparing two assets with the same expected value (obtained with riskless rates as discount rates) from a simulation, we will pick the one with the lower variability in simulated values as the better investment. If we do this, we are assuming that all the risks that we have built into the simulation are relevant for the investment decision. In effect, we are ignoring the line drawn between risks that could have been diversified away in a portfolio and asset-specific risk on which much of modern finance is built. For an investor who is considering investing all her wealth in one asset, this should be reasonable. For a portfolio manager who is comparing two risky stocks that she is considering adding to a diversified portfolio or for a publicly traded company that is evaluating two projects, it can yield misleading results. The rejected stock or project with the higher variance in simulated values may be uncorrelated with the other investments in the portfolio and thus have little marginal risk.

In Practice

The use of probabilistic approaches has become more common with the surge in data availability and computing power. It is typical now to see a capital budgeting analysis, with 20 to 30 additional scenarios, or a Monte Carlo simulation attached to an equity valuation. In fact, the ease with which simulations can be implemented has allowed their use in a variety of new markets.

- **Deregulated electricity markets**—As electricity markets have become deregulated around the world, companies involved in the business of buying and selling electricity have begun using simulation models to quantify the swings in demand and supply of power, and the resulting price volatility. The results have been used to determine how much should be spent on building new power plants and how best to use the excess capacity in these plants.

- **Commodity companies**—Companies in commodity businesses—oil and precious metals, for instance—have used probabilistic approaches to examine how much they should bid for new sources for these commodities, rather than relying on a single best estimate of the future price. Analysts valuing these companies have also taken to modeling the value of these companies as a function of the price of the underlying commodity.

- **Technology companies**—Shifts in technology can be devastating for businesses that end up on the wrong side of the shift. Simulations and scenario analyses have been used to model the effects on revenues and earnings of the entry and diffusion of new technologies.

As we will see in the next chapter, simulations are key components of VaR and other risk management tools used, especially in firms that have to deal with risk in financial assets.

Conclusion

Estimating the risk-adjusted value for a risky asset or investment may seem like an exercise in futility. After all, the value is a function of the assumptions that we make about how the risk will unfold in the future. With probabilistic approaches to risk assessment, we estimate not only an expected value but also get a sense of the range of possible outcomes for value, across good and bad scenarios.

- In the most extreme form of scenario analysis, we look at the value in the best-case and worst-case scenarios and contrast it with the expected value. In its more general form, we estimate the value under a small number of likely scenarios, ranging from optimistic to pessimistic.

- Decision trees are designed for sequential and discrete risks, where the risk in an investment is considered into phases and the risk in each phase is captured in the possible outcomes and the probabilities that they will occur. A decision tree provides a complete assessment of risk and can be used to determine the optimal courses of action at each phase and an expected value for an asset today.

- Simulations provide the most complete assessments of risk because they are based on probability distributions for each input (rather than a single expected value or just discrete outcomes). The output from a simulation takes the form of an expected value across simulations and a distribution for the simulated values.

With all three approaches, the keys are to avoid double-counting risk (by using a risk-adjusted discount rate and considering the variability in estimated value as a risk measure) or making decisions based on the wrong types of risk.

APPENDIX 6.1

Statistical Distributions

Every statistics book provides a listing of statistical distributions with their properties, but browsing through these choices can be frustrating to anyone without a statistical background, for two reasons. First, the choices seem endless, with dozens of distributions competing for our attention, with little or no intuitive basis for differentiating between them. Second, the descriptions tend to be abstract and emphasize statistical properties such as the moments, characteristic functions, and cumulative distributions. In this appendix, we will focus on the aspects of distributions that are most useful when analyzing raw data and trying to fit the right distribution to that data.

Fitting the Distribution

When confronted with data that needs to be characterized by a distribution, it is best to start with the raw data and answer four basic questions that can help in the characterization. The first relates to whether the data can take on only *discrete values or whether the data is continuous*. Whether a new pharmaceutical drug gets FDA approval or not is a discrete value, but the revenues from the drug represent a continuous variable. The second looks at the *symmetry of the data* and if there is asymmetry, which direction it lies in. In other words, are positive and negative outliers equally likely, or is one more likely than the other? The third question is whether there are *upper or lower limits on the data*. Some data items, like revenues, cannot be lower than zero, whereas others, like operating margins, cannot exceed a value (100 percent). The final and related question relates to the *likelihood of observing extreme values* in the distribution. In some data, the extreme values occur very infrequently, whereas in others, they occur more often.

Is the Data Discrete or Continuous?

The first and most obvious categorization of data should be on whether the data is restricted to taking on only discrete values or if it is continuous. Consider the inputs into a typical project analysis at a firm. Most estimates that go into the analysis come from continuous distributions. Market size, market share, and profit margins, for instance, are all continuous variables. There are some important risk factors, though, that can take on only discrete forms, including regulatory actions and the threat of a terrorist attack. In the first case, the regulatory authority may dispense one of two or more decisions that are specified up front; in the latter, we are subjected to a terrorist attack, or we are not.

With discrete data, either the entire distribution can be developed from scratch, or the data can be fitted to a prespecified discrete distribution. With the former, there are two steps to building the distribution. The first is identifying the possible outcomes, and the second is estimating probabilities to each outcome. As we noted in the text, we can draw on historical data or experience as well as specific knowledge about the investment being analyzed to arrive at the final distribution. This process is relatively simple to accomplish when there are a few outcomes with a well-established basis for estimating probabilities but becomes more tedious as the number of outcomes increases. If it is difficult or impossible to build up a customized distribution, it may still be possible to fit the data to one of the following discrete distributions.

- **Binomial distribution**—The binomial distribution measures the probabilities of *the number of successes over a given number of trials* with a specified probability of success in each try. In the simplest scenario of a coin toss (with a fair coin), where the probability of getting a head with each toss is 50 percent and there are 100 trials, the binomial distribution will measure the likelihood of getting anywhere from no heads in 100 tosses (very unlikely) to 50 heads (the most likely) to 100 heads (also very unlikely). The binomial distribution in this case will be symmetric, reflecting the even odds; as the probabilities shift from even odds, the distribution will get more skewed. Figure 6A.1 presents binomial distributions for three scenarios—two with a 50 percent probability of success and one with a 70 percent probability of success and different trial sizes.

  As the probability of success is varied (from 50 percent), the distribution will also shift its shape, becoming positively skewed for probabilities less than 50 percent and negatively skewed for probabilities greater than 50 percent.[17]

- **Poisson distribution**—The Poisson distribution measures *the likelihood of a number of events occurring within a given time interval*, where the key parameter that is required is the average number of events in the given interval (λ). The resulting distribution looks similar to the binomial, with the skewness being positive but decreasing with λ. Figure 6A.2 presents three Poisson distributions, with λ ranging from 1 to 10.

---

17   As the number of trials increases and the probability of success is close to 0.5, the binomial distribution converges on the normal distribution.

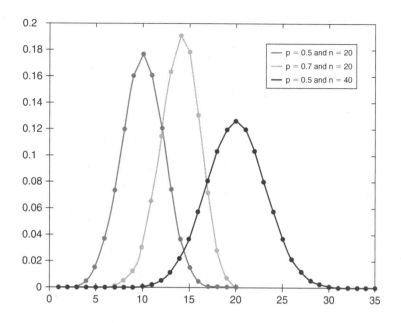

Figure 6A.1: Binomial Distribution

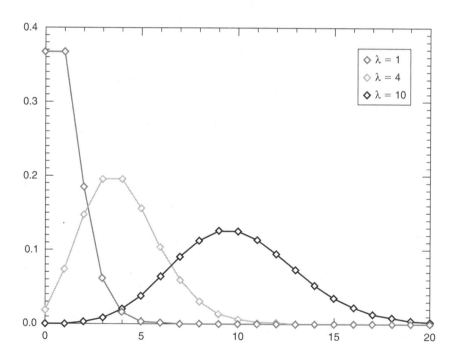

Figure 6A.2: Poisson Distribution

- **Negative binomial distribution**—Returning again to the coin toss example, assume that we hold the number of successes fixed at a given number, and *estimate the number of tries we will have before we reach the specified number of successes.* The resulting distribution is called the *negative binomial,* and it closely resembles the Poisson. In fact, the negative binomial distribution converges on the Poisson distribution but will be more skewed to the right (positive values) than the Poisson distribution with similar parameters.

- **Geometric distribution**—Consider again the coin toss example used to illustrate the binomial. Rather than focusing on the number of successes in n trials, assume that we are measuring the *likelihood of when the first success will occur.* For instance, with a fair coin toss, there is a 50 percent chance that the first success will occur at the first try, a 25 percent chance that it will occur on the second try, and a 12.5 percent chance that it will occur on the third try. The resulting distribution is positively skewed and looks as follows for three different probability scenarios (in Figure 6A.3).

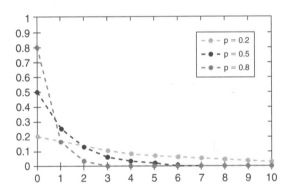

Figure 6A.3: Geometric Distribution

Note that the distribution is steepest with high probabilities of success and flattens out as the probability decreases. However, the distribution is always positively skewed.

- **Hypergeometric distribution**—The hypergeometric distribution measures the probability of a specified number of successes in n trials, *without replacement,* from a finite population. Because the sampling is without replacement, the probabilities can change as a function of previous draws. Consider, for instance, the possibility of getting 4 face cards in a hand of 10, over repeated draws from a pack. Because there are 16 face cards and the total pack contains 52 cards, we can estimate the probability of getting 4 face cards in a hand of 10. Figure 6A.4 provides a graph of the hypergeometric distribution.

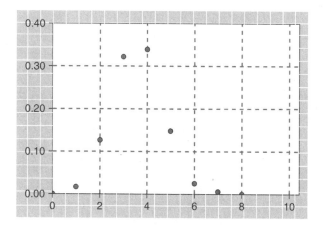

Figure 6A.4: Hypergeometric Distribution

Note that the hypergeometric distribution converges on binomial distribution as the population size increases.

- **Discrete uniform distribution**—This is the simplest of discrete distributions and applies when all the outcomes have an equal probability of occurring. Figure 6A.5 presents a uniform discrete distribution with 5 possible outcomes, each occurring 20 percent of the time.

The discrete uniform distribution is best reserved for circumstances where there are multiple possible outcomes but no information that would allow us to expect that one outcome is more likely than the others.

With continuous data, we cannot specify all possible outcomes because they are too numerous to list, but we have two choices. The first choice is to convert the continuous data into a discrete form and then go through the same process that we went through for discrete distributions of estimating probabilities. For instance, we could take a variable such as market share and break it down into discrete blocks—market share between 3 percent and 3.5 percent, between 3.5 percent and 4 percent, and so on—and consider the likelihood that we will fall into each block. The second choice is to find a continuous distribution that best fits the data and to specify the parameters of the distribution. The rest of this appendix will focus on how to make these choices.

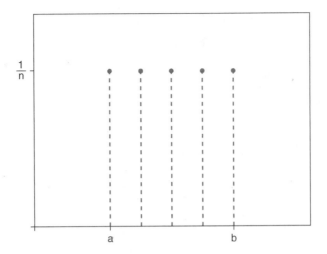

Figure 6A.5: Discrete Uniform Distribution

How Symmetric Is the Data?

Some datasets exhibit symmetry—that is, the upside is mirrored by the downside. The symmetric distribution that most practitioners are familiar with is the normal distribution, shown in Figure 6A.6, for a range of parameters.

The normal distribution has several features that make it popular. First, it can be fully characterized by just two parameters—the mean and the standard deviation—and thus reduces estimation pain. Second, the probability of any value occurring can be obtained simply by knowing how many standard deviations separate the value from the mean; the probability that a value will fall within 2 standard deviations of the mean is roughly 95 percent. The normal distribution is best suited for data that, at the minimum, meets the following conditions:

- There is a strong tendency for the data to take on a central value.

- Positive and negative deviations from this central value are equally likely.

- The frequency of the deviations falls off rapidly as we move further away from the central value.

The last two conditions show up when we compute the parameters of the normal distribution: the symmetry of deviations leads to zero skewness, and the low probabilities of large deviations from the central value reveal themselves in no kurtosis.

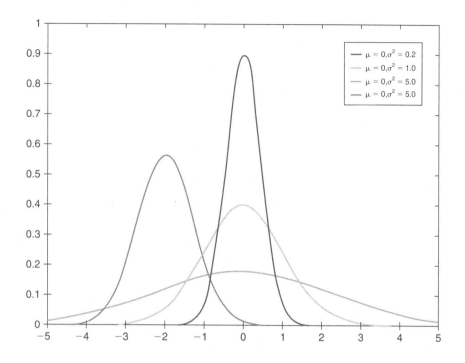

Figure 6A.6: Normal Distribution

We pay a cost, though, when we use a normal distribution to characterize data that is abnormal, because the probability estimates that we obtain will be misleading and can do more harm than good. One obvious problem is when the data is asymmetric, but another potential problem is when the probabilities of large deviations from the central value do not drop off as precipitously as required by the normal distribution. In statistical language, the actual distribution of the data has fatter tails than the normal. Although all symmetric distributions are like the normal in terms of the upside mirroring the downside, they vary in terms of shape, with some distributions having fatter tails than the normal and the others more accentuated peaks. These distributions are characterized as leptokurtic, and we can consider two examples. One is the logistic distribution, which has longer tails and a higher kurtosis (1.2, as compared to 0 for the normal distribution), and the other are Cauchy distributions, which also exhibit symmetry and higher kurtosis and are characterized by a scale variable that determines how fat the tails are. Figure 6A.7 presents a series of Cauchy distributions that exhibit the bias toward fatter tails or more outliers than the normal distribution.

Either the logistic or the Cauchy distributions can be used if the data is symmetric but with extreme values that occur more frequently than we would expect with a normal distribution.

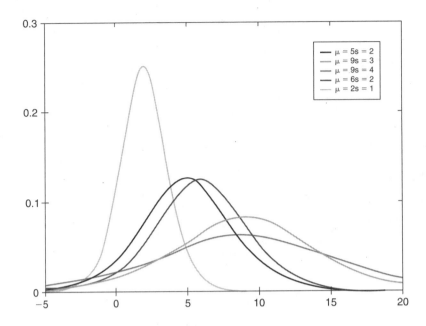

Figure 6A.7: Cauchy Distribution

As the probabilities of extreme values increase relative to the central value, the distribution will flatten out. At its limit, assuming that the data stays symmetric and we put limits on the extreme values on both sides, we end up with the uniform distribution, shown in Figure 6A.8.

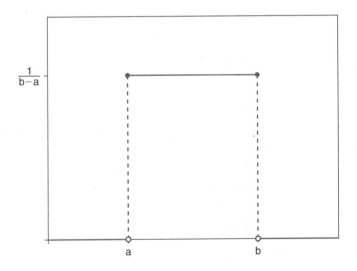

Figure 6A.8: Uniform Distribution

When is it appropriate to assume a uniform distribution for a variable? One possible scenario is when we have a measure of the highest and lowest values that a data item can take but no real information about where within this range the value may fall. In other words, any value within that range is just as likely as any other value.

Most data does not exhibit symmetry and instead skews toward either very large positive or very large negative values. If the data is positively skewed, one common choice is the lognormal distribution, which is typically characterized by three parameters: a shape (σ or sigma), a scale (μ or median), and a shift parameter (θ). When m=0 and θ=1, we have the standard lognormal distribution, and when θ=0, the distribution requires only scale and sigma parameters. As the sigma rises, the peak of the distribution shifts to the left, and the skewness in the distribution increases. Figure 6A.9 graphs lognormal distributions for a range of parameters.

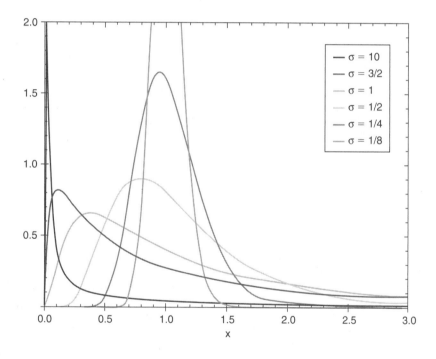

Figure 6A.9: Lognormal Distribution

The Gamma and Weibull distributions are two distributions that are closely related to the lognormal distribution; like the lognormal distribution, changing the parameter levels (shape, shift, and scale) can cause the distributions to change shape and become more or less skewed. In all these functions, increasing the shape parameter pushes the distribution toward the left. In fact, at high values of sigma, the left tail disappears entirely and the outliers are all positive. In this form, all these distributions resemble the exponential, characterized by a location (m) and scale parameter (b), as is clear from Figure 6A.10.

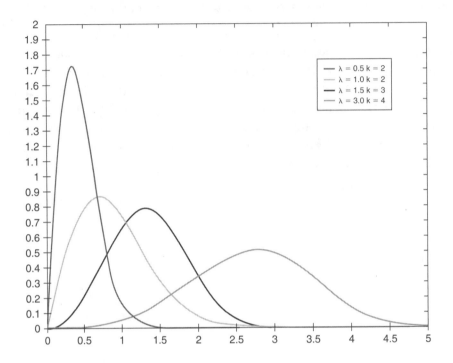

Figure 6A.10: Weibull Distribution

The question of which of these distributions best fits the data depends in large part on how severe the asymmetry in the data is. For moderate positive skewness, where there are both positive and negative outliers but the former are larger and more common, the standard lognormal distribution usually suffices. As the skewness becomes more severe, we may need to shift to a three-parameter lognormal distribution or a Weibull distribution and modify the shape parameter until it fits the data. At the extreme, if there are no negative outliers and only positive outliers in the data, we should consider the exponential function, shown in Figure 6A.11.

If the data exhibits negative slewness, the choices of distributions are more limited. One possibility is the Beta distribution, which has two shape parameters (p and q) and upper and lower bounds on the data (a and b). Altering these parameters can yield distributions that exhibit either positive or negative skewness, as shown in Figure 6A.12.

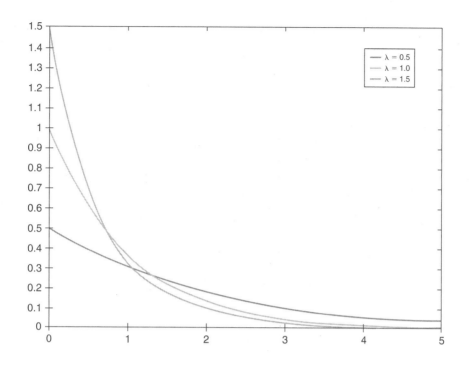

Figure 6A.11: Exponential Distribution

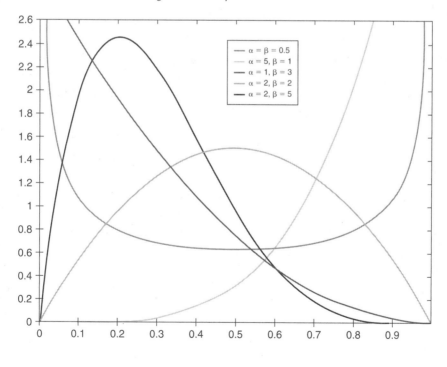

Figure 6A.12: Beta Distribution

Another is an extreme value distribution, which can also be altered to generate both positive and negative skewness, depending on whether the extreme outcomes are the maximum or minimum values; the former yields positive skewness and the latter negative (see Figure 6A.13).

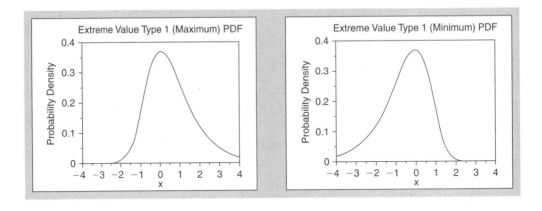

Figure 6A.13: Extreme Value Distributions

Are There Upper or Lower Limits on Data Values?

There are often natural limits on the values that data can take on. As we noted earlier, the revenues and the market value of a firm cannot be negative, and the profit margin cannot exceed 100 percent. Using a distribution that does not constrain the values to these limits can create problems. For instance, using a normal distribution to describe profit margins can sometimes result in profit margins that exceed 100 percent, because the distribution has no limits on either the downside or the upside.

When data is constrained, we need to answer the questions of whether the constraints apply on one side of the distribution or both, and if both, what the limits on values are. After we've answered these questions, we have two choices. One is to find a continuous distribution that conforms to these constraints. For instance, we can use the lognormal distribution to model data, such as revenues and stock prices that are constrained never to be less than zero. For data that has both upper and lower limits, we can use the uniform distribution, if the probabilities of the outcomes are even across outcomes or a triangular distribution (if the data is clustered around a central value). Figure 6A.14 presents a triangular distribution.

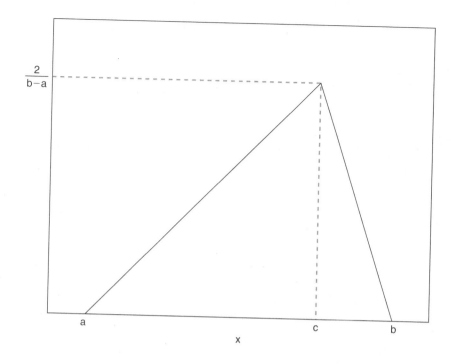

Figure 6A.14: Triangular Distribution

An alternative approach is to use a continuous distribution that normally allows data to take on any value and to put upper and lower limits on the values that the data can assume. Note that the cost of putting these constrains is small in distributions like the normal where the probabilities of extreme values is very small. It increases as the distribution exhibits fatter tails.

How Likely Are You to See Extreme Values of Data, Relative to the Middle Values?

As we noted in an earlier section, a key consideration in which distribution to use to describe the data is the likelihood of extreme values for the data, relative to the middle value. In the case of the normal distribution, this likelihood is small, but it increases as we move to the logistic and Cauchy distributions. Although it may often be more realistic to use the latter to describe real-world data, the benefits of a better distribution fit have to be weighed against the ease with which parameters can be estimated from the normal distribution. Consequently, it may make sense to stay with the normal distribution for symmetric data, unless the likelihood of extreme values increases above a threshold.

The same considerations apply for skewed distributions, although the concern is generally more acute for the skewed side of the distribution. In other words, with a positively skewed distribution, the question of which distribution to use depends on how much more likely large positive values are than large negative values, with the fit ranging from the lognormal to the exponential.

In summary, we cannot answer the question of which distribution best fits data without looking at whether the data is discrete or continuous, symmetric or asymmetric, and where the outliers lie. Figure 6A.15 summarizes the choices in a chart.

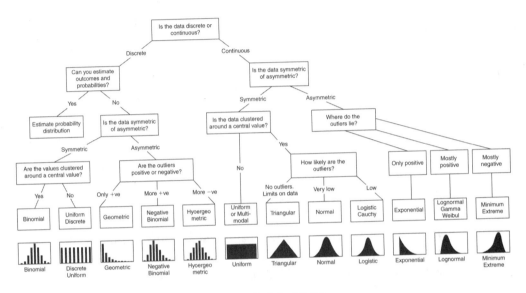

Figure 6A.15: Distributional Choices

Tests for Fit

The simplest test for distributional fit is visual, with a comparison of the histogram of the actual data to the fitted distribution. Consider Figure 6A.16, where we report the distribution of current price earnings ratios for U.S. stocks in early 2007, with a normal distribution superimposed on it.

The distributions are so clearly divergent that the normal distribution assumption does not hold up.

A slightly more sophisticated test is to compute the moments of the actual data distribution—the mean, the standard deviation, skewness, and kurtosis—and to examine them for fit to the chosen distribution. With the price-earnings data in Figure 6A.16, for instance, the moments of the distribution and key statistics are summarized in Table 6A.1.

Because the normal distribution has no skewness and zero kurtosis, we can easily reject the hypothesis that price earnings ratios are normally distributed.

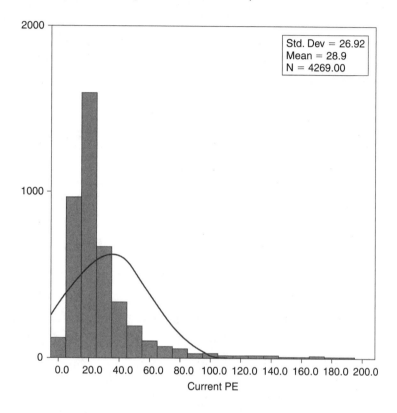

Figure 6A.16: Current PE Ratios for US Stocks–January 2007

Table 6A.1   Current PE Ratio for U.S. Stocks—Key Statistics

	Current PE	**Normal Distribution**
Mean	28.947	
Median	20.952	Median = Mean
Standard deviation	26.924	
Skewness	3.106	0
Kurtosis	11.936	0

The typical tests for goodness of fit compare the actual distribution function of the data with the cumulative distribution function of the distribution that is being used to characterize the data, either to accept the hypothesis that the chosen distribution fits the data or to reject it. Not surprisingly, given its constant use, there are more tests for normality than for any other distribution. The Kolmogorov-Smirnov test is one of the oldest tests of fit for distributions,[18] dating back to 1967. Improved versions of the tests include the Shapiro-Wilk and Anderson-Darling tests. Applying these tests to the current PE ratio yields the unsurprising result that the hypothesis that current PE ratios are drawn from a normal distribution is roundly rejected.

Tests of Normality

Tests of Normality

	Kolmogorov-Simirnov[a]			Shapiro-Wilk		
	Statistic	df	Sig.	Statistic	df	Sig.
Current PE	.204	4269	.000	.671	4269	.000

a. Lilliefors Significance Correction

There are graphical tests of normality, where probability plots can be used to assess the hypothesis that the data is drawn from a normal distribution. Figure 6A.17 illustrates this, using current PE ratios as the dataset.

Given that the normal distribution is one of the easiest to work with, it is useful to begin by testing data for abnormality to see if we can get away with using the normal distribution. If not, we can extend our search to other and more complex distributions.

---

18   The Kolgomorov-Smirnov test can be used to see if the data fits a normal, lognormal, Weibull, exponential, or logistic distribution.

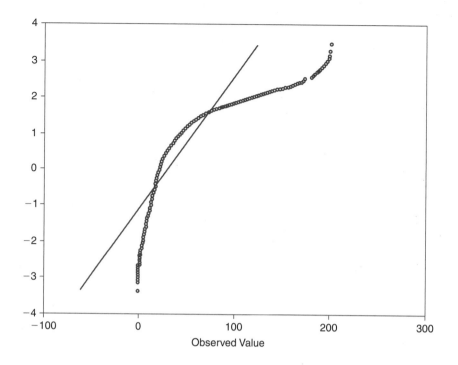

Figure 6A.17: Normal Q-Q Plot of Current PE

Conclusion

Raw data is almost never as well behaved as we would like it to be. Consequently, fitting a statistical distribution to data is part art and part science, requiring compromises along the way. The key to good data analysis is maintaining a balance between getting a good distributional fit and preserving ease of estimation, keeping in mind that the ultimate objective is that the analysis should lead to a better decision. In particular, we may decide to settle for a distribution that less completely fits the data over one that more completely fits it, simply because estimating the parameters may be easier to do with the former. This may explain the overwhelming dependence on the normal distribution in practice, notwithstanding the fact that most data does not meet the criteria needed for the distribution to fit.

7

VALUE AT RISK (VaR)

W hat is the most I can lose on this investment? This is a question that almost every investor who has invested or is considering investing in a risky asset asks at some point in time. Value at risk (VaR) tries to provide an answer, at least within a reasonable bound. In fact, it is misleading to consider VaR to be an alternative to risk-adjusted value and probabilistic approaches. After all, it borrows liberally from both. However, the wide use of VaR as a tool for risk assessment—especially in financial service firms—and the extensive literature that has developed around it push us to dedicate this chapter to its examination.

We begin this chapter with a general description of VaR and the view of risk that underlies its measurement, and we examine the history of its development and applications. We then consider the various estimation issues and questions that have come up in the context of measuring VaR and how analysts and researchers have tried to deal with them. Next, we evaluate variations that have been developed on the common measure, in some cases to deal with different types of risk and in other cases as a response to the limitations of VaR. In the final section, we evaluate how VaR fits into and contrasts with the other risk assessment measures we developed in the previous two chapters.

What Is VaR?

In its most general form, the VaR measures the potential loss in value of a risky asset or portfolio over a defined period for a given confidence interval. Thus, if the VaR on an asset is $100 million at a one-week, 95 percent confidence level, there is a only a 5 percent chance that the value of the asset will drop more than $100 million over any given week. In its adapted form, the measure is sometimes defined more narrowly as the possible loss in value from "normal market risk" as opposed to all risk, requiring that we draw distinctions between normal and abnormal risk as well as between market and nonmarket risk.

Although any entity can use VaR to measure its risk exposure, it is used most often by commercial and investment banks to capture the potential loss in value of their traded portfolios from adverse market movements over a specified period; this can then be compared to their available capital and cash reserves to ensure that the losses can be covered without putting the firms at risk.

Taking a closer look at VaR, there are clearly key aspects that mirror our discussion of simulations in the previous chapter:

- To estimate the probability of the loss, with a confidence interval, we need to define the probability distributions of individual risks, the correlation across these risks, and the effect of such risks on value. In fact, simulations are widely used to measure the VaR for asset portfolios.

- The focus in VaR is clearly on downside risk and potential losses. Its use in banks reflects their fear of a liquidity crisis, where a low-probability catastrophic occurrence creates a loss that wipes out the capital and creates a client exodus. The demise of Long Term Capital Management, the investment fund with top pedigree Wall Street traders and Nobel Prize winners, was a trigger in the widespread acceptance of VaR.

- VaR has three key elements: a specified level of loss in value, a fixed period over which risk is assessed, and a confidence interval. The VaR can be specified for an individual asset, a portfolio of assets, or for an entire firm.

- Although the VaR at financial service firms is specified in terms of market risks—interest rate changes, equity market volatility, and general economic growth—there is no reason why the risks cannot be defined more broadly or narrowly in specific contexts. Thus, we could compute the VaR for a large investment project for a firm in terms of competitive and firm-specific risks and the VaR for a gold mining company in terms of gold price movements.

In the sections that follow, we will begin by looking at the history of the development of this measure, ways in which to compute the VaR, limitations of and variations on the basic measures, and the way VaR fits into the broader spectrum of risk assessment approaches.

A Short History of VaR

Although the term *value at risk* was not widely used prior to the mid 1990s, the origins of the measure lie further back in time. The mathematics that underlie VaR were largely developed in the context of portfolio theory by Harry Markowitz and others, although their efforts were directed toward a different end—devising optimal portfolios for equity investors. In particular, the focus on market risks and the effects of the co-movements in these risks are central to the way VaR is computed.

The impetus for the use of VaR measures, though, came from the crises that beset financial service firms over time and the regulatory responses to these crises. The first regulatory capital requirements for banks were enacted in the aftermath of the Great Depression and the bank failures of the era, when the Securities Exchange Act established the Securities Exchange Commission (SEC) and required banks to keep their borrowings below 2000 percent of their equity capital. In the decades thereafter, banks devised risk measures and control devices to ensure that they met these capital requirements. With the increased risk created by the advent of derivative markets and floating exchange rates in the early 1970s, capital requirements were refined and expanded in the SEC's Uniform Net Capital Rule (UNCR) that was promulgated in 1975, which categorized the financial assets that banks held into 12 classes, based on risk, and required different capital requirements for each based upon risk, ranging from 0 percent for short-term treasuries to 30 percent for equities. Banks were required to report on their capital calculations in quarterly statements that were titled Financial and Operating Combined Uniform Single (FOCUS) reports.

The first regulatory measures that evoked VaR, though, were initiated in 1980, when the SEC tied the capital requirements of financial service firms to the losses that would be incurred, with 95 percent confidence over a 30-day interval, in different security classes. Historical returns were used to compute these potential losses. Although the measures were described as haircuts and not as value or capital at risk, it was clear the SEC was requiring financial service firms to embark on the process of estimating one-month 95 percent VaRs and hold enough capital to cover the potential losses.

At about the same time, the trading portfolios of investment and commercial banks were becoming larger and more volatile, creating a need for more sophisticated and timely risk control measures. Ken Garbade at Banker's Trust, in internal documents, presented sophisticated measures of VaR in 1986 for the firm's fixed income portfolios, based on the covariance in yields on bonds of different maturities. By the early 1990s, many financial service firms had developed rudimentary measures of VaR, with wide variations on how it was measured. In the aftermath of numerous disastrous losses associated with the use of derivatives and leverage between 1993 and 1995, culminating with the failure of Barings, the British investment bank, firms were ready for more comprehensive risk measures. In 1995, J. P. Morgan provided public access to data on the variances of and covariances across various security and asset classes that it had used internally for almost a decade to manage risk, and it allowed software makers to develop software to measure risk. It titled the service RiskMetrics and used the term *value at risk* to describe the risk measure that emerged from the data. The measure found a ready audience with commercial and investment banks and the regulatory authorities overseeing them, who warmed to its intuitive appeal. In the past decade, VaR has become the established measure of risk exposure in financial service firms and has even begun to find acceptance in nonfinancial service firms.

Measuring VaR

Three basic approaches are used to compute VaR, although each approach has numerous variations. The measure can be computed analytically by making assumptions about return distributions for market risks and by using the variances in and covariances across these risks. It can also be estimated by running hypothetical portfolios through historical data or from Monte Carlo simulations. In this section, we describe and compare the approaches.[1]

Variance-Covariance Method

Because VaR measures the probability that the value of an asset or portfolio will drop below a specified value in a particular period, it should be relatively simple to compute if we can derive a probability distribution of potential values. That is basically what we do in the variance-covariance method, an approach that has the benefit of simplicity but is limited by the difficulties associated with deriving probability distributions.

General Description

Consider a simple example. Assume that we are assessing the VaR for a single asset, where the potential values are normally distributed with a mean of $120 million and an annual standard deviation of $10 million. With 95 percent confidence, we can assess that the value of this asset will not drop below $80 million (two standard deviations below the mean) or rise about $120 million (two standard deviations above the mean) over the next year.[2] When working with portfolios of assets, the same reasoning will apply,

---

1   For a comprehensive overview of VaR and its measures, look at Jorion, P. *Value at Risk: The New Benchmark for Managing Financial Risk.* New York: McGraw Hill, 2001. For a listing of every possible reference to the measure, try www.GloriaMundi.org.

2   The 95 percent confidence intervals translate into 1.96 standard deviations on either side of the mean. With a 90 percent confidence interval, we would use 1.65 standard deviations. A 99 percent confidence interval would require 2.33 standard deviations.

but the process of estimating the parameters is complicated by the fact that the assets in the portfolio often move together. As we noted in our discussion of portfolio theory in Chapter 4, "How Do We Measure Risk?," the central inputs to estimating the variance of a portfolio are the covariances of the pairs of assets in the portfolio. In a portfolio of 100 assets, there will be 49,500 covariances that need to be estimated, in addition to the 100 individual asset variances. Clearly, this is not practical for large portfolios with shifting asset positions.

It is to simplify this process that we map the risk in the individual investments in the portfolio to more general market risks, when we compute VaR, and then estimate the measure based on these market risk exposures. This process generally involves four steps:

1. The first step requires us to take each of the assets in a portfolio and map that asset on to simpler, standardized instruments. For instance, a 10-year coupon bond with annual coupons C and face value FV, for instance, can be broken down into 10 zero coupon bonds, with matching cash flows.

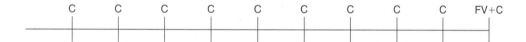

The first coupon matches up to a one-year zero coupon bond with a face value of C, the second coupon matches a two-year zero coupon bond with a face value of C, and so on until the tenth cash flow. The tenth cash flow is matched up with a 10-year zero coupon bond with a face value of FV (corresponding to the face value of the 10-year bond) plus C. The mapping process is more complicated for more complex assets such as stocks and options, but the basic intuition does not change. We try to map every financial asset into a set of instruments representing the underlying market risks. Why bother with mapping? Instead of having to estimate the variances and covariances of thousands of individual assets, we estimate those statistics for the common market risk instruments that these assets are exposed to; there are far fewer of the latter than the former. The resulting matrix can be used to measure the VaR of any asset that is exposed to a combination of these market risks.

2. In the second step, each financial asset is stated as a set of positions in the standardized market instruments. This is simple for the 10-year coupon bond, where the intermediate zero coupon bonds have face values that match the coupons, and the final zero coupon bond has the face value, in addition to the coupon in

that period. As with the mapping, this process is more complicated when working with convertible bonds, stocks, or derivatives.

3. After the standardized instruments that affect the asset or assets in a portfolio have been identified, we have to estimate the variances in each of these instruments and the covariances across the instruments. In practice, we obtain these variance and covariance estimates by looking at historical data. That data is key to estimating the VaR.

4. In the final step, the VaR for the portfolio is computed using the weights on the standardized instruments computed in step 2 and the variances and covariances in these instruments computed in step 3.

Appendix 7.1 provides an illustration of the VaR computation for a six-month dollar/euro forward contract. The standardized instruments that underlie the contract are identified as the six month risk-free securities in the dollar and the euro and the spot dollar/euro exchange rate. The dollar values of the instruments is computed and the VaR is estimated based on the covariances between the three instruments.

Implicit in the computation of the VaR in step 4 are assumptions about the way returns on the standardized risk measures are distributed. The most convenient assumption both from a computational standpoint and in terms of estimating probabilities is normality, and it should come as no surprise that many VaR measures are based on some variant of that assumption. If, for instance, we assume that each market risk factor has normally distributed returns, we ensure that the returns on any portfolio that is exposed to multiple market risk factors will also have a normal distribution. Even those VaR approaches that allow for abnormal return distributions for individual risk factors find ways of ending up with normal distributions for final portfolio values.

The RiskMetrics Contribution

As we noted in an earlier section, the term *value at risk* and the usage of the measure can be traced back to the RiskMetrics service offered by J. P. Morgan in 1995. The key contribution of the service was that it made the variances in and covariances across asset classes freely available to anyone who wanted to access them, thus easing the task for anyone who wanted to compute the VaR analytically for a portfolio. Publications by J. P. Morgan in 1996 describe the assumptions underlying its computation of VaR:[3]

---

3   J. P. Morgan. "RiskMetrics—Technical Document." December 17, 1996.

Zangari, P. "An Improved Methodology for Computing VaR." *J. P. Morgan RiskMetrics Monitor*, Second Quarter 1996.

- Returns on individual risk factors are assumed to follow conditional normal distributions. Although returns themselves may not be normally distributed and large outliers are far too common (that is, the distributions have fat tails), the assumption is that the standardized return (computed as the return divided by the forecasted standard deviation) is normally distributed.

- The focus on standardized returns implies that it is not the size of the return per se that we should focus on but its size relative to the standard deviation. In other words, a large return (positive or negative) in a period of high volatility may result in a low standardized return, whereas the same return following a period of low volatility will yield an abnormally high standardized return.

The focus on normalized returns exposed the VaR computation to the risk of more frequent large outliers than would be expected with a normal distribution. In a subsequent variation, the RiskMetrics approach was extended to cover normal mixture distributions, which allow for the assignment of higher probabilities for outliers. Figure 7.1 contrasts the two distributions.

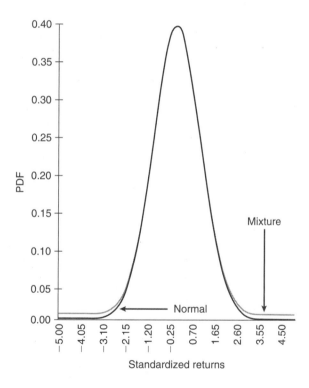

Figure 7.1 Standard normal and normal mixture
probability density functions (PDF)

In effect, these distributions require estimates of the probabilities of outsized returns occurring and the expected size and standard deviations of such returns, in addition to the standard normal distribution parameters. Even proponents of these models concede that estimating the parameters for jump processes, given the infrequently of jumps, is difficult.

Assessment

The strength of the variance-covariance approach is that the VaR is simple to compute after we have made an assumption about the distribution of returns and inputted the means, variances, and covariances of returns. In the estimation process, though, lie the three key weaknesses of the approach.

- **Wrong distributional assumption**—If conditional returns are not normally distributed, the computed VaR will understate the true VaR. In other words, if there are far more outliers in the actual return distribution than would be expected given the normality assumption, the actual VaR will be much higher than the computed VaR.

- **Input error**—Even if the standardized return distribution assumption holds up, the VaR can still be wrong if the variances and covariances that are used to estimate it are incorrect. To the extent that these numbers are estimated using historical data, there is a standard error associated with each of the estimates. In other words, the variance-covariance matrix that is input to the VaR measure is a collection of estimates, some of which have large error terms.

- **Nonstationary variables**—A related problem occurs when the variances and covariances across assets change over time. This nonstationarity in values is common because the fundamentals driving these numbers do change over time. Thus, the correlation between the U.S. dollar and the Japanese yen may change if oil prices increase by 15 percent. This, in turn, can lead to a breakdown in the computed VaR.

Not surprisingly, much of the work that has been done to revitalize the approach has been directed at dealing with these critiques.

First, a host of researchers have examined how best to compute VaR with assumptions other than the standardized normal; we mentioned the normal mixture model in the section "The RiskMetrics Contribution."[4] Hull and White suggest ways of estimating VaR when variables are not normally distributed; they allow users to specify any probability

---

4   Duffie, D., and J. Pan. "An Overview of Value at Risk." Working Paper, Stanford University, 1997. The authors provide a comprehensive examination of different distributions and the parameters that have to be estimated for each one.

distribution for variables but require that transformations of the distribution still fall under a multivariate normal distribution.[5] These and other papers like it develop interesting variations but have to overcome two practical problems. Estimating inputs for non-normal models can be difficult, especially when working with historical data, and the probabilities of losses and VaR are simplest to compute with the normal distribution and get progressively more difficult with asymmetric and fat-tailed distributions.

Second, other research has been directed at bettering the estimation techniques to yield more reliable variance and covariance values to use in the VaR calculations. Some suggest refinements on sampling methods and data innovations that allow for better estimates of variances and covariances looking forward. Others posit that statistical innovations can yield better estimates from existing data. For instance, conventional estimates of VaR are based on the assumption that the standard deviation in returns does not change over time (*homoskedasticity*). Engle argues that we get much better estimates by using models that explicitly allow the standard deviation to change over time (*heteroskedasticity*).[6] In fact, he suggests two variants—autoregressive conditional heteroskedasticity (ARCH) and generalized autoregressive conditional heteroskedasticity (GARCH)—that provide better forecasts of variance and, by extension, better measures of VaR.[7]

One final critique that can be leveled against the variance-covariance estimate of VaR is that it is designed for portfolios that have a linear relationship between risk and portfolio positions. Consequently, it can break down when the portfolio includes options, because the payoffs on an option are not linear. In an attempt to deal with options and other nonlinear instruments in portfolios, researchers have developed *Quadratic VaR* measures.[8] These quadratic measures, sometimes categorized as delta-gamma models (to contrast with the more conventional linear models, which are called delta-normal), allow researchers to estimate the VaR for complicated portfolios that include options and option-like securities such as convertible bonds. The cost, though, is that the math-

---

5   Hull, J., and A. White. "Value at Risk When Daily Changes Are Not Normally Distributed." *Journal of Derivatives*, Vol. 5, 9–19, 1998.

6   Engle, R. "GARCH 101: The Use of ARCH and GARCH Models in Applied Econometrics." *Journal of Economic Perspectives*, Vol. 15, 157–168, 2001.

7   He uses the example of a $1,000,0000 portfolio composed of 50 percent NASDAQ stocks, 30 percent Dow Jones stocks, and 20 percent long bonds, with statistics computed from March 23, 1990 to March 23, 2000. Using the conventional measure of daily standard deviation of 0.83 percent computed over a 10-year period, he estimates the value at risk in a day to be $22,477. Using an ARCH model, the forecasted standard deviation is 1.46 percent, leading to VaR of $33,977. Allowing for the fat tails in the distribution increases the VaR to $39,996.

8   Britten-Jones, M. and S. M. Schaefer. "Non-Linear Value-at-Risk." *European Finance Review*, Vol. 2, 161–187, 1999.

     Rouvinez, C. "Going Greek with VAR." *Risk*, Vol. 10, 57–65, 1997.

ematics associated with deriving the VaR become complicated, and some of the intuition is lost along the way.

Historical Simulation

Historical simulations represent the simplest way of estimating the VaR for many portfolios. In this approach, the VaR for a portfolio is estimated by creating a hypothetical time series of returns on that portfolio, obtained by running the portfolio through actual historical data and computing the changes that would have occurred in each period.

General Approach

To run a historical simulation, we begin with time series data on each market risk factor, just as we would for the variance-covariance approach. However, we do not use the data to estimate variances and covariances looking forward, because the changes in the portfolio over time yield all the information we need to compute the VaR.

Cabedo and Moya provide a simple example of the application of historical simulation to measure the VaR in oil prices.[9] Using historical data from 1992 to 1998, they obtained the daily prices in Brent Crude Oil and graphed the prices in Figure 7.2.

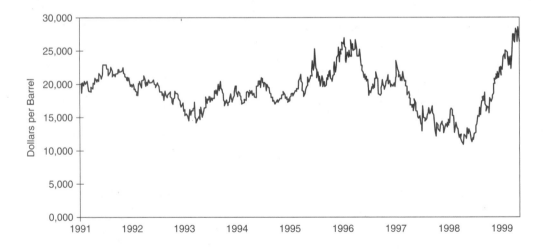

Figure 7.2: Price/barrel for Brent Crude Oil – 1992-99

---

9   J. D. Cabedo and I. Moya. "Estimating Oil Price Value at Risk Using the Historical Simulation Approach." *Energy Economics*, Vol. 25, 239–253, 2003.

They separated the daily price changes into positive and negative numbers and analyzed each group. With a 99 percent confidence interval, the positive VaR was defined as the price change in the 99th percentile of the positive price changes and the negative VaR as the price change at the 99th percentile of the negative price changes.[10] For the period they studied, the daily VaR at the 99th percentile was about 1 percent in both directions.

The implicit assumptions of the historical simulation approach are visible in this simple example. The first assumption is that the approach is agnostic when it comes to distributional assumptions, and the VaR is determined by the actual price movements. In other words, there are no underlying assumptions of normality driving the conclusion. The second is that each day in the time series carries an equal weight when it comes to measuring the VaR, a potential problem if there is a trend in the variability—lower in the earlier periods and higher in the later periods, for instance. The third is that the approach is based on the assumption of history repeating itself, with the period used providing a full and complete snapshot of the risks that the oil market is exposed to in other periods.

Assessment

Although historical simulations are popular and relatively easy to run, they do come with baggage. In particular, the underlying assumptions of the model give rise to its weaknesses.

- **Past is not prologue**—Although all approaches to estimating VaR use historical data, historical simulations are much more reliant on them than the other approaches for the simple reason that the VaR is computed entirely from historical price changes. There is little room to overlay distributional assumptions (as we do with the variance-covariance approach) or to bring in subjective information (as we can with Monte Carlo simulations). The example provided in the previous section with oil prices provides a classic example. A portfolio manager or corporation that determined its oil price VaR, based on 1992 to 1998 data, would have been exposed to much larger losses than expected over the 1999 to 2004 period as a long period of oil price stability came to an end and price volatility increased.

- **Trends in the data**—A related argument can be made about the way in which we compute VaR, using historical data, in which all data points are weighted equally. In other words, the price changes from trading days in 1992 affect the VaR in the

---

10   By separating the price changes into positive and negative changes, they allow for asymmetry in the return process where large negative changes are more common than large positive changes, or vice versa.

same proportion as price changes from trading days in 1998. To the extent that there is a trend of increasing volatility even within the historical period, we will understate the VaR.

- **New assets or market risks**—Although this could be a critique of any of the three approaches for estimating VaR, the historical simulation approach has the most difficulty dealing with new risks and assets for an obvious reason: there is no historic data available to compute the VaR. Assessing the VaR to a firm from developments in online commerce in the late 1990s would have been difficult to do, because the online business was in its nascent stage.

The trade-off that we mentioned earlier is therefore at the heart of the historic simulation debate. The approach saves us the trouble and related problems of having to make specific assumptions about distributions of returns, but it implicitly assumes that the distribution of past returns is a good and complete representation of expected future returns. In a market where risks are volatile and structural shifts occur at regular intervals, this assumption is difficult to sustain.

Modifications

As with the other approaches to computing VaR, modifications to the approach have been suggested, largely directed at taking into account some of the criticisms mentioned in the previous section.

- **Weighting the recent past more**—A reasonable argument can be made that returns in the recent past are better predictors of the immediate future than are returns from the distant past. Boudoukh, Richardson, and Whitelaw present a variant on historical simulations, where recent data is weighted more, using a decay factor as their time-weighting mechanism.[11] In simple terms, each return, rather than being weighted equally, is assigned a probability weight based on its recency. In other words, if the decay factor is .90 and the most recent observation has the probability weight p, the observation prior to it will be weighted 0.9p, the one before that will be weighted 0.81p, and so on. In fact, the conventional historical simulation approach is a special case of this approach, where the decay factor is set to 1. Boudoukh et al. illustrate the use of this technique by computing the VaR for a stock portfolio, using 250 days of returns, immediately before and after the market crash on October 19, 1987.[12] With historical simulation, the VaR for this portfolio is for all practical purposes unchanged the

---

11   Boudoukh, J., M. Richardson, and R. Whitelaw,. "The Best of Both Worlds." *Risk*, Vol. 11, 64–67, 1998.

12   The Dow dropped 508 points on October 19, 1987, approximately 22 percent.

day after the crash because it weights each day (including October 19) equally. With decay factors, the VaR very quickly adjusts to reflect the size of the crash.[13]

- **Combining historical simulation with time series models**—Earlier in this section, we referred to a VaR computation by Cabado and Moya for oil prices using a historical simulation. In the same paper, they suggested that better estimates of VaR could be obtained by fitting a time series model through the historical data and using the parameters of that model to forecast the VaR. In particular, they fit an autoregressive moving average (ARMA) model to the oil price data from 1992 to 1998 and use this model to forecast returns with a 99 percent confidence interval for the holdout period of 1999. The actual oil price returns in 1999 fall within the predicted bounds 98.8 percent of the time, in contrast to the 97.7 percent of the time that they do with the unadjusted historical simulation. One reason for the improvement is that the measured VaR is much more sensitive to changes in the variance of oil prices with time series models, than with the historical simulation, as can be seen in Figure 7.3.

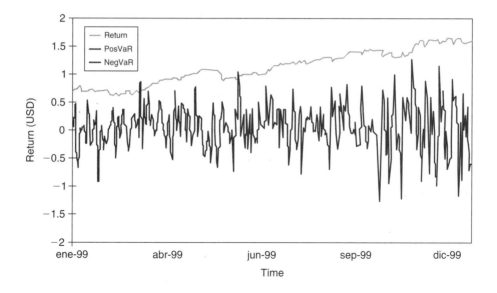

Figure 7.3: Value at Risk Estimates (99%) from Time Series Models

---

13 With a decay factor of 0.99, the most recent day will be weighted about 1 percent (instead of 1/250). With a decay factor of 0.97, the most recent day will be weighted about 3 percent.

Note that the range widens in the later part of the year in response to the increasing volatility in oil prices, as the time series model is updated to incorporate more recent data.

- **Volatility updating**—Hull and White suggest a different way of updating historical data for shifts in volatility. For assets where the recent volatility is higher than historical volatility, they recommend that the historical data be adjusted to reflect the change. Assume, for illustrative purposes, that the updated standard deviation in prices is 0.8 percent and that it was only 0.6 percent when estimated with data from 20 days ago. Rather than use the price change from 20 days ago, they recommend scaling that number to reflect the change in volatility; a 1 percent return on that day would be converted into a 1.33 percent return ($\frac{0.8}{0.6}*1\%$). Their approach requires day-specific estimates of variance that change over the historical period, which they obtain by using GARCH models.[14]

Note that all of these variations are designed to capture shifts that have occurred in the recent past but are underweighted by the conventional approach. None of them is designed to bring in the risks that are out of the sampled historical period (but are still relevant risks) or to capture structural shifts in the market and the economy. In a paper comparing the different historical simulation approaches, Pritsker notes the limitations of the variants.[15]

Monte Carlo Simulation

In the previous chapter, we examined the use of Monte Carlo simulations as a risk assessment tool. These simulations also happen to be useful in assessing VaR, with the focus on the probabilities of losses exceeding a specified value rather than on the entire distribution.

General Description

The first two steps in a Monte Carlo simulation mirror the first two steps in the Variance-covariance method where we identify the market risks that affect the asset or assets in a portfolio and convert individual assets into positions in standardized instruments. It is in the third step that the differences emerge. Rather than compute the variances and covariances across the market risk factors, we take the simulation route, where we

---

14 Hull, J. and A. White. "Incorporating Volatility Updating into the Historical Simulation Method for Value at Risk." *Journal of Risk*, Vol. 1, 5–19, 1998.

15 Pritsker, M. "The Hidden Dangers of Historical Simulation." Working Paper, SSRN, 2001.

specify probability distributions for each of the market risk factors and specify how these market risk factors move together. Thus, in the example of the six-month dollar/euro forward contract that we used earlier, the probability distributions for the 6-month zero coupon $ bond, the 6-month zero coupon euro bond, and the dollar/euro spot rate will have to be specified, as will the correlation across these instruments.

Although the estimation of parameters is easier if we assume normal distributions for all variables, the power of Monte Carlo simulations comes from the freedom we have to pick alternate distributions for the variables. In addition, we can bring in subjective judgments to modify these distributions.

After the distributions are specified, the simulation process starts. In each run, the market risk variables take on different outcomes, and the value of the portfolio reflects the outcomes. After a repeated series of runs, numbering usually in the thousands, we will have a distribution of portfolio values that can be used to assess VaR. For instance, assume that we run a series of 10,000 simulations and derive corresponding values for the portfolio. We can rank these values from highest to lowest, and the 95 percent percentile VaR will correspond to the 500th lowest value and the 99th percentile to the 100th lowest value.

Assessment

Much of what was said about the strengths and weaknesses of the simulation approach in the previous chapter apply to its use in computing VaR. Quickly reviewing the criticism, a simulation is only as good as the probability distribution for the inputs that are fed into it. Although Monte Carlo simulations are often touted as more sophisticated than historical simulations, many users directly draw on historical data to make their distributional assumptions.

In addition, as the number of market risk factors increases and their comovements become more complex, Monte Carlo simulations become more difficult to run for two reasons. First, we now have to estimate the probability distributions for hundreds of market risk variables rather than just the handful that we talked about in the context of analyzing a single project or asset. Second, the number of simulations that we need to run to obtain reasonable estimates of VaR will have to increase substantially (to the tens of thousands from the thousands).

We can see the strengths of Monte Carlo simulations when we compare them to the other two approaches for computing VaR. Unlike the variance-covariance approach, we do not have to make unrealistic assumptions about normality in returns. In contrast to the historical simulation approach, we begin with historical data but are free to bring in both subjective judgments and other information to improve forecasted probability distributions. Finally, Monte Carlo simulations can be used to assess the VaR for any type of portfolio and are flexible enough to cover options and option-like securities.

Modifications

As with the other approaches, the modifications to the Monte Carlo simulation are directed at its biggest weakness, which is its computational bulk. To provide a simple illustration, a yield curve model with 15 key rates and 4 possible values for each will require 1,073,741,824 simulations (4^{15}) to be complete. The modified versions narrow the focus, using different techniques, and reduce the required number of simulations.

- **Scenario simulation**—One way to reduce the computation burden of running Monte Carlo simulations is to do the analysis over a number of discrete scenarios. Frye suggests an approach that can be used to develop these scenarios by applying a small set of prespecified shocks to the system.[16] Jamshidan and Zhu suggest what they called scenario simulations where they use principal component analysis as a first step to narrow the number of factors. Rather than allow each risk variable to take on all the potential values, they look at likely combinations of these variables to arrive at scenarios. The values are computed across these scenarios to arrive at the simulation results.[17]

- **Monte Carlo simulations with variance-covariance method modification**—The strength of the variance-covariance method is its speed. If we are willing to make the required distributional assumption about normality in returns and have the variance-covariance matrix in hand, we can compute the VaR for any portfolio in minutes. The strength of the Monte Carlo simulation approach is the flexibility it offers users to make different distributional assumptions and deal with various types of risk, but it can be painfully slow to run. Glasserman, Heidelberger, and Shahabuddin use approximations from the variance-covariance approach to guide the sampling process in Monte Carlo simulations and report a substantial savings in time and resources, without appreciable loss of precision.[18]

---

16 Frye, J. "Principals of Risk: Finding Value-at-Risk Through Factor-Based Interest Rate Scenarios." NationsBanc-CRT, 1997.

17 Jamshidian, Farshid, and Yu Zhu. "Scenario Simulation: Theory and Methodology." *Finance and Stochastics*, Vol. 1, 43–67, 1997. In principal component analysis, we look for common factors affecting returns in historical data.

18 Glasserman, P., P. Heidelberger, and P. Shahabuddin. "Efficient Monte Carlo Methods for Value at Risk." Working Paper, Columbia University, 2000.

The trade-off in each of these modifications is simple. We give up some of the power and precision of the Monte Carlo approach but gain in terms of estimation requirements and computational time.

Comparing Approaches

Each of the three approaches to estimating VaR has advantages and comes with limitations. The variance-covariance approach, with its delta normal and delta gamma variations, requires us to make strong assumptions about the return distributions of standardized assets, but it is simple to compute after those assumptions have been made. The historical simulation approach requires no assumptions about the nature of return distributions but implicitly assumes that the data used in the simulation is a representative sample of the risks looking forward. The Monte Carlo simulation approach allows for the most flexibility in terms of choosing distributions for returns and bringing in subjective judgments and external data, but it is the most demanding from a computational standpoint.

Because the product of all three approaches is the VaR, it is worth asking two questions.

- How different are the estimates of VaR that emerge from the three approaches?
- If they are different, which approach yields the most reliable estimate of VaR?

To answer the first question, we have to recognize that the answers we obtain with all three approaches are a function of the inputs. For instance, the historical simulation and variance-covariance methods will yield the same VaR if the historical returns data is normally distributed and is used to estimate the variance-covariance matrix. Similarly, the variance-covariance approach and Monte Carlo simulations will yield roughly the same values if all the inputs in the latter are assumed to be normally distributed with consistent means and variances. As the assumptions diverge, so will the answers. Finally, the historical and Monte Carlo simulation approaches will converge if the distributions we use in the latter are entirely based on historical data.

As for the second, the answer seems to depend both on what risks are being assessed and how the competing approaches are used. As we noted at the end of each approach, variants have been developed within each approach, aimed at improving performance. Many of the comparisons across approaches are skewed by the fact that the researchers doing the comparison are testing variants of an approach that they have developed against alternatives. Not surprisingly, they find that their approaches work better than the alternatives. Looking at the unbiased studies of the alternative approaches, the evidence is mixed. Hendricks compared the VaR estimates obtained using the variance-covariance and historical simulation approaches on 1,000 randomly selected foreign exchange portfolios.[19] He used nine measurement criteria, including the mean squared error (of the actual loss against the forecasted loss) and the percentage of the outcomes covered. He concluded that the different approaches yield risk measures that are roughly comparable, and they all cover the risk that they are intended to cover, at least up to the 95 percent confidence interval. He did conclude that all the measures have trouble capturing extreme outcomes and shifts in underlying risk. Lambadrais, Papadopoulou, Skiadopoulus, and Zoulis computed the VaR in the Greek stock and bond market with historical Monte Carlo simulations. They found that although historical simulation overstated the VaR for linear stock portfolios, the results were less clear-cut with nonlinear bond portfolios.[20]

In short, the question of which VaR approach is best can be answered by looking at the task. If we are assessing the VaR for portfolios that do not include options, over short periods (a day or a week), the variance-covariance approach does a reasonably good job, notwithstanding its heroic assumptions of normality. If the VaR is being computed for a risk source that is stable and where there is substantial historical data (commodity prices, for instance), historical simulations provide good estimates. In the most general case of computing VaR for nonlinear portfolios (which include options) over longer periods, where the historical data is volatile and nonstationary and the normality assumption is questionable, Monte Carlo simulations do best.

Limitations of VaR

Although VaR has acquired a strong following in the risk management community, there is reason to be skeptical of its accuracy as a risk management tool and its use in decision making. Researchers have taken issue with VaR on many dimensions, and we will categorize the criticism into those dimensions.

VaR Can Be Wrong

There is no precise measure of VaR, and each measure comes with its own limitations. The result is that the VaR that we compute for an asset, portfolio, or firm can be wrong, and sometimes, the errors can be large enough to make VaR a misleading measure of risk

---

19   Hendricks, D. "Evaluation of Value-at-Risk Models Using Historical Data." *Economic Policy Review*, Vol. 2, 39–70. Federal Reserve Bank of New York, 1996.

20   Lambadiaris, G., L. Papadopoulou, G. Skiadopoulos, and Y. Zoulis. "History or Simulation?" www.risk.net, 2000.

exposure. The reasons for the errors can vary across firms and for different measures and include the following.

- **Return distributions**—Every VaR measure makes assumptions about return distributions, which, if violated, result in incorrect estimates of the VaR. With delta-normal estimates of VaR, we are assuming that the multivariate return distribution is the normal distribution, because the VaR is based entirely on the standard deviation in returns. With Monte Carlo simulations, we get more freedom to specify different types of return distributions, but we can still be wrong when we make those judgments. Finally, with historical simulations, we are assuming that the historical return distribution (based upon past data) is representative of the distribution of returns looking forward.

  There is substantial evidence that returns are not normally distributed and that not only are outliers more common in reality but that they are much larger than expected, given the normal distribution. In chapter 4, we noted Mandelbrot's critique of the mean-variance framework and his argument that returns followed power law distributions. His critique extended to the use of VaR as the risk measure of choice at financial service firms. Firms that use VaR to measure their risk exposure, he argued, would be under prepared for large and potentially catastrophic events that are extremely unlikely in a normal distribution but seem to occur at regular intervals in the real world.

- **History may not a good predictor**—All measures of VaR use historical data to some degree or the other. In the variance-covariance method, historical data is used to compute the variance-covariance matrix that is the basis for the computation of VaR. In historical simulations, the VaR is entirely based on the historical data with the likelihood of value losses computed from the time series of returns. In Monte Carlo simulations, the distributions don't have to be based on historical data, but it is difficult to see how else they can be derived. In short, any VaR measure will be a function of the period over which the historical data is collected. If that period was a relatively stable one, the computed VaR will be a low number and will understate the risk looking forward. Conversely, if the period examined was volatile, the VaR will be set too high. Earlier in this chapter, we provided the example of VaR for oil price movements and concluded that VaR measures based on the 1992–1998 period, where oil prices were stable, would have been too low for the 1999–2004 period, when volatility returned to the market.

- **Nonstationary correlations**—Measures of VaR are conditioned on explicit estimates of correlation across risk sources (in the variance-covariance and

Monte Carlo simulations) or implicit assumptions about correlation (in historical simulations). These correlation estimates are usually based on historical data and are extremely volatile. We can obtain one measure of how much they move by tracking the correlations between widely following asset classes over time. Figure 7.4 graphs the correlation between the S&P 500 and the 10-year Treasury bond returns, using daily returns for a year, every year from 1990 to 2005.

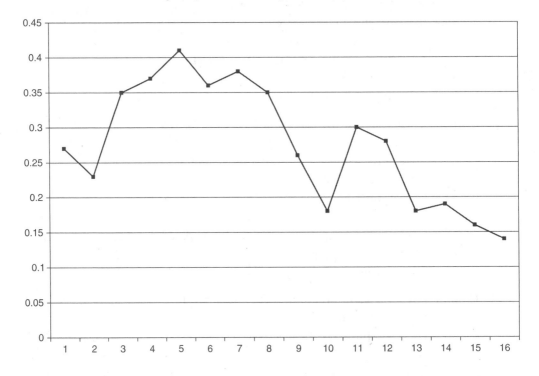

Figure 7.4: Time Series of Correlation between Stock and Bond Returns

Skintzi, Skiadoupoulous, and Refenes show that the error in VaR increases as the correlation error increases and that the effect is magnified in Monte Carlo simulations.[21]

One indicator that VaR is subject to judgment comes from the range of values that analysts often assign to the measure, when looking at the same risk for the same entity. Different assumptions about return distributions and different historical periods can yield different values for VaR.[22] In fact, different measures of VaR can be derived for a

21   Skintzi, V. D., G. Skiadoubpoulous, and A. P. N. Refenes. "The Effect of Misestimating Correlation on Value at Risk." *Journal of Alternative Investments*, Spring 2005.

22   Beder, T. S. "VAR: Seductive But Dangerous." *Financial Analysts Journal.*, September-October 1995.

portfolio even when we start with the same underlying data and methodology.[23] A study of VaR measures used at large bank-holding companies to measure risk in their trading portfolios concluded that they were much too conservatively set and were slow to react to changing circumstances; in fact, simple time series models outperformed sophisticated VaR models in predictions. The study concluded that the computed VaR was more a precautionary number for capital at risk than a measure of portfolio risk.[24] In defense of VaR, it should be pointed out that the reported VaRs at banks are correlated with the volatility in trading revenues at these banks and can be used as a proxy for risk (at least from the trading component).[25]

Narrow Focus

Although many analysts like VaR because of its simplicity and intuitive appeal, relative to other risk measures, its simplicity emanates from its narrow definition of risk. Firms that depend on VaR as the only measure of risk can not only be lulled into a false sense of complacency about the risks they face but can also make decisions that are not in their best interests.

- **Type of risk**—VaR measures the likelihood of losses to an asset or portfolio due to market risk. Implicit in this definition is the narrow definition of risk, at least in conventional VaR models. First, risk is almost always considered to be a negative in VaR. Although there is no technical reason we cannot estimate potential profits that we can earn with 99 percent probability, VaR is measured in terms of potential losses and not gains. Second, most VaR measures are built around market risk effects. Again, although there is no reason we cannot look at the VaR, relative to all risks, practicality forces us to focus on just market risks and their effects on value. In other words, the true VaR can be much greater than the computed VaR if we consider political risk, liquidity risk, and regulatory risks that are not built into the VaR.

- **Short term**—VaR can be computed over a quarter or a year, but it is usually computed over a day, a week, or a few weeks. In most real-world applications, therefore, the VaR is computed over short periods, rather than longer ones.

---

23 Marshall, Chris, and Michael Siegel. "Value at Risk: Implementing a Risk Measurement Standard." *Journal of Derivatives*, Vol. 4, No. 3, 91–111, 1997. Different measures of value at risk are estimated using different software packages on the J.P. Morgan RiskMetrics data and methodology.

24 Berkowitz, J., and J. O'Brien. "How Accurate Are Value at Risk Models at Commercial Banks?" *Journal of Finance*, Vol. 57, 1093–1111, 2002.

25 Jorion, P. "How Informative Are Value-at-Risk Disclosures?" *The Accounting Review*, Vol. 77, 911–932., 2002.

There are three reasons for this short-term focus. The first is that the financial service firms that use VaR often are focused on hedging these risks on a day-to-day basis and are thus less concerned about long-term risk exposures. The second is that the regulatory authorities, at least for financial service firms, demand to know the short-term VaR exposures at frequent intervals. The third is that the inputs into the VaR measure computation, whether it is measured using historical simulations or the variance-covariance approach, are easiest to estimate for short periods. In fact, as we noted in the previous section, the quality of the VaR estimates quickly deteriorates as we go from daily to weekly to monthly to annual measures.

- **Absolute value**—The output from a VaR computation is not a standard deviation or an overall risk measure but is stated in terms of a probability that the losses will exceed a specified value. As an example, a VaR of $100 million with 95 percent confidence implies that there is only a 5 percent chance of losing more than $100 million. The focus on a fixed value makes it an attractive measure of risk to financial service firms that worry about their capital adequacy. By the same token, it is what makes VaR an inappropriate measure of risk for firms that are focused on comparing investments with different scales and returns; for these firms, more conventional scaled measures of risk (such as standard deviation or betas) that focus on the entire risk distribution will work better.

In short, VaR measures look at only a small slice of the risk that an asset is exposed to, and a great deal of valuable information in the distribution is ignored. Even if the VaR assessment is correct that the probability of losing more than $100 million is less than 5 percent, would it not make sense to know the most we could lose in that catastrophic range (with less than 5 percent probability)? It should, after all, make a difference whether our worst possible loss was $1 billion or $150 million. Looking back at Chapter 6 on probabilistic risk assessment approaches, VaR is closer to the worst-case assessment in scenario analysis than it is to the fuller risk assessment approaches.

Suboptimal Decisions

Even if VaR is correctly measured, it is not clear that using it as the measure of risk leads to more reasoned and sensible decisions on the part of managers and investors. In fact, there are two strands of criticism against the use of VaR in decision making. The first is that making investment decisions based on VaR can lead to overexposure to risk, even when the decision makers are rational and VaR is estimated precisely. The other is that managers who understand how VaR is computed can game the measure to report superior performance while exposing the firm to substantial risks.

- **Overexposure to risk**—Assume that managers are asked to make investment decisions, while having their risk exposures measured using VaR. Basak and Shapiro note that such managers will often invest in more risky portfolios than managers who do not use VaR as a risk assessment tool. They explain this counterintuitive result by noting that managers evaluated based on VaR will be much more focused on avoiding the intermediate risks (under the probability threshold), but that their portfolios are likely to lose far more under the most adverse circumstances. Put another way, by not bringing in the magnitude of the losses once we exceed the VaR cutoff probability (90 percent or 95 percent), we are opening ourselves to the possibility of very large losses in the worst-case scenarios.[26]

- **Agency problems**—Like any risk measure, VaR can be gamed by managers who have decided to make an investment and want to meet the VaR risk constraint. Ju and Pearson note that because VaR is generally measured using past data, traders and managers who are evaluated using the measure will have a reasonable understanding of its errors and can take advantage of them. Consider the example of the VaR from oil price volatility that we estimated using historical simulation earlier in the chapter; the VaR was understated because it did not capture the trending up in volatility in oil prices toward the end of the period. A canny manager who knows this can take on far more oil price risk than is prudent while reporting a VaR that looks like it is under the limit.[27] It is true that all risk measures are open to this critique, but by focusing on an absolute value and a single probability, VaR is more open to this game playing than other measures.

Extensions of VaR

The popularity of VaR has given rise to numerous variants of it, some designed to mitigate problems associated with the original measure and some directed toward extending the use of the measure from financial service firms to the rest of the market.

---

26 Basak, S., and A. Shapiro. "Value-at-Risk Based Management: Optimal Policies and Asset Prices." *Review of Financial Studies*, Vol. 14 , 371–405, 2001.

27 Ju, X., and N. D. Pearson. "Using Value-at-Risk to Control Risk Taking: How Wrong Can You Be?" Working Paper, University of Illinois at Urbana-Champaign, 1998.

There are modifications of VaR that adapt the original measure to new uses but remain true to its focus on overall value. Hallerback and Menkveld modified the conventional VaR measure to accommodate multiple market factors and computed what they call a component VaR, breaking down a firm's risk exposure to different market risks. They argued that managers at multinational firms can use this risk measure not only to determine where their risk is coming from but to manage it better in the interests of maximizing shareholder wealth.[28] In an attempt to bring in the possible losses in the tail of the distribution (beyond the VaR probability), Larsen, Mausser, and Uryasev estimate what they call a conditional VaR, which they define as a weighted average of the VaR and losses exceeding the VaR.[29] This conditional measure can be considered an upper bound on the VaR and may reduce the problems associated with excessive risk taking by managers. Finally, some note that VaR is just one aspect of an area of mathematics called extreme value theory, and that there may be better and more comprehensive ways of measuring exposure to catastrophic risks.[30]

The other direction that researchers have taken is to extend the measure to cover metrics other than value. The most widely used of these is cash flow-at-risk (C-FaR). Although VaR focuses on changes in the overall value of an asset or portfolio as market risks vary, C-FaR is more focused on the operating cash flow during a period and market-induced variations in it. Consequently, with C-FaR, we assess the likelihood that operating cash flows will drop below a prespecified level; an annual C-FaR of $100 million with 90 percent confidence can be read to mean that there is only a 10 percent probability that cash flows will drop by more than $100 million during the next year. Herein lies the second practical difference between VaR and C-FaR: whereas VaR is usually computed for very short time intervals—days or weeks—C-FaR is computed over much longer periods—quarters or years.

Why focus on cash flows rather than value? First, for a firm that has to make contractual payments (interest payments, debt repayments, and lease expenses) during a particular period, it is cash flow that matters; after all, the value can remain relatively stable while cash flows plummet, putting the firm at risk of default. Second, unlike financial service firms where the value measured is the value of marketable securities, which can be converted into cash at short notice, value at a nonfinancial service firm takes the form of real investments in plant, equipment, and other fixed assets, which are far more difficult

---

28   Hallerback, W. G., and A. J. Menkveld. "Analyzing Perceived Downside Risk: The Component Value-at-Risk Framework." Working Paper, 2002.

29   Larsen, N., H. Mausser, and S. Ursyasev. "Algorithms for Optimization of Value-at-Risk." Research Report, University of Florida, 2001.

30   Embrechts, P. "Extreme Value Theory: Potential and Limitations as an Integrated Risk Management Tool." Working Paper (listed on GloriaMundi.org), 2001.

to monetize. Finally, assessing the market risks embedded in value, although relatively straightforward for a portfolio of financial assets, can be much more difficult to do for a manufacturing or technology firm.

How do we measure C-FaR? Although we can use any of the three approaches described for measuring VaR—variance-covariance matrices, historical simulations, and Monte Carlo simulations—the process becomes more complicated if we consider all risks and not just market risks. Stein, Usher, LaGattuta, and Youngen developed a template for estimating C-FaR using data on comparable firms, where comparable is defined in terms of market capitalization, riskiness, profitability, and stock-price performance. They used the template to measure the risk embedded in the earnings before interest, taxes, and depreciation (EBITDA) at Coca Cola, Dell, and Cignus (a small pharmaceutical firm).[31] Using regressions of EBITDA as a percent of assets across the comparable firms over time, for a 5 percent worst case, they estimated that EBITDA would drop by $5.23 per $100 of assets at Coca Cola, $28.50 for Dell, and $47.31 for Cygnus. They conceded that although the results look reasonable, the approach is sensitive to the definition of comparable firms and is likely to yield estimates with error.

Less common adaptations extend the measure to cover earnings at risk (EaR) and stock prices at risk (SPaR). These variations are designed by what the researchers view as the constraining variable in decision making. For firms that are focused on earnings per share and ensuring that it does not drop below some prespecified floor, it makes sense to focus on EaR. For other firms, where a drop in the stock price below a given level gives risk to constraints or delisting, SPaR is the relevant risk control measure.

VaR as a Risk Assessment Tool

In the last three chapters, we have considered a range of risk assessment tools. In Chapter 5, "Risk-Adjusted Value," we introduced risk and return models that attempted either to increase the discount rate or reduce the cash flows (certainty equivalents) used to value risky assets, leading to risk-adjusted values. In Chapter 6, "Probabilistic Approaches: Scenario Analysis, Decision Trees, and Simulations," we considered probabilistic approaches to risk assessment, including scenario analysis, simulations, and decision trees, where we considered most or all possible outcomes from a risky investment and used that information in valuation and investment decisions. In this chapter, we introduced VaR, touted by its adherents as a more intuitive, if not better, way of assessing risk.

---

31   Stein, J. C., S. E. Usher, D. LaGattuta, and J. Youngen. "A Comparables Approach to Measuring Cashflow-at-Risk for Non-Financial Firms." Working Paper, National Economic Research Associates, 2000.

From our perspective, and it may very well be biased, VaR seems to be a throwback and not an advance in thinking about risk. Of all the risk assessment tools that we have examined so far, it is the most focused on downside risk, and even within that downside risk, at a very small slice of it. It seems foolhardy to believe that optimal investment decisions can flow out of such a cramped view of risk. VaR seems to take a subset of the information that comes out of scenario analysis (the close to worst-case scenario) or simulations (the fifth percentile or tenth percentile of the distribution) and throw the rest of it out. Some would argue that presenting decision makers with an entire probability distribution rather than just the loss that they will make with 5 percent probability will lead to confusion, but if that is the case, there is little hope that such individuals can be trusted to make good decisions in the first place with any risk assessment measure.

How then can we account for the popularity of VaR? A cynic would attribute it to an accident of history where a variance-covariance matrix, with a dubious history of forecasting accuracy, was made available to panicked bankers, reeling from a series of financial disasters wrought by rogue traders. Consultants and software firms then filled in the gaps and sold the measure as the magic bullet to stop runaway risk taking. The usage of VaR has also been fed by three factors specific to financial service firms. The first is that these firms have limited capital, relative to the huge nominal values of the leveraged portfolios that they hold; small changes in the latter can put the firm at risk. The second is that the assets held by financial service firms are primarily marketable securities, making it easier to break risks down into market risks and compute VaR. Finally, the regulatory authorities have augmented the use of the measure by demanding regular reports on VaR exposure. Thus, although VaR may be a flawed and narrow measure of risk, it is a natural measure of short-term risk for financial service firms, and there is evidence that it does its job adequately.

For nonfinancial service firms, there is a place for VaR and its variants in the risk toolbox, but more as a secondary measure of risk rather than a primary measure. Consider how payback (the number of years that it takes to make our money back in an investment) has been used in conventional capital budgeting. When picking between two projects with roughly equivalent net present value (or risk-adjusted value), a cash-strapped firm will pick the project with the speedier payback. By the same token, when picking between two investments that look equivalent on a risk-adjusted basis, a firm should pick the investment with less cash flow or VaR. This is especially true if the firm has large amounts of debt outstanding, and a drop in the cash flows or value may put the firm at risk of default.

Conclusion

Value at risk (VaR) has developed as a risk assessment tool at banks and other financial service firms in the past decade. Its usage in these firms has been driven by the failure of the risk tracking systems used until the early 1990s to detect dangerous risk taking on the part of traders. VaR offered a key benefit: a measure of capital at risk under extreme conditions in trading portfolios that could be updated on a regular basis.

Although the notion of VaR is simple—the maximum amount that we can lose on an investment over a particular period with a specified probability—there are three ways to measure VaR. In the first, we assume that the returns generated by exposure to multiple market risks are normally distributed. We use a variance-covariance matrix of all standardized instruments representing various market risks to estimate the standard deviation in portfolio returns and compute the VaR from this standard deviation. In the second approach, we run a portfolio through historical data—a historical simulation—and estimate the probability that the losses exceed specified values. In the third approach, we assume return distributions for each of the market risks and run Monte Carlo simulations to arrive at the VaR. Each measure comes with its own pluses and minuses. The variance-covariance approach is simple to implement, but the normality assumption can be tough to sustain. Historical simulations assume that the past time periods used are representative of the future, and Monte Carlo simulations are time and computation intensive. All three yield VaR measures that are estimates and subject to judgment.

We understand why VaR is a popular risk assessment tool in financial service firms, where assets are primarily marketable securities, there is limited capital at play, and a regulatory overlay emphasizes short-term exposure to extreme risks. We are hard pressed to see why VaR is of particular use to nonfinancial service firms, unless they are highly levered and risk default if cash flows or value fall below a prespecified level. Even in those cases, it would seem to us to be more prudent to use all the information in the probability distribution rather than a small slice of it.

APPENDIX 7.1

Example of VaR Calculations: Variance—Covariance Approach

In this appendix, we will compute the VaR of a six-month forward contract, going through four steps: the mapping of the standardized market risks and instruments underlying this security, a determination of the positions that we would need to take in the standardized instruments, the estimation of the variances and covariances of these instruments, and the computation of the VaR in the forward contract.

1. The first step requires us to take each of the assets in a portfolio and map that asset on to simpler, standardized instruments. Let's consider the example of a six-month dollar/euro forward contract. The market factors affecting this instrument are the six-month risk-free rates in each currency and the spot exchange rate. The financial instruments that proxy for these risk factors are the six-month zero coupon dollar bond, the six-month zero coupon euro bond, and the spot $/euro.

2. Each financial asset is stated as a set of positions in the standardized instruments. To make the computation for the forward contract, we assume that the forward contract requires us to deliver $12.7 million dollars in 180 days and receive 10 million euros in exchange. We assume, in addition, that the current spot rate is $1.26/euro and that the annualized interest rates are 4 percent on a six-month zero coupon dollar bond and 3 percent on a six-month zero coupon euro bond. We can compute the positions in the three standardized instruments as follows.

   Value of short position in zero coupon dollar bond:

   $$= \frac{\$12.7}{(1.04)^{180/360}} = -\$12.4534 \text{ million}$$

   Value of long position in zero coupon euro bond (in dollar terms) holding spot:

   $$\text{rate fixed} = \text{Spot \$/Eu}\frac{\text{Euro Forward}}{(1+r_{\text{Euro}})^t} = 1.26 * \frac{10 \text{ million}}{(1.03)^{180/360}} = \$12.4145 \text{ million}$$

   Value of spot euro position (in dollar terms) holding euro rate fixed:

$$= \text{Spot \$/Eu} \frac{\text{Euro Forward}}{(1+r_{\text{Euro}})^t} = 1.26 * \frac{10 \text{ million}}{(1.03)^{180/360}} = \$12.4145 \text{ million}$$

Note that the last two positions are equal because the forward asset exposes us to risk in the euro in two places. Both the riskless euro rate and the spot exchange rate can change over time.

3. After identifying the standardized instruments that affect the asset or assets in a portfolio, we have to estimate the variances in each of these instruments and the covariances across the instruments. Considering again the six-month \$/euro forward contract and the three standardized instruments we mapped that investment onto, we assume that the variance/covariance matrix (in daily returns) across those instruments is as follows.[32]

	Six-Month \$ Bond	Six-Month Euro Bond	Spot \$/Euro
Six-month \$ bond	0.0000314		
Six-month euro bond	0.0000043	0.0000260	
Spot \$/euro	0.0000012	0.0000013	0.0000032

In practice, these variance and covariance estimates are obtained by looking at historical data.

4. We can now compute the VaR for the portfolio using the weights on the standardized instruments computed in step 2 and the variances and covariances in these instruments computed in step 3. For instance, we can compute the daily variance of the 6-month \$/euro forward contract as follows (X_j is the position in standardized asset j and σ_{ij} is the covariance between assets i and j):

Variance of forward contract=

$$X_1^2\sigma_1^2 + X_2^2\sigma_2^2 + X_3^2\sigma_3^2 + 2X_1X_2\sigma_{12} + 2X_2X_3\sigma_{23} + +2X_1X_3\sigma_{13}$$

$$= (-12.4534)^2(0.0000314) + (12.4145)^2(0.0000260) + (12.4145)^2(0.0000032) + 2(-12.4534)$$
$$(12.4145)(0.0000043) + 2(12.4145)(12.4145)(0.0000013) + 2(-12.4534)(12.4145)(0.0000012)$$

$$= \$0.0111021 \text{ million}$$

---

32 The covariance of an asset with itself is the variance. Thus, the values on the diagonal represent the variances of these assets; the daily return variance in the six-month \$ bond is 0.0000314. The off-diagonal values are the covariances; the covariance between the spot \$/euro rate and the six-month \$ bond is 0.0000012.

Daily standard deviation of forward contract $= 0.0111021^{1/2} = \$105,367$

If we assume a normal distribution, we can now specify the potential VaR at a 90 percent confidence interval on this forward contract to be $173,855 for a day.

VaR $= \$105,367^* \ 1.65 = \$173,855$

8

REAL OPTIONS

T he approaches that we have described in the past three chapters for assessing the effects of risk, for the most part, have focused on the negative effects of risk. Put another way, they have all focused on the downside of risk, and they miss the opportunity component that provides the upside. The real options approach is the only one that gives prominence to the upside potential for risk, based on the argument that uncertainty can sometimes be a source of additional value, especially to those who are poised to take advantage of it.

We begin this chapter by describing in very general terms the argument behind the real options approach, noting its foundations in two elements—the capacity of individuals or entities to learn from what is happening around them, and their willingness and the ability to modify behavior based on that learning. We then describe the various forms that real options can take in practice and how they can affect the way we assess the value of investments and our behavior. In the last section, we consider some of the potential pitfalls in using the real options argument and how it can best be incorporated into a portfolio of risk assessment tools.

The Essence of Real Options

To understand the basis of the real options argument and the reasons for its allure, it is easiest to go back to decision trees, the risk assessment tool that we unveiled in Chapter 6, "Probabilistic Approaches: Scenario Analysis, Decision Trees, and Simulations." Consider a simple example of a decision tree in Figure 8.1.

Given the equal probabilities of up and down movements and the larger potential loss, the expected value for this investment is negative.

Expected value = 0.50 (100) + 0.5 (−120) = −$10

Now contrast this with the slightly more complicated two-phase decision tree in Figure 8.2.

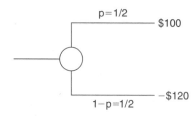

Figure 8.1: Simple Decision Tree

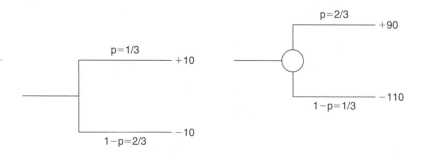

Figure 8.2: Two-Phase Decision Tree

Note that the total potential profits and losses over the two phases in the tree are identical to the profit and loss of the simple tree in Figure 8.1; our total gain is $100, and our total loss is $120. Note also that the cumulative probabilities of success and failure remain at the 50 percent that we used in the simple tree. When we compute the expected value of this tree, though, the outcome changes:

$$\text{Expected value} = (2/3)\,(-10) + 1/3\,[10+(2/3)(90) + (1/3)(-110)] = \$4.44$$

What is it about the second decision tree that changes a potentially bad investment in the first tree to a good investment in the second? We would attribute the change to two factors. First, by allowing for an initial phase where we get to observe the cash flows on a first and relatively small try at the investment, we allow for learning. Thus, getting a bad outcome in the first phase (−10 instead of +10) is an indicator that the overall investment is more likely to be money losing than money making. Second, we act on the learning by abandoning the investment, if the outcome from the first phase is negative; we will call this *adaptive behavior*.

In essence, the value of real options stems from the fact that when investing in risky assets, we can learn from observing what happens in the real world and adapting our behavior to increase our potential upside from the investment and to decrease the possible downside. Consider again the Chinese symbol for risk as a combination of danger and opportunity that we used in Chapter 1, "What Is Risk?." In the real option framework, we use updated knowledge or information to expand opportunities while reducing danger. In the context of a risky investment, we can take three potential actions based on this updated knowledge. The first is that we build on good fortune to increase our possible profits; this is the *option to expand*. For instance, a market test that suggests that consumers are far more receptive to a new product than expected could be used as a basis for expanding the scale of the project and speeding its delivery to the market. The second is that we scale down or even abandon an investment when the information we receive contains bad news; this is the *option to abandon* and can allow us to cut our losses. The third is to hold off on making further investments, if the information we receive suggests ambivalence about future prospects; this is the *option to delay or wait*. We are, in a sense, buying time for the investment, hoping that product and market developments will make it attractive in the future.

We would add one final piece to the mix that is often forgotten but is just as important as the learning and adaptive behavior components in terms of contributing to the real options arguments. The value of learning is greatest when we are the only ones to have access to that learning and can act on it. After all, the expected value of knowledge that is public, where anyone can act on that knowledge, will be close to zero. We will term this third condition *exclusivity* and use it to scrutinize when real options have the most value.

Real Options, Risk-Adjusted Value, and Probabilistic Assessments

Before we embark on a discussion of the options to delay, expand, and abandon, it is important that we consider how the real options view of risk differs from how the approaches laid out in the previous three chapters look at risk, and the implications for the valuation of risky assets.

When computing the risk-adjusted value for risky assets, we generally discount the expected cash flows using a discount rate adjusted to reflect risk. We use higher discount rates for riskier assets and thus assign a lower value for any given set of cash flows. In the process, we are faced with the task of converting all possible outcomes in the future into one expected number. The real options critique of discounted cash flow valuation can be boiled down simply. The expected cash flows for a risky asset, where the holder of the asset can learn from observing what happens in early periods and adapting behavior, will be understated because it will not capture the diminution of the downside risk from the option to abandon and the expansion of upside potential from the options to expand and delay. To provide a concrete example, assume that we are valuing an oil company and we estimate the cash flows by multiplying the number of barrels of oil that we expect the company to produce each year by the expected oil price per barrel. Although we may have reasonable and unbiased estimates of both these numbers (the expected number of barrels produced and the expected oil price), what we are missing in our expected cash flows is the interplay between these numbers. Oil companies can observe the price of oil and adjust production accordingly; they produce more oil when oil prices are high and less when oil prices are low. In addition, their exploration activity will ebb and flow as the oil price moves. Consequently, their cash flows computed across all oil price scenarios will be greater than the expected cash flows used in the risk-adjusted value calculation, and the difference will widen as the uncertainty about oil prices increases. So, what would real options proponents suggest? They would argue that the risk-adjusted value, obtained from conventional valuation approaches, is too low and that a premium should be added to it to reflect the option to adjust production inherent in these firms.

The approach that is closest to real options in terms of incorporating adaptive behavior is the decision tree approach, where the optimal decisions at each stage are conditioned on outcomes at prior stages. The two approaches, though, will usually yield different values for the same risky asset for two reasons. The first is that the decision tree approach is built on probabilities and allows for multiple outcomes at each branch, whereas the real option approach is more constrained in its treatment of uncertainty. In its binomial version, there can be only two outcomes at each stage, and the probabilities are not specified. The second is that the discount rates used to estimate present values in decision trees, at least in conventional usage, tend to be risk adjusted and not conditioned on which branch of the decision tree we are looking at. When computing the value of a diabetes drug in a decision tree, in Chapter 6, we used a 10 percent cost of capital as the discount rate for all cash flows from the drug in both good and bad outcomes. In the real options approach, the discount rate will vary depending on the branch of the tree being analyzed. In other words, the cost of capital for an oil company if oil prices increase may very well be different from the cost of capital when oil prices decrease. Copeland and Antikarov provide a persuasive proof that the value of a risky asset will be the same under real options and decision trees, if we allow for path-dependent discount rates.[1]

Simulations and real options are not so much competing approaches for risk assessment as they are complementary. Two key inputs into the real options valuation—the value

---

1   Copeland, T. E., and V. Antikarov. "Real Options: A Practitioner's Guide." Texere, New York, 2003. For an alternate path to the same conclusion, see Brandao, L. E., J. S. Dyer, and W. J. Huhn. "Using Binomial Decision Trees to Solve Real-Option Valuation Problems." *Decision Analysis*, Vol. 2, 69–88, 2005. They use the risk-neutral probabilities from the option pricing model in the decision tree to solve for the option's value.

of the underlying asset and the variance in that value—are often obtained from simulations. To value a patent, for instance, we need to assess the present value of cash flows from developing the patent today and the variance in that value, given the uncertainty about the inputs. Because the underlying product is not traded, it is difficult to get either of these inputs from the market. A Monte Carlo simulation can provide both values.

Real Option Examples

As we noted in the introductory section, three types of options are embedded in investments—the option to expand, delay, and abandon an investment. In this section, we will consider each of these options and how they may add value to an investment, as well as potential implications for valuation and risk management.

The Option to Delay an Investment

Investments are typically analyzed based on their expected cash flows and discount rates at the time of the analysis; the net present value computed on that basis is a measure of its value and acceptability at that time. The rule that emerges is a simple one: Negative net present value investments destroy value and should not be accepted. Expected cash flows and discount rates change over time, however, and so does the net present value. Thus, a project that has a negative net present value now may have a positive net present value in the future. In a competitive environment, in which individual firms have no special advantages over their competitors in taking projects, this may not seem significant. In an environment in which a project can be taken by only one firm (because of legal restrictions or other barriers to entry to competitors), however, the changes in the project's value over time give it the characteristics of a call option.

Basic Setup

In the abstract, assume that a project requires an initial up-front investment of X, and that the present value of expected cash inflows computed right now is V. The net present value of this project is the difference between the two.

$$NPV = V - X$$

Now assume that the firm has exclusive rights to this project for the next n years, and that the present value of the cash inflows may change over that time, because of changes in either the cash flows or the discount rate. Thus, the project may have a negative net present value right now, but it could still be a good project if the firm waits. Defining V again as the present value of the cash flows, the firm's decision rule on this project can be summarized as follows.

If $V > X$ Take the project: Project has a positive net present value.

$V < X$ Do not take the project: Project has a negative net present value.

If the firm does not invest in the project, it incurs no additional cash flows, although it will lose what it originally invested in getting exclusive rights. This relationship can be presented in a payoff diagram of cash flows on this project, as shown in Figure 8.3, assuming that the firm holds out until the end of the period for which it has exclusive rights to the project:[2]

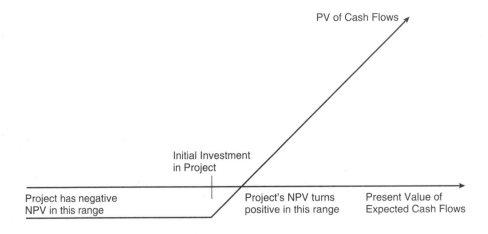

Figure 8.3: The Option to Delay an Investment

Note that this payoff diagram is that of a call option—the underlying asset is the investment, the strike price of the option is the initial outlay needed to initiate the investment, and the life of the option is the period for which the firm has rights to the investment. The present value of the cash flows on this project and the expected variance in this present value represent the value and variance of the underlying asset.

---

2   McDonald, R., and D. Siegel. "The Value of Waiting to Invest." *Quarterly Journal of Economics*, Vol. 101, 707–728, 2002.

Valuing an Option to Delay

On the surface, the inputs needed to value the option to delay are the same as those needed for any option. We need the value of the underlying asset, the variance in that value, the time to expiration on the option, the strike price, the riskless rate, and the equivalent of the dividend yield (cost of delay).

- **Value of the underlying asset**—In this case, the underlying asset is the investment itself. The current value of this asset is the present value of expected cash flows from initiating the project now, not including the up-front investment. This can be obtained by doing a standard capital budgeting analysis. There is likely to be a substantial amount of error in the cash flow estimates and the present value, however. Rather than being viewed as a problem, this uncertainty should be viewed as the reason why the project delay option has value. If the expected cash flows on the project were known with certainty and were not expected to change, there would be no need to adopt an option pricing framework, because there would be no value to the option.

- **Variance in the value of the asset**—The present value of the expected cash flows that measure the value of the asset will change over time, partly because the potential market size for the product may be unknown, and partly because technological shifts can change the cost structure and profitability of the product. The variance in the present value of cash flows from the project can be estimated in one of three ways.

First, if similar projects have been introduced in the past, the variance in the cash flows from those projects can be used as an estimate. This may be the way that a consumer product company like Gillette might estimate the variance associated with introducing a new blade for its razors.

Second, probabilities can be assigned to various market scenarios, cash flows estimated under each scenario, and the variance estimated across present values. Alternatively, the probability distributions can be estimated for each of the inputs into the project analysis—the size of the market, the market share, and the profit margin, for instance—and simulations used to estimate the variance in the present values that emerge.

Third, the variance in the market value of publicly traded firms involved in the same business (as the project being considered) can be used as an estimate of the variance. Thus, the average variance in firm value of firms involved in the software business can be used as the variance in present value of a software project.

The value of the option is largely derived from the variance in cash flows—the higher the variance, the higher the value of the project delay option. Thus, the value of an option to delay a project in a stable business is less than the value of a similar option in an environment where technology, competition, and markets are changing rapidly.

- **Exercise price on option**—A project delay option is exercised when the firm owning the rights to the project decides to invest in it. The cost of making this investment is the exercise price of the option. The underlying assumption is that this cost remains constant (in present value dollars) and that any uncertainty associated with the product is reflected in the present value of cash flows on the product.

- **Expiration of the option and the riskless rate**—The project delay option expires when the exclusive rights to the project lapse; investments made after the project rights expire are assumed to deliver a net present value of zero as competition drives returns down to the hurdle rate. The riskless rate to use in pricing the option should be the rate that corresponds to the expiration of the option. Although option life can be estimated easily when firms have the explicit right to a project (through a license or a patent, for instance), it becomes far more difficult to obtain when firms only have a competitive advantage to take a project.

- **Cost of delay (dividend yield)**—There is a cost to delaying taking a project, after the net present value turns positive. Because the project rights expire after a fixed period, and excess profits (which are the source of positive present value) are assumed to disappear after that time as new competitors emerge, each year of delay translates into one less year of value-creating cash flows.[3] If the cash flows are evenly distributed over time, and the exclusive rights last n years, the cost of delay can be written as follows.

$$\text{Annual cost of delay} = \frac{1}{n}$$

Thus, if the project rights are for 20 years, the annual cost of delay works out to 5 percent a year. Note, though, that this cost of delay rises each year, to 1/19 in year 2, 1/18 in year 3, and so on, making the cost of delaying exercise larger over time.

---

3   A value-creating cash flow is one that adds to the net present value because it is in excess of the required return for investments of equivalent risk.

Practical Considerations

Although it is quite clear that the option to delay is embedded in many investments, there are several problems associated with the use of option pricing models to value these options. First, the *underlying asset in this option, which is the project, is not traded*, making it difficult to estimate its value and variance. We have argued that the value can be estimated from the expected cash flows and the discount rate for the project, albeit with error. The variance is more difficult to estimate, however, because we are attempting the estimate a variance in project value over time.

Second, the *behavior of prices over time may not conform to the price path assumed by the option pricing models.* In particular, the assumption that prices move in small increments continuously (an assumption of the Black-Scholes model), and that the variance in value remains unchanged over time, may be difficult to justify in the context of a real investment. For instance, a sudden technological change may dramatically change the value of a project, either positively or negatively.

Third, *there may be no specific period for which the firm has rights to the project.* For instance, a firm may have significant advantages over its competitors, which may, in turn, provide it with the virtually exclusive rights to a project for a period. The rights are not legal restrictions, however, and could erode faster than expected. In such cases, the expected life of the project itself is uncertain and only an estimate. Ironically, uncertainty about the expected life of the option can increase the variance in present value, and through it, the expected value of the rights to the project.

Applications of Option to Delay

The option to delay provides interesting perspectives on two common investment problems. The first is in the valuation of patents, especially those that are not viable today but could be viable in the future; by extension, this will also allow us to look at whether investments in R&D expenses are delivering value. The second is in the analysis of natural resource assets—vacant land, undeveloped oil reserves, and so on.

Patents

A product patent provides a firm with the right to develop and market a product. The firm will do so only if the present value of the expected cash flows from the product sales exceed the cost of development as shown in Figure 8.4. If this does not occur, the firm can shelve the patent and not incur further costs. If I is the present value of the costs of developing the product and V is the present value of the expected cash flows from development, the payoffs from owning a product patent can be written as such.

Payoff from owning a product patent $= V - I$ if $V > I$

                                                 $= 0$ if   if $V \leq I$

Thus, a product patent can be viewed as a call option, where the product is the underlying asset.[4]

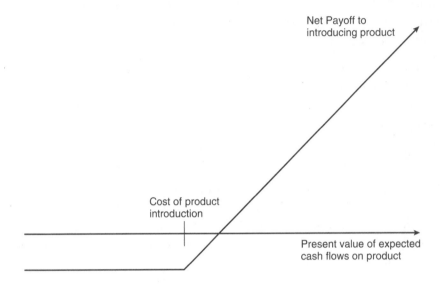

Figure 8.4: Payoff to Introducing Product

We will illustrate the use of option pricing to value Avonex, a drug to treat multiple sclerosis, right after it had received FDA approval in 1997, but before its parent company, Biogen, had decided whether to commercialize the drug. We arrived at the following estimates for use in the option pricing model.

- An internal analysis of the drug at the time, based on the potential market and the price that the firm can expect to charge, yielded a present value of expected cash flows of $3.422 billion, prior to considering the initial development cost.

- The initial cost of developing the drug for commercial use was estimated to be $2.875 billion, if the drug was introduced immediately.

- The firm had the patent on the drug for the next 17 years, and the 17-year Treasury bond rate was 6.7 percent.

---

4   Schwartz, E. "Patents and R&D as Real Options." Working Paper, Anderson School at UCLA, 2004.

- The average historical variance in market value for publicly traded biotechnology firms was 0.224.

- It was assumed that the potential for excess returns exists only during the patent life, and that competition will wipe out excess returns beyond that period. Thus, any delay in introducing the drug, after it is viable, will cost the firm one year of patent-protected excess returns. (For the initial analysis, the cost of delay will be 1/17; the following year, it will be 1/16; the year after, 1/15; and so on.)

Based on these assumptions, we obtained the following inputs to the option pricing model.

Present value of cash flows from introducing drug now = S = $3.422 billion

Initial cost of developing drug for commercial use = K = $2.875 billion

Patent life = t = 17 years
Riskless rate = r = 6.7 percent (17-year Treasury bond rate)

Variance in value = $\sigma^2 = 0.224$

Expected cost of delay = y = 1/17 = 5.89 percent

Using these inputs in an option pricing model, we derived a value of $907 million for the option,[5] which can be considered the real options value attached to the patent on Avonex. To provide a contrast, the net present value of this patent is only $547 million.

NPV = $3,422 million – $2,875 million = $547 million

The time premium of $360 million ($907 million – $547 million) on this option suggests that the firm will be better off waiting rather than developing the drug immediately, the cost of delay notwithstanding. However, the cost of delay will increase over time and make exercise (development) more likely. Note also that we are assuming that the firm is protected from all competition for the life of the patent. In reality, there are other pharmaceutical firms working on their own drugs to treat multiple sclerosis, and that can affect both the option value and the firm's behavior. In particular, if we assume that a competitor has a drug working through the FDA pipeline, and that drug is expected to reach the market in six years, the cost of delay will increase to 16.67 percent (1/6), and the option value will dissipate.

---

5   This value was derived from using a Black-Scholes model with these inputs. With a binomial model, the estimated value increases slightly to $915 million.

The implications of viewing patents as options can be significant. First, it implies that nonviable patents and technologies will continue to have value, especially in businesses where there is substantial volatility. Second, it indicates that firms may hold off on developing viable patents if they feel that they gain more from waiting than they lose in terms of cash flows. This behavior will be more common if there is no significant competition on the horizon. Third, the value of patents will be higher in risky businesses than in safe businesses, because option value increases with volatility. If we consider R&D to be the expense associated with acquiring these patents, this would imply that research should have its biggest payoff when directed to areas where less is known and there is more uncertainty. Consequently, we should expect pharmaceutical firms to spend more of their R&D budgets on gene therapy than on flu vaccines.[6]

Natural Resource Options

In a natural resource investment, the underlying asset is the natural resource, and the value of the asset is based on two variables: the estimated quantity, and the price of the resource. Thus, in a gold mine, the value of the underlying asset is the value of the estimated gold reserves in the mine, based on the current price of gold. In most such investments, there is an initial cost associated with developing the resource; the difference between the value of the asset extracted and the cost of the development is the profit to the owner of the resource (see Figure 8.5). Defining the cost of development as X and the estimated value of the developed resource as V, the potential payoffs on a natural resource option can be written as follows.

$$\text{Payoff on natural resource investment} = V - X \quad \text{if } V > X$$
$$= 0 \quad \text{if } V \leq X$$

Thus, the investment in a natural resource option has a payoff function similar to a call option.[7]

To value a natural resource investment as an option, we need to estimate a number of variables:

---

6   Pakes, A. "Patents as Options: Some Estimates of the Value of Holding European Patent Stocks." *Econometrica*, Vol. 54, 755, 784, 1986. Although this paper does not explicitly value patents as options, it examines the returns investors would have earned investing in companies that derive their value from patents. The return distribution resembles that of a portfolio of options, with most investments losing money but the winners providing disproportionate gains.

7   Brennan, M., and E. Schwartz. "Evaluating Natural Resource Investments." *The Journal of Business*, Vol. 58, 135–157, 1985.

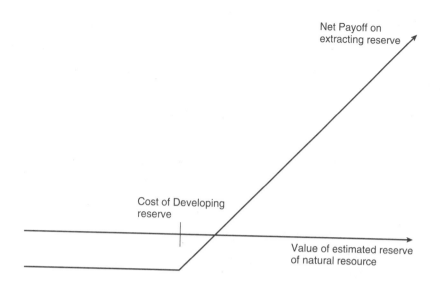

Figure 8.5: Payoff from Developing Natural Resource Reserves

- **Available reserves of the resource**—Because this is not known with certainty at the outset, we have to estimate it. In an oil tract, for instance, geologists can provide reasonably accurate estimates of the quantity of oil available in the tract.

- **Estimated cost of developing the resource**—The estimated development cost is the exercise price of the option. Again, we have to use a combination of knowledge about past costs and the specifics of the investment to come up with a reasonable measure of development cost.

- **Time to expiration of the option**—The life of a natural resource option can be defined in one of two ways. First, if the ownership of the investment has to be relinquished at the end of a fixed period, that period will be the life of the option. In many offshore oil leases, for instance, the oil tracts are leased to the oil company for several years. The second approach is based on the inventory of the resource and the capacity output rate, as well as estimates of the number of years it would take to exhaust the inventory. Thus, a gold mine with a mine inventory of 3 million ounces and a capacity output rate of 150,000 ounces a year will be exhausted in 20 years, which is defined as the life of the natural resource option.

- **Variance in value of the underlying asset**—The variance in the value of the underlying asset is determined by two factors—variability in the price of the resource, and variability in the estimate of available reserves. When the quantity of the reserve is known with certainty, the variance in the underlying asset's value depends entirely on the variance in the price of the natural resource. In the more realistic case in which the quantity of the reserve and the oil price can change over time, the option becomes more difficult to value; here, the firm may have to invest in stages to exploit the reserves.

- **Cost of delay**—The net production revenue as a percentage of the market value of the reserve is the equivalent of the dividend yield and is treated the same way in calculating option values. An alternative way of thinking about this cost is in terms of a cost of delay. When a natural resource option is viable or in-the-money (value of the reserves > cost of developing these reserves), the firm, by not exercising the option, is costing itself the production revenue it could have generated by developing the reserve.

An important issue in using option pricing models to value natural resource options is the effect of development lags on the value of these options. Because the resources cannot be extracted instantaneously, a time lag has to be allowed between the decision to extract the resources and the actual extraction. A simple adjustment for this lag is to reduce the value of the developed reserve to reflect the loss of cash flows during the development period. Thus, if there is a one-year lag in development, the current value of the developed reserve is discounted back one year at the net production revenue/asset value ratio[8] (which we also called the *dividend yield above*).[9]

To illustrate the use of option pricing to value natural reserves, consider an offshore oil property with an estimated reserve of 50 million barrels of oil; the cost of developing the reserve is expected to be $600 million, and the development lag is two years. The firm has the rights to exploit this reserve for the next 20 years, and the marginal value per barrel of oil is $12 currently[10] (price per barrel – marginal cost per barrel). Once developed, the net production revenue each year will be 5 percent of the value of the reserves. The riskless rate is 8 percent, and the variance in ln (oil prices) is 0.03. Given this information, the inputs to the option pricing model can be estimated as follows.

---

8   Intuitively, it may seem like the discounting should occur at the risk-free rate. The simplest way of explaining why we discount at the dividend yield is to consider the analogy with a listed option on a stock. Assume that on exercising a listed option on a stock, we had to wait six months for the stock to be delivered to us. What we lose is the dividends we would have received over the six-month period by holding the stock. Hence, the discounting is at the dividend yield.

9   Brennan, M. J., and E. S. Schwartz. "Evaluating Natural Resource Investments." *Journal of Business*, Vol. 58, 135–157, 1985.

10   For simplicity, we will assume that although this marginal value per barrel of oil will grow over time, the present value of the marginal value will remain unchanged at $12 per barrel. If we do not make this assumption, we will have to estimate the present value of the oil that will be extracted over the extraction period.

Current value of the asset = S = Value of the developed reserve discounted back the length of the development lag at the dividend yield = $12 * 50 / (1.05)^2 = $544.22

If development is started today, the oil will not be available for sale until two years from now. The estimated opportunity cost of this delay is the lost production revenue over the delay period—hence, the discounting of the reserve back at the dividend yield.

Exercise price = Cost of developing reserve = $600 million
(assumed to be both known and fixed over time)

Time to expiration on the option = 20 years

In this example, we assume that the only uncertainty is in the price of oil; the variance, therefore, becomes the variance in oil prices.

Variance in the value of the underlying asset (oil) = 0.03

Riskless rate = 8 percent

Dividend yield = net production revenue / value of reserve = 5 percent

Based on these inputs, the option pricing model yields an estimate of value of $97.08 million.[11] This oil reserve, although not viable at current prices, is still a valuable property because of its potential to create value if oil prices go up.[12]

The same type of analysis can be extended to any other commodity company (gold and copper reserves, for instance) and even to vacant land or real estate properties. The owner of vacant land in Manhattan can choose whether and when to develop the land and will make that decision based on real estate values.[13]

What are the implications of viewing natural resource reserves as options? The first is that the value of a natural resource company can be written as a sum of two values: the conventional risk-adjusted value of expected cash flows from developed reserves and

---

11   This is the estimate from a Black-Scholes model, with a dividend yield adjustment. Using a binomial model yields an estimate of value of $101 million.

12   Paddock, J. L., D. R. Siegel, and J. L. Smith. "Option Valuation of Claims on Real Assets: The Case of Offshore Petroleum Leases." *Quarterly Journal of Economics*, Vol. 103 (3), 479–508, 1988. This paper provides a detailed examination of the application of real options to value oil reserves. They applied the model to examine the prices paid for offshore oil leases in the United States in 1980 and concluded that companies overpaid (relative to the option value).

13   Quigg, L. "Empirical Testing of Real Option-Pricing Models." *Journal of Finance*, Vol. 48, 621–640, 1993. The author examined transaction data on 2,700 undeveloped and 3,200 developed real estate properties between 1976 and 1979 and found evidence of a premium arising from the option to wait in the former.

the option value of undeveloped reserves. Although both will increase in value as the price of the natural resource increases, the latter will increase with increases in price volatility. Thus, the values of oil companies should increase if oil prices become more volatile, even if oil prices themselves do not go up. The second is that conventional discounted cash flow valuation will understate the value of natural resource companies, even if the expected cash flows are unbiased and reasonable because it will miss the option premium inherent in their undeveloped reserves. The third is that development of natural resource reserves will slow down as the volatility in prices increases; the time premium on the options will increase, making exercise of the options (development of the reserves) less likely.

Mining and commodity companies have been at the forefront of using real options in decision making, and their usage of the technology predates the current boom in real options. One reason is that natural resource options come closest to meeting the prerequisites for the use of option pricing models. Firms can learn a great deal by observing commodity prices and can adjust their behavior (in terms of development and exploration) quickly. In addition, if we consider exclusivity to be a prerequisite for real options to have value, that exclusivity for natural resource options derives from their natural scarcity; there is, after all, only a finite amount of oil and gold under the ground and vacant land in Manhattan. Finally, natural resource reserves come closest to meeting the arbitrage/replication requirements that option pricing models are built on; both the underlying asset (the natural resource) and the option can often be bought and sold.

The Option to Expand

In some cases, a firm takes an investment because doing so allows it either to make other investments or to enter other markets in the future. In such cases, it can be argued that the initial investment provides the firm with an option to expand; therefore, the firm should be willing to pay a price for such an option. Consequently, a firm may be willing to lose money on the first investment because it perceives the option to expand as having a large enough value to compensate for the initial loss.

To examine this option, assume that the present value of the expected cash flows from entering the new market or taking the new project is V, and the total investment needed to enter this market or take this project is X. Further, assume that the firm has a fixed time horizon, at the end of which it has to make the final decision on whether to take advantage of this opportunity. Finally, assume that the firm cannot move forward on this opportunity if it does not take the initial investment. This scenario implies the option payoffs shown in Figure 8.6.

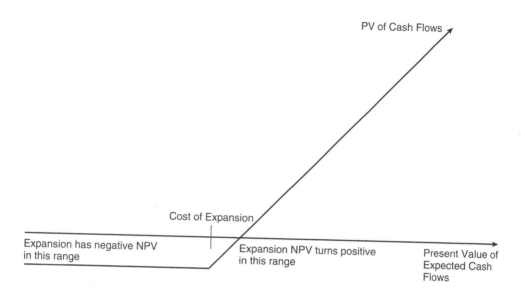

Figure 8.6: The Option to Expand a Project

Notice that, at the expiration of the fixed time horizon, the firm will enter the new market if the present value of the expected cash flows at that point in time exceeds the cost of entering the market.

Consider a simple example of an option to expand. Disney is considering starting a Spanish version of the Disney Channel in Mexico and estimates the net present value of this investment to be –$150 million. Although the negative net present value would normally suggest that rejecting the investment is the best course, assume that if the Mexican venture does better than expected, Disney plans to expand the network to the rest of South America at a cost of $500 million. Based on its current assessment of this market, Disney believes that the present value of the expected cash flows on this investment is only $400 million (making it a negative net present value investment as well). The saving grace is that the latter present value is an estimate, and Disney does not have a firm grasp of the market; a Monte Carlo simulation of the investments yields a standard deviation of 50 percent in value. Finally, assume that Disney will have to make this expansion decision within five years of the Mexican investment, and that the five-year risk-free rate is 4 percent. The value of the expansion option can now be computed using the inputs.

S = Present value of expansion cash flows = $400 million

K = Cost of expansion = $500 million

σ = Standard deviation in value (from simulation) = 50 percent t = 5 years

r = 4 percent

The resulting option value is $167 million. Adding this to the net present value of the initial investment in Mexico (-$150 million) yields the conclusion that Disney should go ahead with the investment, notwithstanding its negative net present value.[14]

The practical considerations associated with estimating the value of the option to expand are similar to those associated with valuing the option to delay. In most cases, firms with options to expand have no specific time horizon by which they have to make an expansion decision, making these open-ended options, or, at best, options with arbitrary lives. Even when a life can be estimated for the option, neither the size nor the potential market for the product may be known, and estimating either can be problematic. To illustrate, consider the Disney example just discussed. Although we adopted a period of five years, at the end of which the Disney must decide one way or another on its future expansion into South America, it is entirely possible that this time frame is not specified at the time the store is opened. Furthermore, we have assumed that both the cost and the present value of expansion can be estimated initially. In reality, the firm may not have good estimates for either before making the first investment, because it does not have much information on the underlying market.

Implications

Firms implicitly use the option to expand to rationalize taking investments that have negative net present value but provide significant opportunities to tap into new markets or sell new products. The option pricing approach adds rigor to this argument by estimating the value of this option, and provides insight into those occasions when it is most valuable. In general, the option to expand is clearly more valuable in more volatile businesses with higher returns on projects (such as biotechnology or computer software) than in stable businesses with lower returns (such as housing, utilities, or automobiles). Specifically, the option to expand is at the basis of arguments that an investment should be made because of strategic considerations or that large investments should be broken into smaller phases. It can also be considered a rationale for why firms may accumulate cash or hold back on borrowing, thus preserving financial flexibility.

---

14   This value was computed using the Black-Scholes model. A binomial model yields a similar value.

Strategic Considerations

In many acquisitions or investments, the acquiring firm believes that the transaction will give it competitive advantages in the future. These competitive advantages range the gamut and include these:

- **Entry into a growing or large market**—An investment or acquisition may allow the firm to enter a large or potentially large market much sooner than it otherwise would have been able to do so. A good example of this would be the acquisition of a Mexican retail firm by a U.S. firm, with the intent of expanding into the Mexican market.

- **Technological expertise**—In some cases, the acquisition is motivated by the desire to acquire a proprietary technology that will allow the acquirer to expand either its existing market or into a new market.

- **Brand name**—Firms sometimes pay large premiums over market price to acquire firms with valuable brand names. They believe these brand names can be used for expansion into new markets in the future.

Although all these potential advantages may be used to justify initial investments that do not meet financial benchmarks, not all of them create valuable options. The value of the option is derived from the degree to which these competitive advantages, assuming that they do exist, translate into sustainable excess returns. Consequently, these advantages can be used to justify premiums only when the acquiring firm believes that it has some degree of exclusivity in the targeted market or technology. Two examples can help illustrate this point. A developed market telecomm firm should be willing to pay a premium for a Chinese telecomm firm if the latter has exclusive rights to service a large segment of the Chinese market; the option to expand in the Chinese market could be worth a significant amount.[15] On the other hand, a developed market retailer should be wary about paying a real option premium for an Indian retail firm, even though it may believe that the Indian market could grow to be a lucrative one. The option to expand into this lucrative market is open to all entrants and not just to existing retailers; therefore, it may not translate into sustainable excess returns.

Multistage Projects/Investments

When entering new businesses or making new investments, firms sometimes have the option to enter the business in stages. Although doing so may reduce potential upside, it

---

15 A note of caution needs to be added here. If the exclusive rights to a market come with no pricing power—in other words, the Government will set the price charged to customers—it may very well translate into zero excess returns (and no option value).

also protects the firm against downside risk by allowing it, at each stage, to gauge demand and decide whether to go on to the next stage. In other words, a standard project can be recast as a series of options to expand, with each option depending on the previous one. Two propositions follow.

- Some projects that do not look good on a full investment basis may be value creating if the firm can invest in stages.

- Some projects that look attractive on a full investment basis may become even more attractive if taken in stages.

The gain in value from the options created by multistage investments has to be weighed against the cost. Taking investments in stages may allow competitors who decide to enter the market on a full scale to capture the market. It may also lead to higher costs at each stage, because the firm is not taking full advantage of economies of scale.

Several implications emerge from viewing this choice between multistage and one-time investments in an option framework. The projects where the gains will be largest from making the investment in multiple stages include these.

- **Projects that have significant barriers to entry from competitors entering the market**—Thus, a firm with a patent on a product or other legal protection against competition pays a much smaller price for starting small and expanding as it learns more about the product.

- **Projects characterized by significant uncertainty about the size of the market and the eventual success of the project**—Here, starting small and expanding allows the firm to reduce its losses if the product does not sell as well as anticipated and to learn more about the market at each stage. This information can then be useful in subsequent stages in both product design and marketing. This has been used as an argument for why venture capitalists invest in young companies in stages. They do it partly to capture the value of waiting/learning at each stage and partly to reduce the likelihood that the entrepreneur will be too conservative in pursuing risky (but good) opportunities.[16]

- **Projects that need a substantial investment in infrastructure (large fixed costs) and high operating leverage**—Because the savings from doing a project in multiple stages can be traced to investments needed at each stage, they are likely to be greater in firms where those costs are large. Capital-intensive projects as well as projects that require large initial marketing expenses (a new brand

---

16 Hsu, Y. "Staging of Venture Capital Investment: A Real Options Analysis." Working paper, University of Cambridge, 2002.

name product for a consumer product company) gain more from the options created by taking the project in multiple stages.

Growth Companies

In the stock market boom in the 1990s, we witnessed the phenomenon of young, start-up, Internet companies with large market capitalizations but little to show in terms of earnings, cash flows, or even revenues. Conventional valuation models suggested that it would be difficult, if not impossible, to justify these market valuations with expected cash flows. In an interesting twist on the option-to-expand argument, some argued that investors in these companies were buying options to expand and be part of a potentially huge e-commerce market, rather than stock in conventional companies.[17]

Although the argument is alluring and serves to pacify investors in growth companies who may feel that they are paying too much, there are clearly dangers in making this stretch. The biggest one is that the "exclusivity" component that is necessary for real options to have value is being given short shrift. Consider investing in an Internet stock in 1999 and assume that we were paying a premium to be part of a potentially large online market in 2008. We can assume further that this market comes to fruition. Could we have partaken in this market without paying that upfront premium for a dot-com company? We don't see why not. After all, GE and Nokia were just as capable of being part of this online market, as were any number of new entrants into the market.[18]

Financial Flexibility

When making decisions about how much to borrow and how much cash to return to stockholders (in dividends and stock buybacks), managers should consider the effects such decisions will have on their capacity to make new investments or meet unanticipated contingencies in future periods. Practically, this translates into firms maintaining excess debt capacity or larger cash balances than are warranted by current needs, to meet unexpected future requirements. Although maintaining this financing flexibility has value to firms, it also has costs; the large cash balances might earn below-market returns and expose them to hostile takeovers, and excess debt capacity implies that the firm is giving up some value by maintaining a higher cost of capital.

Using an option framework, it can be argued that a firm that maintains a large cash balance and preserves excess debt capacity is doing so to have the option to invest in unexpected projects with high returns that may arise in the future. To value financial

---

17   Schwartz, E. S., and M. Moon. "Rational Pricing of Internet Companies Revisited." *The Financial Review*, 36, 7–26, 2001. A simpler version of the same argument was made in Mauboussin, M. "Get Real: Using Real Options in Security Analysis." CSFB Publication, June 23, 1999.

18   This argument is fleshed out in my book, *The Dark Side of Valuation*, published by Prentice-Hall.

flexibility as an option, consider the following framework: a firm has expectations about how much it will need to reinvest in future periods, based on its own past history and current conditions in the industry. On the other side of the ledger, a firm also has expectations about how much it can raise from internal funds and its normal access to capital markets in future periods. Actual reinvestment needs can be very different from the expected reinvestment needs; for simplicity, we will assume that the capacity to generate funds is known to the firm. The advantage (and value) of having excess debt capacity or large cash balances is that the firm can meet any reinvestment needs in excess of funds available using its excess debt capacity and surplus cash. The payoff from these projects, however, comes from the excess returns that the firm expects to make on them.

Looking at financial flexibility as an option yields valuable insights on when financial flexibility is most valuable. Using the framework developed earlier, for instance, we would argue that the following.

- Other things remaining equal, firms operating in businesses where projects earn substantially higher returns than their hurdle rates should value flexibility more than those that operate in stable businesses where excess returns are small. This would imply that firms that earn large excess returns on their projects can use the need for financial flexibility as the justification for holding large cash balances and excess debt capacity.

- Because a firm's ability to fund these reinvestment needs is determined by its capacity to generate internal funds, other things remaining equal, financial flexibility should be worth less to firms with large and stable earnings, as a percent of firm value. Young and growing firms that have small or negative earnings, and therefore much lower capacity to generate internal funds, will value flexibility more. As supporting evidence, note that technology firms usually borrow very little and accumulate large cash balances.

- Firms with limited internal funds can still get away with little or no financial flexibility if they can tap external markets for capital—bank debt, bonds, and new equity issues. Other things remaining equal, the greater the capacity (and willingness) of a firm to raise funds from external capital markets, the less should be the value of flexibility. This may explain why private or small firms, which have far less access to capital, will value financial flexibility more than larger firms. The existence of corporate bond markets can also make a difference in how much flexibility is valued. In markets where firms cannot issue bonds and have to depend entirely on banks for financing, there is less access to capital and a greater need to maintain financial flexibility.

- The need for and the value of flexibility is a function of how uncertain a firm is about future reinvestment needs. Firms with predictable reinvestment needs should value flexibility less than firms in sectors where reinvestment needs are volatile on a period-to-period basis.

In conventional corporate finance, the optimal debt ratio is the one that minimizes the cost of capital and has little incentive for firms to accumulate cash balances. This view of the world, though, flows directly from the implicit assumption we make that capital markets are open and can be accessed with little or no cost. Introducing external capital constraints, internal or external, into the model leads to a more nuanced analysis where rational firms may borrow less than optimal and hold back on returning cash to stockholders.

The Option to Abandon an Investment

The final option to consider here is the option to abandon a project when its cash flows do not measure up to expectations. One way to reflect this value is through decision trees, as evidenced in Chapter 6. The decision tree has limited applicability in most real-world investment analyses; it typically works only for multistage projects, and it requires inputs on probabilities at each stage of the project. The option pricing approach provides a more general way of estimating and building the value of abandonment into investment analysis. To illustrate, assume that V is the remaining value on a project if it continues to the end of its life, and L is the liquidation or abandonment value for the same project at the same point in time. If the project has a life of n years, the value of continuing the project can be compared to the liquidation (abandonment) value. If the value from continuing is higher, the project should be continued; if the value of abandonment is higher, the holder of the abandonment option could consider abandoning the project.

$$\text{Payoff from owning an abandonment option} \quad = 0 \qquad \text{if } V > L$$

$$= L - V \qquad \text{if } V \leq L$$

These payoffs are graphed in Figure 8.7, as a function of the expected value from continuing the investment.

Unlike the prior two cases, the option to abandon takes on the characteristics of a put option.

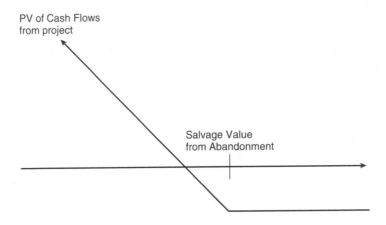

PV of Cash Flows
from project

Salvage Value
from Abandonment

Figure 8.7: The Option to Abandon a Project

Let's consider a simple example. Assume that a firm is considering taking a 10-year project that requires an initial investment of $100 million in a real estate partnership, where the present value of expected cash flows is $110 million. Although the net present value of $10 million is small, assume that the firm has the option to abandon this project anytime in the next 10 years by selling its share of the ownership to the other partners in the venture for $50 million. Assume that the variance in the present value of the expected cash flows from being in the partnership is 0.09.

We can estimate the value of the abandonment option by determining the characteristics of the put option.

Value of the underlying asset (S) = PV of cash flows from project = $110 million

Strike price (K) = salvage value from abandonment = $50 million

Variance in underlying asset's value = 0.06

Time to expiration = period for which the firm has abandonment option = 10 years

The project has a 25-year life and is expected to lose value each year; for simplicity, we will assume that the loss is linear (4 percent per year).

Loss in value each year = $1/n = 1/25 = 4$ percent

Assume that the 10-year riskless rate is 6 percent. We can estimate the value of the put option as follows:

Call value = $110 \exp^{(-.04)(10)} (0.9737) - 50 (\exp^{(-0.06)(10)} (0.8387)$
= $84.09 million

Put value = $84.09 - 110 + 50 \exp^{(-0.06)(10)}$ = $1.53 million

We have to add the value of this abandonment option to the net present value of the project of $10 million, yielding a total net present value with the abandonment option of $11.53 million. Note, though, that abandonment becomes a more and more attractive option as the remaining project life decreases, because the present value of the remaining cash flows will decrease.

In the preceding analysis, we assumed, rather unrealistically, that the abandonment value was clearly specified up front and that it did not change during the life of the project. This may be true in some specific cases, in which an abandonment option is built into the contract. More often, however, the firm has the option to abandon, and the salvage value from doing so has to be estimated (with error) up front. Further, the abandonment value may change over the life of the project, making it difficult to apply traditional option pricing techniques. Finally, it is entirely possible that abandoning a project may not bring in a liquidation value but may create costs instead; a manufacturing firm may have to pay severance to its workers, for instance. In such cases, it would not make sense to abandon unless the present value of the expected cash flows from continuing with the investment were even more negative.

Implications

The fact that the option to abandon has value provides a rationale for firms to build in operating flexibility to scale back or terminate projects if they do not measure up to expectations. It also indicates that firms that focus on generating more revenues by offering their customers the option to walk away from commitments may be giving up more than they gain, in the process.

Escape Clauses

When a firm enters into a long-term risky investment that requires a large up-front investment, it should do so with the clear understanding that it may regret making this investment fairly early in its life. Being able to get out of such long-term commitments that threaten to drain more resources in the future is at the heart of the option to abandon. It is true that some of this flexibility is determined by the business; getting out of bad investments is easier to do in service businesses than in heavy infrastructure businesses. However, it is also true that firms can take actions at the time of making these investments that give them more choices if things do not go according to plan.

The first and most direct way is to build operating flexibility contractually with those parties that are involved in the investment. Thus, contracts with suppliers may be written on an annual basis, rather than long term, and employees may be hired on a temporary basis, rather than permanently. The physical plant used for a project may be leased on a short-term basis, rather than bought, and the financial investment may be made in stages rather than as an initial lump sum. Although there is a cost to building in this flexibility, the gains may be much larger, especially in volatile businesses. The initial capital investment can be shared with another investor, presumably with deeper pockets and a greater willingness to stay with the investment, even if it turns sour. This provides a rationale for joint venture investing, especially for small firms that have limited resources; finding a cash-rich, larger company to share the risk may well be worth the cost.

None of these actions is costless. Entering into short-term agreements with suppliers and leasing the physical plant may be more expensive than committing for the life of the investment, but that additional cost has to be weighed against the benefit of maintaining the abandonment option.

Customer Incentives

Firms that are intent on increasing revenues sometimes offer abandonment options to customers to induce them to buy their products and services. As an example, consider a firm that sells its products on multiyear contracts and offers customers the option to cancel their contracts at any time, with no cost. Although this may sweeten the deal and increase sales, there is likely to be a substantial cost. In the event of a recession, customers who are unable to meet their obligations are likely to cancel their contracts. In effect, the firm has made its good times better and its bad times worse; the cost of this increased volatility in earnings and revenues has to be measured against the potential gain in revenue growth to see if the net effect is positive.

This discussion should also act as a cautionary note for those firms that are run with marketing objectives such as maximizing market share or posting high revenue growth. Those objectives can often be accomplished by giving valuable options to customers— salespeople will want to meet their sales targets and are not particularly concerned about the long-term costs they may create with their commitments to customers—and the firm may be worse off as a consequence.

Switching Options

Although the abandonment option considers the value of shutting down an investment entirely, it is worth examining an intermediate alternative. Firms can sometimes alter production levels in response to demand, and being able to do so can make an investment more valuable. Consider, for instance, a power company that is considering a new plant to generate electricity. Assume that the company can run the plant at full capacity and produce 1 million kilowatt hours of power, or run it at half capacity (and substantially less cost) and produce 500,000 kilowatt hours of power. In this case, the company can observe both the demand for power and the revenues per kilowatt-hour and decide whether it makes sense to run at full or half capacity. We can then compare the value of this switching option to the cost of building in this flexibility in the first place.

The airline business provides an interesting case study in how different companies manage their cost structure and the payoffs to their strategies. One reason that Southwest Airlines has been able to maintain its profitability in a deeply troubled sector is that it has made cost flexibility a central component in its decision process. From its choice of using only one type of aircraft for its entire fleet[19] to its refusal, for the most part, to fly into large urban airports (with high gate costs), the company's operations have created the most flexible cost structure in the business. Thus, when revenues dip (as they inevitably do at some point in time when the economy weakens), Southwest is able to trim its costs and stay profitable while other airlines teeter on the brink of bankruptcy.

Caveats on Real Options

The discussion on the potential applications of real options should provide a window into why they are so alluring to practitioners and businesses. In essence, we are ignoring the time-honored rules of capital budgeting, which include rejecting investments that have negative net present value, when real options are present. Not only does the real options approach encourage you to make investments that do not meet conventional financial criteria, but it also makes it more likely that you will do so, the less you know about the investment. Ignorance, rather than being a weakness, becomes a virtue because it increases the uncertainty in the estimated value and the resulting option value. To prevent the real options process from being hijacked by managers who want to rationalize bad (and risky) decisions, we have to impose some reasonable constraints on when it can be used and, when it is used, how to estimate its value.

The first restraint is that not all investments have options embedded in them, and not all options, even if they do exist, have value. To assess whether an investment creates valuable options that need to be analyzed and valued, we need to answer three key affirmatively.

- **Is the first investment a prerequisite for the later investment/expansion?** If not, how necessary is the first investment for the later investment/expansion?

---

19 From its inception until recently, Southwest used the Boeing 737 as its workhorse, thus reducing its need to maintain different maintenance crews at each airport it flies into.

Consider our earlier analysis of the value of a patent or the value of an undeveloped oil reserve as options. A firm cannot generate patents without investing in research or paying another firm for the patents, and it cannot get rights to an undeveloped oil reserve without bidding on it at a government auction or buying it from another oil company. Clearly, the initial investment here (spending on R&D, bidding at the auction) is required for the firm to have the second option. Now consider the Disney expansion into Mexico. The initial investment in a Spanish channel provides Disney with information about market potential, without which presumably it is unwilling to expand into the larger South American market. Unlike the patent and undeveloped reserves illustrations, the initial investment is not a prerequisite for the second, although management might view it as such. The connection gets even weaker when we look at one firm acquiring another to have the option to be able to enter a large market. Acquiring an Internet service provider to have a foothold in the Internet retailing market or buying a Brazilian brewery to preserve the option to enter the Brazilian beer market would be examples of such transactions.

- **Does the firm have an exclusive right to the later investment/expansion?** If not, does the initial investment provide the firm with significant competitive advantages on subsequent investments? The value of the option ultimately derives not from the cash flows generated by the second and subsequent investments, but from the excess returns generated by these cash flows. The greater the potential for excess returns on the second investment, the greater the value of the option. The potential for excess returns is closely tied to how much of a competitive advantage the first investment provides the firm when it takes subsequent investments. At one extreme, again, consider investing in research and development to acquire a patent. The patent gives the firm that owns it the exclusive rights to produce that product, and if the market potential is large, the right to the excess returns from the project. At the other extreme, the firm might get no competitive advantages on subsequent investments, in which case, it is questionable as to whether there can be any excess returns on these investments. In reality, most investments will fall in the continuum between these two extremes, with greater competitive advantages being associated with higher excess returns and larger option values.

- **How sustainable are the excess returns?** In a competitive marketplace, excess returns attract competitors, and competition drives out excess returns. The more sustainable the competitive advantages possessed by a firm, the greater the value of the options embedded in the initial investment. The sustainability of competitive advantages is a function of two forces. The first force is the nature of the competition; other things remaining equal, competitive advantages fade much more quickly in sectors where there are aggressive competitors and new entry into the business is easy. The second force is the nature of the competitive advantage. If the resource controlled by the firm is finite and scarce (as is the case with natural resource reserves and vacant land), the competitive advantage is likely to be sustainable for longer periods. Alternatively, if the competitive advantage comes from being the first mover in a market or technological expertise, it will come under assault far sooner. The most direct way of reflecting this in the value of the option is in its life; the life of the option can be set to the period of competitive advantage, and only the excess returns earned over this period count toward the value of the option.

The second restraint is that when real options are used to justify a decision, the justification has to be in more than qualitative terms. In other words, managers who argue for investing in a project with poor returns or paying a premium on an acquisition based on real options should be required to value these real options and show, in fact, that the economic benefits exceed the costs. There will be two arguments made against this requirement. The first is that real options cannot be easily valued, because the inputs are difficult to obtain and often noisy. The second is that the inputs to option pricing models can be easily manipulated to back up whatever the conclusion might be. Although both arguments have some basis, an estimate with error is better than no estimate at all, and the process of quantitatively trying to estimate the value of a real option is, in fact, the first step to understanding what drives its value.

We should add one final note of caution about the use of option pricing models to assess the value of real options. Option pricing models, whether they are of the binomial or Black-Scholes variety, are based on two fundamental precepts: replication and arbitrage. For either to be feasible, we have to be able to trade on the underlying asset and on the option. This is easy to accomplish with a listed option on a traded stock; we can trade on both the stock and the listed option. It is much more difficult to pull off when valuing a patent or an investment expansion opportunity; neither the underlying asset (the product that emerges from the patent) nor the option itself is traded. This does not mean that we cannot estimate the value of a patent as an option, but it does indicate that monetizing this value will be much more difficult to do. In the Avonex example from earlier in this chapter, the option value for the patent was $907 million, whereas the conventional risk-adjusted value was only $547 million. Much as you may believe in the former as the right estimate of value, it is unlikely that any potential buyer of the patent will come close to paying that amount.

Real Options in a Risk Management Framework

Given the different perspective on risk brought into the picture by real options, how do we fit this approach into the broader set of risk assessment tools, and what role, if any, should it play in risk management? Although some real options purists view it as the answer to all the problems that we face in managing risk, a more nuanced conclusion is merited.

Real options have made an important contribution to the risk management debate by bringing in the potential upside in risk to offset the hand wringing generated by the downside. It can also be viewed as a bridge between corporate finance and corporate strategy. Historically, the former has been focused on how best to assess the value of risky assets in the interests of maximizing firm value, and the latter on the sources of competitive advantages and market potential. The real option framework allows us to bring the rigors of financial analysis to corporate strategic analysis and link it with value creation and maximization. Finally, the real options approach reveals the value of maintaining flexibility in both operating and financial decisions. By preserving the flexibility to both scale up an investment in good scenarios and to scale down or abandon the same investment in down scenarios, a firm may be able to turn a bad investment into a good one.

As we noted earlier in the chapter, though, the value of real options is greatest when we have exclusivity and dissipates quickly in competitive environments. Consequently, real options will be most useful to firms that have significant competitive advantages and can therefore assume that they will be able to act alone or at least much earlier than their competition in response to new information. It should come as no surprise that the real options approach has been used longest and with the most success, by mining and commodity companies. The danger with extending the real options framework to all firms is that it will inevitably be used to justify bad investments and decisions.

The real options approach in risk management should not replace risk-adjusted values or Monte Carlo simulations but should be viewed more as a supplement or a complement to these approaches.[20] After all, to assess the value of Avonex, we began with the risk-adjusted present value of the expected cash flows from the drug. Similarly, to analyze the Disney expansion opportunity in South America, we drew on the output from Monte Carlo simulations.

---

20 For an example of how simulations and real options complement each other, see Gamba, A. "Real Options Valuation: A Monte Carlo Approach." Working Paper, SSRN, 2002.

Conclusion

In contrast to the approaches that focus on downside risk—risk-adjusted value, simulations, and value at risk (VaR)—the real options approach brings an optimistic view to uncertainty. Although conceding that uncertainty can create losses, it argues that uncertainty can also be exploited for potential gains and that updated information can be used to augment the upside and reduce the downside risks inherent in investments. In essence, we are arguing that the conventional risk-adjustment approaches fail to capture this opportunity and that we should be adding an option premium to the risk-adjusted value.

In this chapter, we considered three potential real options and applications of each. The first is the option to delay, in which a firm with exclusive rights to an investment has the option of deciding when to take that investment and to delay taking it, if necessary. The second is the option to expand, whereby a firm may be willing to lose money on an initial investment, in the hope of expanding into other investments or markets further down the road. The third is the option to abandon an investment, if it looks like a money loser, early in the process.

Although it is clearly appropriate to attach value to real options in some cases—patents, reserves of natural resources, or exclusive licenses—the argument for an option premium gets progressively weaker as we move away from the exclusivity inherent in each of these cases. In particular, a firm that invests into an emerging market in a money-losing enterprise, using the argument that that market is a large and potentially profitable one, could be making a serious mistake. After all, the firm could be right in its assessment of the market, but absent barriers to entry, it may not be able to earn excess returns in that market or keep the competition out. Not all opportunities are options, and not all options have significant economic value.

APPENDIX 8.1

Basics of Options and Option Pricing

An option provides the holder with the right to buy or sell a specified quantity of an underlying asset at a fixed price (called a *strike price* or an *exercise price*) at or before the expiration date of the option. Because it is a right and not an obligation, the holder can choose not to exercise the right and allow the option to expire. There are two types of options: call options and put options.

Option Payoffs

A *call option* gives the buyer of the option the right to buy the underlying asset at a fixed price, called the strike or the exercise price, at any time prior to the expiration date of the option. The buyer pays a price for this right. If, at expiration, the value of the asset is less than the strike price, the option is not exercised and expires worthless. If, on the other hand, the value of the asset is greater than the strike price, the option is exercised—the buyer of the option buys the stock at the exercise price, and the difference between the asset value and the exercise price comprises the gross profit on the investment. The net profit on the investment is the difference between the gross profit and the price paid for the call initially. A payoff diagram illustrates the cash payoff on an option at expiration. For a call, the net payoff is negative (and equal to the price paid for the call) if the value of the underlying asset is less than the strike price. If the price of the underlying asset exceeds the strike price, the gross payoff is the difference between the value of the underlying asset and the strike price, and the net payoff is the difference between the gross payoff and the price of the call. This is illustrated in Figure 8A.1.

A *put option* gives the buyer of the option the right to sell the underlying asset at a fixed price, again called the strike or exercise price, at any time prior to the expiration date of the option. The buyer pays a price for this right. If the price of the underlying asset is greater than the strike price, the option will not be exercised and will expire worthless. If, on the other hand, the price of the underlying asset is less than the strike price, the owner of the put option will exercise the option and sell the stock at the strike price, claiming the difference between the strike price and the market value of the asset as the gross profit. Again, netting out the initial cost paid for the put yields the net profit from the transaction. A put has a negative net payoff if the value of the underlying asset exceeds the strike price, and it has a gross payoff equal to the difference between the strike price and the value of the underlying asset if the asset value is less than the strike price. This concept is summarized in Figure 8A.2.

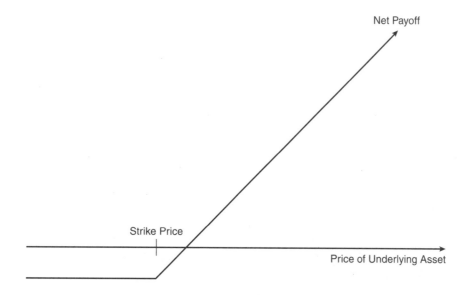

Figure 8A.1: Payoff on Call Option

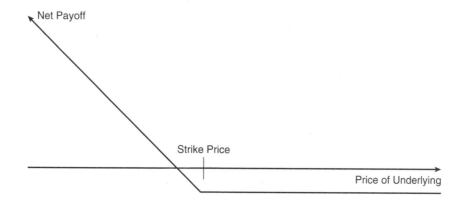

Figure 8A.2: Payoff on Put Option

We need to make one final distinction. Options are usually categorized as American or European. A primary distinction between two is that American options can be exercised at any time prior to its expiration, whereas European options can be exercised only at expiration. The possibility of early exercise makes American options more valuable than otherwise similar European options; it also makes them more difficult to value. One compensating factor enables the former to be valued using models designed for the latter. In most cases, the time premium associated with the remaining life of an option and transactions costs makes early exercise suboptimal. In other words, the holders of in-the-money options will generally get much more by selling the option to someone else than by exercising the options.[21]

Determinants of Option Value

The value of an option is determined by a number of variables relating to the underlying asset and financial markets.

- **Current value of the underlying asset**—Options are assets that derive value from an underlying asset. Consequently, changes in the value of the underlying asset affect the value of the options on that asset. Because calls provide the right to buy the underlying asset at a fixed price, an increase in the value of the asset will increase the value of the calls. Puts, on the other hand, become less valuable as the value of the asset increases.

- **Variance in value of the underlying asset**—The buyer of an option acquires the right to buy or sell the underlying asset at a fixed price. The higher the variance in the value of the underlying asset, the greater the value of the option. This is true for both calls and puts. Although it may seem counterintuitive that an increase in a risk measure (variance) should increase value, options are different from other securities because buyers of options can never lose more than the price they pay for them; in fact, they have the potential to earn significant returns from large price movements.

---

21 Although early exercise is not optimal generally, there are at least two exceptions to this rule. One is a case where the underlying asset pays large dividends, thus reducing the value of the asset, and any call options on that asset. In this case, call options may be exercised just before an ex-dividend date, if the time premium on the options is less than the expected decline in asset value because of the dividend payment. The other exception arises when an investor holds both the underlying asset and deep in-the-money puts on that asset when interest rates are high. In this case, the time premium on the put may be less than the potential gain from exercising the put early and earning interest on the exercise price.

- **Dividends paid on the underlying asset**—The value of the underlying asset can be expected to decrease if dividend payments are made on the asset during the life of the option. Consequently, the value of a call on the asset is a decreasing function of the size of expected dividend payments, and the value of a put is an increasing function of expected dividend payments. A more intuitive way of thinking about dividend payments, for call options, is as a cost of delaying exercise on in-the-money options. To see why, consider an option on a traded stock. Once a call option is in-the-money—that is, the holder of the option will make a gross payoff by exercising the option—exercising the call option will provide the holder with the stock and entitle him to the dividends on the stock in subsequent periods. Failing to exercise the option will mean that these dividends are foregone.

- **Strike price of option**—A key characteristic used to describe an option is the strike price. In the case of calls, whereby the holder acquires the right to buy at a fixed price, the value of the call will decline as the strike price increases. In the case of puts, whereby the holder has the right to sell at a fixed price, the value will increase as the strike price increases.

- **Time to expiration on option**—Both calls and puts become more valuable as the time to expiration increases. This is because the longer time to expiration provides more time for the value of the underlying asset to move, increasing the value of both types of options. Additionally, in the case of a call, where the buyer has to pay a fixed price at expiration, the present value of this fixed price decreases as the life of the option increases, increasing the value of the call.

- **Riskless interest rate corresponding to life of option**—Because the buyer of an option pays the price of the option up front, an opportunity cost is involved. This cost depends on the level of interest rates and the time to expiration on the option. The riskless interest rate also enters into the valuation of options when the present value of the exercise price is calculated, because the exercise price does not have to be paid (received) until expiration on calls (puts). Increases in the interest rate increase the value of calls and reduce the value of puts.

Table 8A.1 summarizes the variables and their predicted effects on call and put prices.

Table 8A.1   Summary of Variables Affecting Call and Put Prices

Factor	Effect on Call Value	Effect on Put Value
Increase in underlying asset's value	Increases	Decreases
Increase in strike price	Decreases	Increases
Increase in variance of underlying asset	Increases	Increases
Increase in time to expiration	Increases	Increases
Increase in interest rates	Increases	Decreases
Increase in dividends paid	Decreases	Increases

Option Pricing Models

Option pricing theory has made vast strides since 1972, when Black and Scholes published their path-breaking paper providing a model for valuing dividend-protected European options. Black and Scholes used a *replicating portfolio*—a portfolio composed of the underlying asset and the risk-free asset that had the same cash flows as the option being valued—to come up with their final formulation. Although their derivation is mathematically complicated, there is a simpler binomial model for valuing options that draws on the same logic.

The Binomial Model

The *binomial option pricing model* is based on a simple formulation for the asset price process, in which the asset, in any period, can move to one of two possible prices. The general formulation of a stock price process that follows the binomial is shown in Figure 8A.3.

In this figure, S is the current stock price. The price moves up to Su with probability p and down to Sd with probability 1 – p in any time period.

The objective in creating a replicating portfolio is to use a combination of risk-free borrowing/lending and the underlying asset to create the same cash flows as the option being valued. The principles of arbitrage apply here, and the value of the option must be equal to the value of the replicating portfolio. In the case of the general formulation, where stock prices can either move up to Su or down to Sd in any period, the replicating portfolio for a call with strike price K will involve borrowing $B and acquiring Δ of the underlying asset, where

Δ = Number of units of the underlying asset bought = $(C_u - C_d)/(Su - Sd)$

where

C_u = Value of the call if the stock price is Su

C_d = Value of the call if the stock price is Sd

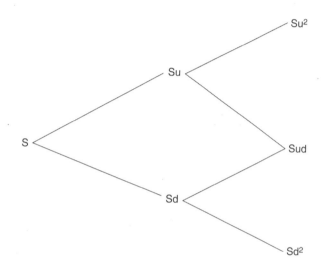

Figure 8A.3: General Formulation for Binomial Price Path

In a multiperiod binomial process, the valuation has to proceed iteratively—that is, starting with the last period and moving backward until the current point in time. The portfolios replicating the option are created at each step and valued, providing the values for the option in that period. The final output from the binomial option pricing model is a statement of the value of the option in terms of the replicating portfolio, composed of Δ shares (option delta) of the underlying asset and risk-free borrowing/lending.

Value of the call = current value of underlying asset * option delta – borrowing needed to replicate the option

Consider a simple example. Assume that the objective is to value a call with a strike price of 50, which is expected to expire in two periods, on an underlying asset whose price currently is 50 and is expected to follow a binomial process.

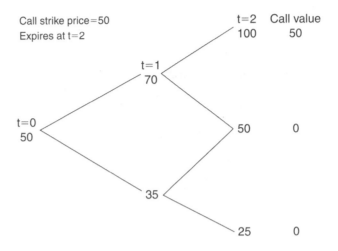

Now assume that the interest rate is 11 percent. In addition, define the following:

Δ = Number of shares in the replicating portfolio

B = Dollars of borrowing in replicating portfolio

The objective is to combine Δ shares of stock and B dollars of borrowing to replicate the cash flows from the call with a strike price of $50. We can do this iteratively, starting with the last period and working back through the binomial tree.

1. Start with the end nodes and work backward:

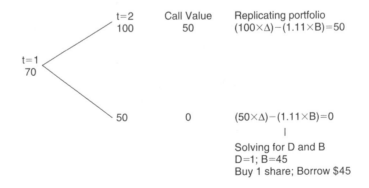

Thus, if the stock price is $70 at t = 1, borrowing $45 and buying one share of the stock will give the same cash flows as buying the call. The value of the call at t = 1, if the stock price is $70, is therefore

Value of call = value of replicating position = 70 Δ − B = 70 − 45 = 25

Considering the other leg of the binomial tree at t = 1,

If the stock price is 35 at t = 1, the call is worth nothing.

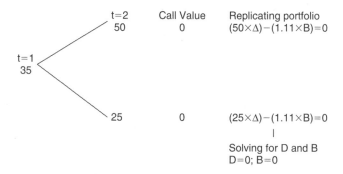

2. Move backward to the earlier time and create a replicating portfolio that will provide the cash flows for the option.

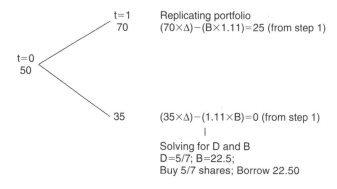

In other words, borrowing $22.50 and buying 5/7 of a share will provide the same cash flows as a call with a strike price of $50. The value of the call therefore has to be the same as the value of this position.

Value of call = value of replicating position = 5/7 × Current stock price − $22.50
= $13.20

The binomial model provides insight into the determinants of option value. The value of an option is not determined by the expected price of the asset but by its current price, which, of course, reflects expectations about the future. This is a direct consequence of arbitrage. If the option value deviates from the value of the replicating portfolio, investors can create an arbitrage position—that is, one that requires no investment, involves no risk, and delivers positive returns. To illustrate, if the portfolio that replicates the call costs more than the call does in the market, an investor could buy the call, sell the replicating portfiolio, and be guaranteed the difference as a profit. The cash flows on the two positions will offset each other, leading to no cash flows in subsequent periods. The option value also increases as the time to expiration is extended, as the price movements (u and d) increase, and with increases in the interest rate.

The Black-Scholes Model

The binomial model is a discrete-time model for asset price movements, including an interval (t) between price movements. As the interval is shortened, the limiting distribution, as t approaches 0, can take one of two forms. If as t approaches 0, price changes become smaller, the limiting distribution is the normal distribution, and the price process is a continuous one. If as t approaches 0, price changes remain large, the limiting distribution is the Poisson distribution—that is, a distribution that allows for price jumps. The Black-Scholes model applies when the limiting distribution is the normal distribution,[22] and it explicitly assumes that the price process is continuous.

The Model

The original Black and Scholes model was designed to value European options, which were dividend protected. Thus, neither the possibility of early exercise nor the payment of dividends affects the value of options in this model. The value of a call option in the Black-Scholes model can be written as a function of the following variables:

S = Current value of the underlying asset

K = Strike price of the option

t = Life to expiration of the option

r = Riskless interest rate corresponding to the life of the option

---

22 Stock prices cannot drop below zero because of the limited liability of stockholders in publicly listed firms. Therefore, stock prices, by themselves, cannot be normally distributed, because a normal distribution requires some probability of infinitely negative values. The distribution of the natural logs of stock prices is assumed to be log-normal in the Black-Scholes model. This is why the variance used in this model is the variance in the log of stock prices.

σ^2 = Variance in the ln (value) of the underlying asset

The model itself can be written as follows.

Value of call = $S\,N\,(d_1) - K\,e^{-rt}\,N(d_2)$

where

$$d_1 = \frac{\ln\left(\dfrac{S}{K}\right) + \left(r + \dfrac{\sigma^2}{2}\right)t}{\sigma\,\sqrt{t}}$$

$$d_2 = d_1 - \sigma\,\sqrt{t}$$

The process of valuation of options using the Black-Scholes model involves the following steps.

1. The inputs to the Black-Scholes are used to estimate d_1 and d_2.

2. The cumulative normal distribution functions, $N(d1)$ and $N(d2)$, corresponding to these standardized normal variables are estimated.

3. The present value of the exercise price is estimated, using the continuous time version of the present value formulation.

    Present value of exercise price = $K\,e^{-rt}$

4. The value of the call is estimated from the Black-Scholes model.

The determinants of value in the Black-Scholes are the same as those in the binomial: the current value of the stock price, the variability in stock prices, the time to expiration on the option, the strike price, and the riskless interest rate. The principle of replicating portfolios that is used in binomial valuation also underlies the Black-Scholes model. In fact, embedded in the Black-Scholes model is the replicating portfolio:

Value of call = $\quad S\,N\,(d_1) \quad\quad\quad\quad\quad - K\,e^{-rt}\,N(d_2)$

$\quad\quad\quad\quad\quad$ Buy $N(d_1)$ shares $\quad$ Borrow this amount

$N(d1)$, which is the number of shares needed to create the replicating portfolio, is called the *option delta*. This replicating portfolio is self-financing and has the same value as the call at every stage of the option's life.

Model Limitations and Fixes

The version of the Black-Scholes model presented earlier does not take into account the possibility of early exercise or the payment of dividends, both of which impact the value of options. Adjustments exist, which although not perfect, provide partial corrections to value.

Dividends

The payment of dividends reduces the stock price. Consequently, call options will become less valuable and put options more valuable as dividend payments increase. One approach to dealing with dividends is to estimate the present value of expected dividends paid by the underlying asset during the option life and subtract it from the current value of the asset to use as "S" in the model. Because this becomes impractical as the option life becomes longer, we would suggest an alternate approach. If the dividend yield (y = dividends / current value of the asset) of the underlying asset is expected to remain unchanged during the life of the option, the Black-Scholes model can be modified to consider dividends.

$$C = S\,e^{-yt}\,N(d_1) - K\,e^{-rt}\,N(d_2)$$

where

$$d_1 = \frac{\ln\left(\dfrac{S}{K}\right) + (r - y + \dfrac{\sigma^2}{2})\,t}{\sigma\,\sqrt{t}}$$

$$d_2 = d_1 - \sigma\,\sqrt{t}$$

From an intuitive standpoint, the adjustments have two effects. First, the value of the asset is discounted back to the present at the dividend yield to take into account the expected drop in value from dividend payments. Second, the interest rate is offset by the dividend yield to reflect the lower carrying cost from holding the stock (in the replicating portfolio). The net effect will be a reduction in the value of calls, with the adjustment, and an increase in the value of puts.

Early Exercise

The Black-Scholes model is designed to value European options, whereas most options that we consider are American options, which can be exercised anytime before expiration. Without working through the mechanics of valuation models, an American option should always be worth at least as much and generally more than a European option because of the early exercise option. There are three basic approaches for dealing with the possibility of early exercise. The first is to continue to use the unadjusted Black-Scholes and regard the resulting value as a floor or conservative estimate of the true value. The second approach is to value the option to each potential exercise date. With options on stocks, this requires that we value options to each ex-dividend day and chooses the maximum of the estimated call values. The third approach is to use a modified version of the binomial model to consider the possibility of early exercise.

Although it is difficult to estimate the prices for each node of a binomial, there is a way to use variances estimated from historical data to compute the expected up and down movements in the binomial. To illustrate, if σ^2 is the variance in ln (stock prices), the up and down movements in the binomial can be estimated as follows.

$$u = \text{Exp} \left[(r - \sigma^2/2)(T/m) + \sqrt{(\sigma^2 T/m)} \right]$$

$$d = \text{Exp} \left[(r - \sigma^2/2)(T/m) - \sqrt{(\sigma^2 T/m)} \right]$$

where u and d are the up and down movements per unit time for the binomial, T is the life of the option, and m is the number of periods within that lifetime. Multiplying the stock price at each stage by u and d will yield the up and down prices. We can use these to value the asset.

The Impact of Exercise on the Value of the Underlying Asset

The derivation of the Black-Scholes model is based on the assumption that exercising an option does not affect the value of the underlying asset. This may be true for listed options on stocks, but it is not true for some types of options. For instance, the exercise of warrants increases the number of shares outstanding and brings fresh cash into the firm, both of which will affect the stock price. The expected negative impact (dilution) of exercise will decrease the value of warrants compared to otherwise similar call options. The adjustment for dilution in the Black-Scholes to the stock price is fairly simple. The stock price is adjusted for the expected dilution from the exercise of the options. In the case of warrants, for instance

Dilution-adjusted $S = (S\, n_S + W\, n_W) / (n_S + n_w)$

where

S = Current value of the stock $\qquad$ n_W = Number of warrants outstanding

W = Market value of warrants outstanding $\quad$ n_S = Number of shares outstanding

When the warrants are exercised, the number of shares outstanding will increase, reducing the stock price. The numerator reflects the market value of equity, including both stocks and warrants outstanding. The reduction in S will reduce the value of the call option.

There is an element of circularity in this analysis, because the value of the warrant is needed to estimate the dilution-adjusted S, and the dilution-adjusted S is needed to estimate the value of the warrant. We can resolve this problem by starting the process with an estimated value of the warrant (say, the exercise value), and then iterating with the new estimated value for the warrant until there is convergence.

Valuing Puts

We can derive the value of a put from the value of a call with the same strike price and the same expiration date through an arbitrage relationship that specifies the following.

$$C - P = S - K e^{-rt}$$

where C is the value of the call, and P is the value of the put (with the same life and exercise price).

This arbitrage relationship can be derived fairly easily and is called *put-call parity*. To see why put-call parity holds, consider creating the following portfolio.

- Sell a call and buy a put with exercise price K and the same expiration date "t."

- Buy the stock at current stock price S.

The payoff from this position is riskless and always yields K at expiration (t). To see this, assume that the stock price at expiration is S^*.

Position	Payoffs at t if $S^* > K$	Payoffs at t if $S^* < K$
Sell call	$-(S^* - K)$	0
Buy put	0	$K - S^*$
Buy stock	S^*	S^*
Total	K	K

Because this position yields K with certainty, its value must be equal to the present value of K at the riskless rate ($K e^{-rt}$).

$$S + P - C = K e^{-rt}$$

$$C - P = S - K e^{-rt}$$

This relationship can be used to value puts. Substituting the Black-Scholes formulation for the value of an equivalent call,

Value of put = $S\,e^{-yt}\,(N(d_1) - 1) - K\,e^{-rt}\,(N(d_2) - 1)$

where

$$d_1 = \frac{\ln\left(\dfrac{S}{K}\right) + (r - y + \dfrac{\sigma^2}{2})\,t}{\sigma\,\sqrt{t}}$$

$$d_2 = d_1 - \sqrt{t}$$

CHAPTERS 9–12

Risk Management: The Big Picture

The last four chapters in this book represent the heart of the book, insofar as they are focused directly on risk management, rather than on the economic underpinnings of risk aversion or on risk assessment. We begin in Chapter 9, "Risk Management: The Big Picture," by defining our objective in risk management as increasing the value of the businesses we run, rather than reducing or increasing risk exposure, and follow up by developing a valuation framework that incorporates all the elements of risk management. We end the chapter by arguing that the key to successful risk management in a business is the decomposition of risk into risk that should be passed on to investors in the company, risk to be hedged or avoided, and risk to be exploited. Chapter 10, "Risk Management: Profiling and Hedging," examines the first two components and presents a framework for determining not only which risks should be hedged but also what tool (insurance, derivatives) to use in hedging risk. Chapter 11, "Strategic Risk Management," draws on corporate strategy and competitive advantages to analyze which risks should be exploited by a business and what the payoff is to this risk exposure. Chapter 12, "Risk Management: First Principles," concludes both the section and the book by drawing lessons for risk management from across the book.

Because these chapters represent a straddling of valuation, corporate finance, and corporate strategy, the language reflects the diversity of views. There are portions that draw heavily on financial theory (when we look at the link between value and risk, for instance) and sections that are almost entirely qualitative (the strategic assessments of risk).

Chapter	Questions for Risk Management
9	What is the objective in risk management?
	How do we get a complete picture of the consequences of risk management?
10	What are the risks that should be passed to investors and why?
	What are the risks that a business should hedge?
	Which hedging tools should you choose when hedging risk?

Chapter	Questions for Risk Management
11	What are the risks that should be exploited by a business?
	What is the payoff to exploiting risk?
12	What are the general propositions that should govern risk management?

9

RISK MANAGEMENT: THE BIG PICTURE

L et us take stock of what we have established so far. Human beings are risk averse, although they sometimes behave in quirky ways when confronted with uncertainty, and risk affects value. The tools to assess risk have become more sophisticated, but the risks we face have also multiplied and become more complex. What separates business success from failure, though, is the capacity to be judicious about which risks to pass through to investors, which risks to avoid, and which risks to exploit.

In Chapter 1, "What Is Risk?," we also noted that risk hedging has taken far too central a role in risk management. In this chapter, we will draw a sharper distinction between risk hedging, which is focused on reducing or eliminating risk, and risk management, where we have a far broader mission of reducing some risks, ignoring other risks, and seeking out still others. We commence our examination of risk management as a process by developing a framework for evaluating its effects on value. We begin by assessing the way risk is considered in conventional valuation and then examine three ways in which we can more completely incorporate the effects of risk on value. In the first, we stay within a discounted cash flow framework but examine the way both risk hedging and savvy risk management can affect cash flows, growth, and overall value. In the second, we try to incorporate the effects of risk hedging and management on value through relative valuation—that is, by looking at how the market prices companies that follow different risk management practices. In the final approach, we adapt some of the techniques that we introduced in the context of real options to assess both the effects of risk hedging and risk taking on value.

Risk and Value: The Conventional View

How does risk show up in conventional valuations? To answer this question, we will look at the two most commonly used approaches to valuation. The first is *intrinsic* or *discounted cash flow valuation*, where the value of a firm or asset is estimated by discounting the expected cash flows back to the present. The second is *relative valuation*, where the value of a firm is estimated by looking at the way the market prices similar firms.

Discounted Cash Flow Valuation

In a conventional discounted cash flow valuation model, the value of an asset is the present value of the expected cash flows on the asset. In this section, we will consider the basic structure of a discounted cash flow model, discuss how risk shows up in the model, and consider the implications for risk management.

Structure of DCF Models

When we are valuing a business, we can apply discounted cash flow valuation in one of two ways. First, we can discount the expected cash flow to equity investors at the cost of equity to arrive at the value of equity in the firm; this is *equity valuation*.

$$\text{Value of Equity} = \sum_{t=1}^{t=\infty} \frac{\text{Expected Cashflow to Equity in period t}}{(1+\text{Cost of Equity})^t}$$

Note that adopting the narrowest measure of the cash flow to equity investors in publicly traded firms gives us a special case of the equity valuation model—the dividend discount model. A broader measure of free cash flow to equity (FCFE) is the cash flow left over after capital expenditures, working capital needs, and debt payments have been made; this is the *free cash flow to equity*.

Second, we can discount the cash flows generated for all claimholders in the firm, debt as well as equity, at the weighted average of the costs demanded by each—the cost of capital—to value the entire business.

$$\text{Value of Firm} = \sum_{t=1}^{t=\infty} \frac{\text{Expected Free Cashflow to Firm}_t}{(1+\text{Cost of Capital})^t}$$

We define the cash flow to the firm as being the cash flow left over after operating expenses, taxes, and reinvestment needs, but before any debt payments (interest or principal payments).

Free cash flow to firm (FCFF) = After-tax operating income – Reinvestment needs

The two differences between cash flow to equity and cash flow to firm become clearer when we compare their definitions. The FCFE begins with net income, which is after interest expenses and taxes, whereas the FCFF begins with after-tax operating income, which is before interest expenses. Another difference is that the FCFE is after net debt payments, whereas the FCFF is before net debt cash flows. What exactly does the FCFF measure? On the one hand, it measures the cash flows generated by the assets before any financing costs are considered and thus is a measure of operating cash flow. On the other, the FCFF is the cash flow used to service all claim holders' needs for cash—interest and principal payments to debt holders and dividends and stock buybacks to equity investors.

Because we cannot estimate cash flows forever, we usually simplify both equity and firm valuation models by assuming that we estimate cash flows for only a period and estimate a terminal value at the end of that period. Applying this to the firm valuation model from earlier would yield the following:

$$\text{Value of firm=} \sum_{t=1}^{t=N} \frac{\text{Expected Cashflow to Firm}_t}{(1+\text{Cost of Capital})^t} + \frac{\text{Terminal Value of Business}_N}{(1+\text{Cost of Capital})^N}$$

How can we estimate the terminal value? Although a variety of approaches exist in practice, the approach that is most consistent with a discounted cash flow approach is based on the assumption that cash flows will grow at a constant rate beyond year N and estimating the terminal value as follows:

$$\text{Terminal value of business}_{t=N} = \frac{\text{Expected Cashflow in year N+1}}{(\text{Cost of Capital - Stable (Constant) Growth Rate})}$$

We can use a similar computation to estimate the terminal value of equity in an equity valuation model.

Risk Adjustment in Discounted Cash Flow Models

In conventional discounted cash flow models, the effect of risk is usually isolated to the discount rate. In equity valuation models, the cost of equity becomes the vehicle for risk adjustment, with riskier companies having higher costs of equity. In fact, if we use the capital asset pricing model to estimate the cost of equity, the beta used carries the entire burden of risk adjustment. In firm valuation models, more components are affected by risk—the cost of debt also tends to be higher for riskier firms, and these firms often cannot afford to borrow as much leading to lower debt ratios—but the bottom line is that the cost of capital is the only input in the valuation where we adjust for risk.[1]

The cash flows in discounted cash flow models represent expected values, estimated either by making the most reasonable assumptions about revenues, growth, and margins for the future or by estimating cash flows under a range of scenarios, attaching probabilities for each of the scenarios and taking the expected values across the scenarios.[2] In summary, then, Table 9.1 captures the risk adjustments in equity and firm valuation models.

Table 9.1   Risk Adjustment in a DCF Model: Equity and Firm Valuation

	Expected Cash Flows	**Discount Rate**
Equity DCF model	Not adjusted for risk. Represent expected cash flows to equity.	Cost of equity increases as exposure to market (nondiversifiable) risk increases. Unaffected by exposure to firm-specific risk.
Firm DCF model	Not adjusted for risk. Represent expected cash flows to all claimholders of the firm.	In addition to the cost of equity effect (see above), the cost of debt will increase as the default risk of the firm increases, and the debt ratio may be a function of risk.

As we noted in Chapter 5, "Risk-Adjusted Value," the alternative to this approach is the certainty-equivalent approach, where we discount the certainty-equivalent cash flows at the risk-free rate to arrive at the value of a business or asset. However, we still capture the risk effect entirely in the adjustment (downward) that we make to expected cash flows. In fact, if we are consistent about the way we define risk and measure risk premiums, the two approaches yield equivalent risk-adjusted values.

The Payoff to Risk Management in a DCF World

If the only input in a discounted cash flow model that is sensitive to risk is the discount rate, and the only risk that matters when it comes to estimating discount rates is *market risk* (or risk that cannot be diversified away), the payoff to hedging risk in terms

---

1   Even this adjustment becomes moot for those who fall back on the Miller Modigliani formulation where the firm value and cost of capital are unaffected by financial leverage.

2   As noted in Chapter 6, this will work only when the scenarios cover all possibilities. This will not work if you look at only a subset of possible scenarios..

of higher value is likely to be limited, and the payoff to risk management will be difficult to trace. In this section, we will consider the value effects of both hedging and managing firm-specific and market risk.

Risk Hedging and Value

Firms are exposed to myriad firm-specific risk factors. In fact, about 75 to 80 percent of the risk in a publicly traded firm comes from firm-specific factors, and some managers do try to hedge or reduce their exposure to this risk.[3] Consider the consequences of such actions on expected cash flows and discount rates in a DCF model.

- Because hedging risk, using either insurance products or derivatives, is not cost-less, the expected cash flows will be lower for a firm that hedges risk than for an otherwise similar firm that does not.

- The cost of equity of this firm will be unaffected by the risk reduction because it reflects only market risk.

- The cost of debt may decrease, because default risk is affected by both firm-specific and market risk.

- The proportion of debt that the firm can use to fund operations may expand because of the lower exposure to firm-specific risk.

With these changes in mind, we can state two propositions about the effects of hedging firm-specific risk on value. The first is that an all-equity-funded firm that expends resources to reduce its exposure to firm-specific risk will see its value decrease as a consequence. This follows directly from the fact that the expected cash flows will be lower for this firm, and there is no change in the cost of equity because of the risk reduction. Because the firm has no debt, the positive effects of risk management on the cost of debt and debt capacity are nullified. The second is that a firm that uses debt to fund operations can see a payoff from hedging its exposure to firm-specific risk in the form of a lower cost of debt, a higher debt capacity, and a lower cost of capital. The benefits will be greatest for firms that are both highly levered and are perceived as having high default risk. This proposition follows from the earlier assertions made about cash flows and discount rates. For firm value to increase because of prudent risk hedging, the cost of capital has to decrease by enough to overcome the costs of risk hedging (which reduce the cash flows). Because the savings take the form of a lower cost of debt and a higher debt ratio, a firm that is AAA rated and gets only 10 percent of its funding from debt will see little or no savings in the cost of capital resulting from the risk reduction. In contrast,

---

3   The R-squared of the regression of stock returns against market indices is a measure of the proportion of the risk that is market risk. The average R-squared across all U.S. companies is between 20 and 25 percent.

a firm with a BB rating that raises 60 percent of its capital from debt will benefit more from risk hedging.

Firms can also hedge their exposure to market risk. In particular, the expansion of the derivatives markets gives a firm that is so inclined the capacity to hedge against interest rate, inflation, foreign currency, and commodity price risks. As with the reduction of firm-specific risk, a firm that reduces its exposure to market risk will see its cash flows decrease (as a result of the cost of hedging market risk) and its cost of debt decline (because of lower default risk). In addition, though, the beta in the CAPM (or betas in a multifactor model) and the cost of equity will also decrease. As a result, the effects of hedging market risk on firm value are more ambiguous. The cost of buying protection against market risk reduces cash flows, but hedging against market risk reduces the discount rate used on the cash flows. If risk-hedging products are fairly priced in the marketplace, the benefits will exactly offset the cost leading to no effect on value.

For the hedging of market risk to pay off, different markets have to be pricing risk differently, and one or more of them has to be wrong. Although we talk about markets as a monolith, four markets are at play here. The first is the equity market, which assesses the value of a stock based on the exposure of a company to market risk. The second is the bond market, which assesses the value of bonds issued by the same company based on its evaluation of default risk. The third is the derivatives market, where we can buy options and futures on market risk components like exchange rate risk, interest rate risk, and commodity price risk. The fourth is the insurance market, where insurance companies offer protection for a price against some of the same market risks. If all four markets price risk equivalently, there would be no payoff to risk hedging. However, if it's possible to buy risk protection cheaper in the insurance market than in the traded equities market, publicly traded firms will gain by buying insurance against risk. Alternatively, if we can hedge against interest rate risk at a lower price in the derivatives market than in the equity market, firms will gain by using options and futures to hedge against risk.

Considering how the reduction of firm-specific risk and market risk affect value, it is quite clear that if the view of the world embodied by the discounted cash flow model is right—that is, that investors in companies are diversified, have long time horizons, and care only about market risk, managers overmanage risk. The only firms that should be hedging risk should be ones that have substantial default risk and high debt or ones that have found a way to hedge market risk at below-market prices.

Risk Taking and Value

If risk reduction generally is considered too narrowly in conventional valuation, risk taking is either not considered at all or enters implicitly through the other inputs into a valuation model. A firm that takes advantage of risk to get a leg up on its competition may be able to generate larger excess returns and higher growth for a longer period and thus have a higher value. If the inputs to a valuation come from historical data, it is possible that we are incorporating the effects of risk management into value by extrapolating from the past, but the adjustment to value is not explicit.

In particular, we would be hard pressed, with conventional discounted cash flow models, to effectively assess the effects of a change in risk management policy on value. Firms that wonder whether they should hedge foreign currency risk or insure against terrorist attacks will get little insight from discounted cash flow models, where the only input that seems sensitive to such decisions is the discount rate.

Relative Valuation Models

For better or worse, most valuations are relative, where a stock is valued based on how similar companies are priced by the market. In practice, relative valuations take the form of a multiple and comparable firms; a firm is viewed as cheap if it trades at 10 times earnings when comparable companies trade at 15 times earnings. Although the logic of this approach seems unassailable, the problem lies in the definition of comparable firms and how analysts deal with the inevitable differences across these firms.

Structure of Relative Valuation

There are three basic steps in relative valuation. The first step is picking a multiple to use for comparison. Although there are dozens of multiples that analysts use, they can be categorized into four groups.

- **Multiples of earnings**—The most widely used of the earnings multiples remains the price earnings ratio, where the market value of equity is divided by equity earnings (net income). However. enterprise value, where the market value of debt and equity are aggregated and cash netted out to get a market estimate of the value of operating assets (enterprise value), has acquired a significant following among analysts. Enterprise value is usually divided by operating income or earnings before interest, taxes, depreciation, and amortization (EBITDA) to arrive at a multiple of operating income or cash flow.

- **Multiples of book value**—Here again, the market value of equity can be divided by a book value of equity to estimate a price-to-book ratio, or the enterprise value can be divided by the book value of capital to arrive at a value-to-book ratio.

- **Multiples of revenues**—In recent years, as the number of firms in the market with negative earnings (and even negative book value for equity) have proliferated, analysts have switched to multiples of revenues, stated either in equity terms (price-to-sales) or enterprise value (enterprise value-to-sales).

- **Multiples of sector-specific variables**—Some multiples are sector specific. For instance, dividing the market value of a cable company by the number of subscribers that it has will yield a value-to-subscriber ratio, and dividing the market value of a power company by the kilowatt-hours of power produced will generate a value per kwh.

When deciding which multiple to use in a specific sector, analysts usually stick with conventional practice. For example, revenue multiples are widely used for retail firms, enterprise value to EBITDA multiples for heavy infrastructure companies, and price-to-book ratios for financial service firms.

The second step in relative valuation is the selection of comparable firms. A comparable firm is one with cash flows, growth potential, and risk similar to the firm being valued. It would be ideal if we could value a firm by looking at how an identical firm—in terms of risk, growth, and cash flows—is priced in the market. Because two firms are almost never identical in the real world, however, analysts define comparable firms to be other firms in the firm's business or businesses. If there are enough firms in the industry to allow for it, this list is pruned further using other criteria; for instance, only firms of similar size may be considered.

The last step in the process is the comparison of the multiple across comparable firms. Because it is impossible to find firms identical to the one being valued, we have to find ways of controlling for differences across firms on these variables. In most valuations, this part of the process is qualitative. The analyst, having compared the multiples, will tell a story about why a particular company is undervalued, relative to comparables, and why the fact that it has less risk or higher growth augments this recommendation. In some cases, analysts may modify the multiple to take into account differences on a key variable. For example, many analysts divide the PE ratio by the expected growth rate in earnings to come up with a PEG ratio. Arguing that this ratio controls for differences in growth across firms, they will use it to compare companies with different growth rates.

Risk Adjustment in Relative Valuation Models

If risk adjustment in discounted cash flow models is too narrow and focuses too much on the discount rate, risk adjustment in relative valuation can range from being nonexistent at worst to being haphazard and arbitrary at best.

- In its nonexistent form, analysts compare the pricing of firms in the same sector without adjusting for risk, making the implicit assumption that the risk exposure is the same for all firms in a business. Thus, the PE ratios of software firms may be compared with each other with no real thought given to risk because of the assumption that all software firms are equally risky.

- Relative valuations that claim to adjust for risk do so in arbitrary ways. Analysts will propose a risk measure, with little or no backing for its relationship to value, and then compare companies on this measure. They will then follow up by adjusting the values of a company that look risky on this measure. If that sounds harsh, consider an analyst who computes PE ratios for software companies and then proceeds to argue that firms that have less volatile earnings or consistently meet analyst estimates should trade at a premium on the sector because they are little risky. Unless this is backed up by evidence that this is indeed true, it is an adjustment with no basis in fact.

The Payoff to Risk Hedging in Relative Valuation Models

If the assessment of risk in relative valuations is nonexistent or arbitrary, it should come as no surprise that firms that try to improve their relative value will adopt risk management practices that correspond to analyst measures of risk. If analysts consider all firms in a sector to be equally risky and the market prices stocks accordingly, there will be no payoff to reducing risk, and firms will not hedge against risk. In contrast, if earnings stability becomes the proxy measure for risk used by analysts and markets, firms will expend their resources smoothing out earnings streams by hedging against all kinds of risk. If meeting analyst estimates of earnings becomes the proxy for risk, firms will be eager for risk management products that increase the odds that they will beat earnings estimates in the next quarter.

The nature of risk adjustment in relative valuation therefore makes it particularly susceptible to gaming by firms. We would argue that one of the reasons for the accounting scandals at U.S. firms in 1999 and 2000 was that managers at risky firms created facades of stability for short-sighted analysts, using both derivatives and accounting sleight of hand.

Expanding the Analysis of Risk

The sanguine view that firm-specific risk is diversifiable and therefore does not affect value is not shared by many managers. Top executives at firms continue to believe that conventional valuation models take too narrow a view of risk and that they don't fully factor in the consequences of significant risk exposure. In this section, we will consider ways in which we can expand the discussion of risk in valuation.

Discounted Cash Flow Valuation

In the first part of this chapter, we noted that the adjustment for risk in conventional discounted cash flow valuation is narrowly focused on the discount rate. In this section, we consider the potential effects of risk (and its management) on other inputs in the model.

The Drivers of DCF Value

The value of a firm can generally be considered a function of four key inputs. The first is the cash flow from assets in place or investments already made. The second is the expected growth rate in the cash flows during what we can term a period of both high growth and excess returns (where the firm earns more than its cost of capital on its investments). The third is the time before the firm becomes a stable-growth firm earning no excess returns. The final input is the discount rate reflecting both the risk of the investment and the financing mix used by the firm.

- **Cash flow to the firm**—Most firms have assets or investments that they have already made, generating cash flows. To the extent that these assets are managed more efficiently, they can generate more earnings and cash flows for the firm. Isolating the cash flows from these assets is often difficult in practice because of the intermingling of expenses designed to generate income from current assets and to build up future growth. We would define cash flows from existing investments as follows.

Cash flow from existing assets = after-tax operating income generated by assets + depreciation of existing assets – capital maintenance expenditures – change in noncash working capital

Note that capital maintenance expenditures refer to the portion of capital expenditures designed to maintain the earning power of existing assets.[4]

- **Expected growth from new investments**—Firms can generate growth in the short term by managing existing assets more efficiently. To generate growth in the long term, though, firms have to invest in new assets that add to the earnings

---

4   Many analysts assume that capital maintenance is equal to depreciation. If we do that, the cash flow equation simplifies to just after-tax operating income and noncash working capital.

stream of the company. The expected growth in operating income is a product of a firm's *reinvestment rate*—that is, the proportion of the after-tax operating income that is invested in net capital expenditures and changes in noncash working capital, and the quality of these reinvestments, measured as the return on the capital invested.

Expected growth$_{EBIT}$ = reinvestment rate * return on capital

where

$$\text{Reinvestment Rate} = \frac{\text{Capital Expenditure - Depreciation} + \Delta \text{ Non-cash WC}}{\text{EBIT (1 - tax rate)}}$$

Return on capital = After-tax Operating Income / capital invested

The capital expenditures referenced here are total capital expenditures and thus include both maintenance and new capital investments. A firm can grow its earnings faster by increasing its reinvestment rate or its return on capital or by doing both. Higher growth, though, by itself does not guarantee a higher value because these cash flows are in the future and will be discounted back at the cost of capital. For growth to create value, a firm has to earn a return on capital that exceeds its cost of capital. As long as these excess returns last, growth will continue to create value.

- **Length of the excess return/high growth period**—It is clearly desirable for firms to earn more than their cost of capital, but it remains a reality in competitive product markets that excess returns fade over time for two reasons. The first is that these excess returns attract competitors, and the resulting price pressure pushes returns down. The second is that as firms grow, their larger size becomes an impediment to continued growth with excess returns. In other words, it gets more and more difficult for firms to find investments that earn high returns. As a general rule, the stronger the barriers to entry, the longer a firm can stretch its excess return period.

- **Discount rate**—As noted in Chapter 5, where we discussed the topic at greater length, the discount rate reflects the riskiness of the investments made by a firm and the mix of funding used. By holding constant the other three determinants—cash flows from existing assets, growth during the excess return phase, and the length of the excess return phase—we can reduce the discount rate to raise the firm value.

In summary, then, to value any firm, we begin by estimating cash flows from existing investments and then consider how long the firm will be able to earn excess returns and how high the growth rate and excess returns will be during that period. When the excess returns fade, we estimate a terminal value and discount all of the cash flows, including the terminal value, to the present to estimate the value of the firm. Figure 9.1 summarizes the process and the inputs in a discounted cash flow model.

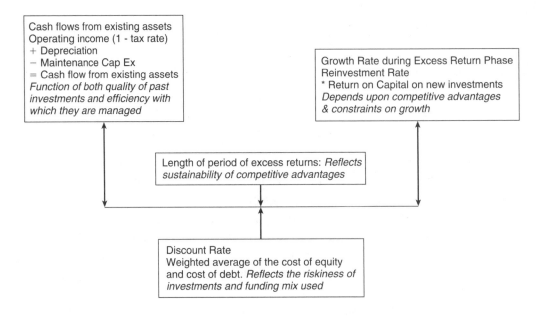

Figure 9.1: Determinants of value

With these inputs, it is quite clear that for a firm to increase its value, it has to do one or more of the following.

- Generate more cash flows from existing assets

- Grow faster or more efficiently during the high growth phase

- Lengthen the high growth phase

- Lower the cost of capital

To the extent that risk management can help in these endeavors, it can create value.

Risk and DCF Value: A Fuller Picture

To get a more complete sense of how risk affects value, we have to look at its impact not just on the discount rate but also on the other determinants of value. In this section, we will begin by revisiting our discussion of the relationship between discount rates and risk. Then we will move on to consider the effects of risk on cash flows from existing assets, growth during the excess return phase, and the length of the excess return phase. In each section, we will draw a distinction between the effects of risk hedging and risk management on value, and argue that the latter has a much wider impact on value.

Discount Rates

In the first part of this chapter, we consider two ways in which risk hedging can affect discount rates. Although reducing exposure to firm-specific risk has no effect on the cost of equity, reducing the exposure to market risk will reduce the cost of equity. Reducing exposure to any risk, firm specific or market, can reduce default risk and thus the cost of debt. In this section, we will add one more potential effect of risk hedging.

Consider a firm that is a small, closely held public company or a private business. It is clear that the assumption that the marginal investor is well diversified and cares about only market risk falls apart in this case. The owner of the private business and the investors in the small, public company are likely to have significant portions of their wealth invested in the company and will therefore be exposed to both market and firm-specific risk. Consequently, the cost of equity will reflect both types of risk. At the limit, if the owner of a business has 100 percent of her wealth invested in it, the cost of equity will reflect not the market risk in the investment (which is the beta in the CAPM or the betas in multifactor models) but its total risk.[5] For such a firm, the reduction of firm-specific risk will result in a lower cost of equity. If we accept this rationale, the payoff to risk management should be greater for private firms and for closely held publicly traded firms than it is for publicly traded firms with dispersed stock holdings. The cost of equity for a private business will decrease when firm-specific risk is reduced, whereas the cost of equity for a publicly traded firm with diversified investors will be unaffected. If we assume that the cost of reducing firm-specific risk is the same for both firms, the effects of reducing firm-specific risk will be much more positive for private firms. Note, though, this does not imply that value will always increase for private firms when they reduce firm-specific risk. That will still depend on whether the cost of reducing risk exceeds the benefits (lower cost of equity and cost of capital).

The relationship between risk management and discount rates is more complicated. Because risk management can sometimes lead to more exposure to at least some types of

---

5   In fact, the beta for a private firm can be written as follows:

Total beta = market beta/correlation between the firm and the market index

For example, if the market beta for chemical companies is 0.80 and the correlation between chemical companies and the market is 0.40, the total beta for a private chemical company would be 2.0.

risk where the firm believes that it has a competitive edge, it is possible that the costs of equity and capital will rise as a consequence. Although this, by itself, would reduce value, the key to effective risk management is that there is a more than compensating payoff elsewhere in the valuation in the form of higher cash flows or higher growth.

Cash Flows from Existing Assets

At the outset, it is difficult to see a payoff from risk hedging on cash flows from existing assets. After all, the investments have already been made, and the efficiency with which they are managed has nothing to do with whether the risk is hedged or not. The only possible benefit from risk hedging is that the firm may be able to save on taxes paid for two reasons. First, smoothing out earnings over time can lower taxes paid, especially if income at higher levels is taxed at a higher rate. Second, the tax laws may provide benefits to hedgers by allowing them full tax deductions for hedging expenses, while not taxing the benefits received. For instance, insurance premiums paid may be tax deductible, but insurance payouts may not be taxed. We will return to examine these potential tax benefits in the next chapter in more detail.

If risk hedging can increase cash flows by reducing taxes paid, risk management may allow a firm to earn higher operating margins on its revenues. A consumer product firm that is better than its competition at meeting and overcoming the risks in emerging markets may be able to exploit turmoil in these markets to generate higher market shares and profits.

Expected Growth During High Growth/Excess Returns Phase

The expected growth during the high growth/excess returns phase comes from two inputs: the reinvestment rate and the return on capital. Both risk hedging and risk management can affect these inputs, and through them the expected growth rate.

Consider risk hedging first. If managers accept every positive net present value investment that they are presented with, there would clearly be no benefit from hedging risk. In practice, though, it has been widely argued that managers in some firms underinvest, and there is empirical evidence to support this view. Although there are many reasons given for underinvestment, ranging from the unwillingness of companies to issue new equity to the prevalence of capital constraints, the risk aversion of managers also plays a role. Managers have a substantial amount of human capital invested in the companies that they manage. Consequently, they may be much more concerned about firm-specific risk than diversified stockholders in the firm. After all, if the firm goes bankrupt because of firm-specific risk, it is only one of several dozen investments for diversified investors, but it can be catastrophic for the managers in the firm. Building on this theme, managers may avoid taking good investments—investments with returns on capital that exceed the cost of capital and positive net present value—because of the presence of firm-specific risk in those investments. An example will be a U.S.-based company that avoids taking investments in Mexico, even though the expected returns look good, because the managers are concerned about exchange rate risk. This behavior will lower the reinvestment rate and the expected growth rate for this firm. If we can give these managers the tools for managing and reducing the exposure to firm-specific risk, we can remove the disincentive that prevents them from reinvesting. The net result will be a higher reinvestment rate and a higher expected growth rate.

If we tie growth to excess returns, the payoff to risk hedging should be greater for firms with weak corporate governance structures and managers with long tenure. Managers with long tenure at firms are more likely to have substantial human capital invested in the firm, and whether they are likely to get away with turning away good investments will largely be a function of how much power stockholders have to influence their decisions. A long-term CEO with a captive board can refuse to invest in emerging markets because he views them as too risky and can get away with that decision. Without condoning his behavior, we would argue that providing protection against firm-specific risks may help align the interests of stockholders and managers and lead to higher firm value.

The effect of risk management on growth is both broader and more difficult to trace. A company that takes advantage of the opportunities generated by risk will be able to find more investments (higher reinvestment rate) and earn a higher return on capital on those investments. The problem, however, is in disentangling the effects of risk management on expected growth from those of other factors, such as brand name value and patent protection.

Length of the High Growth/Excess Returns Period

A firm with high growth and excess returns will clearly be worth much more if it can extend the period for which it maintains these excess returns. Because the length of the high growth period is a function of the sustainability of competitive advantages, we have to measure the impact of risk hedging and management on this dimension. One possible benefit to risk hedging and smoother earnings is that firms can use their stable (and positive) earnings in periods where other firms are reporting losses to full advantage. Thus, a gold mining stock that hedges against gold price risk may be able to use its positive earnings and higher market value in periods when gold prices are down to buy out their competitors, who don't hedge and thus report large losses at bargain basement prices. This will be especially true in markets where access to capital is severely constrained.

The payoff from risk management, though, should be much greater. Firms that are better at strategically managing their exposure to firm-specific risks may find that this by itself is a competitive advantage that increases both their excess returns and the period for which they can maintain them. Consider, for instance, a pharmaceutical firm. A significant portion of its value comes from new products in the pipeline (from basic research to FDA approval and commercial production), and a big part of its risk comes from the pipeline drying up. A pharmaceutical company that manages its R&D more efficiently, generating more new products and getting them to the market quicker, will have a decided advantage over another pharmaceutical firm that has allowed its research pipeline to run dry or become uneven with too many products in early research and too few close to commercial production.

Building on this link between risk and value, the payoff to risk management should be greater for firms that are in volatile businesses with high returns on capital on investment. For risk management to pay off as excess returns over longer periods, firms have to be in businesses where investment opportunities can be lucrative but are not predictable. In fact, the reason the value added to managing the pipeline in the pharmaceutical business is so high is because the payoff to research is uncertain. The FDA approval process is fraught with pitfalls, but the returns to a successful drug are immense. Table 9.2 summarizes the effects of risk hedging and risk management on the different components of value.

Table 9.2   Risk Hedging, Risk Management, and Value

Valuation Component	Effect of Risk Hedging	Effect of Risk Management
Costs of equity and capital	The cost of equity for private and closely held firms will be reduced. The cost of debt will be reduced for heavily levered firms with significant distress risk.	This may increase the costs of equity and capital if a firm increases its exposure to risks where it feels it has a differential advantage.
Cash flow to the firm	The cost of risk hedging will reduce earnings. Smoothing out earnings may reduce taxes paid over time.	More effective risk management may increase operating margins and increase cash flows.
Expected growth rate during high growth period	Reducing risk exposure may make managers more comfortable taking risky (and good) investments. Increasing the reinvestment rate will increase the growth.	Exploiting opportunities created by risk will allow the firm to earn a higher return on capital on its new investments.

Valuation Component	Effect of Risk Hedging	Effect of Risk Management
Length of high growth period	There will be no effect of risk hedging.	Strategic risk management can be a long-term competitive advantage and can increase the length of the growth period.

Relative Valuation

Although discounted cash flow models allow for a great deal of flexibility when it comes to risk management, they also require information on the specific effects of risk hedging and risk management on the inputs to the models. One way to bypass this requirement is to look at whether the market rewards companies that hedge or manage risk and, if it does, to estimate how much of a price we are willing to pay for either risk hedging or risk management.

Payoff to Risk Hedging in Relative Valuation

A firm that hedges risk more effectively should have more stable earnings and stock prices. If the market values these characteristics, as proponents of risk hedging argue, the market should attach a much higher value to this firm than to a competitor that does not hedge risk. To examine whether this occurs, we could look at a group of comparable companies and either identify the companies that we know use risk-hedging products or come up with quantifiable measures of the effects of risk hedging; two obvious choices would be earnings variability and stock price variability. We can then compare the market values of these companies to their book value, revenues, or earnings and relate the level of these multiples to the risk-hedging practices of these firms. If risk hedging pays off in higher value, firms that hedge risk and reduce earnings or price variability should trade at higher multiples than firms that do not.

Let us consider a simple example. In Table 9.3, we have listed the price-to-book and enterprise value-to-sales ratios of gold and silver mining stocks in the United States in November 2003. We have also reported the return on equity for each stock. About 80 percent of the stocks in the sample reported negative earnings in 2002. The beta[6] and standard deviation in stock prices[7] are used as measures of the market risk and total risk respectively in these companies. In the final column, the compounded annual return

---

6   The betas are estimated using five years of weekly returns against the S&P 500.

7   The standard deviations are annualized estimates based on five years of weekly returns on the stock.

that investors would have earned on each of these stocks between November 1998 and November 2003 is reported.

Table 9.3   Gold Mining Companies Valuation Multiples and Risk

Company Name	PBV	EVS	ROE	Beta	Standard Deviation in Stock Prices	5-Year Return
IAMGOLD Corp.	5.50	9.28	6.91%	−0.26	64.99%	14.51%
Ashanti Goldfields Company Lim	3.63	3.93	14.50%	0.11	63.22%	6.75%
Silver Standard Resources Inc.	5.93	6.55	0.00%	0.19	78.28%	35.94%
Barrick Gold	3.44	5.69	0.00%	0.31	38.19%	−0.58%
Anglo Gold Ltd. ADR	5.31	5.78	0.00%	0.33	51.23%	18.64%
Compania de Minas Buena ventura	8.98	23.15	0.00%	0.58	42.21%	33.63%
Crystallex Intl Corp	2.66	6.63	−39.55%	0.86	77.60%	40.73%
Campbell Resources	1.79	6.50	−45.54%	−1.78	144.37%	2.95%
Cambior Inc.	3.92	3.08	0.00%	−0.59	76.29%	−12.38%
Richmont Mines	2.81	1.37	12.91%	−0.14	59.68%	11.73%
Miramar Mining Corp.	2.08	5.63	0.00%	0.02	70.72%	15.12%
Golden Star Res	14.06	17.77	20.65%	−0.73	118.29%	39.24%
Royal Gold	5.50	23.99	8.93%	−0.26	65.70%	35.02%
Agnico-Eagle Mines	2.08	8.15	−1.00%	−0.25	50.92%	18.24%
Newmont Mining	3.32	7.30	0.00%	0.17	53.80%	16.35%
Stillwater Mining	1.16	3.06	0.00%	2.18	79.20%	−14.10%
Glamis Gold Ltd	5.07	22.23	3.63%	−0.71	53.67%	40.38%
Meridian Gold Inc	2.61	8.72	7.54%	0.30	51.99%	20.68%
Teck Cominco Ltd. 'B'	1.20	1.90	1.19%	0.49	40.44%	7.86%
DGSE Companies Inc	2.40	0.68	12.50%	1.17	86.20%	−9.86%
Bema Gold Corporation	4.61	21.45	−6.19%	−0.76	81.91%	24.27%
Hecla Mining	26.72	7.35	−19.49%	−0.16	78.12%	6.77%
Canyon Resources	2.25	3.48	−22.64%	−0.15	83.07%	5.15%
Placer Dome	3.18	6.01	6.60%	0.42	54.11%	0.82%
Aur Resources Inc.	1.94	2.83	2.25%	0.65	51.80%	10.92%
Coeur d'Alene Mines	17.40	10.45	−105.71%	0.64	79.53%	−8.63%
Apex Silver Mines	3.87	4.77	−6.56%	0.52	42.08%	8.47%
Black Hawk Mining Inc.	3.21	2.60	−30.47%	0.20	74.36%	1.73%

Three interesting findings emerge from this table. The first is that even a casual perusal indicates that there are a large number of companies with negative betas, which isn't surprising because gold prices and the equity markets moved in opposite directions for much of the period (1998–2003). At the same time, there are companies with not just positive betas but fairly large positive betas, indicating that these companies hedged at least some of the gold price risk over the period. Finally, there is no easily detectable link between betas and standard deviations in stock prices. There are companies with negative betas and high standard deviations as well as companies with positive betas and low standard deviations.

To examine whether the pricing of these companies is affected by their exposure to market and total risk, we estimated the correlations between the multiples (price-to-book and EV/sales) and the risk variables. The correlation matrix is reported in Table 9.4.

Table 9.4   Correlation Matrix: Value Versus Risk: Gold Mining: November 2003

	PBV	EV/S	BETA	Standard Deviation	Earnings Stability	5-Year Return
PBV	1.000	.303	−.122	.196	.074	.078
EV/S		1.000	−.347	.011	−.094	.711**
BETA			1.000	−.424*	.013	−.296
Standard deviation				1.000	.065	−.064
Earnings stability					1.000	−.313
5-year return						1.000

** Correlation is significant at the 0.01 level (2-tailed).
 * Correlation is significant at the 0.05 level (2-tailed).

Only two of the correlations are statistically significant. First, companies with higher betas tended to have lower standard deviations. These are the companies that hedged away gold price risk, pushing their betas from negative to positive territory, and became less risky on a total risk basis (standard deviation). Second, companies with high enterprise value-to-sales ratios had much higher returns over the past five years, which perhaps explains why they trade at lofty multiples. The absence of correlation is more telling about the payoff or lack thereof to risk management in this sector. Both the price-to-book and enterprise value-to-sales ratios are negatively correlated with beta and positively correlated with standard deviation in stock prices, although the correlations are not statistically significant. In other words, the companies that hedged risk and lowered their stock price volatility did not trade at higher multiples. In fact, these firms may have been punished by the market for their risk-hedging activities. There was also no correlation between the stability of earnings[8] and the valuation multiples. There is also no evidence to indicate that the hedging away of gold price risk had any effect on overall stock returns.

Does this mean that risk hedging does not pay off? We are not willing to make that claim, based on this sample. After all, gold mining stocks are a small and fairly unique subset of the market. It is possible that risk hedging pays off in some sectors, but the question has to be answered by looking at how the market prices stocks in these sectors and what risk measure it responds to. The onus has to be on those who believe that risk hedging is value enhancing to show that the market sees it as such. We will return to this issue in far more depth in the next chapter.

Payoff to Risk Management in Relative Valuation

If the market does not attach much value to risk hedging, does it value risk management? As with the risk-hedging case, we can begin with a group of comparable firms and try to come up with a quantifiable measure of risk management. We can then relate how the market values stocks to this quantifiable measure.

We will face bigger challenges establishing a link (or lack thereof) between risk management and value than we do with risk hedging. Unlike risk hedging, where the variability in earnings and value can operate as a proxy for hedging, it is difficult to come up with good proxies for the quality of risk management. Furthermore, these proxies are likely to be industry specific. For instance, the proxy for risk management in the pharmaceutical firm may be the size and balance in the product pipeline. In the oil business, it may a measure of the speed with which the firm can ramp up its production of oil if oil prices go up.

Option Pricing Models

There is a third way of looking at the value of both risk hedging and risk management, and that is to use option pricing models. As we will argue in this section, risk hedging is essentially the equivalent of buying a put option against specific eventualities, whereas risk management gives the firm the equivalent of a call option. In fact, much of our

---

8   The variance in quarterly earnings over the previous five years was used to measure earnings stability.

discussion of real options in Chapter 8, "Real Options," can be considered an examination of the value of strategic risk taking.

An Option Pricing View of Risk Hedging

Consider a $100 million valued firm that buys risk-hedging products to ensure that its value does not drop below $80 million. In effect, it is buying a put option, where the underlying asset is the unhedged value of the firm's assets, and the strike price is the lower bound on the value. The payoff diagram for risk hedging as a put option is shown in Figure 9.2.

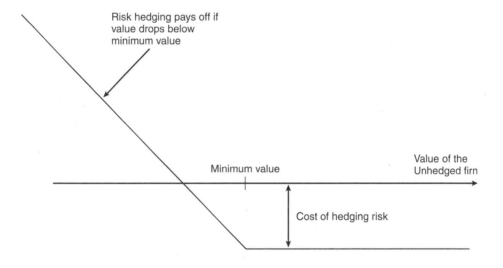

Figure 9.2: Payoff diagram for risk hedging

If we can estimate a standard deviation in firm value, we can value this put option and, by doing so, attach a value to risk hedging. Because this protection will come with a cost, we can then consider the trade-off. If the cost of adding the protection is less than the value created by the protection, risk hedging will increase the value of the firm.

Value of firm after risk management =   Value of firm without risk hedging

+ Value of put (risk hedging)

- Cost of risk hedging

To provide a measure of the value of risk hedging, consider again the example of the firm with a value of $100 million that wants to hedge against the possibility that its value may drop below $80 million. Assume that the standard deviation in firm value[9] is 30 percent and that the one-year riskless rate is 4 percent. If we value a one-year put option with these characteristics, using a standard Black-Scholes model, we arrive at a value of $2.75, or 2.75 percent of firm value. That would indicate that this firm can spend up to 2.75 percent of its value to hedge against the likelihood that value will drop below $80 million. The value of risk hedging can be estimated as a function of both the degree of protection demanded (as a percent of existing firm value) and the standard deviation in firm value. Table 9.5 provides these estimates.

Table 9.5   Value of Risk Hedging as a Percent of Firm Value

Protection Boundary	Standard Deviation in Firm Value				
	10%	20%	30%	40%	50%
80%	0.01%	0.78%	2.75%	5.34%	8.21%
85%	0.07%	1.48%	4.03%	7.03%	10.21%
90%	0.31%	2.55%	5.65%	9.00%	12.43%
95%	0.95%	4.06%	7.59%	11.22%	14.86%
100%	2.29%	6.04%	9.87%	13.70%	17.50%

For instance, the value of protecting against losing more than 10% of value can be worth 9% of its value to a firm with a 40% standard deviation in value. The value of hedging risk increases as the volatility in firm value increases and with the degree of protection against downside risk. The cost of hedging risk can be compared to these values to assess whether it makes sense to hedge risk in the first place.

We can extend this process to cover risk hedging that is focused on earnings, but the problem that we run into is one that we referenced in the earlier section on discounted cash flow valuation. Without a model to link earnings to value, we cannot value risk hedging as a put against value declining. Simplistic models such as assuming a constant PE ratio as earnings go up and down can lead to misleading conclusions about the value of hedging.

---

9   The standard deviation in firm value will generally be much lower than the standard deviation in stock prices (equity value) for any firm with substantial leverage. In fact, the standard deviation in firm value can be written as follows : $\sigma^2_{Firm\,value} = (E/(D+E))^2\sigma^2_{Equity} + (D/(D+E))^2\sigma^2_{Debt} + 2((E/(D+E))(D/(D+E))\sigma_{Equity}\sigma_{Debt}$

Looking at the trade-off between the cost and value of risk hedging yields the proposition that risk hedging is most likely to generate value when investors cannot find traded instruments in the market that protect against the risk. This proposition emerges from our belief that if investors can find securities in the market that protect against risk, it is unlikely (although not impossible) that companies could buy risk protection for less. Because it is easier for investors to buy protection against certain types of risk—such as currency, interest rate, and commodity risk—than against others, such as political risk—this would indicate that risk hedging is likely to have a much larger payoff when employed to reduce exposure to the latter.

An Option Pricing View of Risk Management

If risk hedging creates the equivalent of a put option for the firm, risk management creates the equivalent of a call option. This is because risk management is centered on taking advantage of the upside created because of uncertainty. Consider a simple example. Assume that we operate an oil company and that we are considering whether to invest in new refineries and facilities designed to help us increase our oil production quickly to take advantage of higher oil prices. We are looking at a call option, whose value will be tied to both the variance in oil prices and the amount of additional production (and cash flows) we will generate if oil prices increase.

In fact, although much of the real option literature has been focused on valuation issues and applying option pricing models to valuing real options such as patents or oil reserves, real options also offer an effective framework for examining the costs and benefits of risk management. Using the option framework would lead us to argue that risk management is likely to generate the most value for firms that operate in volatile businesses with substantial barriers to entry. The first part of the proposition—higher volatility—follows from viewing risk management as a call option, because options increase in value with volatility. Significant barriers to entry allow firms that take advantage of upside risk to earn substantial excess returns for longer periods.

A Final Assessment of Risk Management

Two extreme views dominate the risk management debate, and they are both rooted in risk hedging. One perspective, adopted by portfolio theorists and believers in efficient markets, is that risk hedging on the part of firms is almost always useless and will generally decrease value. Although proponents of this view will concede that there are potential tax benefits (although they are likely to be small) and possibly a savings in distress cost, they will argue that diversified investors can manage risk exposure in their portfolios much more effectively and with lower costs than managers in the individual firms.

At the other extreme are those who sell risk-hedging products and essentially argue that reducing risk will reduce earnings variability and almost always yield a payoff to firms in the form of higher stock prices. Neither side seems to make a meaningful distinction between risk hedging and risk management.

When Does Risk Hedging Pay Off?

Based on our discussion in this chapter, we think that there is an intermediate view that makes more sense. Risk hedging is most likely to generate value for smaller, closely held firms or for firms with substantial debt and distress costs. It is also most likely to create value if it is focused on hedging risks where investors cannot buy risk protection through market-traded securities. The increase in value is most likely to come from a lower cost of capital, although there may be a secondary benefit in managers being more willing to invest in high risk, high return projects (higher growth). Risk hedging is unlikely to create value for firms that are widely held by diversified investors and those focused on risk where market protection is easy to obtain. Table 9.6 summarizes our conclusions.

Table 9.6   Payoff to Risk Hedging

Marginal Investor Is...	Risk Being Reduced Is...	Market Risk Protection Exists	Firm Is Highly Leveraged	Effect on Cash Flows	Effect on Growth	Effect on Discount Rate	Effect on Value
Diversified	Firm-specific risk	Yes	No	Negative (cost of risk reduction)	None	None	Negative
Diversified	Firm-specific risk	No	Yes	Negative	None	May reduce (lower cost of debt and capital)	Neutral to negative
Diversified	Market risk	Yes	No	Negative	None	Reduce	Neutral to negative
Diversified	Market risk	No	Yes	Negative	None	Reduce	Neutral to positive
Not diversified	Firm-specific risk	Yes	No	Negative		Reduce	Neutral
Not diversified	Firm-specific risk	No	Yes	Negative	Positive	Reduce	Neutral to positive
Not diversified	Market risk	Yes	No	Negative	None	Reduce	Neutral to positive
Not diversified	Market risk	No	Yes	Negative	Positive	Reduce	Positive

Using this matrix, it is clear that risk hedging should be used sparingly by firms that are widely held by institutional investors, are not highly leveraged, and are exposed to market risks where investors can buy risk protection easily.

When Does Risk Management Pay Off?

All firms are exposed to risk and should therefore consider risk management as an integral part of doing business. Effective risk management is more about strategic than financial choices and will show up in value as higher and more sustainable excess returns. The benefits of risk management, though, are likely to be greatest in businesses with the following characteristics:

- **High volatility**—The greater the range of firm-specific risks that a firm is exposed to, the greater the potential for risk management. After all, it is the uncertainty about the future that is being exploited to advantage.

- **Strong barriers to entry**—Because the payoff to risk management shows up as higher returns, it is likely to create more value when new entrants can be kept out of the business either because of infrastructure needs (aerospace, automobiles) or legal constraints such as patents or regulation (pharmaceuticals and financial service firms).

Given that risk management can have such high payoffs, how can we explain the lack of emphasis on it? There are several reasons. The first is that its emphasis on strategic rather than financial considerations pushes it into the realm of corporate strategy. The second is that it is far more difficult to trace the payoff from risk management than it is with risk hedging. Those who sell risk-hedging products can point to the benefits of less volatile earnings and even less downside risk in value, but those pushing for risk management have to talk in terms of excess returns in the future.

Risk Hedging Versus Risk Management

We have made much of the difference between risk hedging and risk management in this chapter and the consequences for value. In Table 9.7, we summarize the discussion in this chapter.

Table 9.7   Risk Management Versus Risk Hedging—A Summary

	Risk Hedging	Risk Management
View of risk	Risk is a danger.	Risk is a danger and an opportunity.
Objective	To protect against the downside of risk.	To exploit the upside created by uncertainty.
Functional emphasis	Financial.	Strategic, stretching across all functions.
Process	Product oriented. Primarily focused on the use of derivatives and insurance to hedge against risks.	Process oriented. Identify key risk dimensions and try to develop better ways of handling and taking advantage of these risks than the competition.
Measure of success	Reduce volatility in earnings, cash flows, or value.	Higher value.
Type of real option	Put option (insurance against bad outcomes).	Call option (taking advantage of high volatility to create good outcomes).
Primary effect on value	Lower discount rate.	Higher and more sustainable excess returns.
Likely to make sense for	Closely held and private firms or publicly traded firms with high financial leverage and substantial distress costs.	Firms in volatile businesses with significant potential for excess returns (if successful).

Developing a Risk Management Strategy

Given the discussion of risk hedging and risk management in this chapter, we see five steps that every firm should take to deal with risk effectively.

1. **Make an inventory of possible risks**—The process has to begin with an inventory of all the potential risks that a firm is exposed to. This will include risks that are specific to the firm, risks that affect the entire sector, and macroeconomic risks that influence the value.

2. **Decide whether to hedge or not**—We have argued through this chapter that risk hedging is not always optimal and will reduce value in many cases. Having

made an inventory of risks, the firm has to decide which risks it will attempt to hedge and which ones it will allow to flow through to its investors. The size of the firm, the type of stockholders that it has, and its financial leverage (exposure to distress) will all play a role in making this decision. In addition, the firm has to consider whether investors can buy protection against the risks in the market on their own.

3. **Choose risk-hedging products**—If a firm decides to hedge risk, it has a number of choices. Some of these choices are market traded (currency and interest rate derivatives, for example), some are customized solutions (prepared by investment banks to hedge against risk that may be unique to the firm), and some are insurance products. The firm has to consider both the effectiveness of each of the choices and the costs.

4. **Determine the risk or risks that you understand better or deal with better than your competitors**—This is the step where the firm moves from risk hedging to risk management and from viewing risk as a threat to risk as a potential opportunity. Why would one firm be better at dealing with certain kinds of risk than its competitors? It may have to do with experience. A firm that has operated in emerging markets for decades clearly will have a much better sense of both what to expect in a market meltdown and how to deal with it. It may also come from the control of a resource—physical or human—that provides the company an advantage when exposed to the risk. Having access to low-cost oil reserves may give an oil company an advantage in the event of a drop in oil prices, and having a top-notch legal staff may give a tobacco company a competitive advantage when it comes to litigation risk.

5. **Devise strategies to take advantage of your differential advantage in the long term**—In the final step in the process, firms build on their competitive edge and lay out what they will do to create the maximum benefit. The oil company with low-cost reserves may decide that it will use its cost advantage the next time oil prices drop to acquire oil companies with higher-cost reserves and high leverage.

Risk hedging and risk management are not mutually exclusive strategies. In fact, we consider risk hedging to be part of broader risk management strategy where protecting against certain types of risk and trying to exploit others go hand in hand. We would argue that most firms do not have comprehensive strategies when it comes to dealing with risk. Consider the way each step in this process is handled currently and the entity it is handled by. The risk inventory, if it is done, is usually the responsibility of the managers of a company. These managers often bring in a narrow perspective of risk, based on their own experiences, and tend to miss some important risks and overweigh others.

The advice on what type of risks to hedge (step 2) is usually offered by the same entities (investment banks and insurance companies) that then offer their own risk-hedging products (step 3) as the ideal solutions. Because of the conflict of interests, too much risk is hedged at many large firms and too little at smaller firms, and the risk-hedging products chosen are almost never the optimal ones. The last two steps are usually viewed as the domain of strategists in the firm and the consultants that work with them. The limitation with this setup, though, is that strategic advice tends to gloss over risk and focus on rewards. Consequently, strategies that focus on higher profitability and higher growth often dominate strategies built around taking advantage of risk. Table 9.8 summarizes the five steps, the state of play at the moment, and potential opportunities for complete risk management advice.

Table 9.8 Steps in Developing a Risk Strategy: Potential Problems and Possible Opportunities

	What Is It?	Who Does It Now?	Limitations/Problems	Possible Improvements
Step 1	Make an inventory of all of the risks that the firm is faced with firm specific, sector, and market.	Internal. Managers of firms do this now, but often haphazardly and in reaction to events.	Managers may be good at identifying firm-specific problems but may not be very good at assessing sector or market risks. They may miss some risks and inflate others.	A team with sector expertise and experience can do a much more comprehensive job.
Step 2	Decide what risks should be hedged and what should not.	Managers of the firm with significant input (and sales pitches) from investment bankers and insurance companies.	Conflict of interest. Not surprisingly, the investment banker or insurance company will want managers to over hedge risk and argue that their products are the best ones.	Look for unbiased advice on both components; in effect, you want an outsider with no ax to grind to assess risk hedging products to find the cheapest and best alternatives.
Step 3	For the risks to be hedged, pick the risk-hedging products that can be derivatives or insurance products.			
Step 4	Determine the risk dimensions where you have an advantage over your competitors either because you understand the risk better or you control a resource.	If it occurs, it is usually part of strategic management and consultants and is packaged with other strategic objectives.	Risk gets short shrift since the focus is on rewards. In other words, strategies that offer higher growth will win out over ones that emphasize risk advantages.	Develop a team that focuses only on strategic risk taking. Draw on services that offer advice purely on this dimension.
Step 5	Take strategic steps to ensure that you can use this risk advantage to gain over your competition.			

Conclusion

There is too much of a focus on risk hedging and not enough attention paid to risk management at firms. This is troubling because the payoff to risk hedging is likely to be small even for firms where it makes sense and is often negative at many large publicly traded firms with diversified investors. In contrast, the payoff to risk management can be substantial to a far larger subset of firms.

In this chapter, we have laid out the fundamental differences between risk hedging and risk management and set up a template for the comprehensive management of risk. The real work, though, will have to occur at the level of each firm because the right path to adopt will depend on the firm's competitive advantages and the sector it operates in. Unlike risk hedging, which is viewed as the job of the finance function, risk management should be on the agenda of everyone in the firm. In today's world, the key to success lies not in avoiding risk but in taking advantage of the opportunities it offers. As businesses confront the reality of higher volatility, they have to get out of a defensive crouch when it comes to risk and think of ways in which they can exploit the risk to advantage in a global marketplace.

10

RISK MANAGEMENT: PROFILING AND HEDGING

To manage risk, we first have to understand the risks that we are exposed to. This process of developing a risk profile thus requires an examination of both the immediate risks from competition and product market changes as well as the more indirect effects of macroeconomic forces. We will begin this chapter by looking at ways in which we can develop a complete risk profile for a firm, where we outline all the risks that a firm is exposed to and estimate the magnitude of the exposure.

In the second part of this chapter, we turn to a key question of what we should do about these risks. In general, we have three choices. First, we can do nothing and let the risk pass through to investors in the business—stockholders in a publicly traded firm and the owners of private businesses. Second, we can try to protect ourselves against the risk using a variety of approaches—using options and futures to hedge against specific risks, modifying the way we fund assets to reduce risk exposure or buying insurance. Third, we can intentionally increase our exposure to some of the risks because we feel that we have significant advantages over the competition. In this chapter, we will consider the first two choices and hold off on the third choice until Chapter 11, "Strategic Risk Management."

Risk Profile

Every business faces risks, and the first step in managing risk is making an inventory of the risks that we face and getting a measure of the exposure to each risk. In this section, we examine the process of developing a risk profile for a business and consider some of the potential pitfalls. There are four steps involved in this process. In the first step, we list all risks that a firm is exposed to, from all sources and without consideration to the type of risk. We categorize these risks into broad groups in the second step and analyze the exposure to each risk in the third step. In the fourth step, we examine the alternatives available to manage each type of risk and the expertise that the firm brings to dealing with the risk.

Step 1: List the Risks

Assume that we run a small company in the United States, packaging and selling premium coffee beans to customers. We may buy our coffee beans in Columbia, sort and package them in California, and ship them to our customers all over the world. In the process, we are approached to a multitude of risks. There is the risk of political turmoil in Columbia, compounded by the volatility in the dollar-peso exchange rate. Our packaging plant in California may sit on top of an earthquake fault line and be staffed with unionized employees, exposing us to the potential for both natural disasters and labor troubles. Our competition comes from other small businesses offering their own gourmet coffee beans and from larger companies like Starbucks that may be able to get better deals because of higher volume. On top of all of this, we have to worry about the overall demand for coffee ebbing and flowing, as customers choose between a wider array of drinks and worry about the health concerns of too much caffeine consumption.

Not surprisingly, the risks we face become more numerous and complicated as we expand our business to include new products and markets, and listing them all can be exhausting. At the same time, though, we have to be aware of the risks we face before we can begin analyzing them and deciding what to do about them.

Step 2: Categorize the Risks

A listing of all risks that a firm faces can be overwhelming. One step toward making the risks manageable is to sort them into broad categories. Categorizing the risks organizes them into groups and is a key step toward determining what to do about them. In general, we can categorize risks based on the following criteria:

- **Market versus firm-specific risk**—In keeping with our earlier characterization of risk in risk and return models, we can categorize risk into risk that affects one or a few companies (firm-specific risk) and risk that affects many or all companies (market risk). The former can be diversified away in a portfolio, but the latter will persist even in diversified portfolios; in conventional risk and return models, the former have no effect on expected returns (and discount rates), whereas the latter do.

- **Operating versus financial risk**—We can categorize risk as coming from a firm's financial choices (its mix of debt and equity and the types of financing that it uses) or from its operations. An increase in interest rates or risk premiums would be an example of the former, whereas an increase in the price of raw materials used in production would be an example of the latter.

- **Continuous risks versus event risk**—Some risks are dormant for long periods and manifest themselves as unpleasant events that have economic consequences, whereas other risks create continuous exposure. Consider again the coffee bean company's risk exposure in Columbia. A political revolution or nationalization of coffee estates in Columbia would be an example of event risk, whereas the changes in exchange rates would be an illustration of continuous risk.

- **Catastrophic risk versus smaller risks**—Some risks are small and have a relatively small effect on a firm's earnings and value, whereas others have a much larger impact, with the definition of small and large varying from firm to firm. Political turmoil in its Indian software operations will have a small impact on Microsoft, with its large market cap and cash reserves allowing it to find alternative sites, but it will have a large impact on a small software company with the same exposure.

Some risks may not be easily categorized, and the same risk can switch categories over time; however, it still pays to categorize.

Step 3: Measure Exposure to Each Risk

A logical follow-up to categorizing risk is measuring exposure to risk. To make this measurement, though, we first have to decide what it is that risk affects. At its simplest level, we can measure the effect of risk on the earnings of a company. At its broadest level, we can capture the risk exposure by examining how the value of a firm changes as a consequence.

Earnings versus Value Risk Exposure

It is easier to measure earnings risk exposure than value risk exposure. Numerous accounting rules govern the way companies should record and report exchange rate and interest rate movements. Consider, for instance, how we deal with exchange rate movements. From an accounting standpoint, the risk of changing exchange rates is captured in what is called *translation exposure*, which is the effect of these changes on the current income statement and the balance sheet. In making translations of foreign operations from the foreign to the domestic currency, we need to address two issues. The first is whether financial statement items in a foreign currency should be translated at the current exchange rate or at the rate that prevailed at the time of the transaction. The second is whether the profit or loss created when the exchange rate adjustment is made should be treated as a profit or loss in the current period or deferred until a future period.

Accounting standards in the United States apply different rules for translation depending on whether the foreign entity is a self-contained unit or a direct extension of the parent company. For the first group, FASB 52 requires that an entity's assets and liabilities be converted into the parent's currency at the prevailing exchange rate. The increase or decrease in equity that occurs because of this translation is captured as an unrealized foreign exchange gain or loss and will not affect the income statement until the underlying assets and liabilities are sold or liquidated. For the second group, only the monetary assets and liabilities[1] have to be converted, based on the prevailing exchange rate, and the net income is adjusted for unrealized translations gains or losses.

Translation exposure matters from the narrow standpoint of reported earnings and balance sheet values. The more important question, however, is whether investors view these translation changes as important in determining firm value, or whether they view them as risk that will average out across companies and across time. The answers to this question are mixed. In fact, several studies suggest that earnings adjustments caused purely by exchange rate changes do not affect the stock prices of firms.

Although translation exposure is focused on the effects of exchange rate changes on financial statements, *economic exposure* attempts to look more deeply at the effects of such changes on firm value. These changes, in turn, can be broken down into two types. *Transactions exposure* looks at the effects of exchange rate changes on transactions and projects that have already been entered into and denominated in a foreign currency. *Operating exposure* measures the effects of exchange rate changes on expected future cash flows and discount rates, and, thus, on total value.

In his book on international finance, Shapiro presents a time pattern for economic exposure, in which he notes that firms are exposed to exchange rate changes at every stage in the process from developing new products for sale abroad, to entering into contracts to sell these products, to waiting for payment on these products.[2] To illustrate, a weakening of the U.S. dollar will increase the competition among firms that depend on export

---

1   Monetary assets include cash, marketable securities, and some short-term assets such as inventory. They do not include real assets.

2   Shapiro, A. *Multinational Financial Management* (Seventh Edition). New York: John Wiley, 1996.

markets, such as Boeing, and increase their expected growth rates and value, while hurting those firms that need imports as inputs to their production process.

Measuring Risk Exposure

We can measure risk exposure in subjective terms by assessing whether the impact of a given risk will be large or small (but not specifying how large or small) or in quantitative terms where we attempt to provide a numerical measure of the possible effect. This section considers both approaches.

Qualitative Approaches

When risk assessment is done for strategic analysis, the impact is usually measured in qualitative terms. Thus, a firm will be found to be vulnerable to country risk or exchange rate movements, but the potential impact will be categorized on a subjective scale. Some of these scales are simple and have only two or three levels (high, average, and low impact), whereas others allow for more gradations (risk can be scaled from 1–10).

No matter how these scales are structured, we will be called on to make judgments about where individual risks fall on this scale. If the risk being assessed is one that the firm is exposed to on a regular basis, say currency movements, we can look at its impact on earnings or market value on a historical basis. If the risk being assessed is a low-probability event on which there is little history, as is the case for an airline exposed to the risk of terrorism, the assessment has to be based on the potential impact of such an incident.

Although qualitative scales are useful, the subjective judgments that go into them can create problems because two analysts looking at the same risk can make very different assessments of their potential impact. In addition, the fact that the risk assessment is made by individuals, based on their judgments, exposes it to all the quirks in risk assessment that we noted earlier in this book. For instance, individuals tend to weight recent history too much in making assessments, leading to an overestimation of exposure from recently manifested risks. Thus, companies overestimate the likelihood and impact of terrorist attacks right after well-publicized attacks elsewhere.

Quantitative Approaches

If risk manifests itself over time as changes in earnings and value, we can assess a firm's exposure to risk by looking at its history. In particular, we can correlate changes in a firm's earnings and value with potential risk sources to see both whether they are affected by the risks and by how much. Alternatively, we can arrive at estimates of risk exposure by looking at firms in the sector in which we operate and their sensitivity to changes in risk measures.

Risk matters to firms because it affects their profitability and consequently their value. Thus, the simplest way of measuring risk exposure is to look at the past and examine how earnings and firm value have moved over time as a function of the prespecified risk. If we contend, for instance, that a firm is cyclical and is exposed to the risk of economic downturns, we should be able to back up this contention with evidence that it has been adversely impacted by past recessions.

Consider a simple example where we estimate how much risk Walt Disney Inc. is exposed to from changes in a number of macroeconomic variables, using two measures: Disney's *firm value* (the market value of debt and equity) and its operating income. We begin by collecting past data on firm value, operating income, and the macroeconomic variables against which we want to measure its sensitivity. In the case of Disney, we look at four macroeconomic variables—the level of long-term rates measured by the 10-year Treasury bond rate, the growth in the economy measured by changes in real GDP, the inflation rate captured by the consumer price index, and the strength of the dollar against other currencies (estimated using the trade-weighted dollar value). In Table 10.1, we report the earnings and value for Disney at the end of each year from 1982 to 2003 with the levels of each macroeconomic variable.

Firm value = market value of equity + book value of debt

After we have collected this data, we can estimate the sensitivity of firm value to changes in the macroeconomic variables by regressing changes in firm value each year against changes in each of the variables.

- Regressing changes in firm value against changes[3] in interest rates over this period yields the following result (with t statistics in brackets).

  Change in firm value = 0.2081   −4.16 (Change in interest rates)
                  (2.91)   (0.75)

  Every 1 percent increase in long-term rates translates into a loss in value of 4.16 percent, although the statistical significant is marginal.

- Is Disney a cyclical firm? One way to answer this question is to measure the sensitivity of firm value to changes in economic growth. Regressing changes in firm value against changes in the real gross domestic product (GDP) over this period yields the following result.

---

3   To ensure that the coefficient on this regression is a measure of duration, we compute the change in the interest rate as follows: $(r_t - r_{t-1})/(1 + r_{t-1})$. Thus, if the long-term bond rate goes from 8 percent to 9 percent, we compute the change to be $(.09 - .08) / 1.08$.

Table 10.1   Disney's Firm Value and Macroeconomic Variables

Period	Operating Income	Firm Value	Treasury Bond Rate	Change in Rate	GDP (Deflated)	% Change in GDP	CPI	Change in CPI	Weighted Dollar	% change in $
2003	$2,713	$68,239	4.29%	0.40%	10493	3.60%	2.04%	0.01%	88.82	−14.51%
2002	$2,384	$53,708	3.87%	−0.82%	10128	2.98%	2.03%	−0.10%	103.9	−3.47%
2001	$2,832	$45,030	4.73%	−1.20%	9835	−0.02%	2.13%	−1.27%	107.64	1.85%
2000	$2,525	$47, 717	6.00%	0.30%	9837	3.53%	3.44%	0.86%	105.68	11.51%
1999	$3,580	$88,558	5.68%	−0.21%	9502	4.43%	2.56%	1.05%	94.77	−0.59%
1998	$3,843	$65,487	5.90%	−0.19%	9099	3.70%	1.49%	−0.65%	95.33	0.95%
1997	$3,945	$64,236	6.10%	−0.56%	8774	4.79%	2.15%	-0.82%	94.43	7.54%
1996	$3,024	$65,489	6.70%	0.49%	8373	3.97%	2.99%	0.18%	87.81	4.36%
1995	$2,262	$54,972	6.18%	−1.32%	8053	2.46%	2.81%	0.19%	84.14	−1.07%
1994	$1,804	$33, 071	7.60%	2.11%	7860	4.30%	2.61%	−0.14%	85.05	−5.38%
1993	$1,560	$22,694	5.38%	−0.91%	7536	2.25%	2.75%	−0.44%	89.89	4.26%
1992	$1,287	$25,048	6.35%	−1.01%	7370	3.50%	3.20%	0.27%	86.22	−2.31%
1991	$1,004	$17, 122	7.44%	−1.24%	7121	−0.14%	2.92%	−3.17%	88.26	4.55%
1990	$1,287	$14,963	8.79%	0.47%	7131	1.68%	6.29%	1.72%	84.42	−11.23%
1989	$1,109	$16, 015	8.28%	−0.60%	7013	3.76%	4.49%	0.23%	95.10	4.17%
1988	$ 789	$ 9,195	8.93%	−0.60%	6759	4.10%	4.25%	−0.36%	91.29	−5.34%
1987	$ 707	$ 8,371	9.59%	2.02%	6493	3.19%	4.63%	3.11%	96.44	−8.59%
1986	$ 281	$ 5,631	7.42%	−2.58%	6292	3.11%	1.47%	−1.70%	105.50	−15.30%
1985	$ 206	$ 3,655	10.27%	−1.11%	6102	3.39%	3.23%	−0.64%	124.56	−10.36%
1984	$ 143	$ 2,024	11.51%	−0.26%	5902	4.18%	3.90%	−0.05%	138.96	8.01%
1983	$ 134	$ 1,817	11.80%	1.20%	5665	6.72%	3.95%	−0.05%	128.65	4.47%
1982	$ 141	$ 2,108	10.47%	−3.08%	5308	−1.16%	4%	−4.50%	123.14	6.48%

Firm Value = Market Value of Equity + Book Value of Debt

Change in firm value = 0.2165   + 0.26 (GDP growth)
           (1.56)   (0.07)

Disney's value as a firm has not been affected significantly by economic growth. Again, to the extent that we trust the coefficients from this regression, this would suggest that Disney is not a cyclical firm.

- To examine the way Disney is affected by changes in inflation, we regressed changes in firm value against changes in the inflation rate over this period with the following result.

Change in firm value = 0.2262   + 0.57 (Change in inflation rate)
           (3.22)   (0.13)

Disney's firm value is unaffected by changes in inflation because the coefficient on inflation is not statistically different from zero.

- We can answer the question of how sensitive Disney's value is to changes in currency rates by looking at how the firm's value changes as a function of changes in currency rates. Regressing changes in firm value against changes in the dollar over this period yields the following regression.

Change in firm value = 0.2060   −2.04 (Change in dollar)
                      (3.40)   (2.52)

Statistically, this yields the strongest relationship. Disney's firm value decreases as the dollar strengthens.

In some cases, it is more reasonable to estimate the sensitivity of operating cash flows directly against changes in interest rates, inflation, and other variables. For Disney, we repeated the analysis using operating income as the dependent variable, rather than firm value. Because the procedure for the analysis is similar, we summarize the conclusions here.

- Regressing changes in operating income against changes in interest rates over this period yields the following result.

Change in operating income = 0.2189   + 6.59 (Change in interest rates)
                            (2.74)   (1.06)

Disney's operating income, unlike its firm value, has moved with interest rates. Again, this result has to be considered in light of the low t statistics on the coefficients. In general, regressing operating income against interest rate changes should yield a lower estimate of duration than the firm value measure, for two reasons. One is that income tends to be smoothed out relative to value, and the other is that the current operating income does not reflect the effects of changes in interest rates on discount rates and future growth.

- Regressing changes in operating income against changes in real GDP over this period yields the following regression.

Change in operating income = 0.1725   + 0.66 (GDP growth)
                            (1.10)   (0.15)

Disney's operating income, like its firm value, does not reflect sensitivity to overall economic growth, confirming the conclusion that Disney is not a cyclical firm.

- Regressing changes in operating income against changes in the dollar over this period yields the following regression.

Change in operating income = 0.1768   −1.76 (Change in dollar)
                                         (2.42)   (1.81)

Disney's operating income, like its firm value, is negatively affected by a stronger dollar.

- Regressing changes in operating income against changes in inflation over this period yields the following result.

Change in operating income = 0.2192   +9.27 (Change in inflation rate)
                                         (3.01)   (1.95)

Unlike firm value, which is unaffected by changes in inflation, Disney's operating income moves strongly with inflation, rising as inflation increases. This would suggest that Disney has substantial pricing power, allowing it to pass through inflation increases into its prices and operating income.

The question of what to do when operating income and firm value have different results can be resolved fairly simply. The former provides a measure of earnings risk exposure and is thus narrow, whereas the latter captures the effect not only on current earnings but also on future earnings. It is possible, therefore, that a firm can be exposed to earnings risk from a source but that the value risk is muted, as is the alternative where the risk to current earnings is low but the value risk is high.

Two key limitations are associated with the firm-specific risk measures described in the previous section. First, they make sense only if the firm has been in its current business for a long time and expects to remain in it for the foreseeable future. In today's environment, in which firms find their business mixes changing from period to period as they divest some businesses and acquire new ones, it is unwise to base too many conclusions on a historical analysis. Second, the small sample sizes used tend to yield regression estimates that are not statistically significant (as is the case with the coefficient estimates that we obtained for Disney from the interest rate regression). In such cases, we might want to look at the characteristics of the industry in which a firm plans to expand, rather than using past earnings or firm value as a basis for the analysis.

To illustrate, we looked at the sector estimates[4] for each of the sensitivity measures for the four businesses that Disney is in: movies, theme parks, entertainment, and consumer product businesses. Table 10.2 summarizes the findings.

---

4   These sector estimates were obtained by aggregating the firm values of all firms in a sector on a quarter-by-quarter basis going back 12 years, and then regressing changes in this aggregate firm value against changes in the macroeconomic variable each quarter.

Table 10.2   Sector Sensitivity to Macroeconomic Risks

| | Coefficients on Firm Value Regression | | | | |
	Interest Rates	GDP Growth	Inflation	Currency	Disney Weights
Movies	−3.70	0.56	1.41	−1.23	25.62%
Theme parks	−6.47	0.22	−1.45	−3.21	20.09%
Entertainment	−4.50	0.70	−3.05	−1.58	49.25%
Consumer products	−4.88	0.13	−5.51	−3.01	5.04%
Disney	−4.71	0.54	−1.71	−1.89	100%

These bottom-up estimates suggest that firms in the business are negatively affected by higher interest rates (losing 4.71 percent in value for every 1 percent change in interest rates), and that firms in this sector are relatively unaffected by the overall economy. Like Disney, firms in these businesses tend to be hurt by a stronger dollar, but, unlike Disney, they do not seem have much pricing power. (Note the negative coefficient on inflation.) The sector averages also have the advantage of more precision than the firm-specific estimates and can be relied on more.

Step 4: Analyze the Risks

After we have listed, categorized, and measured risk exposure, the last step in the process requires us to consider the choices we can make in dealing with each type of risk. Although we will defer the full discussion of which risks should be hedged and which should not to the next section, we will prepare for that discussion by first outlining what our alternatives are when it comes to dealing with each type of risk and follow up be evaluating our expertise in dealing with that risk.

There is a whole range of choices when it comes to hedging risk. We can try to reduce or eliminate risk through our investment and financing choices, through insurance, or by using derivatives. Not all choices are feasible or economical with all risks, and it is worthwhile making an inventory of the available choices with each one. The risk associated with nationalization cannot be managed using derivatives and can be only partially insured against; the insurance may cover the cost of the fixed assets appropriated but not against the lost earnings from these assets. In contrast, exchange rate risk can be hedged in most markets with relative ease using market-traded derivatives contracts.

A tougher call involves assessing how well we deal with different risk exposures. A hotel company may very well decide that its expertise is not in making real estate judgments but in running hotels efficiently. Consequently, it may decide to hedge against the former while being exposed to the latter.

To Hedge or Not to Hedge?

Assume now that we have a list of all the risks that we are exposed to, have categorized these risks, and have measured our exposure to each one. A fundamental and key question that we have to answer is which of these risks we want to hedge against and which we want to either pass through to our investors or exploit. To make this judgment, we have to consider the potential costs and benefits of hedging; in effect, we hedge those risks where the benefits of hedging exceed the costs.

The Costs of Hedging

Protecting ourselves against risk is not costless. Sometimes, as is the case of buying insurance, the costs are explicit. At other times, as with forwards and futures contracts, the costs are implicit. In this section, we consider the magnitude of explicit and implicit costs of hedging against risk and how these costs may weigh on the final question of whether to hedge in the first place.

Explicit Costs

Most businesses insure against at least some risk, and the costs of risk protection are easy to compute. They take the form of the insurance premiums that we have to pay to get the protection. In general, the trade-off is simple. The more complete the protection against risk, the greater the cost of the insurance. In addition, the cost of insurance will increase with the likelihood and the expected impact of a specified risk. A business located in coastal Florida will have to pay more to insure against floods and hurricanes than one in the Midwest.

Businesses that hedge against risks using options can also measure their hedging costs explicitly. A farmer who buys put options to put a lower bound on the price that he will sell his produce has to pay for the options. Similarly, an airline that buys call options on fuel to make sure that the price paid does not exceed the strike price will know the cost of buying this protection.

Implicit Costs

The hedging costs become less explicit as we look at other ways of hedging against risk. Firms that try to hedge against risk through their financing choices—using peso debt to fund peso assets, for instance—may be able to reduce their default risk (and consequently their cost of borrowing), but the savings are implicit. Firms that use futures and forward contracts also face implicit costs. A farmer who buys futures contracts to lock in a price for his produce may face no immediate costs (in contrast with the costs of buying put options) but will have to give up potential profits if prices move upward.

The way in which accountants deal with explicit as opposed to implicit costs can make a difference in which hedging tool is chosen. Explicit costs reduce the earnings in the period in which the protection is acquired, whereas the implicit costs manifest themselves only indirectly in future earnings. Thus, a firm that buys insurance against risk will report lower earnings in the period that the insurance is bought, whereas a firm that uses futures and forward contracts to hedge will not take an earnings hit in that period. The effect of the hedging tool used will manifest itself in subsequent periods, with the latter reducing profitability in the event of upside risk.

The Benefits of Hedging

Firms may choose to hedge risks for several reasons, which can be broadly categorized into five groups. First, as we noted in the previous chapter, the tax laws may benefit those who hedge risk. Second, hedging against catastrophic or extreme risk may reduce the likelihood and the costs of distress, especially for smaller businesses. Third, hedging against risks may reduce the underinvestment problem prevalent in many firms as a result of risk-averse managers and restricted capital markets. Fourth, minimizing the exposure to some types of risk may provide firms with more freedom to fine-tune their capital structure. Finally, investors may find the financial statements of firms that do hedge against extraneous or unrelated risks to be more informative than firms that do not.

Tax Benefits

A firm that hedges against risk may receive tax benefits for doing so, relative to an otherwise similar firm that does not hedge against risk. As we noted in Chapter 9, "Risk Management: The Big Picture," there are two sources for these tax benefits. One flows from the smoothing of earnings that is a consequence of effective risk hedging; with risk hedging, earnings will be lower than they would have been without hedging, during periods where the risk does not manifest itself, and higher in periods where there is risk exposure. To the extent that the income at higher levels is taxed at higher rates, there will be tax savings over time to a firm with more level earnings. To see why, consider a tax schedule, where income beyond a particular level (say $1 billion) is taxed at a higher rate—that is, a windfall profit tax. Because risk management can be used to smooth out income over time, it is possible for a firm with volatile income to pay less in taxes over time because of risk hedging. Table 10.3 illustrates the tax paid by the firm, assuming a tax rate of 30 percent for income below $1 billion and 50 percent above $1 billion.

Table 10.3   Taxes Paid: With and Without Risk Management

Year	Without Risk Management		With Risk Management	
	Taxable Income	Taxes Paid	Taxable Income	Taxes Paid
1	$600	$180	$800	$240
2	$1,500	$550	$1,200	$400
3	$400	$120	$900	$270
4	$1,600	$600	$1,200	$400
Total	$4,100	$1,450	$4,100	$1,310

Risk hedging has reduced the taxes paid over four years by $140 million. Although it is true that we have not reflected the cost of risk hedging in the taxable income, the firm can afford to spend up to $140 million and still come out with a value increase. The tax benefits in the previous example were predicated on the existence of a tax rate that rises with income (convex tax rates). Even in its absence, though, firms that go from making big losses in some years to big profits in other years can benefit from risk hedging to the extent that they get their tax benefits earlier. In a 1999 study, Graham and Smith provide some empirical evidence on the potential tax benefits to companies from hedging by looking at the tax structures of U.S. firms. They estimate that about half of all U.S. firms face convex effective tax functions (where tax rates risk with income), about a quarter have linear tax functions (where tax rates do not change with income), and a quarter actually have concave tax functions (where tax rates decrease with income). They also note that firms with volatile income near a kink in the statutory tax schedule and firms that shift from profits in one period to losses in another are most likely to have convex tax functions. Using simulations of earnings, they estimate the potential tax savings to firms and conclude that although they are fairly small, they can generate tax savings that are substantial for a quarter of the firms with convex tax rates. In some cases, the savings amounted to more than 40 percent of the overall tax liability.[5]

The other potential tax benefit arises from the tax treatment of hedging expenses and benefits. At the risk of oversimplification, there will be a tax benefit to hedging if the cost of hedging is fully tax deductible but the benefits from insurance are not fully taxed. As a simple example, consider a firm that pays $2.5 million in insurance premiums each year for three years and receives an expected benefit of $7.5 million at the third year. Assume that the insurance premiums are tax deductible but that the insurance payout is not taxed. In such a scenario, the firm will clearly gain from hedging. Mains (1983) uses a variation of this argument to justify the purchase of insurance by companies. He cites an Oil Insurance Association brochure titled "To Insure or Not to Insure" that argues that self-insured property damages are deductible only to the extent of the book value but that income from insurance claims is tax free as long as it is used to repair or replace the destroyed assets. Even if used elsewhere, firms only have to pay the capital gains tax on the difference between the book value of the asset and the insurance settlement. Because the capital gains tax rate is generally lower than the income tax rate, firms can reduce their tax payments by buying even fairly priced insurance.[6]

Better Investment Decisions

In a perfect world, the managers of a firm would consider each investment opportunity based on its expected cash flows and the risk that that investment adds to the investors in the firm. They would not be swayed by risks that can be diversified away by these investors, substantial though these risks may be, and capital markets would stand ready to supply the funds needed to make these investments.

As we noted in Chapter 9, frictions can cause this process to break down. In particular, there are two problems that affect investment decisions that can be traced to the difference between managerial and stockholder interests.

- **Managerial risk aversion**—Managers may find it difficult to ignore risks that are diversifiable, partly because their compensation and performance measures are still affected by these risks and partly because so much of their human capital is tied up in these firms. Consequently, they may reject investments that add value to the firm because the firm-specific risk exposure is substantial.

- **Capital market frictions**—A firm that has a good investment that it does not have cash on hand to invest in will have to raise capital by either issuing new

---

5   Graham, J. R., and C. W. Smith. "Tax Incentives to Hedge." *Journal of Finance*, Vol. 54, 2242–2262., 1999.

6   Mains, B. "Corporate Insurance Purchases and Taxes." *Journal of Risk and Insurance*, Vol. 50, 197–223, 1983.

equity or by borrowing money. In a well-cited paper, Myers and Majluf note that firms that depend on new stock issues to fund investments will tend to under-invest because they have to issue the new shares at a discount; the discount can be attributed to the fact that markets cannot easily distinguish between firms raising funds for good investments and those raising funds for poor investments, and the problem is worse for risky companies.[7] If firms depend on bank debt for funding investments, it is also possible that these investments cannot be funded because access to loans is affected by firm-specific risks. Froot, Scharfstein, and Stein generalize this argument by noting that the firms that hedge against risk are more likely to have stable operating cash flows and are thus less likely to face unexpected cash shortfalls. Consequently, they are less dependent on external financing and can stick with long-term capital investment plans and increase value.[8]

By allowing managers to hedge firm-specific risks, risk hedging may reduce the number of good investments that are rejected either because of managerial risk aversion or because of lack of access to capital.

Distress Costs

Every business, no matter how large and healthy, faces the possibility of distress under sufficiently adverse circumstances. Although bankruptcy can be the final cost of distress, the intermediate costs of being perceived to be in trouble are substantial as well. Customers may be reluctant to buy our products, suppliers will impose stricter terms, and employees are likely to look for alternative employment, creating a death spiral from which it is difficult to recover. These "indirect" costs of distress can be very large, and

---

7   Myers, S.C. and N.S. Majluf, "Corporate Financing and Investment Decisions when Firms have Information that Investors do not have," *Journal of Financial Economics*, v13, 187-221, 1984.

8   Froot, K. A., D. S. Scharfstein, and J. C. Stein. "Risk Management: Coordinating Corporate Investment and Financing Policies." *Journal of Finance*, 48(5): 1629–1658, Year.

Froot, K., D. Schartstein, and J. Stein. "A Framework for Risk Management." *Harvard Business Review*, Vol. 72, No. 59, 71, 1994.

studies that try to measure these costs estimate that they range from 20 percent to 40 percent of firm value.[9]

Given the large costs of bankruptcy, it is prudent for firms to protect themselves against risks that may cause distress by hedging against them. In general, these will be risks that are large relative to the size of the firm and its fixed commitments (such as interest expenses). As an example, although large firms with little debt, like Coca Cola, can easily absorb the costs of exchange rate movements, smaller firms and firms with larger debt obligations may very well be pushed to their financial limits by the same risk. Consequently, it makes sense for the latter to hedge against risk.[10]

The payoff from lower distress costs show up in value in one of two ways. In a conventional discounted cash flow valuation, the effect is likely to manifest itself as a lower cost of capital (through a lower cost of debt) and a higher value. In the adjusted present value approach, the expected bankruptcy costs will be reduced because of the hedging. To the extent that the increase in value from reducing distress costs exceeds the cost of hedging, the value of the firm will increase. Note that the savings in distress costs from hedging are likely to manifest themselves in substantial ways only when distress costs are large. Consequently, we would expect firms that have borrowed money and are exposed to significant operating risk to be better candidates for risk hedging. Kale and Noe make this point when they note that risk hedging can actually reduce value at low debt ratios, because any gains from reduced distress costs are likely to be small and overwhelmed by the costs of hedging. In contrast, they note that hedging can increase firm value for firms that are optimally levered and thus carry significant debt loads with concurrent distress costs.[11]

---

9   Shapiro, A., and S. Titman. "An Integrated Approach to Corporate Risk Management." *Midland Corporate Finance Journal*, Vol. 3, 41–55, 1985.

   For an examination of the theory behind indirect bankruptcy costs, see Opler, T. and S. Titman. "Financial Distress and Corporate Performance." *Journal of Finance*, 49, 1015–1040, 1994.

   For an estimate on how large these indirect bankruptcy costs are in the real world, see Andrade, G., and S. Kaplan. "How Costly Is Financial (Not Economic) Distress? Evidence from Highly Leveraged Transactions That Become Distressed." *Journal of Finance*, 53, 1443–1493, 1998. The authors look at highly levered transactions that subsequently became distressed and conclude that the magnitude of these costs ranges from 10 to 23 percent of firm value.

10 Smith, C. W., and R. Stulz. "The Determinants of Firm's Hedging Policies." *Journal of Financial and Quantitative Analysis*, 20 (4): 391–405, 1985.

   Stulz, R. "Optimal Hedging Policies." *The Journal of Financial and Quantitative Analysis*, Vol. 19, 127–140, 1984.

11 Kale, J. R., and T. H. Noe. "Corporate Hedging under Personal and Corporate Taxation." *Managerial and Decision Economics*, Vol. 11, 199–205, 1990.

Capital Structure

Closely related to the reduced distress cost benefit is the tax advantage that accrues from additional debt capacity. Firms that perceive themselves as facing less distress costs are more likely to borrow more. As long as borrowing creates a tax benefit, this implies that a firm that hedges away large risks will borrow more money and have a lower cost of capital. The payoff will be a higher value for the business.[12]

The evidence on whether hedging does increase debt capacity is mixed. In supporting evidence, one study documents a link between risk hedging and debt capacity by examining 698 publicly traded firms between 1998 and 2003. This study notes that firms that buy property insurance (and thus hedge against real estate risk) borrow more money and have lower costs of debt than firms that do not.[13] Another study provides evidence on why firms hedge by looking at firms that use derivatives. The researchers conclude that these firms do so not in response to convex tax functions but primarily to increase debt capacity and that the these tax benefits add approximately 1.1 percent in value to these firms. The study also finds that firms with more debt are more likely to hedge and that hedging leads to higher leverage.[14] However, there is other research that contests these findings. To provide one instance, Gercy, Minton, and Schraud examine firms that use currency derivatives and find no link between their usage and higher debt ratios.[15]

Informational Benefits

Hedging away risks that are unrelated to the core business of a firm can also make financial statements more informative, and investors may reward the firm with a higher value. Thus, the changes in earnings for a multinational that hedges exchange rate risk will reflect the operating performance of the firm rather than the luck of the draw when it comes to exchange rates. Similarly, a hotel management company that has hedged away or removed its real estate risk exposure can be judged on the quality of the hotel management services that it provides and the revenues generated, rather than the profits or losses created by movements in real estate prices over time.

---

12   Leland, H. "Agency Costs, Risk Management, and Capital Structure." *Journal of Finance*, Vol. 53, 1213–1243, 1998. He combined the investment and financing arguments in arguing that firms can increase value by hedging. Firms that precommit to hedging against risk can borrow more money and lower their costs of capital.

13   Zou, H., and M. B. Adams. "Debt Capacity, Cost of Debt, and Corporate Insurance." Working Paper, ssrn.com, 2004.

14   Graham, J. R. and D. A. Rogers. "Do Firms Hedge in Response to Tax Incentives?" *Journal of Finance*, Vol. 57, 815–839, 2002.

15   Geczy, C., B. A. Minton, and C. Schrand. "Why Firms Use Currency Derivatives." *Journal of Finance*, Vol. 52, 1323–1354, 1997.

In a 1995 paper, DeMarzo and Duffie explore this issue in more detail by looking at both the informational advantages for investors when companies hedge risk and the effect of how much of the hedging behavior is disclosed to investors. They note that the benefit of hedging is that it allows investors to gauge management quality more easily by stripping extraneous noise from the process. They also note a possible cost when investors use the observed variability in earnings as a measure of management quality; in other words, investors assume that firms with more stable earnings have superior managers. If managers are not required to disclose hedging actions to investors, they may have the incentive to hedge too much risk; after all, hedging reduces earnings variability and improves managerial reputation.[16]

The Prevalence of Hedging

A significant number of firms hedge their risk exposures, with wide variations in which risks are hedged and which tools are used for hedging. In this section, we will look at some of the empirical and survey evidence of hedging among firms.

Who Hedges?

In 1999, Mian studied the annual reports of 3,022 companies and found that 771 of these firms did some risk hedging during the course of the year. Of these firms, 543 disclosed their hedging activities in the financial statements and 228 mentioned using derivatives to hedge risk but provided no disclosure about the extent of the hedging. Looking across companies, he concluded that larger firms were more likely to hedge than smaller firms, indicating that economies of scale allow larger firms to hedge at lower costs.[17] As supportive evidence of the large fixed costs of hedging, note the results of a survey that found that 45 percent of Fortune 500 companies used at least one full-time professional for risk management and that almost 15 percent used three or more full-time equivalents.[18]

---

16   DeMarzo, P. M., and D. Duffie. "Corporate Incentives for Hedging and Hedge Accounting." *The Review of Financial Studies*, Vol. 8, 743–771, 1995.

17   Mian, S. I. "Evidence on Corporate Hedging Policy." *Journal of Financial and Quantitative Analysis*, Vol. 31, 419–439, 1996.

18   Dolde, W. "The Trajectory of Corporate Financial Risk Management." *Journal of Applied Corporate Finance*, Vol. 6, 33–41, 1993.

In an examination of risk management practices in the gold mining industry, Tufano makes several interesting observations.[19] First, almost 85 percent of the firms in this industry hedged some or a significant portion of gold price risk between 1990 and 1993. Figure 10.1 summarizes the distribution of the proportion of gold price risk hedged by the firms in the sample. Note that 7 of the 48 firms examined hedged no risk, but 7 firms at the other extreme hedged more than 50% of the gold production against price changes.

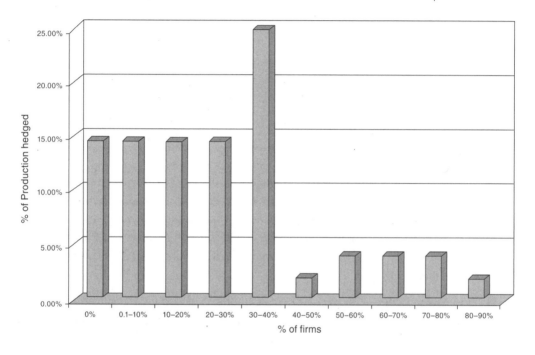

Figure 10.1: Production Hedging at Gold Mining Companies: 1990–93

Second, firms where managers hold equity options are less likely to hedge gold price risk than firms where managers own stock in the firm. Finally, the extent of risk management is negatively related to the tenure of a company's CFO; firms with long-serving CFOs manage less risk than firms with newly hired CFOs.

---

19   Tufano, P. "Who Manages Risk? An Empirical Examination of Risk Management Practices in the Gold Mining Industry." *Journal of Finance*, Vol. 51, 1097–1137, 1996.

What Risks Are Most Commonly Hedged?

Although a significant proportion of firms hedge against risk, some risks seem to be hedged more often than others. In this section, we will look at the two most widely hedged risks at U.S. companies—exchange rate risk and commodity price risk—and consider how and why firms hedge these risks.

Exchange Rate Risk

Surveys consistently indicate that the most widely hedged risk at U.S. firms remains currency risk. This phenomenon can be attributed to three simple reasons.

- **It is ubiquitous**—It is not just large multinational firms that are exposed to exchange rate risk. Even small firms that derive almost all of their revenues domestically often depend on inputs that come from foreign markets and are thus exposed to exchange rate risk. An entertainment software firm that gets its software written in India for sale in the United States is exposed to variations in the U.S. dollar/ Indian rupee exchange rate.

- **It affects earnings**—Accounting conventions also force firms to reflect the effects of exchange rate movements on earnings in the periods in which they occur. Thus, the earnings per share of firms that do not hedge exchange rate risk will be more volatile than firms that do. Consequently, firms are much more aware of the effects of the exchange rate risk, which may provide a motivation for managing it.

- **It is easy to hedge**—Exchange rate risk can be managed both easily and cheaply. Firms can use an array of market-traded instruments, including options and futures contracts, to reduce or even eliminate the effects of exchange rate risk.

Merck's CFO in 1990, Judy Lewent, and John Kearney described the company's policy on identifying and hedging currency risk. They rationalized the hedging of currency risk by noting that the earnings variability induced by exchange rate movements could affect Merck's capacity to pay dividends and continue to invest in R&D. That's because markets would not be able to differentiate between earnings drops that could be attributed to the managers of the firm and those that were the result of currency risk. A drop in earnings caused entirely by an adverse exchange rate movement, they noted, could cause the stock price to drop, making it difficult to raise fresh capital to cover needs.[20]

---

20   Lewent, J., and J. Kearney. "Identifying Measuring and Hedging Currency Risk at Merck." *Journal of Applied Corporate Finance*, Vol. 2, 19–28, 1990.

Commodity Price Risk

Although more firms hedge against exchange rate risk than commodity risk, a greater percentage of firms that are exposed to commodity price risk hedge that risk. Tufano's study of gold mining companies, cited earlier in this section, notes that most of these firms hedge against gold price risk. Whereas gold mining and other commodity companies use hedging as a way of smoothing out the revenues that they will receive on the output, there are companies on the other side of the table that use hedging to protect themselves against commodity price risk in their inputs. For instance, Hershey's can use futures contracts on cocoa to reduce uncertainty about its costs in the future.

Southwest Airlines's use of derivatives to manage its exposure to fuel price risk provides a simple example of input price hedging and why firms do it. Whereas some airlines try to pass increases in fuel prices to their customers (often unsuccessfully) and others avoid hedging because they feel they can forecast future oil prices, Southwest has viewed it as part of its fiduciary responsibility to its stockholders to hedge fuel price risk. They use a combination of options, swaps, and futures to hedge oil price movements, and they report on their hedging activities in their financial statements.

The motivations for hedging commodity price risk may vary across companies and are usually different for companies that hedge against output price risk (like gold companies) as opposed to companies that hedge against input price risk (such as airlines), but the result is the same. The former are trying to reduce the volatility in their revenues, and the latter are trying to do the same with costs, but the net effect for both groups is more stable and predictable operating income, which presumably allows these firms to have lower distress costs and borrow more. With both groups, there is another factor at play. By removing commodity price risk from the mix, firms are letting investors know that their strength lies not in forecasting future commodity prices but in their operational expertise. A gold mining company is then asking to be judged on its exploration and production expertise, whereas a fuel hedging airline's operating performance will reflect its choice of operating routes and marketing skills.

Does Hedging Increase Value?

Hedging risks has both implicit and explicit costs that can vary depending on the risk being hedged and the hedging tool used, and the benefits include better investment decisions, lower distress costs, tax savings, and more informative financial statements. The trade-off seems simple; if the benefits exceed the costs, we should hedge, and if the costs exceed the benefits, we should not.

This simple setup is made more complicated when we consider the investors of the firm and the costs they face in hedging the same risks. If hedging a given risk creates benefits to the firm, and the hedging can be done either by the firm or by investors in the firm, the hedging will add value only if the cost of hedging is lower to the firm than it is to investors. Thus, a firm may be able to hedge its exposure to sector risk by acquiring firms in other businesses, but investors can hedge the same risk by holding diversified portfolios. The premiums paid in acquisitions will dwarf the transactions costs faced by the latter; this is clearly a case where the risk-hedging strategy will be value destroying. In contrast, consider an airline that is planning to hedge its exposure to oil price risk because it reduces distress costs. Because it is relatively inexpensive to buy oil options and futures and the firm is in a much better position to know its oil needs than its investors, this is a case where risk hedging by the firm will increase value. Figure 10.2 provides a flowchart for determining whether firms should hedge the risks that they are faced with.

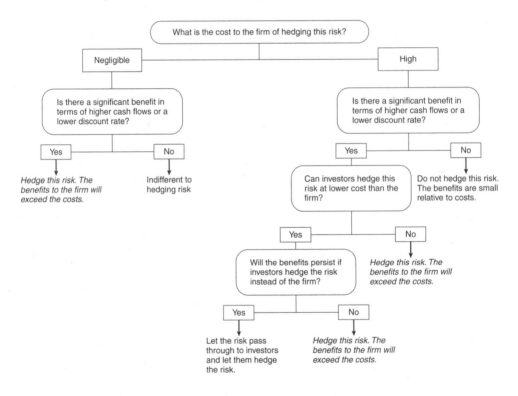

Figure 10.2: To Hedge or not to Hedge?

The evidence on whether risk hedging increases value is mixed. In an article on risk management, Smithson presents evidence that he argues is consistent with the notion that risk management increases value, but the increase in value is small at firms that hedge, and it's not statistically significant.[21] The study by Mian, referenced in the previous section, finds only weak or mixed evidence of the potential hedging benefits—lower taxes and distress costs or better investment decisions. In fact, the evidence in inconsistent with a distress cost model, because the companies with the greatest distress costs hedge the least. Tufano's study of gold mining companies, also referenced in the previous section, finds little support for the proposition that hedging is driven by the value enhancement concerns; rather, he concludes that managerial compensation mechanisms and risk aversion explain the differences in risk management practices across these companies.

In summary, the benefits of hedging are hazy at best and nonexistent at worst when we look at publicly traded firms. Although we have listed many potential benefits of hedging, including tax savings, lower distress costs, and higher debt ratios, there is little evidence that they are primary motivators for hedging at most companies. In fact, a reasonable case can be made that most hedging can be attributed to managerial interests being served rather than increasing stockholder value.

Alternative Techniques for Hedging Risk

If we decide to reduce our exposure to a risk or risks, we can use several approaches. Some of these are integrated into the standard investment and financing decisions that every business has to make; our risk exposure is determined by the assets that we invest in and by the financing that we use to fund these assets. Some have been made available by large and growing derivatives markets, where we can use options, futures, and swaps to manage risk exposure.

Investment Choices

Some of the risk that a firm is exposed to is mitigated by the investment decisions that it makes. Consider retail firms like the Gap and Ann Taylor. One of the risks that they face is related to store location, with revenues and operating income being affected by foot traffic at the mall or street that a store is placed on. This risk is lowered by the fact that these firms also have dozens of store locations in different parts of the country; a less-than-expected foot traffic at one store can be made up for with more-than-expected foot traffic at another.

---

21   Smithson, C. "Does Risk Management Work?" *Risk*, 44–45, 1999.

It is not just the firm-specific risks (like location) that investment decisions can affect. Companies like Citicorp and Coca Cola have argued that their exposure to country risk, created by investing in emerging markets with substantial risk, is mitigated (though not eliminated) by the fact that they operate in dozens of countries. A substandard performance in one country (say Brazil) can be offset by superior performance in another (say India).

Strategists and top managers of firms that diversify into multiple businesses have often justified this push toward becoming conglomerates by noting that diversification reduces earnings variability and makes firms more stable. Although they have a point, we have to draw a distinction between this risk reduction and the examples cited in the previous two paragraphs. Ann Taylor, The Gap, Citicorp, and Coca Cola can all reduce risk through their investment choices without giving up on the base principle of picking good investments. Thus, the Gap can open only good stores and still end up with dozens of stores in different locations. In contrast, a firm that decides to become a conglomerate by acquiring firms in other businesses has to pay significant acquisition premiums. There are usually more cost-effective ways of accomplishing the same objective.

Financing Choices

Firms can affect their overall risk exposure through their financing choices. A firm that expects to have significant cash inflows in yen on a Japanese investment can mitigate some of that risk by borrowing in yen to fund the investment. A drop in the value of the yen will reduce the expected cash inflows (in dollar terms), but there will be at least a partially offsetting impact that will reduce the expected cash outflows in dollar terms.

The conventional advice to companies seeking to optimize their financing choices has therefore been to match the characteristics of debt to the assets funded with the debt. The failure to do so increases default risk and the cost of debt, thus increasing the cost of capital and lowering firm value. Conversely, matching debt to assets in terms of maturity and currency can reduce default risk and the costs of debt and capital, leading to higher firm value.

What are the practical impediments to this debt-matching strategy? First, firms that are restricted in their access to bond markets may be unable to borrow in their preferred mode. Most firms outside and even many firms in the United States have access only to bank borrowing and are thus constrained by what banks offer. If, as is true in many emerging markets, banks are unwilling to lend long term in the local currency, firms with long-term investments will have to borrow short term or in a different currency to fund their needs. Second, there can be market frictions that make it cheaper for a firm to borrow in one market than another; a firm that has a low profile internationally but a strong reputation in its local market may be able to borrow at a much lower rate in the local currency (even after adjusting for inflation differences across currencies). Consequently, it may make sense to raise debt in the local currency to fund investments in other markets, even though this leads to a mismatching of debt and assets. Third, the debt used to fund investments can be affected by views about the overall market; a firm that feels that short-term rates are low, relative to long-term rates, may borrow short term to fund long-term investments with the objective of shifting to long-term debt later.

Insurance

One of the oldest and most established ways of protecting against risk is to buy insurance to cover specific event risk. Just as homeowners buy insurance on their houses to protect against the eventuality of fire or storm damage, companies can buy insurance to protect their assets against possible loss. In fact, it can be argued that, in spite of the attention given to the use of derivatives in risk management, traditional insurance remains the primary vehicle for managing risk.

Insurance does not eliminate risk. Rather, it shifts the risk from the firm buying the insurance to the insurance firm selling it. Smith and Mayers argued that this risk shifting may provide a benefit to both sides, for a number of reasons.[22] First, the insurance company may be able to create a portfolio of risks, thereby gaining diversification benefits that the self-insured firm cannot obtain itself. Second, the insurance company might acquire the expertise to evaluate risk and process claims more efficiently because of its repeated exposure to that risk. Third, insurance companies might provide other services, such as inspection and safety services that benefit both sides. Although a third party could arguably provide the same service, the insurance company has an incentive to ensure the quality of the service.

From ancient ship owners who purchased insurance against losses created by storms and pirates to modern businesses that buy insurance against terrorist acts, the insurance principle has remained unchanged. From the standpoint of the insured, the rationale for insurance is simple. In return for paying a premium, they are protected against risks that have a low probability of occurrence but have a large impact if they do. The cost of buying insurance becomes part of the operating expenses of the business, reducing the

---

22   Smith, C. W., and D. Mayers. "On the Corporate Demand for Insurance." *Journal of Business*, Vol. 55, 281–296, July 1999.

earnings of the company. The benefit is implicit and shows up as more stable earnings over time.

The insurer offers to protect multiple risk takers against specific risks in return for premiums and hopes to use the collective income from these premiums to cover the losses incurred by a few. As long as the risk being insured against affects only a few of the insured at any point in time, the laws of averaging work in the insurer's favor. The expected payments to those damaged by the risk will be lower than the expected premiums from the population. Consequently, we can draw the following conclusions about the effectiveness of insurance.

- It is more effective against individual or firm-specific risks that affect a few and leave the majority untouched and less effective against marketwide or systematic risks.

- It is more effective against large risks than against small risks. After all, an entity can self-insure against small risks and hope that the averaging process works over time. In contrast, it is more difficult and dangerous to self-insure against large or catastrophic risks, because one occurrence can put you out of business.

- It is more effective against event risks, where the probabilities of occurrence and expected losses can be estimated from history, than against continuous risk. An earthquake, hurricane, or terrorist event would be an example of the former, whereas exchange rate risk would be an example of the latter.

Reviewing the conditions, it is easy to see why insurance is most often used to hedge against *acts of God*—events that often have catastrophic effects on specific localities but leave the rest of the population relatively untouched.

Derivatives

Derivatives have been used to manage risk for centuries, but they were available only to a few firms and at high cost, because they had to be customized for each user. The development of options and futures markets in the 1970s and 1980s allowed for the standardization of derivative products, thus allowing access even to individuals who wanted to hedge against specific risk. The range of risks that are covered by derivatives grows each year, and there are very few marketwide risks that we cannot hedge today using options or futures.

Futures and Forwards

The most widely used products in risk management are futures, forwards, options, and swaps. These are generally categorized as derivative products, because they derive their value from an underlying traded asset. Although there are fundamental differences among these products, the basic building blocks for all of them are similar. To examine the common building blocks for each of these products, let us begin with the simplest— the forward contract. In a *forward contract*, the buyer of the contract agrees to buy a product (which can be a commodity or a currency) at a fixed price at a specified period in the future; the seller of the contract agrees to deliver the product in return for the fixed price. Because the forward price is fixed while the spot price of the underlying asset changes, we can measure the cash payoff from the forward contract to both the buyer and the seller of the forward contract at the expiration of the contract as a function of the spot price and present it in Figure 10.3.

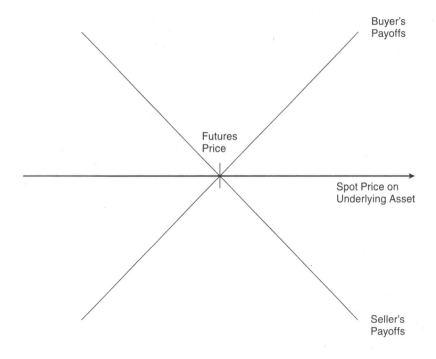

Figure 10.3: Cash Flows on Forward Contract

If the actual price at the time of the expiration of the forward contract is greater than the forward price, the buyer of the contract makes a gain equal to the difference and the seller loses an equivalent amount. If the actual price is lower than the forward price, the buyer takes a loss and the seller gains. Because forward contracts are between private parties, however, there is always the possibility that the losing party may default on the agreement.

A *futures contract*, like a forward contract, is an agreement to buy or sell an underlying asset at a specified time in the future. Therefore, the payoff diagram on a futures contract is similar to that of a forward contract. There are, however, three major differences between futures and forward contracts. First, futures contracts are traded on exchanges, whereas forward contracts are not. Consequently, futures contracts are much more liquid, and there is no default or credit risk; this advantage has to be offset against the fact that futures contracts are standardized and cannot be adapted to meet the firm's precise needs. Second, futures contracts require both parties (buyer and seller) to settle differences on a daily basis rather than waiting for expiration. Thus, if a firm buys a futures contract on oil, and oil prices go down, the firm is obligated to pay the seller of the contract the difference. Because futures contracts are settled at the end of every day, they are converted into a sequence of one-day forward contracts. This can have an effect on their pricing. Third, when a futures contract is bought or sold, the parties are required to put up a percentage of the price of the contract as a "margin." This operates as a performance bond, ensuring there is no default risk.

Options

Options differ from futures and forward contracts in their payoff profiles, which limit losses to the buyers to the prices paid for the options. Recapping our discussion in the appendix to Chapter 8, call options give buyers the rights to buy a specified asset at a fixed price anytime before expiration, whereas put options give buyers the right to sell a specified asset at a fixed price. Figure 10.4 illustrates the payoffs to the buyers of call and put options when the options expire.

The buyer of a call option makes as a gross profit the difference between the value of the asset and the strike price, if the value exceeds the strike price; the net payoff is the difference between this and the price paid for the call option. If the value is less than the strike price, the buyer loses what she paid for the call option. The process is reversed for a put option. The buyer profits if the value of the asset is less than the strike price and loses the price paid for the put if it is greater.

There are two key differences between options and futures. The first is that options provide protection against downside risk, while allowing us to partake in upside potential. Futures and forwards, on the other hand, protect us against downside risk while eliminating upside potential. A gold mining company that sells gold futures contracts to hedge against movements in gold prices will find itself protected if gold prices go down but will also have to forego profits if gold prices go up. The same company will get protection against lower gold prices by buying put options on gold but will still be able to gain if gold prices increase. The second is that options contracts have explicit costs, whereas the cost with futures contracts is implicit; other than transactions and settlement costs associated with day-to-day gold price movements, the gold mining company will face little in costs from selling gold futures, but it will have to pay to buy put options on gold.

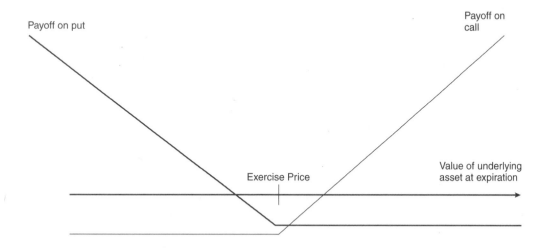

Figure 10.4: Payoff on Call and Put Options at Expiration

Swaps

In its simplest form, titled a plain vanilla swap, we offer to swap a set of cash flows for another set of cash flows of equivalent market value at the time of the swap. Thus, a U.S. company that expects cash inflows in euros from a European contract can swap them for cash flows in dollars, thus mitigating currency risk. To provide a more concrete illustration of the use of swaps to manage exchange rate risk, consider an airline that wants to hedge against fuel price risk. The airline can enter into a swap to pay a fixed price for oil and receive a floating price, with both indexed to fuel usage during a period. During the period, the airline will continue to buy oil in the cash market, but the swap market will make up the difference when prices rise. Thus, if the floating price is $1.00 per gallon and the fixed price is $0.85 per gallon, the floating-rate payer makes a $0.15 per gallon payment to the fixed rate payer.

Broken down to basics, a plain vanilla swap is a portfolio of forward contracts and can therefore be analyzed as such. In recent years, swaps have become increasingly more complex, and many of these more complicated swaps can be written as combinations of options and forward contracts.

Picking the Right Hedging Tool

After firms have decided to hedge or manage a specific risk, they have to pick among competing products to achieve this objective. To make this choice, let us review their costs and benefits.

- *Forward contracts* provide the most complete risk hedging because they can be designed to a firm's specific needs, but only if the firm knows its future cash flow needs. The customized design may result in a higher transaction cost for the firm, however, especially if the cash flows are small, and forward contracts may expose both parties to credit risk.

- *Futures contracts* provide a cheaper alternative to forward contracts, insofar as they are traded on the exchanges and do not have be customized. They also eliminate credit risk, but they require margins and cash flows on a daily basis. Finally, they may not provide complete protection against risk because they are standardized.

- Unlike futures and forward contracts, which hedge both downside and upside risk, *option contracts* provide protection against only downside risk while preserving upside potential. This benefit has to be weighed against the cost of buying the options, however, which will vary with the amount of protection desired. Giddy suggests a simple rule that can be used to determine whether companies should use options or forward contracts to hedge currency risk. If the currency flow is known, Giddy argues, forward contracts provide much more complete protection and should be used. If the currency flow is unknown, options should be used, because a matching forward contract cannot be created.[23]

- In combating event risk, a firm can either *self-insure* or use a *third party insurance* product. Self-insurance makes sense if the firm can achieve the benefits of risk pooling on its own, does not need the services or support offered by insurance companies, and can provide the insurance more economically than the third party.

As with everything else in corporate finance, firms have to make the trade-off. The objective, after all, is not complete protection against risk, but as much protection as makes

---

23   Giddy, I. "Foreign Exchange Options." *Journal of Futures Markets*, Vol. 3, 143–166, 1983.

sense, given the marginal benefits and costs of acquiring it. A survey of the risk products that 500 multinationals in the United States used concluded that forward contracts remain the dominant tool for risk management, at least for currency risk, and that there is a shift from hedging transaction exposure to economic exposure.[24]

Conclusion

This chapter examined the questions of which risks to hedge and which ones to pass through. We began by looking at the process of risk profiling, where we outline the risks faced by a business, categorize those risks, consider the tools available to manage those risks, and analyze the capabilities of the firm in dealing with those risks. We then moved on to look at the costs and benefits of hedging. The costs of hedging can be explicit when we use insurance or put options that protect against downside risk while still providing upside potential and implicit when using futures and forwards, where we give up profit potential if prices move favorably in return for savings when there are adverse price movements. There are five possible benefits from hedging: tax savings either from smoother earnings or favorable tax treatment of hedging costs and payoffs, a reduced likelihood of distress and the resulting costs, higher debt capacity and the resulting tax benefits, better investment decisions, and more informational financial statements.

Although there are potential benefits to hedging and plenty of evidence that firms hedge, there is surprisingly little empirical support for the proposition that hedging adds value. The firms that hedge seem to be motivated less by tax savings or reduced distress costs, and more by managerial interests—compensation systems and job protection are often tied to maintaining more stable earnings. As the tools to hedge risk—options, futures, swaps, and insurance—have multiplied, the purveyors of these tools have become more skilled at selling them to firms that often do not need them or should not be using them.

---

24 Jesswein, K., C. C. Y. Kwok, and W. R. Folks, Jr. "What New Currency Products Are Companies Using and Why?" *Journal of Applied Corporate Finance*, Vol. 8, 103–114, 1995.

11

STRATEGIC RISK MANAGEMENT

hy would risk-averse individuals and entities ever expose themselves intentionally to risk and increase that exposure over time? One reason is that they
believe they can exploit these risks to advantage and generate value. How
else can we explain why companies embark into emerging markets that have substantial
political and economic risk or into technologies where the ground rules change on a
day-to-day basis? By the same token, the most successful companies in every sector and
in each generation—General Motors in the 1920s, IBM in the 1950s and 1960s, Microsoft and Intel in the 1980s and 1990s, and Google in this decade—share a common characteristic. They achieved their success not by avoiding risk but by seeking it out.

Some would attribute the success of these companies and others like them to luck, but
that can explain businesses that are one-time wonders—a single successful product or
service. Successful companies are able to go back to the well again and again, replicating
their success on new products and in new markets. To do so, they must have a template
for dealing with risk that gives them an advantage over the competition. In this chapter,
we consider how best to organize the process of risk taking to maximize the odds of
success. In the process, we will have to weave through many different functional areas
of business, from corporate strategy to finance to operations management, that have
traditionally not been on talking terms.

Why Exploit Risk?

It is true that risk exposes us to potential losses, but it also provides us with opportunities. A simple vision of successful risk taking is that we should expand our exposure
to upside risk while reducing the potential for downside risk. In this section, we will
first revisit the discussion of the payoff to risk taking that we initiated in Chapter 9, "Risk
Management: The Big Picture." Then we will look at the evidence on the success of such
a strategy.

Value and Risk Taking

It is simplest to consider the payoff to risk in a conventional discounted cash flow model. The value of a firm is the present value of the expected cash flows, discounted at a risk-adjusted rate. The value derives from four fundamentals: the cash flows from existing investments, the growth rate in these cash flows over a high growth period accompanied usually by excess returns on new investments, the length of this high growth period, and the cost of funding (capital) both existing and new investments. In this context, the effects of risk taking can manifest in all of these variables:

- The cash flows from existing investments reflect not only the quality of these investments and the efficiency with they are managed, but also the consequences of past decisions made by the firm on how much risk to take and in what forms. A firm that is more focused on which risks it takes, which ones it avoids, and which ones it should pass to its investors may be able not only to determine which of its existing investments it should keep but also generate higher cash flows from these investments. A risk-averse company that is excessively cautious when investing will have fewer investments and report lower cash flows from those investments.

- The excess returns on new investments and the length of the high growth period will be directly affected by decisions on how much risk to take in new investments and how well risk is both assessed and dealt with. Firms that are superior risk takers will generate greater excess returns for longer periods on new investments.

- The relationship between the cost of capital and risk taking will depend in large part on the types of risks the firm takes. While increased exposure to market risk will usually translate into higher costs of capital, higher firm-specific risk may have little or no impact on the costs of capital, especially for firms with diversified investors. Being selective about risk exposure can minimize the impact on discount rates.

The final and most complete measure of good risk taking is whether the value of a firm increases because of its risk taking. That, in turn, will be determined by whether the positive effects of the risk taking—higher excess returns over a longer growth period—exceed the negative consequences—more volatile earnings and a potentially higher cost of capital. Figure 11.1 captures the effects of risk taking on all the dimensions of value.

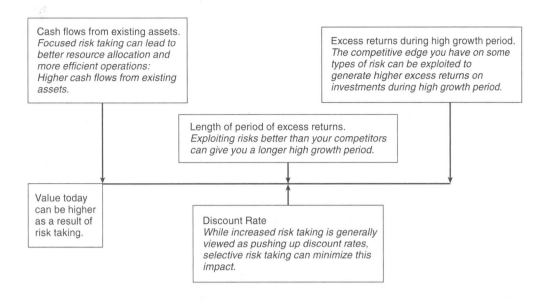

Figure 11.1: Risk Taking and Value

The other way to consider the payoff to risk taking is to use the real options framework developed in Chapter 8, "Real Options." If the essence of good risk taking is that we increase our share of good risk—the upside—while restricting our exposure to bad risk—the downside—it should take on the characteristics of a call option. Figure 11.2 captures the option component inherent in good risk taking:

Figure 11.2: Risk Taking as a Call Option

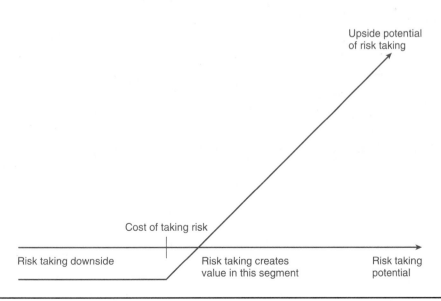

In other words, good risks create significant upside and limited downside. This is the key to why firms seek out risk in the real options framework, whether it is in the context of higher commodity price volatility, if we are an oil or commodity company with undeveloped reserves, or more uncertain markets, if we are a pharmaceutical company considering R&D investments. If we accept this view of risk taking, it will add value to a firm if the price paid to acquire these options is less than the value obtained in return.

Evidence on Risk Taking and Value

It is easy to find anecdotal evidence that risk taking pays off for some individuals and organizations. Microsoft took a risk in designing an operating system for a then-nascent product—the personal computer—but it paid off by making the company one of the most valuable businesses in the world. Google also took a risk when it deviated from industry practice and charged advertisers based on those who actually visited their sites (rather than on total traffic), but it resulted in financial success.[1] The problem with anecdotal evidence is that it can be easily debunked as either luck—Microsoft and Google happened to be at the right place at the right time—or with counter examples of companies that took risks that did not pay off—IBM did take a risk by entering the personal computer business in the 1980s and had little to show for this in terms of profitability and value.

The more persuasive but nuanced evidence for risk taking generating rewards comes from looking at the broader cross section of all investors and firms and the payoff to risk taking. On the one hand, there is clear evidence that risk taking collectively has led to higher returns for both investors and firms. For instance, investors in the United States who chose to invest their savings in equities in the twentieth century generated returns that were significantly higher than those generated by investors who remained invested in safer investments such as government and corporate bonds. Companies in sectors categorized as high risk, with risk defined either in market terms or in accounting terms, have, on average, generated higher returns for investors than lower risk companies. There is persuasive evidence that firms in sectors with more volatile earnings or stock prices have historically earned higher returns than firms in sectors with staid earnings and stable stock prices. Within sectors, there is some evidence, albeit mixed, that risk taking generates higher returns for firms. A study of the 50 largest U.S. oil companies

---

1   Battelle, J. *The Search: How Google and Its Rivals Rewrote the Rules of Business and Transformed Our Culture*. London: Penguin Books, 2005.

between 1981 and 2002, for instance, found that firms that take more risk when it comes to exploration and development earn higher returns than firms that take less.[2]

On the other hand, there is also evidence that risk taking can sometimes hurt companies and that some risk taking, at least on average, seems foolhardy. In a widely quoted study in management journals, a study by Bowman uncovered a negative relationship between risk and return in most sectors, a surprise given the conventional wisdom that higher risk and higher returns go hand-in-hand, at least in the aggregate.[3] This phenomenon, risk taking with more adverse returns, has since been titled the *Bowman paradox* and has been subjected to a series of tests. In follow-up studies, Bowman argued that a firm's risk attitudes may influence risk taking and that more troubled firms often take greater and less justifiable risks.[4] A later study broke down firms into those that earn below and above target level returns (defined as the industry-average return on equity) and noted a discrepancy in the risk/return trade-off. Firms that earned below the target level became risk seekers, and the relationship between risk and return was negative, whereas returns and risk were positively correlated for firms earnings above target-level returns.[5]

In conclusion, then, there is a positive payoff to risk taking, but not if it is reckless. Firms that are selective about the risks they take can exploit those risks to advantage, but firms that take risks without sufficiently preparing for their consequences can be hurt badly. This chapter is designed to lay the foundations for sensible risk assessment, where firms can pick and choose from across multiple risks those risks that they stand the best chance of exploiting for value creation.

How Do You Exploit Risk?

In the process of doing business, it is inevitable that we will be faced with unexpected and often unpleasant surprises that threaten to undercut and even destroy our business. That is the essence of risk, and how we respond to it will determine whether we survive and succeed. In this section, we consider five ways in which we may use risk to gain an advantage over our competitors. The first is access to better and more timely informa-

---

2   Wallis, M. R. "Corporate Risk Taking and Performance: A 20-Year Look at the Petroleum Industry." *Journal of Petroleum Science and Engineering*, v48, 127–140. 2005. Wallis estimates the risk tolerance measure for each of the firms in the sector by looking at the decisions made by the firms in terms of investment opportunities.

3   Bowman, E. H. "A Risk/Return Paradox for Strategic Management." *Sloan Management Review*, Vol. 21, 17–31, 1980.

4   Bowman, E. H. "Risk Seeking by Troubled Firms." *Sloan Management Review*, Vol. 23, 33–42, 1982.

5   Fiegenbaum, A., and H. Thomas. "Attitudes Towards Risk and the Risk-Return Paradox: Prospect Theory Explanations." *Academy of Management Journal*, Vol. 31, 85–106, 1988.

tion about events as they occur and their consequences, allowing us to tailor a superior response to the situation. The second is the speed with which we respond to the changed circumstances in terms of modifying how and where we do business; by acting faster than our competitors, we may be able to turn a threat into an opportunity. The third advantage derives from our experience with similar crises in the past and our knowledge of how the market was affected by those crises, enabling us to respond better than other firms in the business. The fourth derives from having resources—financial and personnel—that allow us to ride out the rough periods that follow a crisis better than the rest of the sector. The final factor is financial and operating flexibility; being able to change our technological base, operations, or financial structure in response to a changed environment can provide a firm with a significant advantage in an uncertain environment. The key with all of these advantages is that we emerge from the crises stronger, from a competitive position, than we were prior to the crisis.

The Information Advantage

During the Second World War, cryptographers employed by the allied army were able to break the code used by the German and Japanese armies to communicate with each other.[6] The resulting information played a crucial rule in the defeat of German forces in Europe and the recapture of the Pacific by the U.S. Navy. Although running a business may not have consequences of the same magnitude, access to good information is just as critical for businesses in the aftermath of crises. In June 2006, for instance, the military seized power in Thailand in a largely bloodless coup while the prime minister of the country was on a trip to the United States. The response of a firm with significant investments in Thailand would have largely depended on what it believed the consequences of the coup to be. The problem, in crises like these, is that good intelligence becomes difficult to obtain, but having reliable information can provide an invaluable edge in crafting the right response.

How can firms that operate in risky businesses or risky areas of the world lay the groundwork for getting superior information? First, they have to invest in *information networks*—human intelligence as the CIA or KGB would have called it in the Cold War era—and vet and nurture the agents in the network well ahead of crises. Lest this be seen as an endorsement of corporate skullduggery, businesses can use their own employees and the entities that they deal with—suppliers, creditors, and joint venture partners—as sources of information. Second, the reliability of the intelligence network has to be tested well before the crisis hits, with the intent of removing the weak links and augmenting

---

6   Code breakers at Bletchley Park solved messages from a large number of Axiscode and cipher systems, including the German Enigma Machine.

its strengths. Third, the network has to be protected from the prying eyes of competitors who may be tempted to raid it rather than design their own. A study of Southern California Edison's experiences in designing an information system to meet power interruptions caused by natural disasters, equipment breakdowns, and accidents made these general recommendations on system design.[7]

- Have a preset crisis team and predetermined action plan ready to go before the crisis hits. This will allow information to get to the right decision makers when the crisis occurs.

- Evaluate how much and what types of information we will need for decision making in a crisis, and invest in the hardware and software to ensure that this information is delivered in a timely fashion.

- Develop early warning information systems that will trigger alerts and preset responses.

As companies invest billions in information technology (IT), one of the questions they should address is how this investment will help in developing an information edge during crises. After all, the key objective of good information technology is not that every employee has an updated computer with the latest operating system on it but that information flows quickly and without distortion through the organization in all directions—from top management to those in the field, from those working in the trenches (and thus in the middle of the crisis) to those at the top and within personnel at each level. Porter and Millar integrate information technology into the standard strategic forces framework and argue that investments in information technology can enhance strategic advantages. In Figure 11.3, we modify their framework to consider the interaction with risk.

As information becomes both more plentiful and easier to access, the challenge that managers often face is not that they do not have enough information but that there is too much, and the information is often contradictory and chaotic. A study by the Economist Intelligence Unit in 2005 confirmed this view, noting that although information is everywhere, it is often disorganized and difficult to act on, with 55 percent of the 120 managers that they surveyed agreeing that information as provided currently is not adequately prioritized. The key to using information to advantage, when confronted with risk, is the presence of a screening mechanism that not only separates reliable from

---

7   Housel, T. J., O. A. El Sawry, and P. F. Donovan. "Information Systems for Crisis Management: Lessons from Southern California Edison." *MIS Quarterly*, Vol. 10, 389–402. Minneapolis: Society for Information Management and The Management Information Systems Research Center, 1986.

unreliable information but also provides decision makers with the tools to make sense of the information.

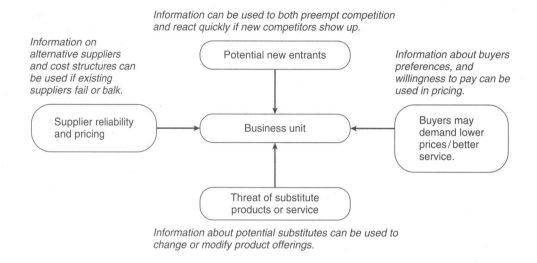

Figure 11.3: Information Technology and Strategic Risks

As a final point, it is worth emphasizing that having better information is one part of successfully exploiting risk, but it is not a sufficient or even necessary precondition. A study of intelligence in military operations found that although good intelligence is a factor in success, it is only one factor, and sometimes armies have failed despite having superior information and succeeded notwithstanding poor information.

The Speed Advantage

When case studies are written of effective responses to crises, whether they are political or economic, they generally highlight the speed of response. One reason Johnson and Johnson was able to minimize the damage ensuing from the Tylenol poisoning scare in the mid 1980s was that it removed bottles of the pills immediately from store shelves and responded with a massive public relations blitz, warning consumers about the dangers, while reassuring them that it had matters under control. In contrast, the Federal Emergency Management Administration (FEMA) was lambasted for the slowness with which it responded to the breaching of levies in New Orleans in 2005, in the aftermath of Hurricane Katrina. J&J's actions did not just reduce the costs from the tampering incident, but the goodwill and credibility gained by their response might have actually made the incident a net benefit for them in the long term.[8] In essence, the company turned into practice the adage that every threat is also an opportunity.

So, what determines the speed of the response? One factor is the quality of the information that we receive about the nature of the threat and its consequences—the information advantage that we noted in the last section is often a key part of reacting quickly. The second factor is recognizing both the potential short-term and long-term consequences of the threat. All too often, entities under threat respond to the near-term effects by going into a defensive posture and either downplaying the costs or denying the risks when they would be better served by being open about the dangers and what they are doing to protect against them. The third factor is understanding the audience and constituencies that we are providing the response for. Johnson and Johnson recognized that the key group that needed reassurance was not analysts worried about the financial consequences but potential future customers. Rather than downplay the threat, which would have been the response that reassured investors, the firm chose to take the highlight the potential dangers and its responses. Although no one template works for every firm, the most successful respondents to crisis maintain a balance among stockholders, customers, and potential or actual victims of the crisis.[9]

In effect, it is not just that we respond quickly to crises but the appropriateness of the response that determines whether we succeed in weathering the crisis and emerging stronger from the experience. The organizational structure and culture of firms also seem to play a role in how effective they are at responding to challenges. An examination of the practices of Japanese manufacturers concluded that firms that responded quickly to market changes tended to share information widely across the organization and its partners and to have small teams that were allowed to make decisions without senior management overview.[10] A study of the decision processes at four firms in the microcomputer industry, with the intent of uncovering the determinants of the speed of this response, found that firms that succeeded were able to straddle paradoxical positions. These successful firms were able to make decisions quickly but carefully, they had pow-

---

8   Johnson and Johnson consistently has ranked at the top of firms for corporate reputation in the years since the Tylenol scare, showing that the way in which we respond to crises can have very long-term consequences.

9   Firms often have to weigh the interests of stockholders against crisis victims. A study that looked at accidents found that stockholders suffer losses when managers are overly accommodating to victims in accidents, but that accommodation is often the best option when companies are embroiled in scandal (and thus cannot blame Mother Nature or external forces). Marcus, A. A. and R. S. Goodman. "Victims and Shareholders: The Dilemma of Presenting Corporate Policy During a Crisis." *Academy of Management Journal*, Vol. 34, 281–305, 1991.

10   Stalk, Jr., G., and T. M. Hout. "Competing Against Time: How Time-Based Competition Is Reshaping Global Markets." New York: *The Free Press*, 1990.

erful CEOs who coexisted with a powerful top management team, and they made innovative and risky decisions while providing for safe and incremental implementation.[11]

The Experience/Knowledge Advantage

Although it is true that no two crises are exact replicas, it is also true that having experienced similar crises in the past can give us an advantage. In economies with high and volatile inflation, for instance, firms develop coping mechanisms ranging from flexible pricing policies to labor contracts that are tied to changing inflation. Thus, a surge in inflation that is devastating to competitors from more mature markets (with stable inflation) is taken in stride by these firms. In a similar vein, firms that are in countries that are subject to frequent currency devaluations or real economic volatility organize themselves in ways that allow them to survive these crises.

How important is experience in dealing with crises? A study of political crises that looked at leaders as diverse as Talleyrand, Wellington, Bismarck, Metternich, and Gromyko, whose stewardship extended across decades and multiple crises, concluded that their lengthy tenure in office made them better as crisis managers.[12] Studies of decision making by board members in a variety of different environments conclude that decisions are made more quickly if decision makers are more experienced.[13] Finally, an analysis of the International Monetary Fund (IMF) as a crisis manager from its inception in 1944 until the peso crisis that hit Mexico in 1994 establishes a similar pattern of improvement, where the organization learned from its mistakes in initial crises to improve its management in subsequent ones. In summary, experience at both the individual and institutional level leads to better and quicker decisions when faced with risk.

How does a firm that does not operate in unstable environments and thus does not have the history acquire this experience? There are at least three possible routes.

- It can do so the painful way by entering new and unfamiliar markets, exposing itself to new risks, and learning from its mistakes. This is the path that many multinational companies have chosen to take in emerging markets. Citigroup,

---

11   Bourgeois, L. J., and K. M. Eisenhardt. "Strategic Decision Processes in High Velocity Environments: Four Cases in the Microcomputer Industry." *Management Science*, Vol. 34, 816–835, 1988.

12   Wallace, M. D., and P. Suedfeld. "Leadership Performance in Crisis: The Longevity-Complexity Link." *International Studies Quarterly*, Vol. 32, 439–451, 1988.

13   Judge, W. Q., and A. Miller. "Antecedents and Outcomes of Decision Speed in Different Environmental Contexts." *Academy of Management Journal*, Vol. 34, 448–483, 1991. Similar results are reported in Vance, S. C. *Corporate Leadership: Boards, Directors and Strategy*. New York: McGraw Hill, 1983.

Nestle, and Coca Cola are all good examples of firms that have been successful with this strategy. The process can take decades, but experience gained internally is often not only cost effective but more engrained in the organization.

- A second route is to acquire firms in unfamiliar markets and use their personnel and expertise. In recent years, this is the path that many firms in developed markets have adopted to enter emerging markets quickly. The perils of this strategy, though, are numerous, beginning with the fact that we have to pay a premium in acquisitions and continuing with the post-merger struggle of trying to integrate firms with two very different cultures. In fact, in the worst-case scenario, multinationals end up with target firms in new markets that are clones and drive away the very talent and experience that they sought to acquire in the first place. Because of these and other factors, there is evidence that these acquisitions are more likely to fail than succeed.[14]

- A third and possibly intermediate solution is to try to hire away or share in the experience of firms that have experience with specific risks. We can do the former by hiring managers or personnel who have crisis experience and the latter by entering into joint ventures. In 2006, eBay provided an illustration of the latter by replacing its main Web site in China, which had been saddled with losses and operating problems, with one run by Beijing-based Tom Online. When eBay entered the Chinese market in 2002, it used its standard technology platform and centralized much of its decision making in the United States, but it found itself unable to adapt quickly the diversity and the speed of change in the market. Tom Online's expertise in the market and its capacity to move quickly were strengths that eBay hoped to draw on in their joint venture.

Even within markets, the importance of knowledge and experience can vary widely across sectors. Professional service firms such as management consultants, investment banks, and advertising agencies are built on the learning and experience that they have accumulated over time. They use the knowledge to attract more customers and to provide better services. In fact, Knowledge Management or KM is the study of how best to

---

14 Studies of cross-border acquisitions find that the record of failure is high. A study of acquisitions by U.S. firms found that cross-border acquisitions consistently delivered lower returns and operating performance than domestic acquisitions; see Moeller, S. B, and F. P. Schlingemann. "Global Diversification and Bidder Gains: A Comparison Between Cross-Border and Domestic Acquisitions." *Journal of Banking and Finance*, Vol. 29, 533–564, 2005. Similar results have been reported for UK firms (Chatterjee, R. and M. Aw. "The Performance of UK Firms Acquiring Large Cross-Border and Domestic Takeover Targets." Judge Institute of Management Studies Research Paper WP07/00, Cambridge, United Kingdom, 2000) and Canadian firms (Eckbo, B. E., and K. S. Thorburn. "Gains to Bidder Firms Revisited: Domestic and Foreign Acquisitions in Canada." *Journal of Financial and Quantitative Analysis*, 35(1), 1–25, 2000.)

use this accumulated know-how and experience in growing and volatile markets as a competitive advantage.[15] To provide an illustration of how firms are marrying accumulated knowledge with advances in information technology, consider the Knowledge On-Line (KOL) system devised by Booz Allen & Hamilton, the consulting firm. The system captures and shares the "best practices" of its more experienced consultants as well as synthesizes the ideas of its experts in ways that can be generalized across clients, with the intent of building on learning over time.

The Resource Advantage

Having the resources to deal with crises as they occur can give a company a significant advantage over its competitors. Consider, for instance, the market meltdown that occurred in Argentina in 2001, when the country defaulted on its foreign currency debt and financial markets in the country essentially shut down. Companies that had the foresight to accumulate large cash balances and liquid assets before the crisis were not only able to survive but also to buy assets owned by more desperate competitors for cents on the dollar. Illustrating the two-tier system that has developed in many emerging markets, Argentine companies with depository receipts (ADRs) listed in the United States were able to use their continued access to capital to establish an advantage over their purely domestic counterparts. Having cash on hand or access to capital proved to be the defining factor in success in this crisis. Firms can draw on other resources to deal with risk, including human capital. An investment bank with more experienced and savvy traders is in a better position to survive a crisis in its primary trading markets and perhaps even profit from the risk.

The link between capital access—either through markets or by having large cash balances—and survival during crises is well established. A study of emerging market companies that list depository receipts on the U.S. stock exchanges notes that the increased access to capital markets allowed these firms to be freer in their investment decisions and less sensitive to year-to-year movements in their cash flows.[16] There was also a consequent increase in stock prices for these companies after cross listings. Similarly,

---

15 Surveys of consulting firms find that a very high percentage of them have tried to build knowledge management systems, marrying information technology advances with the expertise of the people working at these firms.

16 Lins, K., D. Strickland, and M. Zenner. "Do Non-U.S. Firms Issue Equity on U.S. Stock Exchanges to Relax Capital Constraints? *Journal of Financial and Quantitative Analysis*, Vol. 40, 109–134, 2005.

studies of cash balances at companies find evidence that cash holdings are higher at riskier companies in more unstable economies, primarily as protection against risk.[17]

How can firms go about establishing a capital advantage? For private businesses, it can come from being publicly traded, whereas for publicly traded firms, increased capital access can come from opening up their investor base to include foreign investors (by having foreign listings or depository receipts) and from expanding their debt from bank loans to include corporate bonds. Note that there is a cost associated with this increased access to capital; for private business owners, it is the potential loss of control associated with being publicly traded firms, whereas foreign listings, especially for emerging market companies, can increase the need for and the cost of information disclosure as well as put pressure for better corporate governance. Similarly, holding a large cash balance listing may create costs for a company in noncrisis periods; the cash balance will generate low (although riskless) returns and may increase the likelihood that the firm will be taken over.

Flexibility

In the 1920s and 1930s, Ford and General Motors fought the early skirmishes in a decades-long battle to dominate the automobile business. While Henry Ford introduced the Model T Ford, available in one color (black) and one model, and generated the benefits of economies of scale, General Motors adopted a different strategy. The company emphasized a more adaptable design and a production line that could be revamped at short notice to reflect changing customer desires.[18] The flexibility that GM acquired as a consequence allowed them to win that battle and dominate the business for several decades thereafter. In an ironic twist, as oil prices shot up in 2004 and 2005 and GM and Ford struggled to convince customers to keep buying their existing line of SUVs, mini-vans, and other gas guzzlers, Toyota was able to modify its production processes to speed

---

17   Custodio, C., and C. Raposo. "Cash Holdings and Business Conditions." Working Paper, SSRN, 2004. This paper finds strong evidence that financially constrained firms adjust their cash balance to reflect overall business conditions, holding more cash during recessions. Firms that are not financially constrained exhibit the same pattern, but the linkage is much weaker. Their findings are similar to those in another paper by Baum, C. F., M. Caglayan, N. Ozkan, and O. Talvera. "The Impact of Macroeconomic Uncertainty on Cash Holdings for Nonfinancial Service Firms." Working Paper, SSRN, 2004.

18   Alfred Sloan, the CEO of GM, introduced the concept of dynamic obsolescence, where designs and product characteristics were changed on an annual basis, both to reflect changing customer tastes and to influence customers. At the same time, he also hired Harley Earl, a design genius, to invent a "styling bridge" that would allow multiple models to share the same design, thus saving both cost and time in development.

up the delivery of its hybrid entry—the Toyota Prius—and put itself on a path to being the most profitable automobile manufacturer in the world. In both cases, being able to modify production, operating, and marketing processes quickly proved key to being able to take advantage of risk.

Although a flexible response to changing circumstances can be a generic advantage, it can take different forms. For some firms, it can be production facilities that can be adapted at short notice to produce modified products that better fit customer demand; this is the advantage that GM in the 1920s and Toyota in 2005 used to gain market share and profits. Alternatively, firms that have production facilities in multiple countries may be able to move production from one country to another, if faced with risks or higher costs.[19] For other firms, it can be arise from keeping fixed costs low, thus allowing them to adjust quickly to changing circumstances; the budget airlines from Southwest to Ryanair have used this financial flexibility to stay ahead of their more cost-burdened competitors. As with the other competitive advantages that facilitate risk taking, flexibility comes with a cost. A firm that adopts a more open and flexible operating or production process may have to pay more up front to develop these processes or face higher per-unit costs than a firm with a more rigid manufacturing process that delivers better economies of scale. Southwest Airlines, for instance, has traded off the lost revenues from using regional airports (such as Islip in New York and Burbank in Los Angeles) against the flexibility it obtains in costs and scheduling to establish an advantage over its more conventional competitors in the airline business. The value of preserving the flexibility to alter production schedules and get into and out of businesses has been examined widely in the real options literature, presented in more detail in Chapter 8.

In the late 1990s, corporate strategists led by Clayton Christensen at Harvard presented the idea of *disruptive innovations*—that is, innovations that fundamentally change the way in which a business is done. They argued that established firms that generate profits from the established technologies are at a disadvantage relative to upstarts in the business.[20] Christensen distinguished between two types of disruption—low end disruption targeted at customers who do not need the performance valued by customers at the high end (and do not want to pay those prices) and new market disruption targeting customers not served by existing businesses. He used the disk drive business to illustrate his case and presented the process through which a new technology displaces an existing one in five steps (shown in Figure 11.4).

---

19   Kogut, B., and N. Kulatilaka. "Operating Flexibility, Global Manufacturing, and the Option Value of a Multinational Network." *Management Science*, Vol. 40, 123–139, 1994.

20   Christensen, Clayton M. *The Innovator's Dilemma*. Cambridge: Harvard Business School Press, 1997.

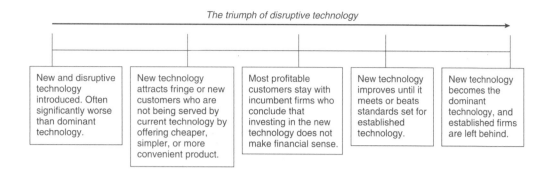

The triumph of disruptive technology

| New and disruptive technology introduced. Often significantly worse than dominant technology. | New technology attracts fringe or new customers who are not being served by current technology by offering cheaper, simpler, or more convenient product. | Most profitable customers stay with incumbent firms who conclude that investing in the new technology does not make financial sense. | New technology improves until it meets or beats standards set for established technology. | New technology becomes the dominant technology, and established firms are left behind. |

Figure 11.4: Disruptive Technology

Christensen's thesis was a provocative one because it suggested that past successes in a business can conspire against a company that tries to adapt to new technology or changes in the way business is done. Those in the disruptive technology school were also able to buttress their arguments by pointing to the advent of online businesses in the dot-com boom and the incapacity of conventional companies to contest young start-ups. Amazon.com was able to take business away from brick and mortar retailers because it could invest itself fully to online retailing, whereas its more established competitors had to weigh the costs created for its existing businesses. As another example of a disruptive technology, consider the growth of the University of Phoenix, an online university aimed at part time and working students who want a university degree at relatively low cost (in both time and resources). Its established competitors—conventional universities—have too much invested in the traditional form of schooling and consider an online university degree to be substandard relative their own offerings to be much of a challenge. The interesting question is whether online universities will be able to use technology to ultimately challenge universities at their own game and eventually beat them.

Although the message delivered by studies of disruptive technologies is sobering for established companies, a few of them have learned ways to thrive even as markets, products, and technologies have changed. In an examination of 66 consumer markets and the survivors and failures within these markets, Tellis and Golder concluded that incumbent companies that survive and beat back upstarts tend to share several characteristics: they prize innovation and are paranoid about challenges, and they are willing to cannibalize existing product lines to introduce new ones.[21] For the former, they provide the examples of Procter and Gamble, Intel, and Microsoft. For the latter, they point to

---

21   Tellis, Gerard J., and Peter N. Golder. *Will and Vision: How Latecomers Grow to Dominate Markets.* New York: McGraw Hill, 2001.

Gillette's willingness to undercut its own shaving market with new razors. An alternative path to success was provided by Apple Computers and its success with both iTunes, a clearly disruptive technology that upended the traditional music retailing business, and the iPod. First, Apple chose to target businesses outside of its own traditional domain, thus reducing the cost to existing business; Apple was primarily a computer hardware and software company when it entered the music business. Second, Apple created an independent iTunes team to make decisions on the music business that would not be contaminated by the history, culture, or business concerns of the computer business. In effect, it created a small, independent company internally, with its innovative zeal and energy, while preserving the resources of a much larger enterprise.

Building the Risk-Taking Organization

Firms that gain an advantage from risk taking do not do so by accident. In fact, successful risk-taking organizations have some key elements in common. First, they succeed in aligning the interests of their decision makers (managers) with the owners of the business (stockholders) so that firms expose themselves to the right risks and for the right reasons. Second, they choose the right people for the task; some individuals respond to risk better than others. Third, the reward and punishment mechanisms in these firms are designed to punish bad risk taking and encourage good risk taking. Finally, the culture of the organizations is conducive to sensible risk taking and is structured accordingly. In this section, we consider all four facets in detail.

Corporate Governance

If there is a key to successful risk taking, it is to ensure that those who expose a business to risk or respond to risk make their decisions with a common purpose in mind—to increase the value of their businesses. If the interests of the decision makers are not aligned with those who own the business, it is inevitable that the business will be exposed to some risks that it should be not be exposed to and not exposed to other risks that it should exploit. In large publicly traded firms, this can be a difficult task. The interests of top management can diverge from those of middle management, and both may operate with objectives that deviate significantly from the stockholders in and the lenders to the corporation.

In recent years, we have seen a spirited debate about corporate governance and why it is important for the future of business. In particular, proponents of strong corporate governance argued that strengthening the oversight that stockholders and directors have over managers allows for change in badly managed firms and thus performs a social good. There is also a risk-related dimension to this discussion of corporate governance. At one end of the spectrum are firms where managers own little or no stake in the equity and make decisions to further their own interests. In such firms, there will often be too little risk taking because the decision makers get little of the upside from risk (because of their limited or nonexistent equity stakes) and too much of the downside (they get fired if the risk does not pay off). A comparison of stockholder-controlled and management-controlled banks found that stockholder-controlled banks were more likely to take risk.[22] In general, managers with limited equity stakes in firms not only invest more conservatively but are more likely to borrow less and hold on to more cash. At the other end of the spectrum are firms where the incumbent managers and key decision makers have too much of their wealth tied up in the firm. These insider-dominated firms, where managers are entrenched, also tend to take less risk than they should for three reasons.

- The key decision makers have more of their own wealth tied up in the firm than diversified investors. Therefore, they worry far more about the consequences of big decisions and tend to be more leery of risk taking; the problem is accentuated when voting rights are disproportionately in incumbent managers' hands.

- Insiders who redirect a company's resources into their own pockets behave like lenders and are thus less inclined to take risk. In other words, they are reluctant to take on risks that may put their perquisites at peril.

- Firms in countries where investors do not have much power also tend to rely on banks for financing instead of capital markets (stock or bonds), and banks restrict risk taking.

The link between corporate governance and risk taking is not only intuitive but is backed up by the evidence. A study of 5,452 firms across 38 countries looked at the link between risk taking and corporate governance by defining risk in terms of standard deviation in operating cash flow over time, as a percent of total assets, and relating this number to measures in corporate governance.[23] Firms that have less insider control in markets where investors were better protected—that is, high in corporate governance—tend to take more risk in operations. These results are reinforced by studies of family-run businesses (that is, publicly traded firms that are controlled and run by the founding families). In a more direct test of how firms are affected by crisis, an examination of

---

22 Saunders, A., E. Strock, and N. G. Travlos. "Ownership Structure, Deregulation, and Bank Risk Taking." *Journal of Finance*, Vol. 45, 643–654, 1990.

23 John, K., L. Litov, and B. Yeung. "Corporate Governance and Managerial Risk Taking: Theory and Evidence." Working Paper, SSRN, 2005.

Korean firms in the aftermath of the 1997 Korean financial crisis found that firms with higher ownership concentration by foreign investors saw a smaller reduction in value than firms with concentrated insider and family ownership, suggesting that the latter didn't respond to risk as well as the former.[24]

Given that there is too little risk taking at either end of this ownership spectrum, the tricky part is to find the right balance. Figure 11.5 illustrates the relationship between corporate ownership and risk taking.

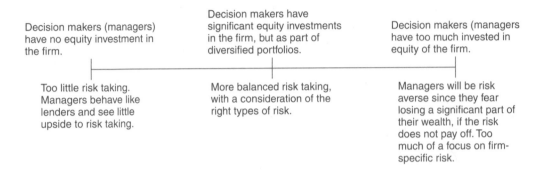

Figure 11.5: Corporate Governance and Risk Taking

The appropriate corporate governance structure for the risk-taking firm would therefore require decision makers to be invested in the equity of the firm but also to be diversified, which is a tough balance to maintain because one often precludes the other. The venture capital and private equity investors who provide equity for young, high-growth firms are perhaps the closest that we get to this ideal. They invest significant amounts in high-growth, high-risk businesses, but they spread their bets across multiple investments, thus generating diversification benefits.

Personnel

All the crisis management and risk analysis courses in the world cannot prepare us for the real event. When confronted with crisis, some people panic, others freeze, but a few thrive and become better decision makers. Keeping a cool head while others losing theirs is a unique skill that cannot be taught easily. These are the individuals that we want

---

24   Baek, J., J. Kang, and K. S. Park. "Corporate Governance and Firm Value: Evidence from the Korean Financial Crisis." Working Paper, 2004.

making decisions during crises. Businesses that manage to hire and keep these people tend to weather risk better and gain advantages over their competitors.

To understand the characteristics of a good crisis manager, it is perhaps best to consider why individuals often make bad decisions when faced with risk. In a study of the phenomenon, Kahneman and Lovallo point to three shortcomings that lead to poor decisions in response to risk.[25]

- **Loss aversion**—In a phenomenon that we examined in Chapter 4, "How Do We Measure Risk?," we noted that individuals weight losses more than equivalent gains when making decisions. Consequently, inaction is favored over action and the status quo over alternatives because loss aversion leads to an avoidance of risks.

- **Near-proportionality**—Individuals seems to be proportionately risk averse. In other words, the cash equivalent that they demand for a 50 percent chance of winning $100 increases close to proportionately as the amount is increased to $1,000 or $10,000 or even $100,000.[26] This behavior is not consistent with any well-behaved risk-aversion function, because the cash equivalent should decrease much more dramatically as the size of the gamble increases. In decision terms, this would imply that managers are unable to differentiate appropriately between small risks (which can be ignored or overlooked) and large risks (which should not be).

- **Narrow decision frames**—Decision makers tend to look at problems one at a time, rather than consider them in conjunction with other choices that they may be facing now or will face in the future. This would imply that the portfolio effect of a series of risky decisions is not factored in fully when evaluating each decision on its own.

In summary, managers have trouble dealing with risk because the possibility of losses skews their decision-making process, their inability to separate small risks from large risks, and the failure to consider the aggregate effect of risky decisions.

---

25   Kahneman, D., and D. Lovallo. "Timid Choices and Bold Forecasts: A Cognitive Perspective on Risk Taking." *Management Science*, Vol. 39, 17–31, 2006.

26   For instance, an individual who accepts $20 with a certainty equivalent for a 50 percent chance of winning $50 will accept close to $200 for a 50 percent chance of winning $500, and $2,000 for a 50 percent chance of winning $5,000. Kahneman and Lovallo note that the scaling is not perfectly proportional, but it's close enough to provoke questions about rationality.

Good risk takers then have a combination of traits that seem mutually exclusive. They are realists who still manage to be upbeat. They tend to be realistic in their assessments of success and failure but are also confident in their capacity to deal with the consequences. They allow for the possibility of losses but are not overwhelmed or scared by its prospects; in other words, they do not allow the possibility of losses to skew their decision-making processes. They are able to both keep their perspective and see the big picture even as they are immersed in the details of a crisis. In terms of decision making, they frame decisions widely and focus on those details that have large consequences. Finally, they can make decisions with limited and often incomplete information (which is par for the course in crisis) and make reasonable assumptions about the missing pieces.

How can firms seek out and retain such individuals? First, the hiring process should be attuned to finding these crisis managers and include some measure of how individuals will react when faced with risky challenges. Some investment banks, for instance, put interviewees to the test by forcing them to trade under simulated conditions and taking note of how they deal with market meltdowns. Second, good risk takers are often not model employees in stable environments. In fact, the very characteristics that make them good risk takers can make them troublemakers during other periods. Third, it is difficult to hold on to good risk takers when the environment does not pose enough of a challenge for their skills; it is very likely that they will become bored and move on, if they are not challenged. Finally, good risk takers tend to thrive when surrounded by kindred spirits; putting them in groups of more staid corporate citizens can drive them away quickly.[27]

Reward/Punishment Mechanisms

After we have aligned the interests of decision makers with those of claimholders in the firm and hired good risk takers, we have to calibrate the reward and punishment mechanism to reward good risk-taking behavior and punish bad risk-taking behavior. This is a lot harder than it looks because the essence of risk taking is that we lose some or even a significant amount of the time. Consequently, any system that is purely results oriented will fail. Thus, an investment bank that compensates its traders based on the profits and losses that they made on their trades for the firm may pay high bonuses to traders who were poor assessors of risk but were lucky during the period and penalize those traders who made reasoned bets on risk but lost. Although it may be difficult to put into practice, a good compensation system will therefore consider both processes

---

27 This may explain why risk taking is geographically concentrated in small parts of the world—Silicon Valley in California is a classic example. While technology firms grow around the world, Silicon Valley still attracts a disproportionately large share of innovative engineers and software developers.

and results. In other words, a trader who is careful about keeping an inventory of risks taken and the rationale for taking these risks should be treated more favorably than one with chaotic trading practices and little or no explanation for trading strategies used, even if the latter is more successful.

Converting these propositions about compensation into practice can be complicated. In the past three decades, firms in the United States have experimented with different types of compensation to improve risk taking and to counteract the fact that managers, left to their own devices, tend to be risk averse and reject good, risky investments. In fact, managerial risk aversion has been offered as an explanation for conglomerate mergers[28] and excessive hedging against risk.[29] Firms first added bonuses based on profitability to fixed salaries to induce managers to take more upside risk, but they discovered that higher profitability in a period is not always consistent with better risk taking or higher value for the firm. Starting in the 1970s, firms shifted toward equity-based compensation for managers, with stock grants in the company being the most common form. There is mixed evidence regarding whether equity-based compensation increases risk taking among managers. Although some of the earlier studies suggested that equity compensation may result in managers becoming overinvested in firms and consequently more risk averse,[30] a more recent study of a change in Delaware takeover laws concluded that risk taking is lower when managers are not compensated with equity.[31]

In the 1990s, the move toward equity compensation accelerated and shifted to equity options. Because options increase in value as volatility increases, some worried that this would lead to too much risk taking, because it is conceivable that some risky actions can make firms worse off while making options more valuable. In fact, option-based compensation can impact a number of different aspects of corporate finance, including financing and dividend policy; managers who are compensated with options may be less likely to increase dividends or issue new stock because these actions can lower stock prices and thus the value of their options.[32] The research on the link between risk

---

28   Amihud, Y., and B. Lev. "Risk Reduction as a Managerial Motive for Conglomerate Mergers." *Bell Journal of Economics*, Vol. 12, 605–617, 1981.

29   Smith, C. W., and R. M. Stulz. "The Determinants of Firms' Hedging Policies." *Journal of Financial and Quantitative Analysis*. Vol. 20, 391–405, 1985.

30   Ross, S. A. "Compensation, Incentives, and the Duality of Risk Aversion and Riskiness." *Journal of Finance*, Vol. 59, 207–225, 2004.

31   Low, A. "Managerial Risk-Taking Behavior and Equity-Based Compensation." Working Paper, Ohio State University, 2006. This paper concludes that firms where CEO compensation is not tied to equity returns tend to take about 10 percent less risk than firms where compensation is more equity based.

32   MacMinn, R. D., and F. H. Page. "Stock Options and Capital Structure." Working Paper, 2005. This study finds that option-compensated managers are more likely to use debt than equity.

taking and option-based compensation has not been conclusive. Although some studies indicate no perceptible increase in risk taking, others have established a link.[33] A study of oil and gas producers found that firms where managers are compensated with equity options are more likely to involve risky exploration activity and less likely to hedge against oil price risk.[34] An analysis of CEO behavior between 1992 and 1999 also found that increased option grants are associated with higher volatility in stock prices in subsequent years, although the magnitude of the increase is modest.[35] We would hasten to add that the increase in risk taking, by itself, is not bad news, because that is what equity compensation is designed to do. However, there seems to be little evidence in these studies and others that the additional risk taking improves operating performance or leads to higher stock prices.[36]

The debate currently is about the right mix of equity holdings and conventional compensation to offer decision makers to optimize risk taking. If options encourage too much risk taking and stock in the firm too little, is there a different compensation system that can encourage just the "right amount"? Figure 11.6 illustrates the balancing act.

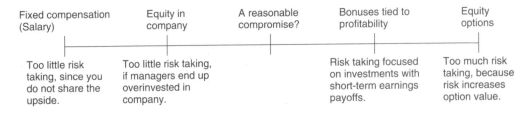

Figure 11.6: Compensation and Risk Taking

As accounting rules on reporting employee option compensation are tightened, more firms are experimenting with restricted stock (with the restrictions applying on trading for periods after the grants), but it is unclear that this will provide a satisfactory

33   Carpenter, J. N. "Does Option Compensation Increase Managerial Risk Appetite?" *Journal of Finance*, Vol. 55, 2311–2331, 2000.

34   Rajgopal, S., and T. Shevlin. "Empirical Evidence on the Relation Between Stock Option Compensation and Risk Taking." Working Paper, University of Washington, 2001.

35   Hanlon, M., S. Rajgopal, and T. Shevlin. "Large Sample Evidence on the Relation Between Stock Option Compensation and Risk Taking." Working Paper, University of Washington, 2004. Similar conclusions are in Guay, W. R. "The Sensitivity of CEO Wealth to Equity Risk: An Analysis of the Magnitude and Determinants." *Journal of Financial Economics*, 1999.

36   Cohen, R., B. J. Hall, and L. M. Viceira. "Do Executive Stock Options Encourage Risk-Taking?" Working Paper, Harvard Business School, 2000.

solution. After all, standard stock issues, restricted stock, and options share a common characteristic: they reward results and not processes; winning leads to big payoffs and losing does not. As we noted, good risk taking will frequently end in failure. If the objective is to reward good risk-taking behavior and punish bad behavior, no matter what the consequences, we are no closer to that objective now than we were three decades ago.

Organization Size, Structure, and Culture

Compensation systems represent one part of a larger story. Organizations can encourage or discourage risk based on how big they are and how they are structured. Also, the culture within can act as an incentive or an impediment to risk taking. Although at least one of these dimensions (size) may seem out of a firm's control, there are ways in which it can come up with creative solutions.

The relationship between the size of a firm and its risk-taking capabilities has been widely debated and researched. Earlier in the chapter, we noted the disadvantage faced by established companies when confronted with a disruptive technology; because they have too much invested in the status quo and tend to react slowly to any challenge to that status quo. At first sight, smaller firms should be more likely to innovate and take risks than larger firms because they have less to lose and more to gain from shaking up established ways of doing business. The evidence, though, suggests that the link between size and risk taking is more ambiguous. A study of small and large airlines found that although small airlines were quicker and more likely to initiate competitive challenges (and thus support the "more risk taking" hypothesis), they were less responsive to competitive challenges than larger airlines. To summarize using sports terminology, small airlines were better at playing offense and large airlines at playing defense.[37] Optimally, we would like to encourage the risk-taking behavior of a small firm with the defensive capabilities of a large one. The Apple experiment with ITunes, referred to earlier in this chapter, may be one way of doing this.

To see the relevance of organizational structure, let us go back to two of the competitive edges that allow firms to succeed at risk taking: timely and reliable information and a speedy response. Although this may be a gross generalization, flatter organizations tend to be better than more hierarchical organizations in handing information and responding quickly. It is revealing that investment banks, operating as they do in markets that are constantly exposed to risk, have flat organizational structures, where newly hired traders on the floor interact with managing directors. In contract, commercial banks,

---

[37] Chen, M., and D.C. Hambrick. "Speed, Stealth, and Selective Attack: How Small Firms Differ from Large Firms in Competitive Behavior." *The Academy of Management Journal*, Vol. 38, 453–482, 1995.

operating in more staid business environments, cultivate multilayered organizations where the employees at the lowest rungs can spend their entire careers in the bank without coming into contact with the bank's top managers. A related issue is how much compartmentalization there is within the organization. In organizations that have to deal with risk on a continuous basis, the lines between different functions and areas of the firm tend to be less firmly drawn, because dealing with risk will require them to collaborate and craft the appropriate response. In contrast, organizations that don't have to deal with crises very often tend to have more rigid separation between different parts of the business.

It is also worth noting that the trend toward diversification among many companies in the sixties and seventies, which created conglomerates such as ITT, GE, and Gulf Western, may have worked against risk-taking behavior. In an admission that this component of corporate strategy had failed, Michael Porter attributed the decline in R&D spending to the presence of large, diversified corporations.[38] A study of corporate R&D investments provided evidence that conglomerates were less willing to innovate, and the reluctance was attributed to their use of internal capital markets (where funds from one part of the business are used to cover investment needs of other parts of the business) as opposed to external markets.[39] This may at least partially explain why the United States, with its abundance of young technology companies, has been able to lay claim to much of the growth in the sector over the past decade, whereas investments in technology have been slower in Europe where much of the investment has had to come from established corporations.

The culture of a firm can also act as an engine for or as a brake on sensible risk taking. Some firms are clearly much more open to risk taking and its consequences, positive as well as negative. One key factor in risk taking is the way the firm deals with failure rather than success; after all, risk takers are seldom punished for succeeding. Thomas Watson, the founder of IBM, said, "The fastest way to succeed is to double your failure rate." Good risk-taking organizations treat failure and success not as opposites but as complements because one cannot exist without the other. Although all of us would like to be successful in our endeavors, the irony is that the odds of success are improved as firms tolerate failure. In a 2002 article in the *Harvard Business Review*, Farson and Keys argue that "failure-tolerant" leaders are an essential piece of successful risk-taking organizations and note that they share these characteristics.

- Every product and endeavor is treated as an experiment that can have positive or negative outcomes.

---

38 Porter, M. "Capital Disadvantage: America's Failing Capital Investment System." Harvard Business Review, 1992.

39 Seru, A. "Do Conglomerates Stifle Innovation?" Working Paper, 2006.

- An experiment that does not yield the desired outcome but was well thought out, planned for, and executed is a success. Conversely, an experiment that generates a good result but is carelessly set up and poorly followed through is a failure.

- The experiments that fail can be mined for important information that can be used to advantage later. Thus, every risky endeavor provides a payoff even when it fails to yield profits in the conventional sense. Even mistakes can be productive.

- Rather than scapegoating individuals after failed experiments, these businesses encourage and reward collaboration.

In short, failure-tolerant leaders engage their employees and use the result of risky experiments, positive and negative, to advantage. If the flip side of risk aversion is irrational risk seeking, firms have to have pieces in place to prevent or at least operate as a check on "bad" risk taking. One piece is to have independent and objective assessments of risky proposals to ensure that project proponents don't push biased analyses through. A second piece is to encourage open debate, where managers are encouraged to challenge each other on assumptions and forecasts. In summary, a willingness to accept the failures that are a natural outcome from taking risk and an openness to challenge proposals, even when they are presented by top management, characterize good risk-taking organizations.

Conclusion

The essence of risk management is not avoiding or eliminating risk but deciding which risks to exploit, which ones to let pass through to investors, and which ones to avoid or hedge. In this chapter, we focused on exploitable risks by presenting evidence on the payoff to taking risk. Although there is evidence that higher risk taking, in the aggregate, leads to higher returns, there is also enough evidence to the contrary (that is, risk taking can be destructive) to suggest that firms should be careful about which risk they expose themselves to.

To exploit risk, we need an edge over our competitors, who are exposed to that same risk. There are five possible sources. One is having more timely and reliable information when confronted with a crisis, allowing us to map out a superior plan of action in response. A second is the speed of the response to the risk, because not all firms, even when provided with the same information, are equally effective at acting quickly and appropriately. A third advantage may arise from experience weathering similar crises in the past. The institutional memories as well as the individual experiences of how the crises unfolded may provide an advantage over competitors who are new to the risk. A fourth advantage is grounded in resources, because firms with access to capital markets or large cash balances, superior technology, and better trained personnel can survive risks better than their competitors. Finally, firms that have more operating, production, or financial flexibility built into their responses, because of choices made in earlier periods, will be better able to adjust than their more rigid compatriots.

In the last part of this chapter, we examined how best to build a good risk-taking organization. We began with a discussion of how well aligned the interests of decision makers are with interests of the owners of the firm; corporate governance can be a key part of good risk taking. We considered the characteristics of effective risk takers and how firms can seek them out and keep them, and the compensation structures that best support risk taking. Finally, we examined the effects of organizational structure and culture on encouraging and nurturing risk taking.

12

RISK MANAGEMENT: FIRST PRINCIPLES

I f there is a theme that runs through this book, it is that risk underlies and affects every decision that a business makes, and that risk management is not just risk hedging. In this chapter, we review what we know about risk in general and how best to deal with it in practice, and we restate 10 principles that should govern both risk assessment and risk management.

1. Risk Is Everywhere

Individuals and businesses have only three choices when it comes to dealing with risk. The first choice is denial: we do not acknowledge that risk exists, and we hope it goes away. In this idealized world, actions and consequences are logical, and there are no unpleasant surprises. The second is fear: we take the opposite tack and allow the existence of risk to determine every aspect of behavior. Cowering behind the protection of insurance and derivatives, we hope to be spared of its worst manifestations. Neither of these approaches puts us in a position to take advantage of risk. But there is a third choice: accept the existence of risk, be realistic about its odds and consequences, and map out the best way to deal with it. This, in our view, is the pathway to making risk an ally rather than an adversary.

Part of why the study of risk is fascinating is that the nature of risk has changed and continues to change over time, making old remedies dated and requiring constant reinvention. In the past 20 years, three broad trends have emerged in the shifting landscape of risk.

- **Risk is global**—As businesses, economies, and markets have become global, so has risk. To illustrate the interconnectedness of markets and the possible "contagion" effects of risk, consider a small but telling example. On February 27, 2007, investors in the United States woke up to the news that stocks in Shanghai had lost 9 percent of their value overnight. In response, not only did the Dow drop more than 400 points (about 4.3 percent), but so did almost every other market in the world.

- **Risk cuts across businesses**—In contrast to earlier times, when risks tended to be sector focused, what happens in one sector increasingly has spillover effects on others. In early 2007, for instance, the laxity with which credit had been offered to customers with poor credit histories opened up that entire market, called the *subprime loan market*, to a potential shakeout. Analysts following Yahoo, the Internet search company, worried that its revenues and earnings would be hurt because so much of the advertising on web sites comes from lenders in the subprime market.

- **Risk comes increasingly from financial markets**—As firms have flocked to financial markets to raise debt and equity and become increasingly sophisticated in their use of the derivatives markets, they have also made themselves more vulnerable to these markets. A firm with healthy operations can be put on the defensive because of unanticipated turbulence in financial markets. Across the worlds, firms are finding that risk can and often does come from financial rather than product markets.

Because risks have become more international, have spread across sectors, and have encompassed both financial and product markets, it should come as no surprise that firms are finder fewer and fewer safe havens. As little as 20 years ago, some firms still operated in relatively secure habitats, protected by governments or geography against competition. They could predict their revenues and earnings with a fair degree of certainty and could make their other decisions on how much to borrow or pay in dividends accordingly. In the United States, large sections of the economy were insulated from risk; the regulated phone and power companies may not have had stellar growth, but they did have solid earnings. In Europe, protection from foreign competition allowed domestic companies in each country to preserve market share and profits even in the face of more efficient competitors overseas.

We need to make one final point about the ubiquity of risk. In the past decade especially, it can be argued that the balance of power between businesses and consumers has shifted decisively in the consumer's favor. Armed with better information and more choices, consumers are getting better terms and, in the process, lowering profits and increasing risk for businesses.

Risk Management Principle 1: Our biggest risks will come from places that we least expect them to come from and in forms that we did not anticipate that they would take. The essence of good risk management is to be able to roll with the punches when confronted with the unexpected.

2. Risk Is Threat and Opportunity

In Chapter 2, "Why Do We Care About Risk?," we presented the Chinese symbol for risk as the combination of danger and opportunity. Again and again, we have returned to this theme with a variety of examples. Market volatility can ruin us or make us wealthy. Changing customer tastes can lay our entire market to waste or allow us to dominate a market. Business failures and large losses come from exposures to large risks, but so do large profits and lasting successes.

The trouble with risk management is that people see one side or the other of risk and respond accordingly. Those who see the bad side of risk—that is, the danger side—either argue that it should be avoided or push for protection (through hedging and insurance) against it. On the other side are those who see risk as upside and argue for more risk taking, not less. Not surprisingly, their very different perspectives on risk will lead these groups to be on opposite sides of almost every debate, with the other side tarred as either "stuck in the mud" or "imprudent."

Risk is a combination of potential upside with significant downside and requires a more nuanced approach. If we accept the proposition that we cannot have one (upside) without the other (downside), we can become more realistic about how we approach and deal with risk. We can also move toward a consensus on which risks we should seek out, because the upside exceeds the downside, and which risks are imprudent, not because we do not like to take risk but because the downside exceeds the upside.

Risk Management Principle 2: Risk is a mix of upside and downside. Good risk management is not about seeking out or avoiding risk but about maintaining the right balance between the two.

3. We Are Ambivalent About Risks and Not Always Rational About the Way We Assess or Deal with Risk

In keeping with risk being a combination of danger and opportunity, we, as human beings, have decidedly mixed feelings about its existence. On the one hand, we fear it and its consequences, whereas on the other we seek it out, hoping to share in the profits.

We see this in the behavior of both investors and businesses, as they seesaw wildly from taking too much risk in one period to too little in the next.

Although the traditional theory on risk has been built on the premise of the "risk-averse" rational investor with a well-behaved preference function, studies of actual risk-taking behavior suggest that our attitudes toward risk taking are more complicated. To begin with, it is true that we are generally risk averse, but the degree of risk aversion varies widely across the population. More troublingly, though, risk aversion seems to vary for the same individual, depending on the way choices are framed and the circumstances of the choice. For instance, an individual who is normally risk averse can become risk seeking when given a chance to make back money lost on a prior gamble. In fact, behavioral economics and finance have developed as disciplines largely because of findings such as these that suggest that our behavior when confronted with risk is not always rational, at least as defined in classical economics, and is often predictable.

Risk Management Principle 3: Managing risk is a human endeavor, and a risk management system is only as good as the people manning it.

4. Not All Risk Is Created Equal

Risk comes from different sources, takes different forms, and has different consequences, but not all risk is created equal when it comes to the way it affects value and how it should be managed. To provide one concrete example, most conventional risk and return models draw a line between risks that affect one or a few firms and are thus diversifiable and risks that affect many or all firms and are not diversifiable. Only the latter risk is rewarded in these models, on the assumption that investors in firms are diversified and can mitigate their exposure to the former.

In fact, we can categorize risk with implications for risk management on a number of other dimensions.

- **Small versus large risks**—Risks can be small or large, depending on the potential impact that they can have on a firm's value. A small risk can be ignored or passed to investors with little or no worry, but a large risk may need to be assessed and managed carefully because of its potential to cause the firm's demise. Given that size is relative, it is entirely possible that the same risk can be small to one firm and be large to another.

- **Symmetric versus asymmetric risks**—Although we described risk as a combination of danger and opportunity, the upside and the downside are not necessarily symmetric. Some risks offer a small chance of a "very large" upside with a high probability of a "limited downside," whereas other risks offer the opposite combination. Why would it matter? In addition to feeding into some established quirks in risk aversion (loss aversion and a preference for large positive payoffs, for instance), it has implication for whether the risk will be managed (risks with large downside are more likely to be insured, even if the probability is small) and how we will manage it (whether we will use options, futures, or insurance).

- **Short term versus long term**—Some risks manifest themselves in the near term, whereas others take longer to affect firm value. Depending on what they see as their competitive advantages, firms may try to exploit long-term risks and protect themselves against short-term risks.

- **Continuous versus discontinuous**—There is some risk that firms are exposed to continuously and that have consequences over even small periods—exchange rates can change and interests rates can move up or down over the next minute. Other risks, such as damage from a terrorist incident or a hurricane, occur infrequently but can create significant damage. Although different risk-hedging tools exist for each, it can be argued that discontinuous risk is both more damaging and more difficult to manage.

Earlier in this book, we suggested that a risk inventory, where we listed all potential risks facing a firm, was a good beginning to the risk management process. Breaking down the risks into its components—firm specific or market, small or large, symmetric or asymmetric (and if so in what way), continuous versus discontinuous, and short term or long term—will make the risk inventory a more useful tool in risk management.

Finally, the saying that risk is in the eye of the beholder does have a foundation. After all, we can look at the risk in an investment through the eyes of the immediate decision makers (the line managers), their superiors (the top managers), or investors in that firm (who are often mutual funds or pension funds). As a generalization, risks that seems huge to middle managers may not seem as large to top managers, who bring a portfolio perspective to the process, and they might be inconsequential to investors in the firm, who have the luxury of having diversification work its wonders for them.

Risk Management Principle 4: To manage risk the right way, we have to pick the right perspective on risk and stay consistent through the process to that perspective. In other words, if we choose to view risk through the eyes of investors in the firm, we will assess risk differently and behave accordingly.

5. Risk Can Be Measured

There is a widespread belief even among risk managers that some risks are too qualitative to be assessed. This notion that some risks cannot be evaluated—either because the likelihood of occurrence is small or the consequences too unpredictable—can be dangerous, because these are exactly the types of risks that have the potential to create damage. As we have argued through this book, the debate should be about what tools to use to assess risk rather than whether they can be assessed. At the risk of sounding dogmatic, all risks can and should be assessed, although the ease and method of assessment can vary across risks.

There are two keys to good risk assessment. The first is better quality and more timely information about the risks as they evolve, so that the element of surprise is reduced. The second is tools such as risk-adjusted discount rates, simulations, scenario analysis, and VaR to convert the raw data into risk measures. On both, it can be argued that we are better off than we were in earlier generations. There is more information available to decision makers, with a larger portion of it being provided in real time. The tools available have also become more accessible and sophisticated, with technology lending a helping hand. Thus, a Monte Carlo simulation that would have required the services of a mainframe computer and been prohibitively costly 30 years ago can be run on a personal computer with a modest outlay.

The advances in risk assessment should not lead to false complacency or to the conclusion that risk management has become easier as a consequence for three reasons. First, as we noted earlier in this chapter, the risks being assessed are also becoming more global and complex, and it is an interesting question as to whether the improvements in information and assessment are keeping up with the evolution of risk. Second, risk management is still a relative game. In other words, it is not just how well a business or investor assesses risk that matters, but how well it does that it relative to the competition. The democratization of information and tools has leveled the playing field and enabled small firms to take on much larger and more resource-rich competitors. Third, as both the data and the tools have become more plentiful, picking the right tool to assess a risk (and it can be different for different risks) has become a more critical component of success at risk management.

> **Risk Management Principle 5:** To pick the right tool to assess risk, we have to understand what the tools share in common, what they do differently, and how to use the output from each tool.

6. Good Risk Measurement/Assessment Should Lead to Better Decisions

Superior information and the best tools for risk assessment add up to little, if they do not lead to better decisions when faced with risk. In many businesses, those who assess risk are not necessarily those who make decisions (often based on those risk assessments), and this separation can lead to trouble. In particular, risk assessment tools are often not tailored to the needs of decision makers and are often misread or misused as a consequence.

The problems have their roots in why we assess risk in the first place. Some believe that assessing risk is equivalent to eliminating it and feel more secure with an analysis that is backed up by a detailed and sophisticated risk assessment. Others use risk assessments, not to make better decisions, but as cover, if things do not work out as anticipated. Still others think that risk assessment will make them more comfortable, when they have to make their final judgments. The reality is that risk assessment makes us aware of risk but does not eliminate it, and it cannot be used as an excuse for poor decisions. Finally, the irony of good risk assessment is that it may actually make us more uncomfortable as decision makers rather than less. More information can often lead to more uncertainty rather than less.

For risk assessments to lead to better decisions, we need to do three things better.

- If risk is assessed and decisions are made by different entities, each one has to be aware of the other's requirements and preferences. Thus, risk assessors have to understand what decision makers see as the major issues and tailor both the tools chosen and the output to these needs and constraints. At the same time, those who make decisions have to recognize the flaws and limitations of the information used by risk assessors and understand at least the broad contours of the tools being used to assess risk.

- The risk assessment tools have to be built around the risks that matter rather than all risks. As we noted in an earlier section, we are faced with dozens of risks, of different types and with different consequences, and some of these risks matter far more than others. Keeping risk assessment focused on that which matters will make it more useful to decision makers; a shorter, more focused risk assessment is more useful than one that is comprehensive but rambling.

- Risk assessment should not become an exercise in testing only the downside or the bad side of risk, even though that may be what worries decision makers the most. A good risk assessment will hold true to the complete measure of risk and provide a picture of both upside potential and downside risk.

In short, for risk assessment to work, decision makers need to both understand and be involved in the risk assessment process, and risk assessors should not be shut out of the decision-making process. The fact that the former tend to be higher in the management hierarchy can make this a difficult task.

> **Risk Management Principle 6:** The tools to assess risk and the output from risk assessment should be tailored to the decision-making process, rather than the other way around.

7. The Key to Good Risk Management Is Deciding Which Risks to Avoid, Which Ones to Pass Through, and Which to Exploit

Investors and businesses face myriad risks, and it is easy to be overwhelmed. The theme of the past three chapters is that for good risk management, some of this risk should be passed to investors, some should be hedged and insured, and some should be actively sought out and used as a source of competitive advantage. Firms that are good at apportioning the risks they face to the right boxes have much better odds of succeeding.

The underlying fundamentals for making these choices are not complicated. We begin with the judgment on which risk or risks we want to exploit because we believe we have an advantage—better information, speedier response, more flexibility, or better resources—over our competition. Looking at the risks we choose not to exploit, we have to weigh the costs of protecting ourselves against the potential benefits from the protection—tax benefits, lower distress costs, and a more rational decision-making process. There are some risks that we may be able to reduce or eliminate through the normal course of our operations and thus are costless to hedge; other risks are costly to hedge. For these risks, the choice becomes complicated especially for publicly traded companies, because they have to compare the costs that they, as companies, would face to the costs that investors in their companies would face to eliminate the same risks. This comparison would lead us to conclude that publicly traded firms are usually better off passing through a significant portion of their firm-specific risk and even s market risk to their investors, rather than incur costs to hedge them. For some risks, though, the company is in a better position than its investors in assessing and hedging the risks. For instance, Boeing has much more information about its exchange rate risk exposure on individual contracts with foreign airlines than its investors, and it can hedge those risks more efficiently.

Risk Management Principle 7: Hedging risk is but a small part of risk management. Determining which risks should be hedged, which should not, and which should be taken advantage of is the key to successful risk management.

8. The Payoff to Better Risk Management Is Higher Value

Risk managers are measured and judged on a number of different dimensions, but the only dimension that matters is how it impacts the value of the business. Good risk management increases value, whereas bad risk management destroys value. Choosing any other measure or objective can only distort the process. Consider a few alternatives. If the success of risk management is measured by how much risk it eliminates from the process, the logical product is that too little risk will be exploited and too much hedged. That is why firms that focus on reducing earnings or stock price volatility or the deviation from analyst forecasts will end up mismanaging risk. What about a higher stock price? It is true that in an efficient market, stock price and the value of equity move hand in hand, but there are two problems with a stock-price focus. The first is that in an inefficient market, where investors may focus on the short term or on the wrong variables (earnings variability, for instance), there may be a positive market response to poor risk-management decisions. That response will fade over time, but the managers who made the decisions would have been rewarded and have moved on (or up) by then. The second is that the value of a business includes the value of its equity and other claimholders in the firm (lenders, in particular). Decisions relating to risk often alter the balance between debt and equity and can sometimes make stockholders better off at the expense of lenders. Hence, the focus should be on the value of the business in its entirety rather than just the equity investors.

So, how do we link risk management to value? To begin with, we need much richer valuation models than the ones in use that tend to put all the focus (at least when it comes to risk) on the discount rate. All the inputs in a conventional valuation model, as we explained in Chapter 9, "Risk Management: The Big Picture"—from cash flows to growth rates to the length of the growth period—should be a function of how well risk is managed in the firm. Only then can we see the full impact on value of increasing exposure to some risks and the consequences of hedging or passing through others. Given that most analysts value firms using earnings multiples and comparables, we need to also consider ways in which we can incorporate the full effects of risk management into these comparisons. Finally, it is worth exploring, as in Chapter 8, "Real Options," how the tools in the real option tool kit can be used to capture the upside potential for risk.

Risk Management Principle 8: To manage risk right, we have to understand the levers that determine the value of a business.

9. Risk Management Is Part of Everyone's Job

For decades, risk management was viewed as a finance function, with the CFO playing the role of risk measurer, assessor, and punisher (for those who crossed defined risk limits). In keeping with this definition, risk management became focused entirely on risk assessment and risk hedging. The elevation of strategic risk management or enterprise risk management in businesses, with its willingness to consider the upside of risk, has come with one unfortunate side cost. Many firms have a person or group in charge of risk management, given primary responsibility for coordinating and managing risk through the organization. Although we applaud the recognition given to risk management, it has also led others in the firm, especially in the other functional areas, to think that the existence of a risk management group has relieved them of the responsibility of having to play a role in managing risk.

Although there are some aspects of risk management—risk assessment mechanics and hedging—that may be finance related and thus logically embedded in Treasury departments, there are many aspects of risk management, especially risk taking, that cut across functional areas. Taking advantage of shifts in customer tastes for a retailer requires the skills of the marketing and advertising departments. Exploiting technological change to revamp production facilities is not something that the Treasury department can do much about but is more the domain of the operations department. In short, every decision made by a firm in any functional area has a risk management component. Although we need a centralized group to aggregate these risks and look at the portfolio, individual decision makers have to be aware of how their decisions play out in the big picture.

Risk Management Principle 9: Managing risk well is the essence of good business practice and is everyone's responsibility.

10. Successful Risk-Taking Organizations Do Not Get There by Accident

As we have noted throughout this chapter and, in fact, all through the book, a lot of moving pieces have to work together consistently for risk management to succeed. The challenge is greater if the success has to be repeated period after period. Not surprisingly, firms that succeed at risk management plan for and are organized to deliver that success.

In Chapter 11, "Strategic Risk Management," we laid out some of the ingredients of the consistently successful risk-taking organization:

- **Alignment of interests**—The key challenge in any firm, especially a large publicly traded one, is that decision making is spread through the organization and different decision makers have different interests. Some managers are motivated by rewards, in compensation tied to profits or stock prices, whereas others may be motivated by fear—that failure may lead to loss of a job. The decisions that they make may reflect those desires or fears and have little to do with what is good for the overall business. To the extent that the interests of different decision makers within the firm can be aligned with those of the owners of the firm with carrots (equity options, stock grants, and so on) or sticks (stronger corporate governance), risk management has a much better chance of succeeding.

- **Good and timely information**—Information is the lubricant for good risk management. If reliable information can be provided in a timely fashion to decision makers who are confronted with risk, they can (although they don't always do) make better decisions. The question of how best to design information systems in the past decade has sometimes become a debate about information technology but really should be focused on improving the response to risk. The test of a good information system should be how well it works during crises at delivering needed information to analysts and decision makers.

- **Solid analysis**—Information, even if it is reliable and timely, is still just data. That data has to be analyzed and presented in a way that makes better decisions possible. Having access to analytical tools such as decision trees and simulations is part of the process, but understanding how the tools work and choosing between them is the more difficult component of success.

- **Flexibility**—If there is one common theme shared by all successful risk takers, it is that they are flexible in their responses to change. They adapt to changed circumstances faster than their competitors, either because they built flexibility into their original design or because they have the technological or financial capacity to do so. Having a flat organizational structure, being a smaller organization, or having less vested in existing technologies all seem to be factors that add to flexibility.

- **People**—Ultimately, good risk management depends on having the right people in the right places when crisis strikes. Good risk-taking organizations seek out people who respond well to risk and retain them with a combination of financial rewards (higher pay, bigger bonuses) and nonfinancial incentives (culture and team dynamics).

Risk Management Principle 10: To succeed at risk management, we have to embed it in the organization through its structure and culture.

Conclusion

As the interconnections between economies and sectors have increased and become more complex, firms have become more exposed to risk, and the need to manage this risk has increased concurrently. Although this increasing exposure to change has put firms at risk, it has also opened new frontiers that they can exploit to profit. Risk is, after all, a combination of threat and opportunity.

Risk management as a discipline has evolved unevenly across different functional areas. In finance, the preoccupation has been with the effect of risk on discount rates, and little attention has been paid to the potential upside of risk until recently; real options represent the first real attempt to bring in the potential profits of being exposed to risk. In strategy, risk management has been a side story to the focus on competitive advantages and barriers to entry. In practice, risk management at most organizations is splintered, with little communication between those who assess risk and those who make decisions based on those risk assessments.

This book is an attempt to bridge the chasm not only between different functional areas—finance, strategy, and operations—but also between different parts of organizations where the responsibility for risk management lies today. In the process, it makes the argument that good risk management lies at the heart of successful businesses everywhere.

INDEX

Page numbers followed by *n* indicate footnotes.

A

abandonment. *See* option to abandon (real options)
absolute value, 222
acts of God, 334
actuarial tables, 70
adaptive behavior, 232
age, effect on risk aversion, 42, 49
airline industry example (scenario analysis), 148-151
Allais, 38
Amaranth (hedge fund), 47
American options
    in Black-Scholes option pricing model, 272-273
    European options versus, 264
Amihud, Y., 120, 122
analysis of data, importance of, 377
analyzing risks in risk profiles, 318-319
ancient civilizations
    insurance in, 70
    measuring risk in, 65-66
Anderson-Darling test, 198
Antikarov, V., 234
Apple, flexibility of, 356
arbitrage pricing model, 84, 95-96, 102
ARCH (autoregressive conditional heteroskedasticity), 209
Arrow-Pratt measure of risk aversion, 36
assessing risk. *See* risk assessment
asset pricing, as measure of risk aversion, 50-57
    bond pricing, 56
    implied equity risk premium, 50-56
    limitations of, 57
    option pricing, 56
asymmetric distributions, 81-82
asymmetric risks, symmetric risks versus, 370
auctions, lotteries versus, 40

B

Bachelier, Louis, 72
Bajaj, M., 140
Bakshi, G., 49
Ball, C. A., 83
Baltussen, G., 60
Banker's Trust, 203
Barbon, Nicholas, 71
Barings (investment bank), 203
Basak, S., 223
Bayes, Thomas, 69
Bayesian statistics, 69-70
Beckers, S., 83
bell curve, 68
Benartzi, Shlomo, 44
Berg, Joyce, 40, 41

Bernasek, A., 49
Bernoulli, Jacob, 35, 38, 68
Bernstein, Peter, 65
best-case scenario analysis, 146
Beta distributions, 192
betting. *See* gambling
bid-ask spreads, 142
binomial option pricing model, 269-270
bionomial distributions, 184
Black-Scholes option pricing model, 270-275
Blume, M. E., 47
Boeing example (scenario analysis), 148-151
bond market, illiquidity cost, 122
bond pricing, as measure of risk aversion, 56
Books on the Game of Chance (Cardano), 66
book value constraints, 174-175
book value multiples, 285
bottom-up beta, 101
Boudoukh, J., 212
Bowman paradox, 345
break-even effect, 45, 62
Buffett, Warren, 73
Byrnes, James, 42

C

C-FaR (cash flow-at-risk), 224-225
Cabedo, J. D., 210, 213
call options, 336
    explained, 262
    payoff diagram of, 236
    risk management as, 301
Camerer, C., 41
capital, access in crises, 352-353
capital market frictions, 322
capital structure benefits of hedging risks, 325
CAPM (capital asset pricing model), 77-78, 89-94, 101-102
Cardano, Girolamo, 66
Card Sharks (game show), 59
cash flow-at-risk (C-FaR), 224-225
cash flow haircuts, for certainty-equivalent cash flows, 109-110
cash flows. *See* discounted cash flow valuation
casinos. *See* gambling
catastrophic risk, small risk versus, 311
categorizing risks, 310-311
Cauchy distributions, 189
certainty-equivalent cash flows, 106-111
    cash flow haircuts for, 109-110
    combining with risk, 115
    combining with risk-adjusted discount rate, 111-116
    risk-adjusted discount rate versus, 110-111

implied equity risk premium, 50-52
  anomalies in, 53-56
  historical risk premium versus, 52-53
increased value, hedging risks for, 329-331
independent trials (experimental design), 37
informational benefits of hedging risks, 325-326
information availability, effect on risk aversion, 41
information mirages, 41
information networks, 346-348, 377
innovation, risk and, 7-8
inputs for discounted cash flow valuation, 288-290
inside information, 76n
institutional structure, effect on risk aversion, 41
insurance
  hedging risks with, 333-334, 338
  view of risk, 70-71
insurance decisions, risk surveys of, 48
Internet companies, option to expand (real options) and, 251
intrinsic valuation. See discounted cash flow valuation
intrinsic value, defined, 100
investment choices, risk surveys of, 47
investment decisions for hedging risks, 322-323, 331-332
irrational behavior, risk aversion and, 369-370
Isaac, Mark, 41
item-specific discount rate, composite discount rate versus, 105

J–K

J. P. Morgan, RiskMetrics service, 203, 206, 208
Jagannathan, M., 124
James, Duncan, 41
Jamshidan, Farshid, 216
Jarrow, R. A., 83
Jeopardy! (game show), 60
Jianakoplos, N. A., 49
Johnson, B. A., 123
Johnson, E. J., 45-46
Ju, X., 223
Jullien, B., 59
jump process distributions, 83

Kachmeimeir, Steven, 39
Kagel, John, 42
Kahneman, D., 35, 41, 43-44, 359
Katrina (hurricane), insurance losses in, 71
Kearny, John, 328
Knight, Frank, 5
Knowledge Management (KM), 351
Kolmogorov-Smirnov test, 198
kurtosis. See fat tails

L

LaGattuta, D., 225
Lambadrais, G., 218
large risks, small risks versus, 370
Larsen, N., 224
Lau, M. I., 43
Laury, Susan, 39, 42-43
law of large numbers, 68

Levin, Dan, 42
Levy, Haim, 42
Lewent, Judy, 328
life cycle risk aversion hypothesis, 49
life tables. See actuarial tables
limits. See constraints
linear tax functions, 321
Lingo (game show), 61
Lintner, John, 77
liquidation, transactions costs and, 118. See also illiquidity discounts
liquidity, value of, 121
List, J. A., 45
listing risks, 310
Ljungquist, A., 124
Lloyd's of London, 71
logistic distributions, 189
lognormal distributions, 191
long-shot bias, 58-59, 62
long-term risks, short-term risks versus, 371
Longstaff, F. A., 121
loss aversion, 62
  in crisis managers, 359
  effect on risk aversion, 44-45
lotteries, auctions versus, 40
Lovallo, D., 359

M

Maher, J. M., 123
Mains, B., 322
Majluf, N. S., 323
male versus female, effect on risk aversion, 42, 49
managerial risk aversion, 322
Mandelbrot, Benoit, 79
marital status, effect on risk aversion, 43, 49
market capitalization, 129
market portfolio, CAPM (capital asset pricing model), 77-78, 89-94
market prices. See asset pricing
market risk
  firm-specific risk versus, 310
  hedging, effect on value, 283-284
  in VaR (value at risk), 221
market risk factors, 84
market structure, effect on risk aversion, 41
market value constraints, 176
Markowitz, Harry, 73, 203
Markowitz approach (risk measurement), 73-77
Markowitz portfolios, 91
Mausser, H., 224
Mayers, D., 333
McCabe, K., 41
McGrattan, E. R., 55
mean, in normal distributions, 68
mean-variance framework, 74-76, 89-94
  challenges to, 78-83
    asymmetric distributions, 81-82
    jump process distributions, 83
    power-law distributions, 79-81
  implications of, 76-77

S

Salane, B., 59
sampling, 68
Sarin, A., 124
scenario analysis, 145
    best-case/worst-case analysis, 146
    comparison with other risk assessment methods, 179-180
    decision making, usage in, 151-152
    examples of, 148-151
    problems with, 152-153
    steps in, 147-148
scenario simulations, modifying Monte Carlo simulations, 216
Schafer, William, 42
Scharfstein, D. S., 323
Schraud, C., 325
Schwartz, A., 41
SEC (Securities Exchange Commission), establishment of, 203
sector-specific variable multiples, 286
sector comparisons, 129
Securities Exchange Act, 203
Securities Exchange Commission (SEC), establishment of, 203
selective risk analysis, full risk analysis versus, 179
self-insurance. *See* insurance
sequential risk. *See* decision trees
Shahabuddin, P., 216
Shapiro, A., 223, 312
Shapiro-Wilk test, 198
Sharpe, Bill, 77
Shehata, Mohamed, 39
short-term focus of VaR, 221
short-term risks, long-term risks versus, 371
Silber, W. L., 123, 139
simplicity of VaR, 221-222
simulations, 164
    book value constraints, 174-175
    comparison with other risk assessment methods, 179-180
    decision making, usage in, 173-174
    earnings and cash flow constraints, 175
    examples of, 168-173
    market value constraints, 176
    problems with, 176-177
    real options versus, 234
    risk-adjusted value and, 177-181
    steps in, 164-168
single-period models for multiperiod projects, 105
size of organization, risk taking and, 363-365
skewness, 82
Skiadoupoulous, G., 218, 220
Skintzi, V. D., 220
Sloan, Alfred, 353n
small risk
    catastrophic risk versus, 311
    large risk versus, 370
Smith, C. W., 321, 333
Smith, R. L., 141

Smithson, C., 330
Southwest Airlines
    flexibility of, 354
    switching options example, 257
SPaR (stock prices at risk), 225
speed of response, 348-350
spice trade, 4
spread, as trading cost, 118
stable Paretian distributions, 80
standard deviations, 68
standardized price, 128
Standard Statistics Bureau, 72
statistical artifacts, 54
statistical controls, 129
statistical distributions, 183
    discrete versus continuous data, 183-187
    extreme data values, 195-196
    limits on data values, 194-195
    for probability distributions, 166-167
    symmetry of data, 188-189, 192-194
    testing for fit, 196-198
statistical risk measures, for financial assets, 71-73
status quo value, 126
Stein, J. C., 225, 323
stock prices at risk (SPaR), 225
strategic risk taking, 9
strike prices (options)
    defined, 262
    effect on option value, 265
    in option to delay (real options), 238
strong law of large numbers, 68n
structure of experimental studies, effect on findings, 40-42
Suarez, F., 49
subgroup differences, effect on risk aversion, 42-43, 62
subjective risk, objective risk versus, 5
Summa de Arithmetica (Pacioli), 66
survey design, measuring risk aversion, 47-48
survey measures of risk aversion, 47-50
    findings, 48-49
    quality of, 49-50
    survey design, 47-48
survival, risk and, 3
survivor bias, 54
sustainability, real options and, 258
swaps, hedging risks with, 337-338
switching options, option to abandon (real options) and, 256-257
symmetric risks, asymmetric risks versus, 370
symmetry of data, 188-189, 192-194
synergy premiums, 127
Szpiro, George, 48

T

tax benefits of hedging risks, 320-322
taxes, in historical risk premiums, 55
technology companies, risk assessment methods in, 181
Tellis, Gerard, 355
terminal value, 281
testing statistical distributions for fit, 196-198

tests of normality, 198
Thaler, R. H., 41, 44-46
Theory of Investment Value (Williams), 74
threat, risk versus, 6
time, effect on equity risk premium, 52-53
time series models, combined with historical simulations, 213
time to expiration, effect on options, 265
Torous, W. N., 83
Toyota, flexibility of, 353
trading costs
    elements of, 118-119
    of private businesses, 120
transactions costs
    liquidation and, 118
    of real assets, 119
transactions exposure, 312
translation exposure, 311-312
treasury bond rate, 51n
Treynor, Jack, 77, 119
Tufano, P., 327
Turnbull, S. M., 105
Tversky, A., 35, 41, 43-44

U

uncertainty, risk and, 5, 6
UNCR (Uniform Net Capital Rule), 203
underlying assets, value of
    effect on options, 264
    in option to delay (real options), 237
Uniform Net Capital Rule (UNCR), 203
updating probabilities information, 69-70
upside risks, 126-127. *See also* duality of risk
Uryasev, S., 224
Usher, S. E., 225
utility functions
    for certainty-equivalent cash flows, 107-108
    empirical evidence. *See* empirical evidence
    quadratic utility function, 75

V

valuation. *See* discounted cash flow valuation; relative valuation
value
    linking to risk management, 375-376
    of options, determining, 264-266
    risk taking and, 342-345
value at risk. *See* VaR
value estimates, for option to delay (real options), 237-238
value risk exposure, earnings risk exposure versus, 311-313
Van den Assem, M., 60

VaR (value at risk)
    explained, 201-202
    extensions of, 223-225
    history of, 202-204
    limitations of, 218-223
    measuring, 204
        comparison of approaches, 217-218
        historical simulations, 210-214
        Monte Carlo simulations, 214-217
        variance-covariance method, 204-210, 228-230
    utility as risk assessment tool, 225-226
variables in simulations
    correlation across, 167
    selecting, 164
variance-covariance method
    combining with Monte Carlo simulations, 216
    compared to historical and Monte Carlo simulations, 217-218
    measuring VaR, 204-210, 228-230
variances in asset value
    effect on options, 264
    in option to delay (real options), 237-238
views of risk. *See* duality of risk

W

waiting. *See* option to delay (real options)
Walt Disney Inc. example
    option to expand (real options), 247-248
    risk exposure measurement, 314-318
Watson, Thomas, 364
weak law of large numbers, 68n
wealth, utility functions. *See* utility functions
Weibull distributions, 191
Weigelt, K., 41
weighted past, 212
White, A., 208, 214
Whitelaw, R., 212
Who Wants to Be a Millionaire? (game show), 61
Wietzman, M., 59
wild randomness, 79
Williams, John Burr, 74
women versus men, effect on risk aversion, 42, 49
Wooders, J., 41
worst-case scenario analysis, 146

X–Z

Yahoo! auctions, eBay auctions versus, 41n
Youngen, J., 225
young versus old, effect on risk aversion, 42, 49

Zhu, Yu, 216
Ziemba, W. T., 58
Zoulis, Y., 218

Cocktail Economics
Discovering Investment Truths from Everyday Conversations
BY VICTOR A. CANTO

Foreword by John Rutledge, Rutledge Capital

Utilizing a technique he learned while teaching economics to MBA students at the University of Chicago, Victor Canto uses anecdotes and easy-to-understand examples, analogies, and metaphors to provide simple, conversational, economic explanations to everyday problems and issues of interest. He then goes a step further by relating the discussions to basic investment principles and uses these examples to develop an investment strategy and process that individual investors can actually apply to their own portfolios. The focus of the book is on three things: 1) How does the economy work and how does understanding the economy help the reader become a better investor? 2) Why is it so important to balance "active" and "passive" investing strategies to become a more successful investor? 3) How can readers "read" economic cycles and make appropriate adjustments to their own portfolios?

ISBN 9780132432733, ©2007, 336 pp., $24.99 USA, $29.99 CAN

Trend Following
How Great Traders Make Millions in Up or Down Markets, New Expanded Edition
BY MICHAEL W. COVEL

"For my staff, Michael's *Trend Following* is required reading."
—From the Foreword by Larry Hite, CEO,
Hite Capital Management

For over 30 years, one trading strategy has consistently delivered extraordinary profits in bull and bear markets alike: *Trend Following.* Just ask the billionaire traders who rely on it...traders like John W. Henry, whose profits bought the Boston Red Sox! In *Trend Following, New Expanded Edition,* you'll meet them. More importantly, you'll discover how to use *Trend Following* in your own portfolio: how to limit risk, employ market discipline, and—when the moment is right—swing for the home run! Want proof it works? This New Expanded Edition includes 100+ pages of easy-to-understand performance charts. Want even more proof? You'll find comprehensive information on backtesting *Trend Following* for yourself.

ISBN 9780136137184, ©2007, 448 pp., $17.99 USA, $21.99 CAN